D0933580

Folklife Studies from the Gilded Age

Object, Rite, and Custom in Victorian America

American Material Culture and Folklife

Simon J. Bronner, Series Editor
Associate Professor of Folklore and American Studies
The Pennsylvania State University at Harrisburg

Other Titles in This Series

Folklife Studies from the Gilded Age
Object, Rite, and Custom in Victorian America

Edited by
Simon J. Bronner

1888-89
AMERICAN
FOLKLORE
SOCIETY
CENTENNIAL
1988-89

U·M·I Research Press

Ann Arbor / London

Produced and distributed by
UMI Research Press
an imprint of
University Microfilms Inc.
Ann Arbor, Michigan 48106

Library of Congress Cataloging in Publication Data

Folklife studies from the gilded age.

    (American material culture and folklife)
    Includes bibliographies and index.
    1. United States—Social life and customs—
1865–1918. 2. Material culture—United States.
3. Folklore—United States. 4. Ethnology—United
States. I. Bronner, Simon J. II. Series.
E168.F69 1987   973   87-25509
ISBN 0-8357-1837-9 (alk. paper)

British Library CIP data is available.

For William Mahar

Contents

Figures

Preface

This book is about a distinctive intellectual fervor during the late nine-teenth century for American studies of material culture and folklife. The fervor was distinctive during this period because of the unprecedented output of publication devoted to the subject, the dedication of the studies to evolutionary doctrine, the predominance of scholarly activity outside of academe, and the connection of the studies to decisions of public policy. Following evolutionary thought, the studies uncovered groups and practices left behind by the progressive "march of civilization," and in the Victorian view, this march stepped to the cosmopolitan beat of industry. Among the favorite constrasts of Victorian writers were those made between modern manners and primitive customs, between scien-tific observations and superstitious rites, between machine-driven inven-tions and preindustrial objects. In making these contrasts, Victorian scholars uncovered many disappearing examples of tradition, and they unveiled much about the preoccupations of the new age.

This book, then, is both a reader for the contributions of these nineteenth-century folklife scholars and the reflections of the society in which the scholars lived and worked. The folklife field itself is a broad one, and the sweeping use of folklore (covering all traditional knowledge, especially narrative expressions, belonging to cultural groups) under which folklife studies were usually placed during the Victorian period deserves coverage. But this reader brings together what I discern as three special concerns of Victorian scholars. It gives special attention to mat-ters of traditional *life* that were studied and related to Victorian society: objects, rites, and customs.

I put together this book because my reading in nineteenth-century periodicals made me realize the pervasiveness of folklife studies in the literature of the period and their effect on the Victorian popular mind. Yet I noticed that these richly suggestive studies were neglected in surveys of cultural and intellectual history, and even in chronicles of the folklife field. The reason for this neglect probably stems from long-standing biases within history and folklife. Evidence in humanistic fields such as cultural and intellectual history has tended toward the imaginative products of arts and literature, rather than the ethnographic writing (characterized by scientific observation) typical of folklife studies, which ironically was a major source for arts and literature of the period. The ethnographic bias of present folklife studies, meanwhile, has commonly led to a lack of historical vision, and the limited historiography of the field has typically asserted that folklife and material culture studies constituted a movement made only within living memory. Or, convinced that these early studies were embarrassingly misguided, folklife scholars have chosen to move ahead rather than look back.

The centennial celebration of the American Folklore Society in 1988–89 and the maturation of folklore studies as a discipline, however, have aroused reflections on the need for more of a historical vision within folklife studies. Too often, nonetheless, students receive the lessons of the past secondhand, rather than from reading original sources. Thus, this book offers the work of Victorian scholars in their own words and it adds historical commentary. It puts under one cover a connected group of scholars who were revered during their time and who deserve our historical and cultural appreciation, but who have not been adequately anthologized. This book reaches out to students of history and American civilization by setting the work of these Victorian scholars against the historical and cultural background of the age. It builds on the historiographical work that I established with *American Material Culture and Folklife* (1985), an earlier title in this series, and with *American Folklore Studies: An Intellectual History* (1986).

I chose essays that sample the work of major figures of folklife studies from the Gilded Age and covered major topics of the field during that time. With the opening essays by Otis Mason and Fletcher S. Bassett and the Philadelphia Chapter of the American Folklore Society, we have the major philosophical and methodological foundations of folklife studies before the turn of the century. The next four essays cover customs, rites, and objects of typical groups discussed in Victorian folklife literature: Pennsylvania-Germans, Chinese-Americans, Appalachians, children, and American Indians. The next five essays also discuss observations of cultural groups, but serve especially to bring forward for discussion particular folklife genres, such as art and ornament, gravemarkers, craft and folk technology, and foodways. The last four essays discuss specific objects and their interpretation for museum settings. Offering closure to the book, Henry Mercer's essay is, in addition to being a discussion of specific objects informed by nineteenth-century folklife studies, a harbinger of post-Victorian folklife research.

Besides making choices on the basis of significance and coverage, I was also moved by practical and aesthetic considerations. I chose essays which have not been reprinted and did not require the reproduction of unavailable photographs. I sought readings that were self-contained essays or public presentations, rather than seeking excerpts from books. I followed this strategy to emphasize essays and addresses, which were favored forms of conveying ideas during the Gilded Age ethnological boom. I looked for a variety of settings which featured folklife essays; I picked essays from the journals of learned societies such as the *Journal of American Folklore* and *American Anthropologist,* and I tapped popular sources like *Atlantic Monthly.* Too, there are essays here from some out-of-the-way sources such as the *Medical and Surgical Reporter* and *Craftsman,* because they make available hidden classics and they underscore the point that folklife studies did indeed pervade Victorian scholarship.

I chose essays that would be informative, naturally, but I also looked for pieces that made for lively reading. For the sake of continuity, some essays with related material were combined to form a single piece. In these chapters, the beginning of a new article is indicated by the addition of two line spaces. Other essays were trimmed or retitled to retain focus. Such changes are clearly described in my headnotes, and do not, I believe, alter the intentions of the original authors. My headnotes are added to the essays to give biographical information on the author, offer background on the theme of the essay, indicate sources for the essay, and make suggestions for further reading.

In the interests of the modern reader, I have added editorial notes where appropriate in the text. The substance of both the editorial notes and the authors' original notes follow the pertinent essays. My notes explain figures or give additional explanation from which the reader may benefit. In order to differentiate between these two types of notes, the editorial additions have been enclosed in brackets and are followed by ''Ed.''

As with any project of this sort, my intellectual debts have piled up, and I want to take this opportunity to single out a few of my creditors. Kenneth L. Ames, chair of the Office of Advanced Studies at the Winterthur Museum, was a guiding light when I was a National Endowment for the Humanities Research Fellow there in 1984. He led me to many revelations about Victorian society. On the folklife side, John Michael Vlach, director of the folklife program at George Washington University, let me tap his sage reflections on folklife historiography. Then there was William K. McNeil, folklorist at the Ozark Folk Center, who on countless occasions offered encouragement along with many historical insights. Not least, I owe the late Richard M. Dorson, a great chronicler of folklore studies, for pointing out the way. I know he would have wanted to see this book.

I benefited, too, from having wonderful colleagues in the American Studies program at the Pennsylvania State University at Harrisburg. John Patterson and Michael Barton freely shared with me their wisdom on American civilization, and they graciously tolerated my enthusiasm.

Managing my searches through troves of nineteenth-century literature was made easier by Ruth Runion, interlibrary loan officer at Penn State Harrisburg, Henry Koretzky, periodicals clerk also at Penn State Harrisburg, and Neville Thompson, librarian at the Winterthur Museum. For making their collections available, I also offer my gratitude to the Smithsonian Institution, the Brooklyn Museum, the University of Pennsylvania Museum, the library and folklore archives at the University of Pennsylvania, the library and Folklore Institute at Indiana University, the National Anthropological Archives, the State Library of Pennsylvania, the Historical Society of Pennsylvania, and the New York State Historical Association.

Special thanks, and my dedication, go to William Mahar, division head of humanities, at Penn State Harrisburg. I am grateful for his blessings on my work, and I am inspired by his example.

Introduction

Simon J. Bronner

My story begins in 1893 at the Chicago World's Fair. The fair, or the World's Columbian Exposition as it was officially called, was the crowning spectacle of the nineteenth century. Set in the nation's fastest growing city and in a country which was a wonder of growth to the world, the fair exuded power and wealth. The gigantic Manufactures Hall, the largest roofed structure ever erected, hailed the great energy given to the age by machinery; and the planned "White City" that was the fair, decked out in classical architecture and decorations, attested to the power of civilized men and science over the savage wilderness. Speaking of the construction of buildings at the fair, one guide exclaimed, "It is not easy to overestimate the stupendous character of this portion of the greatest enterprise of modern times. The utmost power of genius and many millions of money were unitedly brought to bear upon the execution of the infinite details of the general plan." For most observers, the fair was the height of a Victorian civilization that owed much to English manners and society, but which apparently was exceeded in America.[1]

The English originated the idea of the fair with the famed Crystal Palace Exposition in 1851, but Americans elaborated the fair to mass proportions. The Americans converted the idea of a fair as an expositon of industries to a spectacle of modern civilization. At the Chicago World's Fair, as well as at other American fairs that followed, the world was on display, and it was divided into levels of advancement. Back on the Midway behind the main industrial exhibits, aboriginal groups offered their culture as amusement, and excitement, to curious Victorians (figs. I-1 and I-2). "The Australian display," one report noted, "contains illustrations of the Bora initiation ceremonies, and that of Africa[,] representations of disguises employed in sacred rites not yet explained. . . . The Midway Plaisance offers a continued spectacle of various life." A "Turkish

Figure I-1.   Illustration of a Scene on the Midway
          The original caption reads: " 'Baby him talk gumbo.' 'Gug-gug-oo-o-ooo!'
          gurgled the baby. 'Him say me his papa!' exclaimed the savage.''
          (From Thomas Fleming, Around the "Pan" with Uncle Hank: His Trip
          through the Pan-American Exposition *[New York: Nut Shell Publishing
          Co., 1901])*

Figure I-2.   Illustration of a Scene on the Midway
The original caption reads: "Uncle Hank Does the Hula-Hula Dance."
(From Thomas Fleming, Around the "Pan" with Uncle Hank: His
Trip through the Pan-American Exposition *[New York: Nut Shell
Publishing Co., 1901])*

Village," for example, featured an exotic bazaar, mosque, and theater; an Arab encampment showcased wedding ceremonies and mock combats. At the "Algerian and Tunisian Village," an observer admiringly wrote, "native dances were performed in the theatre, in one of which, the so-called 'torture dance,' one of the men dancers ate live scorpions and broken glass, grasped red-hot irons, and drew needles through his flesh, while apparently under the influence of some drug."[2]

Although characterized by their sense of restraint and propriety, Victorians took in these exotic demonstrations with great enthusiasm. Indeed, at the same time that the "White City" was celebrated for its rational order and scientific planning, descriptions of the fair coated it in the fantasy of traditional fairy tales. "The enchanted White City," one guide declared, "the City of Aladdin's palaces—was thus magically springing from the mud of a primeval prairie."[3] One expression of the appeal of primitive custom and magic to Victorians comes from Henry Childs Merwin, who wrote a widely circulated article for *Atlantic Monthly*. Provocatively entitling his essay "On Being Civilized Too Much," Merwin bemoaned the loss of "closeness to nature" and the weakening of primitive instincts in the new industrial civilization. Merwin declared, for example, that the greatest literature—that is, the literature with the most feeling—was created by those who were close to nature. Furthermore, he wrote,

> Savages and children have a natural love for good bright colors. Everybody knows that these colors tend to raise the spirits, and therefore to improve the health. . . . This natural, healthy sense of color may of course be cultivated and trained, so that those who possess it can learn to appreciate the beauty of more delicate shades; and in such persons there will be a happy union of natural taste with cultivation.

But alas, this is vicarious, because "city people hire others to do for them, but country people know how to shift for themselves." Merwin pleaded with his audience to "consult the teamster, the farmer, the wood-chopper, the shepherd, or the drover. You will find him as healthy in mind, as free from fads, as strong in natural impulses, as he was in Shakespeare's time and is in Shakespeare's plays. From his loins, and not from those of the dilettante, will spring the man of the future." The country, the children, and the savages constituted the line-up of the Victorian's "folk," whose anachronistic "expressions" and "productions," as the author called them, were refreshing palliatives for the overcivilized man and woman.[4]

Viewing primitive customs and rites, Victorians felt reassured that they had risen above what they assumed to be their primitive ancestors. Yet, while feeling superior in thought and behavior, they felt at a loss for feeling and instinct. Industrial advancement had its price, so it seemed, and many social advisers thought that the vitality of spirituality and emotion apparent in primitive rites and customs was traded in for the march of civilization. Some social advisers sought out to refine primitive rituals for modern application so as to invigorate the sensibilities of modern cosmopolitans. Often borrowing from the example of masked rites, masquerade events enjoyed a vogue in Victorian society; secret and fraternal societies arose invoking elaborate rituals and codes; and cosmetics and bodily ornaments grew in popularity with the suggestion that they provided primitive sensuality. Game manufacturer Selchow and Righter copyrighted the Asian game of Parcheesi in the 1870s, and the "primitive" game caught on as a Victorian parlor game. Books of fairy tales, peasant myths, and Indian legends were among the best-sellers of the Victorian period, and their compilers, men like Andrew Lang, Hans Christian Andersen, and of course the Grimm Brothers, drew world renown.[5]

This material had come under the name of "folklore" since 1846, when Britisher William John Thoms (1803–85) proposed a "good Saxon compound" for what had previously been referred to in English as popular antiquities and literature. In a letter to *Athenaeum,* a leading weekly review of literature, science, and the arts, Thoms described folklore both as a connected whole—"the Lore of the People" and as separable parts— "manners, customs, observances, superstitions, ballads, proverbs." He wanted to accomplish for the British what the Grimm brothers had done for Germany, and he claimed that

> the present century has scarcely produced a more remarkable book, imperfect as its learned author confesses it to be, than the second edition of the *"Deutsche Mythologie"* and, what is it?—a mass of minute facts, many of which, when separately considered, appear trifling and insignificant,—but, when taken in connection with the system into which his master-mind has woven them, assume a value that he who first recorded them never dream of attributing to them.[6]

In the next issue of the weekly magazine, a department of folklore was established, with Thoms in charge. During the 1850s, books began to appear using "folklore" in their titles: Thomas Sternberg's *The Dialect and Folklore of Northamptonshire* (1851), Jabez Allies's *On the Ancient British, Roman and Saxon Antiquities and Folk-Lore of Worcestershire* (1852), and Thoms's *Choice Notes from "Notes and Queries": Folk Lore* (1859). By 1876, Thoms was signing himself "An Old Folk-Lorist," giving a name to the student of the subject; and the next year, the term was given sanction by the formation in England of the Folk-Lore Society.

The distinctive round of life belonging to the peasants found special attention on the European continent. The emphasis on *life* implied a concern for traditions of subsistence and technology (*lore* emphasized traditions of imagination) and the isolation of traditional cultures. Nonetheless, overlaps existed between studies of lore and life because of the common concern for the beliefs that traditions expressed, and at least in America, matters of folklife were often subsumed under folklore in the belief that the combination of folk and lore literally meant informally gained knowledge of the common people. The use of the Swedish word *folkliv* (folklife) can be traced to 1847, when it appeared in a Swedish book, and the German equivalents of "folklife" regularly appeared after 1806. It is likely that Thoms's term was derived from the German usage. Indeed, practitioners of folklife and folklore equally invoked ethnology (usually under the umbrella of anthropology)—studies of preindustrial cultures—although their studies typically stressed ethnic societies within industrialized countries. Early on, however, German usage stressed the overarching culture of the folk, while English usage stressed the surviving materials of the folk. The British *Handbook of Folklore* (1914) explained, for example, that folklore "has established itself as the generic term under which the traditional Beliefs, Customs, Stories, Songs, and Sayings current among backward peoples, or retained by the uncultured classes of more advanced peoples, are comprehended and included." George Laurence Gomme (1853–1916), in *Ethnology in Folklore* (1892), underscored the point he had made in an earlier version of the handbook: "The essential characteristic of folklore is that it consists of beliefs, customs, and traditions which are far behind civilisation in their intrinsic value to man, though they exist under the cover of a civilised nationality."[7] Something of a combination of life and lore was evident, however, in essays such as W. J. Hoffman's description of Pennsylvania-German folklore in the first volume of the *Journal of American Folklore* (reprinted in this book). Hoffman included objects and customs to describe the distinctive ethnic round of life in central Pennsylvania, in addition to collecting folk stories and language. In 1892, Walther Hough, an ethnologist at the United States National Museum, addressed the American Folklore Society on "Folk-life in and about the National Capital." In 1897, the *Journal of American Folklore* carried Heli Chatelain's "African Folklife," and William Greenough published *Canadian Folk-Life and Folk-Lore.* In 1905, the first general book on American folklife appeared, written by a German, Karl Knortz (1841–1918), who was living in Evansville, Indiana. Entitled *Zur amerikanischen Volkskunde,* the book concentrated on ethnic rites and customs, and covered beliefs, tales, and objects.

American writers on beliefs, customs, and other traditions tended to be most influenced by the English view of folklore, although a strong nod to the German notion of folklife was prevalent in Pennsylvania, as a result of the interest in German scholarship spurred by the region's German heritage. With the absence of a native peasantry, Americans focused their attention on American Indians and various groups that they felt were rich in tradition, such as European and Asian immigrants, Afro-Americans, French-Canadians, Latin American migrants, Appalachians and other isolated mountain or maritime groups, and children. Looking at the life of these groups, American folklorists in the late nineteenth century avidly recorded customs, rites, objects, beliefs, narratives, and songs to compare with folklore collected worldwide. By 1887, Americans had staked their claim to the advancement of the science of folklore. The middle-class intellectual magazine *Open Court* (dedicated to reconciling religion and science) carried an article by Lee J. Vance (1862–1942) entitled "Folk-Lore Studies." He traced its roots to the field collecting of the Grimm brothers in the early nineteenth century. "From that day until this," Vance wrote,

> the by-ways and hedges of all Europe have been more or less ransacked by keen-eyed and inquiring disciples of Grimm, eagerly taking down the marvelous stories as they fell from the lips of the peasantry. What was thus taken down, not only found its way in print, but found thousands of readers. And now the lettered were willing to sit at the feet of the unlettered. Folk-Lore societies were quickly established for the purpose of collecting and preserving these fanciful legends, and its members are now numbered by the hundreds [8]

"What have our American students of Folk-Lore done toward contributing their share to the History of Culture?" Vance asked. His answer revolved around the formation of the American Folklore Society, which became a reality in 1888. It, along with the Chicago Folklore Society formed in 1891 (later renamed the International Folklore Association), organized folklore studies in America. Scattered among the professions and especially among museums, American folklorists devoted their energies, Vance declared, to understanding the "history of progress." Chronicling the growth of American efforts in 1893, Vance counted more members of American folklore societies than any European counterpart. "Prior to 1887," Vance reflected, "the study of popular tradition in America was unorganized. Since then the investigations of special students in different fields have been collated and systematized, and, above all, those interested in the subject have been brought together. Thus today there is a certain *esprit de corps* among American folk-lorists that was unknown some six or eight years ago." The folklore societies had, Vance said, a "social side and function," as well as its work; "already their influence has been felt in many quarters."[9]

Writing again in 1896, Vance claimed that the end of the nineteenth century

> will be marked by the rise and growth of a new science,—the science which studies mankind from the time when the earth and the human family were young down to the present time. This science (whether called Anthropology or Comparative Folk-Lore) studies the progress of man in culture. It reveals the evolution of modern culture from the beliefs and usages of savages and simple-minded folk. Now folk-lore is concerned more particularly with the "survival" of primitive or ancient ideas and customs in modern civilization: that is to say, our study traces the development of tribal custom into national law; of pagan custom into Christian ecclesiastical usage and popular festivals; of sorcery and magic into astrology, and finally into astronomical science; of song and dance into Greek drama and poetry; of nursery tales and *Märchen* into the epic and the modern novel. Again, the end of the nineteenth century is remarkable for the immense number of books devoted to the Folk—to people who have shared . . . least in the general advance. These people are, first, the backward races, as the natives of Australia and our Indian tribes; then the European peasantry, Southern negroes, and others out of touch with towns and schools and railroads.[10]

And so, the Midway of the Chicago World's Fair, with its displays of people who have shared least in the general advance, was put under the charge of the Anthropology department. The department was also responsible for what turned out to be among the most popular exhibits of the fair, a gold-medal-winning display of "folk-lore" consisting of gaming and ritual objects, prepared by Stewart Culin from the University of Pennsylvania (fig. I-3). Other notables from the American Folklore Society also participated in the exhibits of the Anthropology building, among them Franz Boas, Frederic Putnam, and Frank Hamilton Cushing. In the Manufactures Hall, the University of Pennsylvania Museum exhibited "a very complete series of objects illustrating the customs of the Chinese laborers in the United States." Elsewhere, "George F. Kunz displayed under the name of the New York Branch of the American Folk-Lore Society a collection of gems and minerals having a folk-lore significance which were of peculiar interest and value." The Chicago World's Fair, Stewart Culin observed, "afforded the greatest opportunity to the student and collector of folk-lore that has ever been presented upon this continent."[11]

When educational congresses were brought to the fair to honor the pressing issues at the end of the century, folklore again came to the fore. Once more reveling in topping the previous work of Europeans, Fletcher S. Bassett (1847–93) of the Chicago Folklore Society organized the Third International Folklore Congress at the fair. The French and British had hosted the first two, but Bassett (fig. I-4) claimed that the Chicago congress was the "first great International Folk-Lore Congress" because it

Figure 1-3. Exhibit, Designed by Stewart Culin, of Folklore Objects at the Chicago World's Fair, 1893
(University of Pennsylvania Museum)

Figure I-4.   Fletcher S. Bassett
(From The International Folk-Lore Congress of the World's
Columbian Exposition, *edited by Helen Wheeler Bassett and
Frederick Starr [Chicago: Charles H. Sergel Co., 1898])*

boasted more worldwide participation than the other congresses. Bassett gushed when speaking of the growth of folklore studies in the previous few years. "Publications, annual, quarterly, monthly, and weekly, appear in our own city, in Boston, in London, in Ghent, in Antwerp, in Liege, in Helsingfors, in Copenhagen, in Berlin, in Leipsig, in Leyden, in Paris, in Palermo, in Vienna, in Warsaw, in Bombay, and in other cities, devoted to this study, besides others whose columns are largely devoted to Folk-Lore." Bassett then went on to note the special role of folklore studies in American society. "Folk-Lore societies encourage the collection, publication, and study of this important and beneficent information and serve an important purpose in our civilization," Bassett explained. "The labors of the eminent scholars of America in this direction," he offered, "demonstrate that Folk-Lore is far advanced in our midst, in spite of the youth of our existence. . . . Folk-Lore," he emphasized, "has become a subject of the day."[12]

Indeed it had. In studies of folklife, writers described unusual "manners" of "ruder ages" and "removed lands," judged by the rigid middle-class standards of the day. The accounts dwelled on sensuality and emotional bonding in customs and rites, and the deep attachments and meanings apparent in ritual and decorative objects. Folklife showed the closeness of man to nature and the glory of the toiling hand. The sweep of tradition was broad, but Victorians drew three special lines of inquiry related to rapid changes in the social life of the nineteenth century. Related to their concern for the secularization of modern culture, the displacement of religion as a formula for living with science, was the Victorians' search for the meaning and development of spiritual belief. Related to their concern for the rapid industrialization of everyday life was the Victorians' uncovering of primitive "invention," "industry," and "technology." And linked to their concern for the utilitarianism of the rational order brought by industrialization, many Victorians sought out the character of art and decoration in folk tradition. For expansive nations like England and America, folklife studies opened the world for cultural judgment.

Folklife studies dramatized the dilemmas of a rising middle class, raising ambivalence about relations between passing traditions and whirring modernity. Editors of popular magazines sought out folklorists to address the issues that were causing ambivalence for their readers. Leafing through the pages of influential magazines such as *Harper's Monthly, Atlantic Monthly, Century, Nation, Open Court, Outlook, Popular Science Monthly,* and *Overland Monthly,* readers found essays on, among other subjects, primitive inventions and "industry," women's roles in primitive society, beliefs and customs having to do with the supernatural, and the evolution of folk religious objects into play items. Further evidence of the folklore "vogue" is that the two main guides to popular periodicals at the time, *Poole's Index to Periodical Literature* and the *Reader's Guide,* indexed the *Journal of American Folklore.* The number of articles cited under "folklore" reveals a pattern from the founding of the American Folklore Society into the first decade of the twentieth century. *Poole's Index* listed 14 articles on folklore (folk song was listed separately) from 1887 to 1892; from 1892 to 1896, the number jumped to 77, but dropped down to 7 from 1902 to 1905, when *Poole's* ceased publication. The *Reader's Guide* listed a whopping 177 articles for folklore between 1890 and 1909, not counting entries for the *Journal of American Folklore.* In 1905, however, the *Reader's Guide* ceased indexing the journal. In the ensuing years, the *Reader's Guide* doubled the number of periodicals that it indexed, but between 1910 and 1924, the guide listed only 58 articles on folklore. The last decades of the nineteenth century not only have the claim, then, to the Gilded Age, but also to the title of the Ethnological Period, full of folkloristic forays far from the beaten path to answer questions close to home.

The ethnological fervor was driven by evolutionary thought and previous decades of attention to the discoveries of natural history. Charles Darwin's journey in 1835 to collect specimens and observe patterns on the Galapagos Islands triggered, in ethnologist W. J. McGee's words, "the most profound revolution in the history of human thought." Darwin capped many years of mulling over his ideas with the publication in 1859 of *The Origin of Species*. The work was a sensation, although evolutionary principles had already been proposed. Historian of ethnology T. K. Penniman, for example, noted that between 1835 and 1859, "the social scientists, the archeologists and students of material cultures, and the ethnologists and biologists were all coming into relation with each other, and breaking down the compartments in which their sciences were imprisoned from each other. Further, all were trying to find principles of origin and development." McGee also mentions that "the wide and ready acceptance of the Darwinian doctrine was but the coordination of knowledge already gained."[13] Still, Darwin's name and his ideas of "natural selection" became inexorably attached to the boom in natural sciences during the nineteenth century.

Among Darwin's revelations to his Victorian audience was that the past extended far longer than had been proposed by religious leaders, advanced species of life evolved from "lower" forms, and natural laws controlled the evolution. Opening up the long history of nature by collecting, classifying, and arranging specimens into an evolutionary order suggested that creation might be similarly defined for humanity, and hence for culture. With the past apparently remote, however, specialized practitioners with esoteric "scientific" skills became necessary to uncover the past for the public. The social side effects of such changes in thinking were significant. For one, a shortened theological past which had been part of the older wisdom meant that changes in nature and man were necessarily large leaps. The opening of the evolutionary past suggested that the world's beginning was not a literal wholesale creation, but was a metaphor for slow and constant change. While Victorians were feeling that transformative changes were occurring during their time, the new world view provided the security that their era was not a cataclysm, but a climax of steady growth.

During the 1860s, proposals for a social and cultural Darwinism came on the scene touting a cultural hierarchy which showed that the Western industrialized nations had prospered through cultural evolution and "survival of the fittest." Laws of evolution applied to culture affirmed the superiority of Victorian society over primitive groups that Victorians sought to modernize and control. In 1871, Darwin made the connection between his natural laws and social patterns explicit in *The Descent of Man*. Referring to the ethnological adaptations during the 1860s of his work by Edward Tylor, John Lubbock, and John McLennan, Darwin weighed the arguments about whether man, as they claimed, rose culturally as well as naturally. Darwin commented:

To believe that man was aboriginally civilized and then suffered utter degradation in so many regions is to take a pitiably low view of human nature. It is apparently a truer and more cheerful view that progress has been much more general than retrogression; that man has risen, though by slow and interrupted steps, from a lowly condition to the highest standard as yet attained by him in knowledge, morals and religion.

At the conclusion of the book, he endorsed the view of progress that was common to his age: "Man may be excused for feeling some pride at having risen, though not through his own exertions, to the very summit of the organic scale; and the fact of his having thus risen, instead of having been aboriginally placed there, may give him hope for a still higher destiny in the distant future."[14]

Darwin sided with the cheerier and more timely view. I say timely, because of the rapid industrialization and imperialism that claimed the march of evolutionary progress as its justification. Welcoming participants to the Third International Folklore Congress, the president of the Chicago Folklore Society, William Knapp, exclaimed: "We are transforming, almost transformed. . . . Quaint faces, strange costumes, unintelligible tongues, have blended with the dominant civilizations of Western Europe and the New World beyond, while venerable races have made obeisance to the material prosperity of younger and novel institutions." In 1871, Edward Tylor emphasized that "not merely as a matter of curious research, but as an important practical guide to the understanding of the present and the shaping of the future, the investigation into the origin and early development of civilization must be pushed on zealously."[15]

W. J. McGee (1853–1912) noted the particularly favorable response to evolutionary doctrine in America. "The earliest and strongest apostles were Americans," he wrote, and "the free, vigorous and trenchant American mind was peculiarly hospitable to the tenets of the new law; and it was accepted here as the foundation for the cult of science years before it was similarly accepted in Great Britain."[16] America gave a particularly hospitable reception to the social Darwinism of Britisher Herbert Spencer, who made a case for industrial progress and laissez-faire economics on the grounds of Darwin's natural selection. By 1903 more than 368,000 volumes of Spencer's works had been sold in the United States. The popular writings of John Fiske (author of *Myths and Mythmakers*) and William Graham Sumner (author of *Folkways*) applied Spencer liberally in their work. Preacher Henry Ward Beecher wrote Spencer with this observation: "The peculiar condition of American society has made your writings far more fruitful and quickening here than in Europe." For the United States, Beecher felt, where industrialization and its social effects came later than in Europe, nonetheless experienced them more quickly and with greater ripples through the diversity of cultural groups living on America's soil. America was like the Galapagos Islands, many thought, because of its rich variety of cultural species and settings. On such a soil, which to many social critics appeared confused with its thick undergrowth of immigrants, mountaineers, river folk, Indians, and blacks, the evolutionary lens brought into focus a unified, orderly outline. Evolution imposed an order on social change and confusion, which was commonly suffered by the middle class during the Gilded Age.[17]

In 1879, The United States government had established the Bureau of American Ethnology in the Smithsonian Institution to record the natural history of America's culture, particularly its Indians. The Bureau sought out folklore in its field collecting trips as a key to uncovering the savage past of that culture. The Bureau had fashioned, W. J. McGee said, "a New Ethnology, in which men are classified by mind rather than by body, by culture rather than by color." In a popular view of cultural evolution, McGee classified all the world's peoples into stages of development, "namely: (1) savagery, with a social organization resting on kinship reckoned in the female line; (2) barbarism, in which the social organization is based on kinship reckoned in the male line; (3) civilization, in which the organization has a territorial basis; and (4) enlightenment, in which the laws and customs are based on intellectual rights." Again pointing to American conditions to explain the intellectual fervor for this scheme, McGee wrote: "Our physical progress has been great because invention is encouraged by free institutions; our progress in geology has been rapid by reason of intellectual freedom and a vast domain; while our progress in anthropology has been marvelous because of the elevated point of view and an incomparable range of types both of blood and of activity."[18]

Accordingly, folk items such as customs, rites, and objects were treated like natural specimens. Readily observable and repeatable, folk items could be classified by type, compared with similar specimens found elsewhere, arranged into levels, and lines, of development, and analyzed to make statements on origin. Evolutionary doctrine implied a distinctive "control" of the world. Rites and customs were especially significant in illustrating this doctrine and the "mind" of culture because they often appeared unusual or exotic and suggested to the Victorians extraordinary attitudes toward, and beliefs about, man in relation to his environment. At lower levels, rites represented control of the world by supernatural and natural forces, and later in advanced stages, by human, technological forces. The progression of items, many folklorists believed, worked from superstition to science, from primitive rites to refined manners, from exotic customs to rational observances. While societies advance, many folk items persist in practice, although they lose their original significance and intimate connection with the group. In evolutionary theory, the persistence of such customs was analogous to survival of the culturally unfit. The survivals could be collected often in remnant form among civilized folk and could be seen in full flowering among existing "savage" groups such as American Indians. Thus, many studies offered to give the original, racy meanings of curious sayings and objects that once had significance in primitive customs; and others gave a glimpse of the similar ways of thinking among different primitive groups.

The *Journal of American Folklore*'s first editor and founder of the American Folklore Society, William Wells Newell (1839–1907), supported evolutionary doctrine and set up custom as folklore's polestar. Writing up "Topics for Collection of Folk-Lore" for the journal, Newell related the study of food, clothing, and craft to belief and ritual. He attracted the leading lights in this study to fill out the agenda he had proposed (figs. I-5 and I-6). Stewart Culin offered his work on games (which evolved, he thought, from religious divinatory rites) and co-authored with Newell a piece on Afro-American sorcery for the journal.[19] Otis Mason from his station at the Smithsonian Institution was especially prominent in the field, and in addition to specific studies of the development of technology from primitive sources (see his study of traps reprinted in this volume), he contributed a manifesto of the evolutionary work of the folklife scholars with "The Natural History of Folklore" (reprinted in this volume). Readers of the *Journal of American Folklore* as well as *Atlantic Monthly* in the 1890s also became familiar with Fanny Bergen's work in material culture. She published several notes on children's folklife, American regional foodways, and quilt patterns. With her botanist husband, she had authored *A Primer of Darwinism and Organic Evolution* (1890), and she followed that work with books that showed that her folklife research owed to her interest in beliefs and the natural world: *Current Superstitions Collected from the Oral Tradition of English-Speaking Folk* (1896) and *Animal and Plant Lore* (1899). Interest in funerary rites and objects is indicated by notes (reprinted in this volume) by two scientists, chemist H. Carrington Bolton and naturalist Ernest Ingersoll, on the decoration of Afro-American graves. From the society's 1890 meeting in New York came several material culture abstracts related to customs published in the journal, including Frederick Starr's "Folk-Lore of Stone Tools" and George Kunz's "Exhibition of Gems Used as Amulets." Starr also compiled a collection of Mexican pottery masks and other Hispanic ritual artifacts which he later expanded and displayed to the Folk-Lore Society in London.[20]

Figure I-5. Illustration of Proceedings of the American Folklore Society's
Annual Meeting on 28–29 December 1897
The topics discussed by those pictured: W. W. Newell,
"Opportunities for Collecting Folklore in America"; A. S. Chessin,
"Russian Folklore"; C. C. Bombaugh, "Bibliography of Folklore";
and H. C. Bolton, "Relics of Astrology."
(From the Baltimore American)

Figure 1-6.   Illustration Entitled "Leaders of the American Folklore Society,"
from an Article Covering the Congress of American Scientists,
Philadelphia, 29 December 1895

Daniel Brinton is the bearded man in the center with the top hat;
up and to the right of him is Otis Mason; on the fourth stair,
second from the left is Stewart Culin; and on the far left is William Wells Newell.

(From the Philadelphia Inquirer*)*

The American Folklore Society's rival during the 1890s, the Chicago Folklore Society, also showed strong interest in material culture. Just before the Chicago World's Fair, the Chicago Folklore Society published its *Folk-Lore Manual* (excerpted in this volume). Its author, Fletcher Bassett, asserted that "finally, collection may well take the direction of tangible objects—visible proofs of the existence of traditional customs, superstitions and ceremonies." He included in the manual a "List of Objects for a Folklore Collection." He divided the objects into categories of "The House and Its Furnishings," "Personal Objects," including clothing, toys, and games, "The Trades," covering occupational crafts, "Folk-Medicine," and "Charms and Amulets."[21]

Bassett made this concern more explicit in his address to the committee planning the International Folklore Congress. He listed four segments composing the subject matter of folklore: (1) Myths and Traditional Beliefs, (2) Oral Literature and Folk Music, (3) Customs, Institutions, and Ritual, and (4) Artistic, Emblematic, and Economic Folk-Lore. "The fourth division," Bassett declared, "embraces all in the Graphic, Plastic and Industrial Arts, bearing upon the questions pertinent to Folk-Lore." Representing the fourth division in the publication of the Folklore Congress were papers on folk craft and invention, history of the Swastika, and Slavic grave decoration. Representing American work, Washington Matthews (fig. I-7) offered his collection of sacred objects taken from the Navajo (reprinted in this volume). With each item, from a drumstick to ritual cigarettes, he pointed out the sensual ritual uses that the items had within the culture.[22]

Such research projected the interests of an important constituency of the American Folklore Society—the museum professionals. The study of folklore and ethnology arose outside of the academy, which was slow to give up its classical curriculum. If they wanted a full-time occupation in the field, the experts on ethnology found homes in museums. With museum exhibits emphasizing the interpretation of rare and exotic clues to the past, often in arrangements that drew comparisons to the allure of world's fairs and department store displays, many ethnologists were able to find sympathetic and influential homes in museums—most dealing with natural history—for their work.[23] The Museum of Natural History opened in 1869; the United States National Museum, in 1879; the University of Pennsylvania Museum, in 1887; and the Brooklyn Institute Museum and the Field Museum in 1893. Each of these added ethnological sections to their collections. From this vantage, many ethnologists had rare opportunities to reach the public with their ideas, and the ethnologists also benefited from private and governmental funding of great collecting trips, especially to Indian lands out West. The roster of the American Folklore

Figure I-7. Washington Matthews, ca. 1895
(National Anthropological Archives, Smithsonian Institution)

Society featured men and women, therefore, concerned with collections of displayable objects, and the "object lessons" provided by primitive customs and rites for a Victorian public. Between 1890 and 1903, ten presidents of the American Folklore Society, when they took office, held professional affiliations with ethnological museums. Frederic Ward Putnam, head of the Anthropology Department at the Chicago World's Fair, was director of the Peabody Museum. Otis Mason was head curator of ethnology at the United States National Museum and worked closely there with Frank Hamilton Cushing. Cushing also did work for the University of Pennsylvania Museum, the home base of Daniel Brinton and Stewart Culin.

A closer look at the careers of Culin and Mason, probably the two best-known museum men, provides an inkling of the kind of professionals who were known for their folklife studies. Stewart Culin (fig. I-8) was born in Philadelphia in 1858. He graduated from Nazareth Hall, where he fondly recalled being regaled with American Indian tales by an influential teacher. At the age of seventeen, Culin entered his father's merchant business in Philadelphia. He conducted business with Chinese immigrants and learned their language. Reading in the early studies of anthropology, he recorded the distinctive customs of the Chinese in the city. He collected their medicines, games, arts, and religious objects. With the merchant's care for detail and accurate record-keeping, he expanded his collections and interests to cover the entire Orient. He joined and later became secretary of the Numismatic and Antiquarian Society of Philadelphia. As a member of the society, he was influenced by Daniel Brinton, who attracted international acclaim for his prolific writings in archaeology, linguistics, mythology, and religion. Brinton, later to become the first university professor of anthropology, published Culin's article on medical practices of the Chinese in 1887 and encouraged Culin to pursue his studies.

Brinton envisioned a museum at the University of Pennsylvania which would undertake the collection, display, and study of cultural objects. Plans went ahead for the museum in 1887 and Culin left his business to become the first secretary for the Oriental Section in 1890. That same year, he publicized his plans for a "folk-lore museum" (reprinted in this volume). Such a museum, he wrote, "would have an extended field, and might embrace a vast number of objects which do not ordinarily come within the domain of the collector, and yet are most valuable as illustrating customs, myths, and superstitions." He gave as an example the rabbit's foot to bring good luck and the potato and the horse chestnut carried to prevent rheumatism. They are "often quite interesting in themselves," he said, and "if properly arranged and labelled with their special story

Figure I-8.   Stewart Culin, ca. 1895
                (National Anthropological Archives, Smithsonian Institution)

or signification, would form a vastly entertaining collection and a valuable aid in the study to which the Folklore Society is devoted."[24]

In 1892, Culin put together a ballyhooed exhibition of religious objects of the world at the University of Pennsylvania Museum. Largely as a result of the show's success, he was appointed secretary of the American Historical Commission to the World's Exposition in Madrid in 1892. He then rose to the position of director of Archaeology and Paleontology for the university museum. He followed in 1893 with a display of "folklore objects," many garnered from American Folklore Society members, for the Chicago World's Fair. Visitors to the fair marvelled at the exhibit he had assembled in eye catching arrangements. "Folklore most intimately connects this age with the greatest antiquity," exclaimed the *Chicago Record,* "and of folklore no branch so directly informs us of our relation to the people of most ancient days than the games for the different stages in the history of the world."[25]

At the fair, Culin met Frank Hamilton Cushing of the Bureau of American Ethnology, who took great interest in Culin's exhibit and offered to collaborate on a study of Indian games (fig. I-9). The exhibit showed an evolution of religious objects giving way to games. Besides this concern for custom, Culin noticed the ornamental features of his objects. "When we examine the products of man's handicraft," he reflected, "we everywhere find evidences of an aesthetic sense, of an effort, not only at mere utility, but at decoration and ornament, analogous to that which is universal among cultivated people at the present day." His explanation? Ornament stemmed from religion, magic, and superstition—"of the reasoning which led many to attempt through magic to control or influence the forces of nature."[26]

Culin followed the Chicago fair with an exhibition in 1895 of games at another world's fair, the Cotton States and International Exposition at Atlanta, for which he received another gold medal. The exhibit was accompanied by the most extensive catalogue of its time, *Chess and Playing Cards,* which continues to be used today as a reference. Two years later, Culin became the president of the American Folklore Society, and devoted his presidential address specifically to American Indian games. Culin then embarked on lengthy trips to Europe to study the collections of renowned ethnological museums and dispatched reports which were printed in the Philadelphia newspapers. Despite the strong head start of European museums, Culin enthused, American museums could rival and surpass them if the resourcefulness given to building American industry was applied to museum work. He assembled a display of games for the Paris World's Fair of 1900 and bewildered the Europeans by taking the grand prize for exhibits.

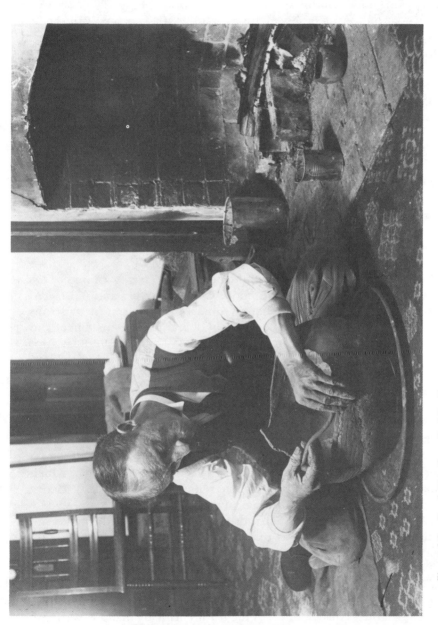

Figure 1-9. Frank Hamilton Cushing Demonstrating Southwest Indian Pottery Techniques for the Bureau of American Ethnology at the Smithsonian Institution, ca. 1895 *(National Anthropological Archives, Smithsonian Institution)*

In 1899 and 1900, Culin grieved over the deaths of his two greatest influences: Daniel Brinton and Frank Hamilton Cushing. To Culin was left the goal of advancing his mentors' studies. He replaced Brinton as lecturer in anthropology and continued Cushing's study of Indian games. In 1900, he left the comforts of his house in Philadelphia to travel west with the Wanamaker Expedition into the Indian territories. The first stop was Tama, Iowa, where he visited the Sac and Fox nations. Observing a tribal feast, his eyes turned to the old men sitting on platforms in the long-houses, their medicine bags hanging from rafters above them. Culin was moved. "These feeble creatures, with strangely wrinkled faces, expressive of patience and suffering and more of life's experience than falls to all the collected multitude of our modern towns," he wrote, "were once the tribal leaders and are still the repositories of the tribal secrets and traditions. One by one, they will be carried to the little graveyard on the hillside and buried with their precious packs, and all their wealth of curious knowledge will be lost to the world forever."[27] Culin rededicated himself after this trip to the study of Indian cultures, and especially their rites and objects (figs. I-10 and I-11).

In 1907, he published his magnum opus of 846 pages, *Games of the North American Indians.* In the book, Culin classified and illustrated American Indian gaming implements in American and European museums according to activity and called upon field observation to document and compare the games across cultures. Writing the chief of the Bureau of American Ethnology, Culin penned, "I might suggest that this is the first serious attempt to compare and study the games of more than one tribe. It is by far the largest collection of data about aboriginal games, whether in the Old World or the New. It is, too, the largest collection of data existing on any particular subject referring to the objective culture of the Indian." The term *objective* appealed to Culin because of its inclusion of "objects," the center of study, and its objectivity, reflecting the stress on a detached "scientific" approach. By this he meant "science which embraces the examination of all man's activities . . . Like modern science generally it is based upon multitudes of more or less minute and widely extended observations, but unlike those sciences such as mathematics and chemistry which we know as exact its formulations are less definite, although no less alluring."[28]

But a few years later, relocated at the Brooklyn Institute Museum (now the Brooklyn Museum), he would refer to his career as "devoted to the study of the material culture of mankind." He accepted more humanism in the "consideration of the things made by man." "We think of them," he wrote, "more in their immediate relation to man himself, not only as expression of his spirit but as retaining in themselves some

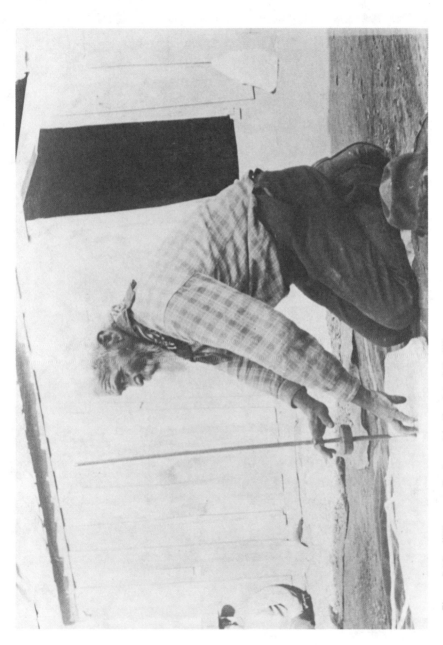

Figure 1-10. "Wampum Boring with Aboriginal Dr Il"
Photo is from Stewart Culin's field journal, 1906, and shows a Pomo Indian from Ukiah, California. *(National Anthropological Archives, Smithsonian Institution. Photo by H. W. Henshaw)*

Figure I-11. "Joseppa, Expert Basketweaver with Jeff, Her Husband" Photo is from Stewart Culin's field journal, 1906. Both are Pomo Indians, from Jokeye, California. *(National Antbropological Archives, Smithsonian Institution. Photo by H. W. Henshaw)*

of the very essence of his life and power. . . . There is something that seems akin to magic in the mastery of things, in this understanding of their language and this power to make them speak and tell their story." That magic, he felt, is "the quality of life to quicken our minds and excite the creative impulse which we designate as art."[29] Culin imagined that the museum would be valuable as industrialization took command, for the museum preserved models for design and a magic inspired by faraway creators filled with the compassion and immediacy of primitive life and power.

Seated in a Paris bistro in 1920, Culin yearned for the glorious vision of the Gilded Age. He watched a drunken display of jazz playing and dancing, and entered the scene in his journal: "I have been among the savages, but a display like this I have never seen." This was not, in his view, social progress. Walking through his museum gallery for one of the last times, he reflected, "It has been my habit as an ethnologist devoted to the study of the material culture of mankind to think of the races of antiquity as younger and not older than the people of our own age; to refresh myself with such contacts as I have had with their minds to feel myself younger and more vital. I have realized my dreams among savages in whose lives and thoughts I have had glimpses of the dawn of the world. I believe one should be free to choose whether the past be seen as a kind of inferno, diversified by murder and punctuated by crime, or as a joyous period of creative effort as I realize it from things of the past which I have made my friends and enticed into telling me their tales."[30]

Besides Stewart Culin, Otis Mason (1838–1908) provides an illustration of the concerns of the new breed of professionals. Born in Maine, and raised in Virginia, Mason (fig. I-12) went to Columbian College (now the George Washington University) in Washington, D.C., receiving, in the tradition of college education at the time, a general knowledge of biblical and classical studies, literature and philosophy. After graduation in 1861, he stayed on to teach natural history, classics, history, English, mathematics, and geography. During the 1870s, he championed "general principles of Natural Science" at the school. By 1880 he was instructor of English and history; when he left in 1884 for the United States National Museum of the Smithsonian Institution, he was listed as professor of anthropology. Among the courses he taught were "Races of Man," "History of Culture," and "History of the Past as Revealed in the Sciences of Archaeology and Folk-Lore."[31]

At the United States National Museum, Mason took up the enormous task of sorting its cultural collections. Claiming fields of folklore and ethnology, Mason used the objects in the collections to establish a cultural history based on the evolutionary principles of natural science. As cultural

Figure I-12. Otis Mason, ca. 1895
(National Anthropological Archives, Smithsonian Institution)

history, Mason's studies were intimately connected to issues of the day, which were being hotly discussed in the nation's capital. Students of primitive and folk culture were naturally involved with such issues, he observed, because they participated in the search for the hidden "secrets of man's origin, progress, and destiny."[32] In 1894, he published *Primitive Travel and Transportation,* a 350-page combination of detailed catalogue of objects in the museum's collection and of the reconstruction of the development of modern transportation industries from "primitive" cultures, mostly American Indian. The study signaled his interest in the roots of industrialization; he argued that increased mobility, both physical and social, in a modernizing nation requires the charting of traditional, passing ways of life, which is best captured in the stable, classifiable item.

The theme of mobility underlay Mason's next work, *Woman's Share in Primitive Culture,* also published in 1894. The moving, socially aspiring "new woman" had by this time raised pressing political and cultural questions. What effect would changes in her traditional roles have on the family and society? Would she be industrious or leisurely, scientific or sentimental? Mason was led to write: "Of the billion and a half human beings on the earth, one half, or about seven hundred million are females. What this vast multitude are doing in the world's activities and what share their mothers and grandmothers, to the remotest generation backward, have had in originating and developing culture, is a question which concerns the whole race."[33] Mason followed the next year with *The Origins of Invention.* Questions of women and industrialism were related, because women's roles in a nation of "mechanicalized" men became a topic of public debate, as did the "feminizing" consequences of genteel middle-class society on work and play.

Mason succeeded Daniel Brinton as the president of the American Folklore Society in 1891. Mason used the opportunity to give "The Natural History of Folklore," a manifesto of evolutionary doctrine applied to folklore studies. "Folk-lore is kept alive by public opinion," he declared, "and is opposed to progress; invention and science are centrifugal, venturesome, individual. This ability to act in common has itself had a historical growth, beginning with such savage acts as beating time to a rude dance, and rising to a grand chorus, a great battle, or a modern industrial establishment employing thousands of men marking time to one master spirit." Reflecting on the appeal of this study, Mason said: "In the last decade of the nineteenth century, when the world was looking forward, it was a relief to vary this mental attitude by occasionally glancing backward, and considering the past as it appeared by its survival in the present." And Mason found many present-day labels to attach to cultural survivals. "Without doubt," he said, "there is also a folk-speech, folk-trades and practices, folk fine art, folk-amusement, folk-festival, folk-ceremonies, folk-customs, folk-government, folk-society, folk-history, folk-poetry, folk-maxims, folk-philosophy, folk-science, and myths or folk-theology. Everything that we have, they have,—they are the back numbers of us.''[34]

At the Chicago World's Fair, Mason recapitulated his argument for a natural history of civilization and the special attention to folk technology which would lead two years later to the publication of *Origins of Invention.* ''The student of folk-lore is supposed to deal . . . with survivals, with customs, with common beliefs and common practices,'' he told the congress. ''He deals chiefly with those who follow suit. He does not frequent patent offices, but places of assembly, and listens to the repetition of things that do not seem to have had an origin, or watches the doing of things that have been done often and often before.'' From this basis, he outlined five evolutionary climbs which explained the rise of invention in modern society. The first is ''the creation of new desires with progress and the greater complexity of each want as it became more exacting.'' Summarized, this evolution is a progress, he said, from naturalism to artificialism. The second evolution is in ''the mental change involved in the act of invention,'' that is, from the assumedly simple observations of nature to the complex uses of a controlled laboratory. The third evolution is the improvement of implements, and the fourth evolution is the growth of public rewards for the inventor. The final evolution is vaguer than the rest; it refers to the organizational development in a society. In Mason's words, it is ''the unfolding of that national, or tribal, or family genius which constitutes the mark by which they have become known.'' Each family of mankind in its native home, Mason concluded, ''has invented a series of arts, the relics of which lie buried in their tombs and place of business. The history of their industries is written in these things. At the same time, by frequent trials and failures, they have invented languages and social structures, philosophies and mythologies, the history of which is written in the sayings and doings of the folk.'' Taken together, this evidence provides the all-important ''evolution of thought in the world.''[35]

Mason's chief disputant, and indeed of the American evolutionists in general, was a young German ethnologist by the name of Franz Boas (1858–1942), who had immigrated to the United States in 1887. Boas's work during the late nineteenth century had much in common with the likes of evolutionists Stewart Culin and Frederic Putnam, with whom he worked at the Chicago World's Fair, and with Otis Mason, for whom he collected Northwest Indian ritual objects in 1894 (fig. I-13). But especially after the turn of the century, when he had established his academic program in anthropology at Columbia University and severed his ties with

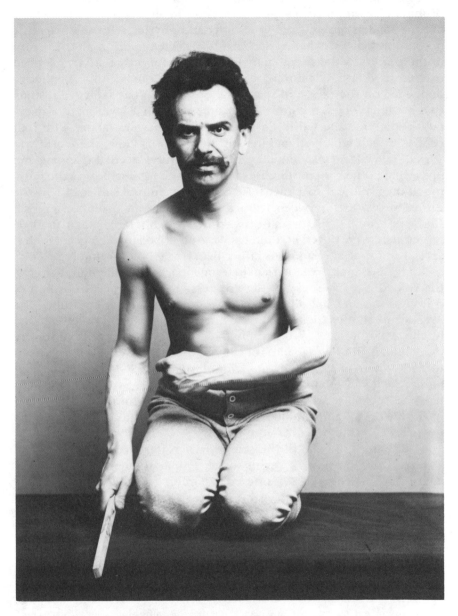

Figure I-13.　Franz Boas Demonstrating a Northwest Indian Ritual for the
Bureau of American Ethnology, ca. 1895
(National Anthropological Archives, Smithsonian Institution)

the American Museum of Natural History, Boas fully embraced a new way of thinking about cultures. Boas used, not the model of natural history, but the models drawn from geography and physics. The new scientific revolution that Boas hailed and that displaced evolution after the turn of the century was ushered in by Einstein's theory of relativity. Applied to culture, relativity assumed that one's view, one's cultural patterns, depended on the time and space one occupied. Boas sketched distinctive patterns for each culture, and came up with a level map of many cultures around the world, instead of an outline of a ladder with four rungs through which all cultures must rise. In his view, the world was varied, heterogeneous, simultaneous; its cultures needed mapping and observing in their totalities, rather than what he thought of as the purging of their cultural specimens. He explained cultural similarities by the diffusion of ideas between cultures rather than an evolutionary rise. Cultures, whether Victorian or Kwakiutl, were not better than another; rather, they were different. Cultures were described by their geographical spread and special conditions rather than by their climb and type. With relativity and a more egalitarian, heterogeneous view of cultural groups, the Gilded Age gave way to the Progressive Era. From his position of power at Columbia University, Boas and his students controlled the American Folklore Society after the turn of the century, and offered the intellectual foundations for twentieth-century views of race and society that supplanted Victorian ideas of cultural evolution. Writing the obituary for Otis Mason in 1908 in the *Journal of American Folklore,* Franz Boas buried the "New Ethnology." Having just taken over as editor of the journal, Boas recognized that Mason's "works assure to him a permanent place in the history of anthropology," while he looked ahead to a long reign for his relativistic brand of ethnography.[36]

But before the end of the century when the "New Ethnology" of Culin and Mason held sway, evolutionary folklife studies had lofty, timely goals. W. J. McGee in 1898 offered a summary of their achievements, which capped, he said, fifty years of Victorian scientific advances. "The main movements," he offered, meant that

> the sources of aesthetics and ethics have been successfully sought, the early steps in the course of industrial development have been traced, the beginnings of law have been analyzed, and the course of human development has been brought to light; and it is now known that the lines of human progress in the arts and industries, in sociology, in language, and in thought are convergent, rather than divergent like the lines of development among beasts and plants, and that the unification of ideas by telegraph and telephone and press is but a ripple marking the course of the great stream of human activity.

The New Ethnology, to which many folklorists held allegiance, laid claim to great advances in scientific progress. "Scientific progress," McGee declared for America, "is so closely interwoven with industrial and social progress that the advance of one cannot be traced without constant reference to the other."[37]

Let me explore, then, the "scientific progress" suggested by studies made to interweave with the realization of industry and women's roles in America. These two themes ran strongly in discussions of the era's tensions and consequently found their way into folklife studies. In George Miller Beard's widely circulated book *American Nervousness* (1881), for example, the author invoked the traditional past to understand the present, for "the moderns differ from the ancient civilizations mainly in these five elements—steam power, the periodical press, the telegraph, the sciences, and the mental activity of women. When civilization, plus these five factors, invades any nation, it must carry nervousness and nervous diseases along with it."[38] Claiming an expertise in the activities of ancient society and their changes in modern civilization, American folklorists provided briefs for a nation that was charged with nervous change.

The labeling by folklorists of primitive and folk activities commonly stressed modernist terms such as *industry* and *invention*. Besides Mason, who used the terms widely, Alexander Chamberlain, the first American Ph.D. in anthropology in 1892, wrote on "Mythology and Folklore of Invention" for the *Journal of American Folklore;* and Thomas Wilson published "Primitive Industry" for the *Smithsonian Institution Annual.* They helped to fashion a distinctive social rhetoric. By connecting manual labor to "primitive industry," no conflict was implied. The development from handicrafts to industry seemed natural. The progressive present set the standard for the primitive past. The lack of conflict is noteworthy, because America during the 1890s was plagued by strikes from hand trades, which were protesting the "unnatural" industrialization of their work. A depression in 1893 brought criticisms that industries had grown out of touch with society and its patterns by overproducing and speculating. In that same year the anthropology building at the Chicago World's Fair held exhibits on "labor-saving devices," "illustrating generally the progress of the amelioration of the condition of life and labor."[39]

From their museums, folklorists actively wrote and exhibited on divisions of culture: the past and the present, industry and craft, men and women. Besides writing on Indian crafts and foodways, Cushing wrote on "primitive motherhood." Culin, meanwhile, regularly wrote in the "For Woman's Entertainment" section of the *Philadelphia Record* and contributed to the *Woman's Home Companion* with articles on folk toys and games, religion, tales, and decoration. "All the world," Culin satirically wrote, "is divided between virilists and feminists and the virilists are no more confined to men than the feminists to women. My theory affords a key to many mysteries. Virilists should marry virilists and feminists, feminists. I know of no better rule for compatibility in married life. There is no more amusing game than picking people out and arranging them properly."[40] Indeed, picking out people and objects and then arranging them properly, usually in an evolutionary scheme, are exactly what this connected group of men and women did.

One popular arrangement claimed that the control of arts and industries had switched through history from women to men. Whereas women manufactured the shelters, clothes, containers, and foods for domestic and community use, large-scale industries under the control of men had taken over these roles. Originally, society was matriarchal but had shifted over time to being patriarchal. Men were hunters and fighters; women were makers and providers. According to Mason, "In contact with the animal world, and ever taking lessons from them, men watched the tiger, the bear, the fox, the falcon—learned their language and imitated them in ceremonial dances. But women were instructed by the spiders, the nest builders, the storers of food and the workers in clay like the mud wasp and the termites." Reacting to Herbert Spencer's division of the history of civilization into, first, an age of militancy, and, later, one of industrialism, Mason asked whether, "instead of an *age,* we should rather say a *sex* of militancy and a *sex* of industrialism." If Victorian women now appeared to be idle and more concerned with leisure, it was no wonder, Mason thought, since they had earned that right from their taxing early industrial efforts. Nonetheless, "at the very beginning of human time she (woman) laid down the lines of her duties, and she has kept to them unremittingly." In 1911, social critic Anna Spencer used Mason's idea to make an argument for women's adaptability to industrial work. Women, she opined, first "attained the discipline of a 'steady job.' The biologic hints of the busy bee, the industrious beaver, the ant, to whose example the human sluggard was long ago commended, all seem to have been taken lightly by the primitive man." She argued that women had the real character of labor, as the term came to be understood for the transforming industrial 1890s. To Anna Spencer, women embodied the character of modernity.[41]

Ambiguity, and a certain amount of ambivalence, remained, however, in the role of work for the sexes and for the age. For all the moralist literature about women's attachment to nature and home, women in larger numbers went out to work before the turn of the century. In 1901, *Cosmopolitan* reported that the modern woman suffered from "restlessness," "usefulness run riot." The section "Topics of the Time" in *Century* magazine asked in 1900, "Are we to see the complete passing away of women of leisure?" After all, the author claimed, "the women who work, in one way or another, because they must work to live, are joined in yearly greater numbers by women who work because they choose to work in order to be independent." Once again, ethnology was invoked: "It is . . . the instinct born of a profound need that leads all societies, once they have emerged from the primitive stage in which the labor of women cannot any more be dispensed with than the labor of men, to make, as it were, a kingdom apart for women of leisure." The conclusion? Women should avoid overwork, and find serenity in a legacy of leisure, which followed an early ethnological stage of toil and struggle.[42]

Writers dwelled on the differences between men's and women's work in primitive culture. George Wharton James (1858–1923) argued in "Primitive Inventions" (reprinted in this volume) that if women were not active in invention for the industrial age, it was because their period of invention had passed. He had collected among Southwest Indians, and he credited basketry, weaving, pottery, house building, and food customs to woman's predominance in primitive culture, and hence to an earlier stage of modern civilization. His study, like so many others at the time, made a connection between the industrial order and folk-culture evidence in regard to men and women. Thorstein Veblen's "The Barbarian Status of Women" is probably best known, but others include "Women and the Occupations" and "Sex in Primitive Industry," by sociologist William Thomas, and Lester Frank Ward's "Our Better Halves." They argued that women, like their children, were treated like primitives. This kind of argument had its widest circulation with the publication of Olive Schreiner's *Woman and Labor,* which in 1912 was one of the ten best sellers in America. In a "strange new world," such as moderns faced, she wrote, women had the choice of becoming a race of "laboring and virile" women, the equals of their ancient ancestors.[43]

Soon after Schreiner's book appeared, however, Elsie Clews Parsons (1875–1941), president of the American Folklore Society in 1919 and 1920, signaled the end of feminist reliance on evolution and the idea of a primitive matriarchal age. In "Femininity and Conventionality," published in 1914, she used the relativistic argument that it is "apprehension of difference rather than actual difference which bulks so large now and always in the social regulation of sex. It is fear of the unlike rather than the fact of it." She argued that as the Victorian reliance on ceremony, convention, and segregation had waned and as the Victorian preoccupation with a usable past had subsided, so, too, would studies emphasizing evolution give way to the examination of social function. But so, too, would studies of a distinctive women's sphere of labor decline as immediate political goals of the age—suffrage and employment opportunities—were met during the 1920s. Looking back on the briefs given earlier, Parsons realized the power of perception in shaping judgments.[44]

The perception of industry could be seen changing, too. No person better serves as a case in point than Mark Twain. It was Twain who, with Charles Dudley Warner in 1873, gave historians the naming of the Gilded Age in the title of a popular novel. A satire about political intrigues in the nation's capital, the book explored the "mere surface play of life" given by growing material prosperity and the undergirding of "custom and the fixed order" within the new cosmopolitan lifestyle. Twain himself came from humble folk roots in Missouri of which he was proud, while late in life he enjoyed the affluent life of a Connecticut Yankee in Hartford in the shadow of the sprawling Colt Arms factory. Early in life he had abandoned the life of an apprentice printer for the romantic lure and lore of the Mississippi riverboats. Turning to writing, he filled his works with vivid sketches of folklife, especially evident in *Huckleberry Finn* (1884). When the American Folklore Society began in 1888, Twain joined and engaged leading folklorists such as Andrew Lang (1844–1912) in correspondence. Twain was also filled with the love of invention and inspired by the promise of technology. He was a sucker for underwriting as many as a hundred new gadgets and manufacturing schemes. He owned the first private telephone in Hartford, grabbed one of the first Remington typewriters for his work, and experimented with phonograph dictation. And perhaps best known is Twain's support during his writing of *A Connecticut Yankee in King Arthur's Court* (1889) for an ill-starred machine that almost drove him to ruin, but which Twain glorified as a "mechanical miracle"—James W. Paige's typesetting machine.

In *Connecticut Yankee,* Twain set out to write a humorous novel tapping into the popular Victorian genre of the medieval fantasy, and applying ethnological ideas, especially about the evolution of invention and industry. He creatively extended the scenarios implied by ethnological writing by putting a civilized, technological man directly in the midst of a barbarian level of evolution. But by the time he finished the novel, and his fortunes with Paige's typesetting machine turned for the worse, his confidence in technology was shaken, and his ethnological fable of industrial progress became darkly clouded.

Twain announces his organizing ethnological principle at the very start of *Connecticul Yankee.* His preface declares that the customs touched on in the tale were "survivals" found at a later time, which can be assumed to have been practiced, befitting ethnological theory, during the sixth century. But Twain concludes, "One is quite justified in inferring that wherever one of these laws and customs was lacking in that remote time, its place was competently filled by a worse one." In an unpublished preface, he made the ethnological case for progress more explicit: "If any are inclined to rail at our present civilization, why—there is no hindering him, but he ought to sometimes contrast it with what went before and take comfort and hope, too." Practical and free of "sentiment," the central character, Hank Morgan, is the bourgeois Yankee, the chief superintendent in a Connecticut arms factory. One of Morgan's workers, who carries the mythical name Hercules, knocks Morgan unconscious in a factory squabble. Morgan wakes up in medieval England, but rather than becoming despondent over his fate, he decides to take commercial advantage of the situation. Helping him is his antiquarian's knowledge of King Arthur's day. Remembering the date of a medieval eclipse was imminent, he threatens the superstitious British with removing the sun if they do not give in to his demands. King Arthur's subjects become alarmed when the moon moves in front of the sun; after they give in to Morgan, the sun reappears from behind the moon. The result is that Morgan is given the title of Sir Boss and control of the economy. He embarks on a campaign for industrial development, on the one hand, and for the destruction of traditional life on the other. At different times he calls King Arthur's subjects "white Indians," "modified savages," "pigmies," "big children," and "great simple-hearted creatures." His plan to have a modern industrial establishment mark time to a master spirit comes finally head to head with the forces of tradition in a great nihilistic battle. He destroys his "civilization-factories," and with a force of 52 boys indoctrinated into his industrial system, he creates a destructive automated battlefield against hundreds of thousands of noble, but hopeless, barbaric Englishmen. Morgan's assistant admits, "We had conquered; in turn we were conquered." This is not the result that the likes of Culin and Mason envisioned for the evolution of industry.

As in the beginning of the novel, Morgan is knocked unconscious late in the story, this time by the legendary figure Merlin, and when he awakens back in the nineteenth century, he romantically yearns for his medieval bride. He smiles, "not a modern smile, but one that must have gone out of use many, many centuries ago." A sense of disillusion and guilt fills Twain, and the views, indeed the dreams, that he held for the development of industry "along existing lines" trouble him. "Death is nothing," he cries out at the end, "let it come, but not with those dreams, not with the torture of those hideous dreams—I cannot endure *that* again." With its finale of destruction, as modernity consumes tradition in evolutionary fashion, it is no wonder that evolutionist Andrew Lang preferred the relatively tame incorporation of folklore in *Huckleberry Finn* to that in *A Connecticut Yankee,* despite Twain's appeal to Lang not to judge the book according to the usual standards of the "cultured classes." "Help me, Mr. Lang," Twain begged, "No voice can reach further than yours in a case of this kind, or carry greater weight of authority."[45] Twain's book testified to the pervasive influence of the evolutionary vision of a technological culture during the late nineteenth century, but at the same time, it foretold its dimming future.

Some events after the turn of the century may have sealed the fate of evolutionary doctrine in folklife studies. A blow to the confidence in the inevitability of progress predicted by evolutionary doctrine, for example, was dealt by World War I. Technological advance brought more destruction, rather than, as many writers had predicted, the obsolescence of war. The world seemed more divided than united, more barbaric than enlightened. A growing bookshelf of works such as *The Decline of the West* (1918) painted a gloomy picture. Many new scholars admitted that perhaps, after all, the evolutionary scheme for culture was wrong; the admission was a way to ward off the prediction of gloom that had been brought by modern warfare and industrial capitalism. Meanwhile, laissez-faire economics, which was the conventional wisdom during the Gilded Age and which depended on evolutionary theory for justification, was under attack. Instead of encouraging progress and competition, a process of natural selection, laissez-faire economics encouraged the maintenance of the status quo and the rise of monopolies. Sociologist Lester Frank Ward arose to stress the rationality of primitive culture and propose that uniform natural laws did not mysteriously control social institutions. Politically created laws, he argued, were necessary to adapt to specific social conditions. Ward presaged the advance of government regulation and planning.[46]

By the 1920s, folklife studies related to industrialism dropped almost completely from view, as Americans either accepted their conversion or lowered their sights from the utopian global vision of evolution to the immediate needs and demands of the pluralistic nation. Symbolic of the triumph of American industrialism at the time was Henry Ford's Model T automobile. Cheap and efficient, more than 740,000 Model Ts were on the road in 1917. Ford had worked hard to ease the nervousness over industrialism. Steeped in country traditions, he refused to admit conflict in his transition to industrial mogul, and he tried to persuade the public to share his commitment to country values in an industrial age. In his industry, he raised wages, offered profit sharing, and emphasized country wholesomeness among workers. For the consumer he bragged about better quality at cheaper prices and improved responsiveness to consumer needs. By the 1920s his system was being hailed as the American System. It needed no justification from the savage past, although Ford did invoke a sense of national tradition, shown in the colonial preindustrial tools and crafts so avidly collected by ethnologist Henry Mercer (see chapter 15), to make a case for a moral industrial order. The relation between Ford's promotion of folk dancing and of traditional American string-band music received national attention as well, but not for its relation to industrialism. Rather, it was a sign of Ford's celebration of the "common man." Ford used living performers, and he obscured the chronology of the past. His nativist version of folklore proclaimed the moral fiber of the industrial present. In 1929, his large outdoor folk museum, Greenfield Village, opened in Dearborn, Michigan, with a combination of industrial and folk exhibits. Ford's industry was the American System, and folklife was a sign of its Americanism, at least until the disillusion of the 1930s tainted Ford's image and cast folklife, much of which was now stressing immigrant and occupational lore, in a less glowing light.[47]

As the twentieth century proceeded, advances in transportation and communication made life seem more immediate; the world, closer; the present, more important.[48] Ethnology came to concentrate less on the span of time and more on spheres of cultures. The turn of the century witnessed a growing diversity of theories to explain the similarity and difference in cultures across the world and within the nation. The spread of folklore seemed to be more the issue at hand than did its origin. As society modernized, so did the use of *folk* grow to describe, not the removed primitive, but rather the nearby man of tradition.

By the 1920s, evolutionary doctrine had mostly disappeared from American writings on folklore. A new generation, pursuing anthropology full-time and weary of the previous generation's dubious grand claims, took the place of the older scientific men and women who had touted evolution so highly. William Wells Newell recognized that evolutionary doctrine which was suited to his generation would not last. In 1901, he wrote in the *Journal of American Folklore:* "From the small body of anthropological students in America during the past decade have been removed many names, some of world-wide reputation, others beloved and admired within their own circle, and the places of these laborers have not as yet been filled."[49] Gone by 1901, for example, were Daniel Brinton, Frank Hamilton Cushing, Fletcher S. Bassett, and John G. Bourke, and six years later Newell himself died. Nineteen hundred also marked Franz Boas's ascent, at the age of forty-two, to the presidency of the American Folklore Society.

Considering Boas's material culture work culminating in his classic *Primitive Art* (1927), Boas's negative influence on studies of folklife might appear surprising. During his tenure as editor from 1908 to 1924, Boas changed the connotation of folklore as the *learning of folk* to *stories of the folk.* Folklore became less of an integrated study and more of a reference to a specific type of oral expression. Boas claimed folklore as the literary part of anthropology; the stuff of folklore hence consisted of myths, tales, and legends. Anthropologist Pliny Earle Goddard's article on the relation between folklore and anthropology for the *Journal of American Folklore* in 1915 echoed Boas's call. Goddard equated folklore as a scholastic discipline with primitive literature. The other parts of culture belonging to the anthropologist are, Goddard wrote, "material culture, ceremonies, and language."[50]

Other factors help explain the decline of material culture and folklife studies as well as evolutionary doctrine. Whereas many museum professionals with a natural interest in artifact collections joined the American Folklore Society in the early years, more academics with less concern for objects later took up the rolls. Representatives from literature, language, and English departments also increased. In the 1920s literary folklorists like Aurelio M. Espinosa and Louise Pound became presidents of the American Folklore Society, and they emphasized the narrative content of folklore, often freeing it from connections to contextual customs and rites. Material culture suffered even within anthropology, because the relativistic ethnology stressed research on social and mental culture over material culture. When the folklife movement in America arose after World War II, the moving force was the Pennsylvania-German folklorists. They looked to continental European research which allowed them to study artifacts and narratives as part of a total cultural distinctiveness. They generally rejected evolutionary doctrine, and sought to describe folk ways of doing things within regional and ethnic enclaves, and not in a grand march of civilization. "Folklife," stressing the integrity and integration of traditional communities and sectarian groups, took on a preservationist character, as analysts seemed to be reacting to the alienation and fragmentation of modern mass culture.[51]

Despite fundamental differences in social views and approaches, some provocative parallels exist between folklore study in the late nineteenth and late twentieth centuries. During the 1890s and the 1960s, popular discussion of "materialism" and rapid technological change translated into a surge of studies of material life. We are far less concerned today with, or convinced by arguments for, origin and evolution from so-called primitives; and the "dynamics" (to quote an oft-used metaphor taken from physics common in today's folklore studies) of behavior among people in all walks of life in the present typically holds the attention of folklorists rather than history of remote, "ruder ages." Questions arising from bureaucratic life, humanistic questions of a custom or person's social function, role, and purpose in a large organization typically take center stage, with nods toward modern concerns of psychological adjustment provided by folk crafts. Nonetheless, the grasp of the early folklife scholars of custom and art's importance in everyday life is still noteworthy—especially when folklore is appreciated for its cultural contexts and aesthetic dimensions. And the precedents that these nineteenth-century scholars set for collection, classification, and display continue into the present, not only in the exhibitionistic treatment of artifacts, but also in the artifactual treatment of oral traditions. Moreover, with these essays in hand set against the background of the Gilded Age, we can usefully reflect on the ways that our scholarly constructions today respond to our historical and cultural climate, and, indeed, to our own *fin de siècle* anxieties.[52]

Consider for a moment that a rage for folklife studies comparable to the one enjoyed during the 1890s swept America during the 1960s. Changes in technology and social structure, and in women's roles, gave rise to soul-searching studies, encompassing folklore, of problems in American society. Now, a deceivingly new trend is to study the ideas, symbols, and beliefs behind the objects which people use in certain situations. To be sure, what is done now and what was done in the 1890s are very different, not least of which is an egalitarian ethic, a pluralistic conception of American culture, in current research.[53] Instead of a unilinear development from primitive to modern technology, current studies stress different technologies responding to conditions of various groups. The dire consequences of some forms of technology have led to a reassessment of folk culture on its own terms for what material, social, and psychological benefits it provides. Indeed, since the 1960s a fervent preservationist spirit has been felt in folklife studies; often folklorists appear to be advocates for the folk, rather than for "industrial progress." Rarely today are folk practices examples of primitive "industry" or "invention"; rather they are "folk arts" in need of "cultural conservation."

Comparisons of the essays in this volume to present practice are inevitable. But the essays stand primarily on their own to give a glimpse of an interesting chapter in American intellectual and cultural history. They are testimonies to the temper of their times, and should be, I believe, read that way. The authors speak to us sincerely about the peoples and traditions they found so fascinating and the issues they found so pressing. They regale us with their love of accumulable facts, their adoration of science, their lofty sense of mission. They provide invaluable documentation of many long-gone traditions that they found active, and curious, in a modernizing society, not to mention documentation of traditions that still persist today.

As I began my story, so I close it here with the Chicago World's Fair. The Anthropology building, along with the hall where the International Congress was held, was reduced to ashes at the close of the fair. Out of the ashes came several important ethnological efforts in the years following—the founding of the Columbian Field Museum, Culin's encyclopedic work on games, and publication of the congress proceedings. The ethnologists came away from the fair as risen stars in the Gilded Age's firmament; they contributed greatly to hailing, one manual declared, the "great achievements in art, in architecture and in manufactures." "The first rude attempts in human art and industry," the guide continued, "are here illustrated, and form a striking contrast to the splendors of modern civilization so lavishly displayed on every side." Reporting on the close of the fair, the guide declared that the result of this great Victorian spectacle was that "Americans are broadened. They saw in what they excel, and in what they are excelled." The fair's "beauties were transient of material, but of influence and memory they can never end. They remain enshrined in the remembrance of the millions who delighted in them, and however dim they may become through the vista of years, always will there by some ray of light reflected into the life and the sense of beauty, from the walls and the domes and the classic glory of the White City, now the Vanishing City."[54] Vanished it may be, along with the glint of the Gilded Age, but the legacy of the intellectual fervor it fostered is vividly expressed in the essays that follow.

Notes

1. Trumbull White and William Igleheart, *The World's Columbian Exposition, Chicago, 1893* (Chicago: J. W. Ziegler, 1893), p. 12; E. Benjamin Andrews, *The History of the Last Quarter-Century in the United States, 1870–1895,* 2 vols. (New York: Charles Scribner's Sons, 1896), I, pp. 227–300. See also David F. Burg, *Chicago's White City of 1893* (Lexington: University Press of Kentucky, 1976); Alan Trachtenberg, *The Incorporation of America: Culture and Society in the Gilded Age* (New York: Hill and Wang, 1982), pp. 208–34; Daniel Walker Howe, ed., *Victorian America* (Philadelphia: University of Pennsylvania Press, 1976); H. Wayne Morgan, ed., *Victorian Culture in America, 1865–1914* (Itasca, Illinois: F. E. Peacock Publishers, 1973); Sean Dennis Cashman, *America in the Gilded Age* (New York: New York University Press, 1984); James Laver, *Manners and Morals in the Age of Optimism, 1848–1914* (New York: Harper and Row, 1966); Howard Mumford Jones, *The Age of Energy: Varieties of American Experience, 1865–1915* (New York: Viking Press, 1971).

2. Robert W. Rydell, *All the World's a Fair: Visions of Empire at American International Expositions, 1876–1916* (Chicago: University of Chicago Press, 1984); "Folk-Lore at the Columbian Exposition," *Journal of American Folklore* 6 (1893): p. 228; Stewart Culin, "Retrospect of the Folk-Lore of the Columbian Exposition," *Journal of American Folklore* 7 (1894): p. 56. See also, the descriptions of the Midway in

White and Igleheart, pp. 561–97; Ben C. Truman, *History of the World's Fair* (Chicago: Ben C. Truman, 1893), pp. 549–79.

3. White and Igleheart, *World's Columbian Exposition,* p. 13

4. Henry Childs Merwin, "On Being Civilized Too Much," *Atlantic Monthly* 79 (June 1897): pp. 838–46. For other examples of popular periodical literature from the nineteenth century dealing with folklore topics, see Bruce Jackson, ed., *The Negro and His Folklore in Nineteenth-Century Periodicals* (Austin: University of Texas Press, 1967); William M. Clements, ed., *Native American Folklore in Nineteenth-Century Periodicals* (Athens: Swallow Press/Ohio University Press, 1986). For the therapeutic uses of folklore and other examples of "antimodernism" during the Gilded Age, see Jackson Lears, *No Place of Grace: Antimodernism and the Transformation of American Culture, 1880–1920* (New York: Pantheon, 1981).

5. See Karen Halttunen, *Confidence Men and Painted Women: A Study of Middle-Class Culture in America, 1830–1870* (New Haven: Yale University Press, 1982), pp. 153–97; Richard Sennett, *The Fall of Public Man: On the Social Psychology of Capitalism* (New York: Vintage Books/Random House, 1976), pp. 188–91; Paula Petrik, "The House That Parcheesi Built: Selchow & Righter," *Business History Review* 60 (1986): pp. 410–37; Lears, *No Place of Grace,* pp. 168–73; Richard M. Dorson, *The British Folklorists: A History* (Chicago: University of Chicago Press, 1968), pp. 202–20; Giuseppe Cocchiara, *The History of Folklore in Europe,* trans. John N. McDaniel (Philadelphia: Institute for the Study of Human Issues, 1981), pp. 220–76; John R. Reed, *Victorian Conventions* (Athens: Ohio University Press, 1975), pp. 29–33, 289–361.

6. William Thoms, "Folklore," in *The Study of Folklore,* ed. Alan Dundes (Englewood Cliffs, New Jersey: Prentice-Hall, 1965), p. 5

7. Charlotte Sophia Burne, *The Handbook of Folklore* (London: Sidgwick & Jackson, 1914), p. 1; George Laurence Gomme, *Ethnology in Folklore* (London: K. Paul, Trench, Trubner, & Co., 1892), p. 2.

8. Lee J. Vance, "Folk-Lore Studies," *Open Court* 1 (1887): p. 612. For Vance's career and views, see Alan Dundes, "Robert Lee J. Vance: American Folklore Surveyor of the 1890's," *Western Folklore* 23 (1964): pp. 27–34.

9. Lee J. Vance, "Folk-Lore Study in America," *Popular Science Monthly* 43 (1893): p. 587.

10. Lee J. Vance, "The Study of Folk-Lore," *Forum* 22 (1896/97): p. 249.

11. Culin, "Retrospect of the Folk-Lore of the Columbian Exposition," p. 51.

12. Fletcher S. Bassett, "The Folk-Lore Congress," in *The International Folk-Lore Congress of the World's Columbian Exposition,* ed. Helen Wheeler Bassett and Frederick Starr (Chicago: Charles H. Sergel, 1898), p. 20. For further discussion of the short-lived, but influential, Chicago Folklore Society and the International Congress, see W. K. McNeil, "The Chicago Folklore Society and the International Folklore Congress of 1893," *Midwestern Journal of Language and Folklore* 11 (1985): pp. 5–19.

13. W. J. McGee, "Fifty Years of American Science," *Atlantic Monthly* 82 (September 1898): p. 317; T. K. Penniman, *A Hundred Years of Anthropology,* 3d ed. (London: G. Duckworth, 1965), p. 19.

14. Charles Darwin, *The Descent of Man,* 2d ed. (New York: A. L. Burt, 1874), pp. 162–65.

For ethnological adaptations of Darwinism, see John Lubbock, *The Origin of Civilisation and the Primitive Condition of Man* (1870; reprint, Chicago: University of Chicago Press, 1978); Edward Tylor, *The Origins of Culture* and *Religion in Primitive Culture* [Originally published in one volume as *Primitive Culture*] (1871; reprint, Gloucester, Mass.: Peter Smith, 1970); John F. McLennan, *Primitive Marriage* (Edinburgh: Adam and Charles Black, 1865). See also George W. Stocking, Jr., *Race, Culture, and Evolution: Essays in the History of Anthropology* (Revised edition, Chicago: University of Chicago Press, 1982), pp. 91–132; George W. Stocking, Jr., *Victorian Anthropology* (New York: Free Press, 1987).

15. William I. Knapp, "Address of Welcome on Behalf of the Chicago Folk-Lore Society," in *International Folk-Lore Congress of the World's Columbian Exposition,* ed. Bassett and Starr, p. 24; Edward Tylor, *The Origins of Culture,* p. 24.

16. McGee, "Fifty Years of American Science," p. 317. See also Daniels, *Science in American Society: A Social History* (New York: Alfred A. Knopf, 1971), pp. 223–45.

17. John Blum et al., *The National Experience: A History of the United States,* 2d. ed. (New York: Harcourt, Brace & World, 1968), p. 452; Robert Hebert Quick, *Essays on Educational Reformers* (New York: D. Appleton, 1896), pp. 439–69; Christine Bolt, *Victorian Attitudes to Race* (London: Routledge & Kegan Paul, 1971); Carl N. Degler, *The Age of the Economic Revolution, 1876–1900* (Glenview, Illinois: Scott, Foresman & Co., 1967), pp. 183–91; Harvey Wish, *Society and Thought in Modern America* (New York: David McKay, 1962), pp. 300–36; Daniels, *Science in American Society,* pp. 223–64.

18. McGee, "Fifty Years of American Science," pp. 318–19.

19. William Wells Newell, "Topics for Collection of Folk-Lore," *Journal of American Folklore* 4 (1891): pp. 151–58; Stewart Culin, "Street Games of Boys in Brooklyn, N.Y.," *Journal of American Folklore* 4 (1891): pp. 221–37; Stewart Culin, "American Indian Games," *Journal of American Folklore* 11 (1898): pp. 245–52; Stewart Culin and William Wells Newell, "Concerning Negro Sorcery in the United States," *Journal of American Folklore* 3 (1890): pp. 281–87. For more on Newell, see Michael J. Bell, "William Wells Newell and the Foundation of American Folklore Scholarship," *Journal of the Folklore Institute* 10 (1973): pp. 7–21; W. K. McNeil, "A History of American Folklore Scholarship before 1908" (Ph.D. Dissertation, Indiana University, 1980), pp. 780–97; William Wells Newell, "On the Field and Work of a Journal of American Folk-Lore," *Journal of American Folklore* 1 (1888): pp. 3–7; William Wells Newell, "Necessity of Collecting the Traditions of Native Races," *Journal of American Folklore* 1 (1888): pp. 162–63; William Wells Newell, "The Study of Folklore," *Transactions of the New York Academy of Sciences* 9 (1890): pp. 134–36; William Wells Newell, *Games and Songs of American Children* (1883; reprint, New York: Dover, 1963). For exemplary books from Newell's time that stressed customs, rites, and objects, see James A. Farrer, *Primitive Manners and Customs* (London: Chatto & Windus, 1879); Leopold Wagner, *Manners, Customs, and Observances: Their Origin and Signification* (London: W. Heinemann, 1894); William S. Walsh, *Curiosities of Popular Customs and of Rites, Ceremonies, Observances, and Miscellaneous Antiquities* (Philadelphia: J. B. Lippincott, 1898).

20. Fanny Bergen, "Pigments Used by Children in Their Play," *Journal of American Folklore* 8 (1895): p. 151; Fanny Bergen, "Poppy Shows," *Journal of American Folklore* 8 (1895): pp. 152–53; Fanny Bergen, "Traditionally American Local Dishes,"

Journal of American Folklore 13 (1900): pp. 65–66; Fanny Bergen, "Some Homely Viands," *Journal of American Folklore* 13 (1900): pp. 292–94; Fanny Bergen, "Quilt Patterns," *Journal of American Folklore* 5 (1892): p. 69; H. Carrington Bolton, "Decoration of Graves of Negroes in South Carolina," *Journal of American Folklore* 4 (1891): p. 214; Ernest Ingersoll, "Decoration of Negro Graves," *Journal of American Folklore* 5 (1892): pp. 68–69; Frederick Starr, "Folk-Lore of Stone Tools," *Journal of American Folklore* 4 (1891): pp. 27–28; George Kunz, "Exhibition of Gems Used as Amulets," *Journal of American Folklore* 4 (1891); pp. 29–31; Frederick Starr, "Presentation to the Folk-Lore Society of Objects Illustrating Mexican Folk-Lore," *Journal of American Folklore* 12 (1899): p. 230.

21. Fletcher S. Bassett, *The Folk-Lore Manual* (Chicago: Chicago Folklore Society, 1892), pp. 12, 82–87.

22. Fletcher S. Bassett, "The World's Congress Auxiliary of the World's Columbian Exposition," in *International Folk-Lore Congress,* ed. Bassett and Starr, pp. 3–6.

23. See George W. Stocking, Jr., ed., *Objects and Others: Essays on Museums and Material Culture* (Madison: University of Wisconsin Press, 1985); William C. Sturtevant, "Does Anthropology Need Museums?" *Proceedings of the Biological Society of Washington* 82 (1969): pp. 619–49; Russell Lewis, "Everything under One Roof: World's Fairs and Department Stores in Paris And Chicago," *Chicago History* 13 (1983): pp. 28–47; Simon J. Bronner, " 'Object Lessons': The Work of Ethnological Museums and Collections," in *Consuming Visions: Accumulation and Display of Goods in America, 1880–1920,* ed. Simon J. Bronner (New York: W. W. Norton, forthcoming). And for accounts during the Gilded Age, see George Dorsey, "The Anthropological Exhibits at the American Museum of Natural History," *Science,* n.s., 25 (1907): pp. 584–89; George Brown Goode, "Museum-History and Museums of History," *Annual Report of the United States National Museum* (Washington, D.C.: Government Printing Office, 1897), pp. 65–81; George Brown Goode, "The Museums of the Future," *Annual Report of the United States National Museum* (Washington, D.C.: Government Printing Office, 1897), pp. 243–61; Harlan I. Smith, "Methods of Collecting Anthropological Material," *Scientific American,* Supplement, 57 (1904): p. 23635.

24. "Folk-Lore Museums," *Journal of American Folklore* 3 (1890): pp. 312–13.

25. Stewart Culin, ed., *Objects Used in Religious Ceremonies and Charms and Implements for Divination* (Philadelphia: University of Pennsylvania, 1892); *Report of the United States Commission to the Columbian Historical Exposition at Madrid, 1892–93* (Washington, D.C.: Government Printing Office, 1895); "A Proposed Folk-Lore Museum," *Journal of American Folklore* 3 (1890): pp. 313–14; "Exhibition of Folk-Lore Objects to Be Made at the Columbian Exposition," *Journal of American Folklore* 5 (1892): pp. 167–68; Stewart Culin, "Exhibit of Games in the Columbian Exposition," *Journal of American Folklore* 6 (1893): pp. 205–27.

26. Stewart Culin, "The Origin of Ornament," *Free Museum of Science and Art Bulletin* 2 (1900): pp. 235–42.

27. Stewart Culin, "A Summer Trip among the Western Indians," *Bulletin of the Free Museum of Science and Art* 3 (1901): p. 2. See also Stewart Culin, "Guide to the Southwestern Indian Hall," *Museum News* 2 (1907): pp. 105–11; Craig D. Bates and Brian Bibby, "Collecting among the Chico Maidu: The Stewart Culin Collection at the Brooklyn Museum," *American Indian Art Magazine* 8 (Autumn 1983): pp. 46–53.

28. Letter to William Henry Holmes from Stewart Culin, November 30, 1906 (Smithsonian Institution Archives); Stewart Culin, "Creation in Art," *Brooklyn Museum Quarterly* 11 (1924): p. 93.

29. Stewart Culin, "The Road to Beauty," *Brooklyn Museum Quarterly* 14 (1927): p. 43; Culin, "Creation in Art," p. 92. See also Simon J. Bronner, "Stewart Culin, 'Museum Magician,' " *Pennsylvania Heritage* 11 (Summer 1985): pp. 4–11.

30. Stewart Culin's field journal, 1920 (Stewart Culin Papers, Brooklyn Museum); Culin, "Road to Beauty," p. 43.

31. Curtis M. Hinsley, Jr., *Savages and Scientists: The Smithsonian Institution and the Development of American Anthropology, 1846–1910* (Washington, D.C.: Smithsonian Institution Press, 1981), pp. 84–94; John Michael Vlach, "Director's Column," *GW Folklife Newsletter* 5 (Spring 1987): pp. 4–5.

32. Otis T. Mason, "The Natural History of Folk-Lore," *Journal of American Folklore* 4 (1891): pp. 97–105.

33. Otis T. Mason, *Woman's Share in Primitive Culture* (New York: D. Appleton, 1894), p. 1.

34. Mason, "Natural History of Folk-Lore," pp. 98, 103.

35. Otis T. Mason, "The Rise of Empiricism," in *International Folk-Lore Congress,* ed. Wheeler and Bassett, pp. 117–24. See also Otis T. Mason, *The Origins of Invention: A Study of Industry among Primitive Peoples* (1895; reprint, Freeport, New York: Books for Libraries Press, 1972).

36. See George W. Stocking, Jr., ed., *A Franz Boas Reader: The Shaping of American Anthropology, 1883–1911* (Chicago: University of Chicago Press, 1974); Franz Boas, *Race, Language and Culture* (New York: Free Press, 1940); Melville Herskovits, *Franz Boas: The Science of Man in the Making* (New York: Charles Scribner's Sons, 1953); Hinsley, *Savages and Scientists,* pp. 98–100; Stocking, *Race, Culture, and Evolution,* pp. 195–233; George W. Stocking, Jr., "The Aims of Boasian Ethnography: Creating the Materials for Traditional Humanistic Scholarship," *History of Anthropology Newsletter* 4 (1977): pp. 4–5; William S. Willis, Jr., "Franz Boas and the Study of Black Folklore," in *The New Ethnicity: Perspectives from Ethnology,* ed. John W. Bennett (St. Paul, Minnesota: West Publishing, 1975), pp. 307–34; Ira Jacknis, "Franz Boas and Exhibits: On the Limitations of the Museum Method of Anthropology," in *Objects and Others,* ed. Stocking, pp. 75–111; McNeil, "A History of American Folklore Scholarship," pp. 866–926; Rosemary Zumwalt, "American Folkloristics: The Literary and Anthropological Roots" (Ph.D. Dissertation, University of California—Berkeley, 1982), pp. 142–202; Susan Dwyer-Shick, "The American Folklore Society and Folklore Research in America, 1888–1940" (Ph.D. Dissertation, University of Pennsylvania, 1979), pp.206–40; Franz Boas, "Otis Tufton Mason," *Journal of American Folklore* 21 (1908): p. 362; Franz Boas, "The History of Anthropology," *Science* 20 (1904): pp. 513–24.

37. McGee, "Fifty Years of American Science," pp. 319, 307. See also Daniels, *Science in American Society,* pp. 246–64.

38. George M. Beard, "Causes of American Nervousness," in *Democratic Vistas, 1860–1880,* ed. Alan Trachtenberg (New York: George Braziller, 1970), p. 238.

39. Alexander F. Chamberlain, "Mythology and Folklore of Invention," *Journal of American Folklore* 17 (1904): pp. 14–22; Thomas Wilson, "Primitive Industry," in *Smithsonian Institution Annual for 1892* (Washington, D.C.: Government Printing Office, 1893), pp. 521–34; Trachtenberg, *Incorporation of America,* pp. 38–69; Truman, *History of the World's Fair,* pp. 260–61.

40. Jesse Green, ed., *Zuñi: Selected Writings of Frank Hamilton Cushing* (Lincoln: University of Nebraska Press, 1979); Frank Hamilton Cushing, "Primitive Motherhood," in *The Work and Words of the National Congress of Mothers* (New York: D. Appleton, 1897), pp. 3–47; Stewart Culin, "The Perfect Collector," typescript (Stewart Culin Papers, Brooklyn Museum).

41. Mason, *Woman's Share in Primitive Culture,* pp. 2–3; Anna Garlin Spencer, "The Primitive Working-Woman," *Forum* 46 (1911): pp. 546–58.

42. Alice Kessler-Harris, *Out to Work: A History of Wage Earning Women in the United States* (New York: Oxford University Press, 1982); Daniel T. Rodgers, *The Work Ethic in Industrial America, 1850–1920* (Chicago: University of Chicago Press, 1974), pp. 182–209; Ella Wheeler Wilcox, "The Restlessness of the Modern Woman," *Cosmopolitan* 31 (1901): pp. 314–17; "Women of Leisure," *Century* 60 (1900): pp. 632–33.

43. George Wharton James, "Primitive Inventions," *Craftsman* 5 (1903): pp. 125–37; Thorstein Veblen, "The Barbarian Status of Women," *American Journal of Sociology* 4 (1899): pp. 503–14; William I. Thomas, "Woman and the Occupations," *American Magazine* 68 (1909): pp. 463–70; William I. Thomas, "Sex in Primitive Industry," *American Journal of Sociology* 4 (1899): pp. 474–88; Lester Frank Ward, "Our Better Halves," *Forum* 6 (1888): pp. 266–75; Olive Schreiner, *Woman and Labor* (New York: Frederick A. Stokes, 1911).

44. Elsie Clews Parsons, "Femininity and Conventionality," *American Academy of Political and Social Science* 56 (1914): pp. 47–53. For Parson's life, see Keith S. Chambers, "The Indefatigable Elsie Clews Parsons—Folklorist," *Western Folklore* 32 (1973): pp. 180–98. For examples of the Victorian preoccupation with the usable ethnological past by women, see Elizabeth Cady Stanton, "The Matriarchate, or Mother-Age," and Susan B. Anthony, "Comments," in *Transactions of the National Council of Women of the United States* (Philadelphia: J. B. Lippincott, 1891), pp. 218–30. See also Sue Samuelson, "Women in the American Folklore Society, 1888–1892," *Folklore Historian* 2 (1985): pp. 3–11.

45. Mark Twain and C. D. Warner, *The Gilded Age,* ed. Herbert Van Thal (1873; reprint, London: Cassell, 1967); Samuel L. Clemens, *A Connecticut Yankee in King Arthur's Court* (1889; reprint, New York: Dodd, Mead & Co., 1960); Henry Nash Smith, *Mark Twain's Fable of Progress: Political and Economic Ideas in "A Connecticut Yankee"* (New Brunswick, New Jersey: Rutgers University Press, 1964); John F. Kasson, *Civilizing the Machine: Technology and Republican Values in America, 1776–1900* (New York: Penguin Books, 1977), pp. 202–15; Mark Twain, *Mark Twain's Letters,* ed. Albert Bigelow Paine, 2 vols. (New York: Harper & Bros., 1929), II, pp. 525–28. See also Herbert L. Sussman, *Victorians and the Machine: The Literary Response to Technology* (Cambridge: Harvard University Press, 1968); Leo Marx, *The Machine in the Garden: Technology and the Pastoral Ideal in America* (London: Oxford University Press, 1964), pp. 319–40.

48   *Introduction*

46. Stephen Kern, *The Culture of Time and Space, 1880–1918* (Cambridge: Harvard University Press, 1983), pp. 104–8, 287–318; Henry Steele Commager, *The American Mind: An Interpretation of American Thought and Character since the 1880s* (New Haven: Yale University Press, 1950), pp. 199–26.

47. See Warren I. Susman, *Culture as History: The Transformation of American Society in the Twentieth Century* (New York: Pantheon, 1984), pp. 131–41; Henry C. Mercer, "The Tools of the Nation Maker," in *A Collection of Papers Read before the Bucks County Historical Society,* vol. 3 (Riegelsville, Pennsylvania: B. F. Fackenthal, Jr., 1909), pp. 469–81.

48. Kern, *Culture of Time and Space,* pp. 10–88; Donald M. Lowe, *History of Bourgeois Perception* (Chicago: University of Chicago Press, 1982), pp. 108–20; Susman, *Culture as History,* pp. 252–70.

49. William Wells Newell, "Resignation," *Journal of American Folklore* 14 (1901): p. 56.

50. Franz Boas, "Mythology and Folklore," in *General Anthropology,* ed. Franz Boas (Boston: D. C. Heath, 1938), pp. 95–123; Gladys Reichard, "Franz Boas and Folklore," in *Franz Boas, 1858–1942* (Memoirs of the American Anthropological Association, no. 61, 1943), pp. 52–57; Pliny Earle Goddard, "The Relation of Folk-Lore to Anthropology," *Journal of American Folklore* 28 (1915): pp. 18–23. See also Regna Darnell, "American Anthropology and the Development of Folklore Scholarship, 1890–1920," *Journal of the Folklore Institute* 10 (1973): pp. 23–39.

51. See Stith Thompson, "American Folklore after Fifty Years," *Journal of American Folklore* 51 (1938): pp. 1–9; "Advances in Folklore Studies," in *Anthropology Today: An Encyclopedic Inventory,* ed. Alfred L. Kroeber (Chicago: University of Chicago Press, 1955), pp. 587–96; Louise Pound, "The Scholarly Study of Folklore," *Western Folklore* 11 (1952): pp. 100–108; William N. Fenton, "The Advancement of Material Culture Studies in Modern Anthropological Research," in *The Human Mirror: Material and Spatial Images of Man,* ed. Miles Richardson (Baton Rouge: LSU Press, 1974), p. 18; Don Yoder, "The Folklife Studies Movement," *Pennsylvania Folklife* 3 (July 1963): pp. 43–46; Richard M. Dorson, ed., *Folklore in the Modern World* (The Hague: Mouton, 1978); Simon J. Bronner, "The Idea of the Folk Artifact," in *American Material Culture and Folklife,* ed. Simon J. Bronner (Ann Arbor, Michigan: UMI Research Press, 1985), pp. 3–39; Simon J. Bronner, *American Folklore Studies: An Intellectual History* (Lawrence: University Press of Kansas, 1986), pp. 94–129; Richard Bauman, "Folklore and the Forces of Modernity," *Folklore Forum* 16 (1983): pp. 153–58.

52. See Barre Toelken, *The Dynamics of Folklore* (Boston: Houghton Mifflin, 1979); Simon J. Bronner, "Visible Proofs: Material Culture Study in American Folkloristics," in *Material Culture: A Research Guide,* ed. Thomas J. Schlereth (Lawrence: University Press of Kansas, 1985), pp. 127–54; *Folklore/Folklife* (Washington: D.C.: American Folklore Society, 1984); Michael Owen Jones, *Exploring Folk Art: Twenty Years of Thought on Craft, Work, and Aesthetics* (Ann Arbor: UMI Research Press, 1987); Dan Ben-Amos, "The Seven Strands of *Tradition:* Varieties in Its Meaning in American Folklore Studies," *Journal of Folklore Research* 21 (1984): pp. 97–131; Henry Glassie, "Folkloristic Study of the American Artifact: Objects and Objectives," in *Handbook of American Folklore,* ed. Richard M. Dorson (Bloomington: Indiana University Press, 1983), pp. 376–83; Robert A. Georges, "The Folklorist as Comparatist," *Western Folklore* 45 (1986): pp. 1–20; Lears, *No Place of Grace,* pp. xi–xiv.

53. See Robert D. Abrahams and Susan Kalčik, "Folklore and Cultural Pluralism," in *Folklore in the Modern World,* ed. Richard M. Dorson, pp. 223–36; Henry Glassie, "The Moral Lore of Folklore," *Folklore Forum* 16 (1983): pp. 123–52.

54. White and Igleheart, *World's Columbian Exposition,* p. 640.

I

Doctrines and Guides

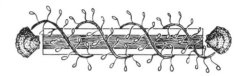

1

The Natural History of Folklore

Otis T. Mason

Otis Mason (1838–1908) was a man of science, speaking in the vogue of his day. Specifically, he believed in applying the tenets of evolutionary natural science to create a cultural history of civilization, a history that would show the development of humankind's mental development and inventive faculty. Addressing the American Folklore Society in this important essay, he made a case for the place of folklore studies in this effort. As curator of the United States National Museum's ethnology section, he had concerns of classification to convey to his audience, and as a leader of the group of ethnologists that used material evidence, he wanted to use customs as the connecting thread between matters of lore and life. "It has been the ruling thought of my life," he reflected two years before his death, "that the people of the world have left their history most fully recorded in the works of their hands," and "his great idea," he said, was that "the true history of our race is written in things . . . the material expressions of the human mind." Because the mind "held in trust the possibilities of the future," the ethnologist's tracing of cultural history becomes crucial, he thought, to examining the issues of the day. He wrote influential works on, for example, invention (*The Origins of Invention,* 1895), transportation (*Primitive Travel and Transportation,* 1894), and women's roles (*Women's Share in Primitive Culture,* 1894). But more than expressing a concern from the vantage of the nation's capital for policy issues, his optimism, and grandiloquent rhetoric, which should be apparent from this essay, were reflections of the society and period in which he wrote.

Mason was an important figure in the American Folklore Society's early years, and in 1891 he became its president. That same year he invited the society to hold its annual meeting in Washington, D.C. The society accepted and held its meeting at Columbian College (now the George Washington University), where Mason taught a course entitled "The History of the Past as Revealed in the Sciences of Archaeology and Folk-Lore." This essay might easily have been the conspectus for the course. It was written for the society's journal, the *Journal of American Folklore* 4 (1891): pp. 97–105.

For readings on Mason's career, see Curtis M. Hinsley, Jr., *Savages and Scientists: The Smithsonian Institution and the Development of American Anthropology,*

1846–1910 (Washington, D.C.: Smithsonian Institution Press, 1981), pp. 83–123; Walter Hough, "Otis Tufton Mason," *American Anthropologist* 20 (1908): pp. 661–67. For background on the evolutionary ideas attached to the development of industrial civilization, see Fred W. Voget, *A History of Ethnology* (New York: Holt, Rinehart and Winston, 1975), pp. 114–64, and my *American Folklore Studies: An Intellectual History* (Lawrence: University Press of Kansas, 1986), pp. 1–38.

*   *   *

The object of this paper is not to discuss natural history in folklore. That is, no doubt a branch of the subject, and its discussion would fill many volumes. Indeed, you will agree with me that there are not many phenomena of nature apparent to the unaided senses which have not over and over again entered into the thoughts and directed the actions of the folk. My purpose is to inquire how the folk-lorist is to bring his work into line with that of other naturalists. . . .

Folk-lore in this discussion means the lore of the folk. The folk include all unlettered men and women and tribes, and even lettered people when they think and act like the folk, rather than in accordance with the rules of science and culture. We all have traditions and manners which we cannot shake off, although we know them to be absurd. The greatest men have had their foibles in this respect, which linked them with the crowd. The folk are: (1) all savages, (2) the old-fashioned people, (3) the children, and (4) all of us when we are old-fashioned.

The lore of the folk includes what they claim to know, and what they do. The boundaries of this definition are not accurately fixed. Omitting the doubtful margin, however, there is enough left that is clearly our territory in common.

Folk-lore has reference to what is customary, what men and women and children think and say and do in common.

There are two kinds of action in every life. If we were left alone, each one would act spontaneously and independently, doing what seemed good in his own eyes. But hemmed in as we are by family, friends, society, government, business, school, church, associations, crafts, and fashion, we find it more convenient to act as others act, and to think as they think, than to originate a new set of actions and thoughts on every occasion. The first kind of actions we perform at our wits' end, the second kind we fall into. We are impelled into the first by inward pressure, natural proclivity; but we are attracted, led, driven into the second.

Now, as it is possible for an individual to repeat an original action until it becomes fixed and automatic, so also may we perform in unison with others, certain actions, until they become easy and agreeable.

Those actions which living beings are induced to perform in common become fixed, characteristic, varietal, specific. They go on surviving and holding over, even after the causes which combined to produce them have ceased to operate.

Those actions which they perform spontaneously give rise to new classes of activity, or they die in the struggle. In the same way custom and invention are the corner-stones of human action. The former becomes folk-lore, the latter progress.

Folk-lore stands for the hereditable part of our activity; invention is the creative, originating part of our action. Folk-lore is crystalloid; invention and science are colloidal. Folk-lore is kept alive by public opinion, and is opposed to progress; invention and science are centrifugal, venturesome, individual.

This ability to act in common has itself had a historic growth, beginning with such savage acts as beating time to a rude dance, and rising to a grand chorus, a great battle, or a modern industrial establishment employing thousands of men marking time to one master spirit.[1]

We shall now show how the methods of the naturalist may be applied to our science with regard to morphology.

If we had a number of crystals laid before us, how would the scientific mineralogist proceed in studying them? His first effort would be to understand and discriminate their forms; the folk-lorist may follow his example, and search for the external, formal distinctions of his material. It is apparent to everybody that unlettered people have, first, their opinions or theories upon many subjects; this he would call folk-thought. It is no less apparent, secondly, that these same people have their practices or ways of doing things, and this he would call folk-custom or wont. Folk-thought and folk-wont added together would make folk-lore. Folk-thought gives rise to the library, folk-wont to the picture gallery and the museum.

Now we cannot separate thought from wont, as some have tried to do. The best plan is to keep the library, the gallery, and the museum under one régime.

Another formal distinction in folk-lore is purely literary. Folk-thought and folk-sayings, on all sorts of subjects, are sometimes in prose, at other times in verse or rhyme. The prose saying may be proverb, maxim, fable, parable, allegory, *märchen,* myth, story; the versified lore may be the same things, besides songs, ballads, counting-out rhymes, epic poems, and other forms.

Some folk-lorists have founded their classifications on these formal characteristics, and indeed this is a very useful method for the collector, the man of business, or the intelligent woman, who is willing to consecrate any amount of leisure to some definite object within the limits of their comprehension. But the scientific student of folk-lore may have to seek other concepts in his final arrangement.

The moment the mineralogist has finished his study of form, he concerns himself about specific gravity and chemical composition. The components of his specimen must be determined and discriminated. All of the distinguished scholars who have given their attention to our subject have attempted classifications of folk-lore after the same fashion, based on analysis.

The chemical solvent, the blow-pipe analysis, are imitated in a suitable method of tabulation. The important elements of the specimen, that is, the dramatis personae and incidents, are laid out for comparison, and the future student will have to do with these. If he is not satisfied with the diagnosis already made, he may, without cost, refer to the original specimen and dissect it for himself. The folk-specimen has this advantage, that no bungling or malicious analyst can destroy it by dissolving it into its elements. The archaeologist who rummages a mound, the palaeontologist who removes a fossil from its associations, the anatomist of a rare animal who destroys the connections of parts, all have closed the door of research. The folk-cabinet is like the piles of enumerators' atlases in the Census Office. The material is ever at hand to be considered.

The refined analysis of the belief, the saying, the action, is to be our reliance in discovering the characteristics upon which a national, scientific classification is to be based.

Supplementary to such work, we have in America the opportunity of better collecting. You can imagine what sort of natural history that would be which one would make up from the desultory mention of travellers, or even from specimens gathered for commercial purposes. You may be pleased to know that the Bureau of Ethnology in Washington, at infinite pains, is gathering the stories of our Indians. The work is done by men who insist on hearing a narrative over and over again until there is no mistake about accuracy; no physicist or mineralogist is more careful than Dr. Dorsey and his colleagues at this point.[2] No attempt has yet been made to combine this material, to anatomize it. As yet there need not be. In all sciences, the period of accurate instrumental, multiplied observation must succeed that by the mere senses, preparatory to higher generalizations. In our science we shall occupy an enviable position if it be possible to have the reputation of accuracy. . . .

In this matter of collecting, there is one subject that I would emphasize again and again, and yet I would use the utmost caution and politeness in calling attention to it. I refer now to *personal equation*.

In every observatory there is accurate record made of each observer's personal equation,—the difference of time between the crossing of a spider line by a star and the recorded time of the observer.

No astronomer would be offended if one were to say to him in a courteous manner, "You do not tell the truth." He would calmly say, "My personal equation is three tenths of a second, minus."

As we approach the more complex sciences, the personal equation varies in all those records which are based on sense perception. In anthropology the variation from truth is not only in number, time, distance, weight, color, and motion, but in the subtile inferences which always accompany sense perceptions. I have witnessed some very curious effects upon the minds of those who overlooked this important matter. There are archaeologists who will not read a word of the old Spanish chroniclers because of their personal aversion to them. You will see everyday examples of this false reading because we have not calmly eliminated the personal equation of the chronicler and accepted the residuum as true. I make no reference here to falsifiers of any kind, and their name is legion, or to those shallow people who obtrude themselves into all sciences. My allusion is to honest people who, for the reason I have assigned, fall short of the truth.

Indeed, I see no reason why the modern collector may not go a step further, carefully study out his own personal equation, and save the reader the trouble by eliminating it himself. That would be a forward step in anthropology, perhaps, for which we are not now prepared.

Beyond the accumulation of most valuable material, what ought to be our next aspiration? Perhaps I may discourage you in this answer. It should not be and cannot be, according to the canons of science, the discovery of mysteries, the guessing of the riddle of existence, or any other great matter. It is simply and prosaically this, that we pursue with fidelity scientific processes, on material carefully collected, by means of refined apparatus; we may hope to know how folk-thoughts and folk-customs came to be what they are, and how they are linked to culture-lore. In coöperation with the archaeologist and the decipherer, the folk-lorist hopes to restore much of the lost history of our race.

Consider the botanist or the zoölogist. By means of much time and money expended, he comprehends the ongoings, the becomings, the changes of nature. The forces behind these things act as far away from his microscopic limit as that is distant from the visible things around him. The folk-lorist, who studies ballads and proverbs and counting-out rhymes, must find out how these things were made, how they grew, the law of their organic development. He will have then arrived at the half-way house of wisdom. But the analysis of each thought, saying, invention, custom, story, and so forth, must be made as carefully as I would have him do his collecting in the first instance. I would invoke the method of the patent attorney, who will take to pieces before your eyes the most complicated machine and show you the order of invention, the chronological order in which each part was added. It is not enough to say that this or that people say or do this or that; we must know exactly what they say or do, and how they say and do it, down to the fastening-off thread.

A word may be added regarding lore-areas. The naturalist who would treat comprehensively a species—for example, our honey-bee—would not be content with giving the creature a binomial name based on anatomy. All that bees are and do would be included in his study. The unfolding of a single life would be as interesting to him as the telling of a tale or the singing of a ballad, would correspond with E. Sidney Hartland's pursuit of the "Outcast Child" in many lands and down the centuries.[3] The points of view in the study of bee-life would be offset by our tracing the lore of the folk into the activities of human life. I do not know of any side from which the one subject may be viewed, that may not be advantageously occupied for the other.

Much attention has been paid in the last few years to biological regions. No naturalist neglects them. You will hear him say again and again that he does not want a mineral, a plant, an egg, a mammal skin or skeleton, if you cannot tell him quite definitely where you got it. Indeed, Dr. Virchow told the German Anthropological Society, in 1889, that a human skull counted for little unless the collector had marked well its source.

Already this fact is recognized, and, as a preparation for the true determination of lore-areas, many volumes are devoted to the folk-lore of regions. I must repeat the warning of our honored president, however, and remind you that topography or chorography for us has a variety of meanings.[4] The term "folk-lore of Norway and Sweden" would mean, for one mind, all the lore of that peninsula, with especial reference to the pressure which long days and nights, mountains, fjords, cold and storm, abundance of fish, and dark forests had exerted over the thoughts, the speech, the ways of men there. That would be topographic lore. For another mind this term would have reference to the unfolding of the nationality and language of the peninsula, which would be demographic lore. And to a third, there would appear a blue-eyed lore and black-eyed lore, based on the distinctions of race or blood, which would be ethnographic. We cannot, in the final count, neglect any of these points of view. Chorography for us means place, race, or people, according to the motive of our search. Besides, a lore-area has frequently a circumscription of its own, smaller or larger than any of those enumerated.

The problem of origins thrusts itself before the eyes of the folk-lorist as well as before the naturalist, the archaeologist, or the historian. In startling fashion, the same language, arts, social structures, beliefs, tales, and mottoes appear in regions far apart. Were they separately created? Did a certain people, like the modern Gypsies, travel about and carry these with them? Did the sayings and doings travel themselves across vast distances by a species of commerce? None of these questions can be answered as long as our material is filled with sediment and foreign bodies. In our own land we shall have to exercise extreme caution. There is scarcely a fraction of territory where the Indian was not a century or more in contact with whites before the recorder made his appearance. In some areas this space of time reaches to three hundred and fifty years. And even the negro race had ample time to introduce its lore to the aborigines before the reporter arrived on the spot. Especially is this true of the aborigines now in the Indian Territory, who were deported from the Southern States only fifty years ago, after remaining in close contact with negroes two hundred years. In the Spanish Americas the contact remains to this moment.

The classifications of folk-lore which I have seen, even those in which the connection with anthropology is recognized, give prominence to the subjective side rather than to the objective side of the inquiry. It is anthropology standing off and regarding the folk, forming opinions about them, and writing books about them. From our point of view, the term "folk-lore" is both subjective and objective. But it is primarily objective. It is the anthropology which the folk hold. It is their beliefs about the heavens above, the earth beneath, and the waters under the earth. Cosmogony, chemistry, physics, botany, zoölogy, and mankind, bodily, intellectual, and spiritual,—whence came the objects and the phenomena involved in these, what is their nature, power, and limitations?

Consider for a moment the range of the science called anthropology. In addition to investigating what man is, it now comprehends all that he does, his activities manifested in speech, in arts of comfort, in arts of pleasure, in social organization, duties and customs, in philosophy, literature, and science, in religion. Without doubt, there is also a folk-speech, folk-trades and practices, folk fine art, folk-amusement, folk-festival, folk-ceremonies, folk-customs, folk-government, folk-society, folk-history, folk-poetry, folk-maxims, folk-philosophy, folk-science, and myths or folk-mythology. Everything that we have, they have,—they are the back numbers of us.

It is true that the cosmogony of the folk overshadows all the beliefs and practices of the folk; the light from the spirit world streams over every thought, and seems to have led some into the error that the folk are only myth-makers. But no one seems to have noticed that also, with the most learned, every object and movement of the present life is reflected back upon the heavenly life. Nothing takes place there that was not enacted here. Every god and minor spirit is a copy of something real. Mythology is only a part of folk-lore, and can be fairly understood only when we have a correct understanding of the culture plain of the myth-teller and his audience. I hope I may be pardoned for repeating that every specialist in anthropology must first go down and sit at the feet of the folk, to be instructed in all the ways of life, and in the proper method of accounting for phenomena.

Most classifications of folk-lore that I have examined have been based on a mixture of classific concepts partly formal, partly functional, and partly metaphysical.[5] For my own part, I have found it better to work the other way, to make collections in the smallest possible classes of folk-lore, just as our museum collectors gather specimens, waiting for these to group themselves as occasion may demand. The linguist will naturally fix his mind on folk-speech,—etymologies, spelling, pronunciation, definition, sentence-making, wherever he may find them. The house-builder, cabinet-maker, tailor, craftsman, doctor, sailor, and others will search out each his share of practical lore. The musician, draughtsman, painter, sculptor, or landscape-gardener will compass sea and land to complete his technic family tree.

Around the governmental organization, the military organization, the family, the community, the guild, the union, cluster traditions and customs, ceremonies, festivals, games, as thick as leaves in the forest. These are capable of separate collection, and naturally fall together. The science of the folk, as before mentioned, falls naturally into cosmogony, sky-lore, weather-lore, mineral-lore, plant-lore, and man-lore, or history and philosophy.

What we call literature had its parent and predecessor in folk-speech. I do not mean now the matter, but the manner of saying. It would not do to speak of the *belles-lettres* of the unlettered. But they hand down by tradition in prose and verse the choicest utterances of their distinguished men, and these are their treasured compositions, and will find their patrons in men of literary taste. The historian especially at this time will search out the methods of recording events among the uncivilized, in order that he may catch a glimpse of the old chroniclers at their work. I have a fancy that, in the near future, the little scraps and shreds of lore will be gathered for historic purposes very much as the archaeologist brings together the materials, tools, pictures, and descriptions of processes, and the products of the humblest industries.

Finally, in the presence of the spirit-world, we contemplate folk-religion, which is what they believe about the spirit world and what they practice in view of that belief. What they believe is *folk-creed;* what they practice is *folk-cult.* Folk-creed and folk-cult constitute folk-religion, just as folk-thought and folk-wont constitute the folk-lore of anything whatever.

By this process of gathering material, with no view to classification, we enable the systematic student to write books on child-lore, moon-lore, flower-lore, rabbit-lore, weather-lore, sea-lore, folk-medicine, or any other line he may select. The lore of a people, a region, a race, includes the whole range of anthropological sciences regarded from the point of view of that people, region, or race. In the same way, world-lore expands the vista to all times and climes. Those who pursue the subject with this ruling conception in mind, take up some *infimus conceptus,* like "counting-out rhymes," and find every example thereof under the sun. I have frequently imagined, for the different lore-areas, cards ruled in squares, with the classific concepts of anthropological science in the vertical column and the objects of folk-thought and folk-custom across the top. In each square the collector, by a number or reference, could indicate the character of the folk-response to the binomial conception. All that Mr. Bolton and other folk-loric globe-trotters would have to do would be to glance over the whole set to see whether he had overlooked any examples.[6] Better still, these indefatigable gentlemen might be induced to fill up many of the vacant squares for us. The world would then form an encyclopaedia folk-lorica.

Some day we may hope to realize Mr. J. S. Stuart-Glennie's definition of folk-lore, that it is our learning about the folk, just as bird-lore is what the folk believe and do about birds. But that will be the last chapter in the book, and can be written only after the natural historian of the human mind declares the information all in, and all the little squares on my cards properly filled up.

Until that time, let us be patient, accurate, unprejudiced, scientific. I remember very well the struggle to bring archaeology within the rules of refined work. . . . Folk-lore, also, has its camp-followers, with whom we should part company at an early day. Above all, let us not forget that all science, and every human industry, custom, and belief, originated with the folk. Before astronomy, was astrology; before physics, were caloric and discrete forces; before chemistry, was alchemy; before biology, was natural history; before anthropology, was mythology: and it may be that some day our own precious oracles will turn out to be old wives' fables.

Notes

1. I am aware that the term "folk-lore" has been employed in two senses: first, to denote the sum of knowledge possessed by any folk, or the traditional material; secondly, to signify knowledge about any folk, or to include inferences and conclusions derived from a study of this material. Clearness would seem to require that the word should be confined, for the present at least, to the first meaning, which it was originally invented to express. Again, there has been, and still is, a question as to whether by the term "folk" should be understood only the illiterate portion of highly cultivated communities, or simply any body of persons forming a community, when regarded as acting and feeling in common. American folk-lorists will probably agree in the opinion that in America, the wider signification will be found useful.

2. [Mason is referring to J. Owen Dorsey (1848–95), a founder of the American Folklore Society, who began working for the Bureau of American Ethnology in 1879. Dorsey was an expert for the bureau in American Indian languages and was a careful collector of Indian myths and customs. See, for example, his "Siouan Sociology," *Bureau of American Ethnology Annual Report for 1894* (Washington, D.C.: Government Printing Office, 1897), pp. 205–44. —*Ed.*]

3. [Mason is here referring to Hartland's "The Outcast Child," *Folklore* 4 (1893): pp. 308–49, a classic study in which Hartland identified types of an internationally known folktale, including the "King Lear" type familiar to us from Shakespeare. —*Ed.*]

4. [Mason is here referring to Daniel Brinton (1837–99), president of the American Folklore Society in 1890. The work that Mason has in mind is probably Brinton's *Races and Peoples: Lectures on the Science of Ethnography* (New York: N.D.C. Hodges, 1890). In the work, Brinton outlined characteristics of several geographically bounded "races"; Mason summarized the work in the Smithsonian Institution's annual report for 1890 (pp. 541–45). Mason's example of the Scandinavian peninsula is probably informed by Brinton's "The Folk-Lore of Yucatan," *Folklore Journal* 1 (1883): pp. 244–56. —*Ed.*]

5. . . . Mr. E. Sidney Hartland has advocated a division into two departments, Folk-thought and Folk-practice or Folk-wont, including in the latter, worship. Mr. J. S. Stuart-Glennie divides the study of man's history into Folk-lore and Culture-life, dividing the former into (1) elements and subjects, embracing folk-beliefs, folk-passions, and folk-traditions, and (2) expressions and records, comprehending folk-customs, folk-sayings, and folk-poesy.

[Mason refers his readers to George Laurence Gomme's *Handbook of Folk-Lore* (London: D. Nutt, 1890) for its classification scheme. Gomme (1853–1916) declared that the "subjects which make up the body of survivals called Folk-Lore" could be placed under four major genres: "1. Superstitious Beliefs and Practices: including those relating to natural objects, as trees, plants, and animals; goblindom, witchcraft, leechcraft, magic, and divination; beliefs relating to future life; and superstitions generally. 2. Traditional Customs: including those relating to festivals, ceremonies, and games, or identified with certain localities. 3. Traditional Narratives: such as nursery tales (or *Marchen*), hero tales, drolls, fables, and apologues; creation, deluge, fire and doom myths; ballads and songs; place legends and traditions. 4. Folk Sayings: as jingles, nursery rhymes, riddles, proverbs, nicknames, and place rhymes." The revision of the *Handbook* in 1914 by Charlotte Burne added objects to the folklorist's purview, but Bassett's *Folklore Manual* (1893), reprinted in this volume, while modeled on Gomme's classification, made a special point of including "folklore objects." Gomme's emphasis on classification by genre, which was conducive to the "comparative" or "natural history" methodology that Mason espoused, dominated both the work of British and American folklorists, but received some challenge from German folklorists who concentrated on culture areas. An attempt at compromise is made in the guide to collectors issued by the Philadelphia Chapter of the American Folklore Society, reprinted in this volume; it divided folklore into genres common among the city's distinct ethnic groups. Another issue was whether to concentrate on the literary forms of lore or whether to take into account the life of groups as they express lore. In his note at this location, Mason singles out the British folklorists for inspiration, but makes special mention of the relation of folklore and what he refers to as "Culture life." Background on the issue, and the opinion that classification is best made along generic lines, was given a few years before Mason's article appeared in Charlotte Burne, "Classification of Folklore," *Folklore Journal* 4 (1886): pp. 158–63; see also Richard M. Dorson, *The British Folklorists* (Chicago: University of Chicago Press, 1968), pp. 316–31, and for Mason's dealings with the subject specifically, see Curtis M. Hinsley, Jr., *Savages and Scientists* (Washington, D.C.: Smithsonian Institution Press, 1981), pp. 109–17. —*Ed.*]

6. [Mason is referring to Henry Carrington Bolton's *The Counting Out Rhymes of Children: Their Antiquity, Origin, and Wide Distribution; A Study in Folk-Lore* (New York: D. Appleton, 1888). The work lists 877 rhymes from around the world. See chapter 9 of this book for writing by Bolton on another topic, and chapter 14 (case 1) for another reference to Bolton's work on counting-out rhymes. —*Ed.*]

2

Notes on Folklore Collecting

Fletcher S. Bassett
Philadelphia Chapter of the American Folklore Society

Using the natural science metaphor during the Gilded Age, folklorists took to "collecting specimens" of tradition out in the "field." Folklorists sought the help of nonprofessionals who with their collecting would contribute to the systematic classification, arrangement, and analysis of the material. Because Americans owed the character of their study to British folklorists, they relied primarily on George Laurence Gomme's *Handbook of Folklore* (1890). But Americans hoped to take the lead in the study of folklore during the 1890s, and the Third International Folklore Congress held at the Chicago World's Fair in 1893 offered them a chance to display their advancement. For the occasion, Fletcher Bassott (1047–93), head of the Chicago Folklore Society (later the International Folklore Association) and organizer of the congress, wrote *The Folk-Lore Manual* (1892), a 3¼ by 5½ inch, 87-page booklet to aid American collectors. Bassett freely admitted to borrowing from Gomme's *Handbook,* but claimed that he particularly "fit this work for the use of the American collector," especially because "Folk-Lore has become a science, and there is a pressing call for more material, fresh from any unworked field." One notable addition in Bassett's manual was a "List of Objects for a Folk-Lore Collection," which consisted primarily of ritual objects. To show the emphasis on the object, rite, and custom that characterized American collections, this section along with an introduction to "how to collect" are reprinted here from *The Folk-Lore Manual* (Chicago: Chicago Folk-Lore Society, 1892), pp. 5–12, 82–87.

Bassett did not live to see many results from his work. He died shortly after the World's Fair closed in 1893, but was at least able to point to the many exhibits of "folklore objects" suggested in his manual, including the one described in chapter 14 of this book, around the fair. The Chicago Folklore Society, which he had formed in 1891, survived through the decade, but without Bassett's strong leadership folded after the turn of the century.

That left the American Folklore Society, founded in 1888, as the strongest voice for American collection of traditions. The society stressed the ethnological connection to folklore studies more strongly than the Chicago Folklore Society, and particularly emphasized the traditions of ethnic groups and Native Americans. Both the Chicago Folklore Society and the American Folklore Society had local branches that were expected to undertake regional collecting. A Philadelphia group in 1889 was the first local branch to form within the American Folklore Society. It was an active group whose activities were outgrowths of longstanding clubs such as the Philadelphia Numismatic and Antiquarian Society devoted to folklore topics. The Philadelphia branch of the folklore society sponsored monthly meetings at which papers were read and "folklore objects" were shown. It organized the first national meeting of the American Folklore Society in 1889, and produced two presidents of the society in Daniel Brinton (in 1890) and Stewart Culin (in 1897). City residents recognized that their city was a composite of traditions; it had an unusually wide array of ethnic settlements within relatively close quarters. The city also boasted an early influential work on field-collected folklore collections, John Fanning Watson's *Annals of Philadelphia and Pennsylvania in the Olden Time* (1830), so it was not surprising that the city inspired the first local guide to the society's folklore collectors.

In 1890, the Philadelphia branch issued the guide as a three-page brochure; excerpts were reprinted in the *Journal of American Folklore* that same year. The guide defined folklore and in its outline of folklore "fields" by ethnic groups, reconciled those concerned within the branch for the life of traditional groups and those interested primarily in the history of folklore forms. The guide was probably largely the work of Stewart Culin, who was the secretary of the branch, and a committee made up of C. Leland Harrison, Richard L. Ashhurst, and Rev. Alfred L. Elwyn. The guide, which makes up the second part of this chapter, is reprinted from the original brochure which I found at the University of Pennsylvania Museum.

For background readings on Bassett's Chicago Folklore Society and the Philadelphia Branch of the American Folklore Society, see W. K. McNeil, "The Chicago Folklore Society and the International Folklore Congress of 1893," *Midwestern Journal of Language and Folklore* 11 (1985): pp. 5–19, and Susan Dwyer-Shick, "The American Folklore Society and Folklore Research in America, 1888–1940" (Ph.D. Dissertation, University of Pennsylvania, 1979), pp. 89–94. And for a humanistic perspective on the history of "field" collecting, see Robert A. Georges and Michael Owen Jones, *People Studying People: The Human Element in Fieldwork* (Berkeley: University of California Press, 1980).

*   *   *

How to Collect Folk-Lore

Any one may collect the oral traditions of the people, but all persons cannot do so successfully. Some carefully abstain from imparting to strangers any of their individual beliefs, superstitions or practices; others will only bestow them upon those in whom they have a certain amount of confidence. Hence, it is important for the collector to obtain the good-will of those from whom he may wish to glean curious scraps of traditional lore. A certain amount of tact is necessary in doing this. It will not do to approach each one in the same way. Some are suspicious of any direct questions; others take alarm at any sort of maneuvering. Each one must judge for himself how to proceed, and a little experience will enable him to acquire the art of commencing aright. Suggestion has been found successful, and will hardly fail to be of great assistance. Many who, at the first blush, can remember nothing of the matter sought, will be reminded of it by some story or superstition, or practice, resembling it in some way. It is often best not to declare yourself anxious to record that which is related, although you may sometimes openly write it down. No one will acknowledge that superstition has any hold in his or her case, but it really exists everywhere. The earnest collector may, under all circumstances, be alert to receive more or less important communications, the amount depending principally upon his knowledge of the subject. The field is practically unworked, and will yield abundant harvests if properly tilled. In every direction are uncollected and unwritten traditions, ripe for the gleaner, and fast passing away. Among the Indians, on plantation and cattle-range, in the factory and on the farm, in the crowded city and in the little village, among miners and sailors, professional men of attainments and uneducated laborers, in busy avocations of men and in the household life of women, among children and gray-hairs—everywhere, folk-lore is abundant, for it is the lore of the people, not of any class, and is to be sought everywhere. Individual judgment and tact must decide how and when, but the opportunities are abundant. The fast-decaying traditions of our native tribes and of the negroes and mixed races are the most important, and work among them, will, perhaps, bring the most abundant results; but there is much to be done in our midst, and among all classes. By far the greater mass of material will be found among women, children and old people. Many of our nursery stories, fairy stories and tales came from the mouths and brains of women, whose imaginative faculties, if not so creative, are more retentive than those of men.

It is well to have some local knowledge of the country, the people and the customs. The dialect in which a story is told must be carefully noted. Every tale should be reported, as nearly as possible, in the exact language of the narrator. Familiarity with the Indian language is essential to a great amount of work among the tribes. The locality should always be reported, and the time when a custom, superstition or ceremony is observed. The name of the narrator, when practicable and fit, (sometimes this is not advisable,) and the name of the collector, should be accurately reported. Write the words and the music of folk-songs, describe costumes, instruments used in dances, festivals and ceremonies, and give drawings or sketches when possible.

Only the reported facts should be given in toto, reserving comments, parallels and comparisons for a separate place, or, at least, noting them, when made, in a careful way, so that they may be readily distinguished from the fresh and original matter. Care will have to be exercised to prevent being imposed upon. Some people, without intending deception, will coincide with any opinion suggested by a stranger, and uncultivated persons usually make it a point of honor not to contradict, but always to agree with, the interlocutor. A fertile imagination will sometimes readily invent this or that tale, riddle, rhyme or proverb, and pass it for some saying current in the mouths of the people.

Sketches and short-hand reports are important adjuncts to the collectors' material. Such are, however, valueless if not faithful, and the imagination must play an unimportant part in their production and use. As faithful adjuncts to eye and ear, the camera and phonograph make folk-lore collecting more complete and valuable. The words, intonations and gestures of the story-teller, the music of the song and dance, and graphic representations of ceremonies, costumes and localities, are, by these accurate instruments, carefully presented. We may now preserve dialects that would, otherwise, be lost to the ear, splendid pageants, that seem commonplace when described in words, and music that even skilled players could not reproduce.

Other Work in Folk-Lore

The collection of folk-lore material is not the only work of the folk-lorist. It is, unquestionably, the most pressing duty, but there is work in the library and at home. Much valuable folk-lore (especially of this country) is, as Mr. G. L. Gomme has pointed out, entombed in obscure works, books of travel little known, and in rare brochures and periodicals. These should be searched for the gems they contain, and research in any line of popular tradition cannot fail to be rewarded by valuable results. Some lines of folk-lore have been explored but little, and the careful student may find remuneration in following any of them to their sources. At present, the co-operation of folk-lorists is doing much in the English Society towards the classification of tales, and work in this direction, with regard to our Indian stories, essentially different from European tales, would seem desirable. An analysis of the customs and superstitions has also been proposed, and will furnish interesting and profitable work. Much remains to be done in the bibliography of folk-lore—a large and constantly growing department, and one in which classification would be most useful to the working folk-lorist.

Finally, collection may well take the direction of tangible objects— visible proofs of the existence of traditional customs, superstitions and ceremonies. A scheme for such a collection is given . . . and it is extremely desirable that the services of such persons as may be willing and able to so do, should be obtained in forwarding in every way such an assemblage of objects interesting and instructive in folk-lore. The list sufficiently indicates the nature of such a museum. . . .

List of Objects for a Folk-Lore Collection

A. *The House and Its Furnishings*

1. Any special buildings, either in models, plans or sketches, devoted to feasts, unusual religious ceremonies, purification ceremonies, or other festal or superstitious rites. Temples, council houses, medicine lodges, dance houses, etc.
2. Curious carvings, images, inscriptions, etc., on roofs, over doors, or in walls of houses. Totem poles; votive inscriptions, curious stained glass, and unusual decorations.
3. Any furniture of curious design and purpose, especially anything containing mythical or mythological sculptures, castings or carvings. Curious instruments of worship, such as chalice, crosiers, prayerwheels, lamps, etc. Odd composite furniture, illustrating any curious phases of life.
4. Cooking utensils. Spits. Fire-place andirons, etc. Curious cake-cutters, etc. Butter-moulds, cheese-moulds, souvenir spoons, carved salad spoons, etc. Indian shell spoons and ladles.
5. Curious instruments of Labor. Spinning-wheels, distaffs. Candle moulds, mild strainers, etc., of odd or ancient pattern.
6. Pottery. Any ware of local note. Battle pitchers, ship pitchers; naval and land battle plates, cups and saucers. Presentation crockery. Crockery with portraits, etc.; with superstitious emblems. Curious foot-warmers. Whistling jugs. Monkeys or evaporating jugs. "Huacos" or pottery found in graves.

B. *Personal Objects*

1. Costumes. Bridal and mourning costumes. Costumes worn at certain ceremonies, such as the ghost dance, green corn dances, and at all feasts. Dress of Medicine-men; of conjurers; of worshippers at any religious ceremony. Curious ancient clothing of every form and material. Indian bead-work clothing. Curiously decorated or embroidered clothing. Uniforms, regalia, and insignia. Curious buckles, buttons, hooks, combs, canes, batons. Wooden shoes, or those of any unusual material or shape. Curious hats, and modes of dressing the hair or beard.

2. Jewels. Engagement rings of curious pattern. Wedding rings. Rings, badges, seals, and insignia of associations, lodges, societies, etc. Rings to cure disease; to ward off sorcery and the evil eye; to cure cramps, etc. Teething rings. Crosses and medals. Political medals; souvenir medals. Pins of curious form and materials; brooches, etc. Lip ornaments.

3. Pipes of peace. Curious pipes of local manufacture, and of improvised materials. Curious and unusual tobacco or snuff boxes. Ceremonial pipes.

4. Musical instruments. Horns, drums, flutes, whistles, rattles, etc., used in religious or other ceremonies. Those used in peculiar dances or feasts.

5. Printed matter. Dream books, almanacs, sorcerers' books, curious calendars, books used in divining, and curious maps, drawings and cuts.

6. Playthings. Curious toys, knucklebones, jack-stones, tops, especially those of savages.

7. Miscellaneous. Curious account-books. Tallies. Souvenir knots. Illiterate records of time, historical events, etc.

C. The Trades

Implements, etc. Any charm placed about the harness of a horse, or on the body of an ox, a cow, or a sheep, or used in stables to preserve them from harm. Charms used to make cows give milk. Agricultural implements having flints, thunder stones, or any charms in their handles. Amulets or charms used by hunters or fishermen. Boats with superstitious images on their hulls or sails.

D. Folk-Medicine

Amulets against disease. Against venomous serpents and stings. Madstones. Amulets and charms against the evil eye; against sorcery; to stop bleeding; for toothache, hemorrhoids, piles, headache, to aid dentition, to cure warts, for carbuncles, and boils, to cure fits and epilepsy, to cure rheumatism, erysipelas, gravel, kidney disease, fever, ague, apoplexy and worms; to affect the flow of milk; to aid in restoring natural functions of body, and in particular to preserve eyesight. Coral used as charm in teething.

E. Miscellaneous Charms and Amulets

Amulets against lightning; against hail; against cyclones; to cure grief and melancholy; against robbers; to prevent drowning and shipwreck. Cauls.

Amulets for good luck to hunters, gamesters and lovers. Amulets, such as celts, etc., used as sorcery stones by Indian Medicine men. Lodestones used by [Voodoo] sorcerers. Gems worn as luck bringers. Amber beads used as incense. Fetishes of jade. Bloodstone charms. Fetishes of gypsum and turquoise used by Pueblos to bring rain. Luck pennies. Horse-shoe charms. Indian charm feathers; charm rings.

Animal charms. Tiger claws, eagle claws, eagles' feathers, sharks' teeth, fish amulets, bone charms, rhinoceros' claw, cock's foot, rabbit's claw, mole's foot, badger skin, snake skin, skull bone, wolf or dog's tooth, snail shell.

Hints for the Local Study of Folk-Lore in Philadelphia and Vicinity

The Committee of The Philadelphia Chapter of The American Folk-Lore Society has prepared the following circular for the guidance of local collectors:—

The expressive term "Folk-lore" has been adopted to designate the collective sum of the knowledge, beliefs, stories, customs, manners, dialects, expessions, and usages of a community which are peculiar to itself, and which, taken together, constitute its individuality when compared with other communities.

Every community is thus separated from its neighbors by numerous peculiarities, which, though they may at first seem trivial, exert in their mass a powerful influence on the life of the individual and the history of the people in the aggregate, or the "folk." Hence, as a handmaid to the science of history and ethnology, and as an aid to the just appreciation of the various elements which go to make up a nation, "Folk-lore" is a study of very considerable importance. It is one, moreover, which appeals to every person, because all can contribute to it from their own experience. It should be the most popular of studies, as its aim is to record the peculiarities in the experiences of every one of us and of our families.

The American Folk-Lore Society was formed about three years ago to collect and preserve the "Folk-lore" of our continent, especially of the United States. The formation of local branches will greatly aid in the accomplishment of this work, and the Philadelphia members of the Society have taken the initiative by creating the Philadelphia Chapter.

It includes both male and female members, and it proposes to devote itself to the special study of the "Folk-lore" of Philadelphia and the region for about a hundred miles around the city.

In order that the scope of its industry may be clearly understood, the Committee present the following schedule of topics, which will be separately discussed at various meetings of the Chapter, and concerning which they urge members to collect all the information within their reach, from newspapers, from private sources, and from personal observation.

Special Subjects for Examination

Anglo-American field
Language—Peculiarities of pronunciation, of grammar, of idioms, and of single words, in and around Philadelphia used by English-speaking families.

Superstitions—Omens, portents, ghost stories, weather-warnings, haunted houses or localities, prognostics, etc., among the whites of English descent; astrologers, fortune-tellers, etc.

Songs (ballads), games, plays (of children), folk-literature, almanacs, dream books, odd local publications.

Africo-American field
Language, the (as above), among the colored people of city and country.

Superstitions—Special attention to relics of Voodoo or Obi rites, conjuring, magic, medical superstition, stories and tales, religious notions or unusual ceremonies (camp-meeting stories), plantation songs.

Local foreign fields
The Chinese Quarter: Its English dialect; worship; imported or adopted rites; games; customs; habits.

The Italian Quarter: Same as for Chinese.

The German Quarter: 1. Pennsylvania German, 2. Immigrant German.

Sailors' Haunts.

Gipsies—Roving tinkers, "tramps," their habits, names, and origin.

The collection of American oral traditions should be regarded as a national duty. To gather materials for history, which are indispensable [sic] to anthropological record, and which unless recorded, will in a few years have irretrievably perished, appears at least as important as the collation of historical records safely lodged in libraries.

Groups and Their Customs

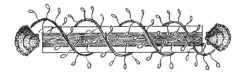

Folklore of the Pennsylvania Germans

W. J. Hoffman

Walter James Hoffman (1846–99), a physician by training, was one of the original staff members of the Bureau of American Ethnology. Assigned to medical positions in Germany and the American West, he developed interests in German-American and American Indian folklife. Eventually he joined the Bureau of American Ethnology in 1879, where he pursued studies of "primitive ritual and primitive art." A native of Reading, Pennsylvania, in the heart of the Pennsylvania "Dutch" country, Hoffman included his observations of Pennsylvania-German folklore in the inaugural volume of the *Journal of American Folklore*. Although his work among the Indians dominated his work for the Bureau of American Ethnology, his obituary commented that his studies of the Pennsylvania Germans were "of particular interest and value." Pennsylvania Germans were of interest to American folklorists, because in the midst of a predominantly British inheritance for the nation, the German communities of central Pennsylvania tenaciously held on to their German traditions. And to "scientific men," their traditions appeared to dwell on superstition and ritual. Hoffman surveys the persistent culture of the Pennsylvania Germans by pointing to the array of folklore they possess set against the background of their cultural history and settlement. He includes folk speech and belief in his survey, and also makes a special point of discussing the foodways, crafts, and architecture of the Pennsylvania Germans, especially as these items relate to custom.

A literature devoted to the folklife of the Pennsylvania-Germans has a long history. Benjamin Rush's *An Account of the Manners of the German Inhabitants of Pennsylvania* in 1798 drew attention to the distinctive customs of the German settlements, and John Fanning Watson in the *Annals of Philadelphia* (1830) described many of their "peculiar" superstitions. "The Pennsylvania Dutch (Properly German)" was the title of a popular series of articles by Phebe Earle Gibbons, which appeared in *Atlantic Monthly* and *Harper's* after 1869, covering festivals, quiltings, manners and customs, and language. But Hoffman's essays beginning with this one in 1888 gave the examination of the Pennsylvania Germans a scientific cast and put it in the frame of evolutionary ideas on culture.

This essay is reprinted from the *Journal of American Folklore* 1 (1888): pp. 125–35. Other articles on the Pennsylvania Germans by Hoffman appeared in the journal in volume 2 (1889): pp. 23–35, 191–202. He also contributed articles on Pennsylvania-German folk medicine to the *Proceedings of the American Philosophical Society* 26 (1889): pp. 187–285 and to *Science* 26 (1893): p. 335. His major work on American Indians was "The Memomini Indians," *Fourteenth Annual Report of the Bureau of American Ethnology* (Washington, D.C.: Government Printing Office, 1896), pp. 3–328. Hoffman's obituary, written by Alexander Chamberlain, appeared in the *Journal of American Folklore* 13 (1900): pp. 44–46. For background on German-American folklife studies, see Don Yoder, "The Folklife Studies Movement," *Pennsylvania Folklife* 13 (July 1963): pp. 43–56, and "Pennsylvania German Folklore Research: A Historical Analysis" and "German Folklore in America: Discussion," in *The German Language in America: A Symposium,* ed. Glenn G. Gilbert (Austin: University of Texas Press, 1971), pp. 70–105, 148–63; Mac E. Barrick, *German-American Folklore* (Little Rock: August House, 1987).

*   *   *

Before describing the customs, folk-medicine and folk-lore of the Pennsylvania Germans, it will be necessary to present a brief sketch of the people to which they relate, and to explain the origin of the dialect generally, though erroneously, denominated "Pennsylvania Dutch."

Swedish settlers appeared at Tinicum Island, on the Delaware River, about the year 1638, where they held possession until 1655, when they were displaced by the Dutch, who in turn (in 1664) were compelled to give way to the English. A few adventurers had already arrived and established themselves where Chester now stands, a year before the arrival of Penn in 1682. Previous to this, numbers of Germans from the Palatinate—Rhenish Bavaria—had been induced to come to England upon the invitation of Queen Anne, the object of the English authorities being the rapid colonization of the new possessions in America; therefore many of the immigrants who came with Penn, and during the following years, were retained for a greater or less period of time to indemnify that government for the expense of transportation and maintenance. Some sold themselves to settlers from the interior, for whom they worked for a specified time. Numbers of these German colonists were transported to Georgia and to New York, but most of them ultimately made their way to Pennsylvania, where their friends had previously settled.

During the years 1683 and 1684 the immigration steadily increased, and was represented chiefly by Welsh, English, and few Dutch, and, above all, by Palatines. According to Proud, some of these lodged in the woods, in hollow trees, and in caves and dug-outs made along the banks of the Delaware and the Wissahickon, while others hastily erected rude huts.[1]

Thousands of new arrivals flocked in between the years 1708 and 1720, these being chiefly Palatines, with a few natives of Würtemberg and Darmstadt. Franconia, Baden, and Saxony were also represented at various intervals. Irish, from the north of Ireland, began to arrive about the year 1719, and the Welsh had been among the first to purchase land of Penn, selecting that on the west bank of the Schuylkill. Previous to 1692, the latter settled six townships in Chester County. The Irish, on the contrary, established themselves on the Lehigh, at a point between the present sites of Bethlehem and Allentown, which was long known as "Craig's Settlement." North of the Blue Mountains, near the Delaware, a few Dutch families from New Jersey and New York took up land, as did also a number of French and Spanish.

Philadelphia County was established in 1682, and on account of the number of Germans at the northern extremity of the settlement that spot received the name of "Germantown," which it still retains. From this point north and west the country was rapidly penetrated and clearings were made, so that during the eighteenth century all that portion of the State east of the Blue Mountains, from the Delaware to Maryland, contained thriving settlements and the beginnings of future cities.

Intermarriage between the various German immigrants, among whom the dialects of the Palatinate, Franconia, etc., predominated, has resulted in the formation of a dialect which is known as "Pennsylvania German." This more strongly resembles some of the Bavarian dialects than any other of the German, as was recognized by the present writer during his service as staff-surgeon in the Prussian army during the war of 1870–71. Although Pennsylvanians read German newspapers and books, they are generally unable to converse in that language, and experience great difficulty in understanding a recent German immigrant, whom they regard in the light of a foreigner, as much as do people of English descent. . . .

Although impracticable in the present paper, to treat of the philologic peculiarities of this dialect, it is necessary to submit a short scheme to facilitate in the proper pronunciation of such words and phrases as may be given from time to time. Consonants are sounded as in English; vowels are short, unless indicated by a line over the vowel prolonged in sound.

a, as in *far, tar*.	i, as in *pit*.
ä, as in *hat*.	ï, as *e* in *neat*.
â, as in *law*.	o, as *u* in *nut*.
ai, as *ai* in *aisle*.	ō, as in *note*.
âi, as *oi* in *oil*.	u, as *u* in *put*.
e, as in *net*.	ū, as *oo* in *fool*.
ē, as *a* in *ale*.	
ch, as in German *nicht*.	
gh, as the soft sound of *g* in *Tagen, schlagen*.	
z is represented by *ts*.	
c " " by *k* or *s*.	

', the acute accent, is used to indicate accented syllables.

ⁿ, the superior *n* indicates a nasalized sound of the letter to which it is attached. This sound appears to be one of the most striking peculiarities of the dialect, and resembles the nasalized *n* of the French language. The final *en* of all German words becomes *a* or *ä*, as schlagen (to strike) = shla'gha; essen (to eat) = es'sä.

It is extremely difficult for people of the rural districts to acquire the proper sound of *j* and *g,* as in the words James and gem, the usual result being *tsh,* as *ch* in Charles; words beginning with *ch* are sounded like the English *j,* and the final *th* becomes *s,* while the same sound as initial, in *this,* becomes *d.*

This dialect is still in common use, particularly in the country and small villages, though through the agency of public schools the English language is rapidly replacing it. As pronounced and spoken by the country folk, the dialect is frequently very amusing to those speaking it in the cities, as the former have a peculiar drawl or prolonged intonation not often heard in business communities, where everything is done with promptness and dispatch. There are marked differences, too, in words and phrases, so that one who is familiar with this dialect can readily distinguish whether the speaker be from Lancaster, or Berks, or Lehigh County.

The descendants of the early German colonists, after having received during several generations the benefits of education and mingling in cultured society, cannot be distinguished from the offspring of other nationalities, and it is only in the rural districts, and in what is frequently termed the "backwoods," that we find the ruder and more primitive customs and superstitions surviving.

The country folks (*bush'lait*) are very averse to the adoption of the usages of polite society, and consequently adhere to many curious customs and manners with great tenacity. A common response, when questioned in regard to this, is, "As my father did, so I do" (*wi děr fádĕr gedú*ⁿ *hŏt, so du ich â*).

Occasional newspaper articles have appeared from time to time purporting to present accounts of the customs and superstitions of this people; but as the writers were generally not of the people, and in addition many were unfamiliar with the dialect, the accuracy of such descriptions may reasonably be questioned.

Many of the customs and superstitions are the remants of what were imported into this country at the time of the first settlements, and it is only natural, therefore, to expect parallels in various portions of Great Britain and on the Continent. Still, the colonists had invariably to adapt themselves to their new environment; and as most of them had no money wherewith to secure the comforts of civilization, they began life *de novo.*

Houses of moderate size were erected upon the clearings, usually having two rooms, sometimes three; the chimney being erected on the inside, as was also the oven. Windows consisted of small square openings, with a sliding board on the inner side, to serve as a shutter. Furniture of all descriptions was home-made and of the most primitive patterns. All clothing was made by the women, and they frequently resorted to buckskin skirts when working in the fields. Squirrel-skin moccasins were considered a luxury, and when the young women went to church on Sunday, in order to make them last as long as possible, they walked barefoot until within sight of the building before putting them on. In time, however, the condition of things and persons improved, so that the account which follows pertains chiefly to the early and middle portion of the present century.

Nearly every farmer raised sufficient flax or hemp for home consumption. The preparation of this, so that the spun fibre could be delivered to the weaver, entailed much labor and time, as many well remember. Wool was also prepared, dyed, and woven for garments and bed-covers. Dyes were made from the bark of trees and from plants. Sassafras bark produced a substantial yellow for woollen materials; a decoction of the bark of the red maple was employed, though a quantity of copperas had to be added. The bark of both the hickory and the oak was employed, chiefly for linen goods, and the loose skins of old onions produced a light yellow. As a substitute for alum, urine was employed, and this was carefully poured into large vessels, until sufficient had accumulated for the desired purpose.

Barns, were then, as now, always larger and frequently more comfortable than the dwelling-house. The ground floor is divided into compartments for the stabling of horses and cattle, one end being left open as a driveway, where farm implements are placed during inclement weather. The main floor, extending over all, is usually from ten to twelve feet above the ground, and is divided into three parts. The middle third is reserved for threshing and the temporary storage of carriages and wagons, while upon either side are located the granaries, above which is stored the hay or straw. The roofs are of shingles. According to an old superstition, the shingles must be nailed on during the waning of the moon, or they will soon curl up and split. It is a common sight to find a horse-shoe nailed upon the lintels of the stable doors, to insure good luck and safety to the animals, and it is still better if the horse-shoe be one that was found upon the highway.

The writer is inclined to believe that this custom had its origin at a time more remote than the superstitions relating to "thirteen at a table" and the "spilling of salt," both of which are generally conceded to have originated at or with the Lord's Supper and consequent events. The

Romans drove nails into the walls of cottages, as an antidote against the plague: for this reason L. Manilius, A.U.C. 390, was named dictator to drive the nail (Brand's "Antiq.," 1882, iii. 18). In Jerusalem, a rough representation of a hand is marked by the natives on the wall of every house whilst in building (Lt. Condor, "Palestine Explor. Fund," January, 1873, p. 16). The Moors generally, and especially the Arabs of Kairwan, employ the marks on their houses as prophylactics, and similar hand-prints are found in El Baird, near Petra.

That these practices and the later use of the horse-shoe originated with the rite of the Passover is probable. The blood upon the door-posts and upon the lintel (Exodus xii. 7) formed the chief points of an arch, and when the horse-shoe was invented it was naturally adopted by the superstitious as conforming to the shape, or outline, upon the primitive doorway, and in time it became the symbol of luck, or "safety to those residing under its protection."

The fence around the barn-yard, as well as others upon the farm, is also made during the waxing of the moon, or the posts will sink and soon rot away (Fayette County). In the eastern part of the State, fences must be made when the horns are turned up, when they will remain; if built when the horns of the moon are directed downward, the posts will sink until the bottom rail touches the ground. So also with the planting of vegetables, etc. Peas, beans, and other plants growing as vines are planted when the horns of the moon are turned up, so that they may grow vigorously. If planted when the horns of the moon are turned down, they will remain low and stunted.[2]

Potatoes are planted in the new moon, so that they will have sufficient light and all strike root; "the sign of the moon must be in the feet" (Mr. Brown, Fayette County). The same authority also says that corn should be planted during the new moon, "when the sign is in the head," so that it may all go to ear. In Lehigh County, the first day of May was the day set apart for planting corn.

Cabbage should be planted on the seventeenth day of March, to insure its heading well.

Cucumbers must be planted in the morning, before sunrise, as otherwise they would be destroyed by bugs.

Wheat must not be cut before full moon, as it will not be fully ripe; "and if Ember-days are high [*sic*] one may expect to obtain a good price therefor." This last is from Mr. L. W. Brown, of Fayette County, but the description is not clear.

A curious belief is still extant in Lehigh County respecting the transplanting of parsley. Should any one obtain one or more plants, and replant them in his own garden, it is believed that such person's death will soon follow.[3]

It is but a few years ago that hogs were slaughtered during the waxing of the moon, as at any other time the meat would shrink and not be as good.[4]

It is still confidently asserted, in many localities, that the cattle kneel and low at midnight before Christmas.

To kill a toad or a barn-swallow will cause the cows to give bloody milk.

In Fayette County, according to my informant, Mr. L. W. Brown, "when a colt opens its mouth for the first time, it drops what is usually called a 'false tongue;' this should be picked up and suspended in the stable, when the colt will always be easily caught when out in pasture."

As counter-charms, the following are still believed in. When corn and beans are reserved for the next year's planting, the cobs, husks and vines are carefully carried out into a field or upon the highway, that they may be quickly destroyed. Should they be burned, the next crop of corn and beans will be attacked by "black fungus" (*brâut*).

To exterminate briers and alders, cut them when the waning moon is in the "sign of the heart."

One will frequently observe, even at this day, the bodies of birds of prey, with outstretched wings, nailed against the gable ends of barns. Birds of this kind, shot upon the farm, were thus exposed to keep away others. A quarter of a century ago it was the custom for the young men to organize a party and shoot all obnoxious birds, and frequently those beneficial to the farmer, on Ascension Day. The origin of this custom, and the reason why that particular day should be selected, is not known.

Corn-husking parties and the merriment incident thereto is well known and indulged in even at this time, but there were also gatherings in the fields at night, after the husking had been completed, one of which the writer witnessed some years ago in Monroe County. In making a journey across the Blue Mountains, the summit was not reached until near midnight, and, just as the country beyond was dimly outlined in the moonlight, occasional strains of music and laughter could be detected floating up from below. Presently large fires were seen, and around them the rapidly moving bodies of the merrymakers. The husking had been completed, and a dance was in progress,—"a genuine jig," as it is termed in that region. The fiddler was seated upon a stump, while the couple who had the "floor" were stationed *vis-à-vis,* and in this position danced out the set, after which their places were taken by another couple. After several rounds, the whole party would promenade round the fire, which served both for illuminating the grounds and to furnish warmth, as it was late in the month of October.

When dances were held in the barn, light was afforded by lanterns and tallow candles. Husking parties (*husk'in matsh'es*) were then held during the day, and the finding of a red ear of corn entitled the finder to kiss any one of the girls present; if a girl found such an ear, and wished to avoid being kissed, she would hide it quickly as possible, though, if discovered, the first of the young men to reach her was entitled to the kiss.

That curious custom of courting termed bundling still survives in a few isolated localities along the eastern foothills of the Blue Mountains. It was rather common during the early portion of the present century, and survived and was considered a not improper practice even until the outbreak of the late war. It is more than probable that the young men discovered the absurdity and indecency of the custom during their enlistment, when they came in contact with more enlightened people, to whom such practice no doubt seemed criminal.

Among the uncultured this form of courtship was conducted with propriety and sincerity, but by the educated classes the proceedings were looked upon as decidedly immodest. No young man was esteemed a desirable beau unless he possessed at least a horse and buggy, so as to be enabled to take his sweetheart to local gatherings on holidays, and to church on Sunday.

Saturday evening was considered the proper time for courting (*shpär'iya*), though this delightful pastime often extended over the whole of Sunday. As before stated, houses were limited as to rooms; and as the distance travelled by the lover was often too great for him to return home late Saturday night, and to be at the command of his *fiancée* on Sunday morning, the matter was compromised by his remaining and sharing her bed. At sunset, the old folks were wont to retire, both to rest from the labors of the day and to save the unnecessary burning of tallow candles, which were homemade and a luxury.

The custom of bundling was, in early times, not confined to Pennsylvania alone, but extended into the New England States, as the following quotation will illustrate. William Smith, in the "Gentleman's Magazine" (1747, p. 211), says: "It must be noted that it is the custom in this country [New England] for young persons between whom there is a courtship, or treaty of marriage, to lye together, the woman having her petticoats on, and the man his breeches; and afterwards, if they do not fall out, they confess the covenant at the church, in the midst of the congregation, and to the minister, who declares the marriage legal; and if anything criminal has been acted, orders a punishment accordingly, sometimes of forty stripes save one."

In Pennsylvania, however, superfluous clothing was frequently dispensed with, and, if a like rule had existed, it would have been rarely found necessary to inflict such punishment.

That bundling received judicial recognition by the Supreme Court of the State of Pennsylvania is evident in the case of Kenderline *v.* Phelin, about the year 1852. This was on appeal from the case tried before Chief Justice Gibson, holding court at nisi prius in Philadelphia, who, in a decision on a point of evidence, ruled "that in that part of the country where the custom was known to prevail, that the female being in bed with a man, or different men, was not conclusive evidence as to her want of chastity;" and, on appeal, the decision was sustained.[5]

Another case, tried at Allentown, resulted in favor of the defendant, for the reason shown in the following extract from "The Pennsylvania Law Journal" (v. 1846, p. 30): "In an action brought to recover damages for the seduction of the plaintiff's daughter, it appeared that the defendant and the daughter slept together on the occasion of the seduction, according to a *custom* which prevailed in the part of the country where they resided (known as bundling), and with the knowledge of the plaintiff: Held, that the knowledge of the plaintiff amounted to connivance, and he could not therefore recover damages."[6]

Thirty years ago it was common, at church, to see all the marriageable girls—or at least those who had lovers—wearing white scarfs or handkerchiefs around their necks, to hide the scarlet blotches caused by the kisses and "love bites" of the preceding evening. When visiting the larger towns, numbers of young couples would stroll along the streets with clasped hands or linked fingers, like children, totally oblivious to all comment from the amused lookers-on, and the writer distinctly remembers seeing such visitors sitting upon the butcher's block, in the public market-place, clasped in each other's arms and sound asleep!—this, too, in the midst of a multitude of people who had been attracted to the town on account of a public demonstration.

The marriage ceremony was generally performed at the minister's residence, and it was he, also who furnished refreshments, consisting of home-made wine and small cakes. The bride and groom, sometimes attended by friends, usually went on horseback, and wedding trips were unknown to most people. Upon the return of the party to the temporary or future home of the newly wedded couple, dancing and other festivites were indulged in until long after midnight.

It was the custom for the bride to furnish the household linen, bedding, etc., the husband being supposed to have secured a house and plat of ground, either by purchase or renting. The habit was never to take an old broom into a new house, as bad luck was sure to follow.[7] It must be a new broom, and first carried across the meadow, to avert any evil consequences.

Both at wedding feasts and upon other occasions it was usual, when dancing, to "dance for flax;" that is, the higher the feet were raised from the floor, the higher would be the host's crop of flax at the next harvest.[8]

The young wife, in the absence of farm help, often lent a helping hand in the heavy work of farming, such as plowing, threshing grain, clearing the fields of large stones, etc. From spring until autumn it was her duty, to gather the various herbs, barks, roots, and flowers supposed to contain medicinal properties, which were subsequently employed in domestic practice, as occasion required. Garden-seeds were also selected for the next year's planting, and, altogether, these various packages and bags, suspended from the rafters of the loft or garret of the house, formed quite important and interesting collection. . . .

"Quiltings" and apple-butter parties were looked forward to by the young folks with much interest. At the former the young women assisted in finishing bed-quilts, which consisted of many-colored patches of calico, and sometimes silks, the evening terminating with a dance and a supper; while, at the latter, much of the day was spent in boiling down cider and paring apples, which were subsequently reduced therein to the proper consistency. As this required constant stirring to avoid burning, the labors sometimes extended far into the night, and were then followed by a dance.

In some localities it is believed that if vinegar be disturbed while the apple-trees bloom it will again turn to cider.

With the exception of very few articles, nearly every variety of food was of farm production. Such as was obtained at the country stores was received in exchange for butter and eggs.

The housewife, sometimes found difficulty in butter-making, the "spell" being believed to be the work of a witch, as every locality boasted of such a personage. The remedy was to plunge a red-hot poker into the contents of the churn, when the spell was broken, and the butter immediately began to form.

To refuse a witch any request was sure to be followed by misfortune. The following incident was related to the writer by Mr. A. F. Berlin, of Allentown, Pennsylvania, who received it at first hand. A farmer who lives at Alburtis, Lehigh County, had two cows. One day an old woman, who lived but a short distance away, and who was suspected of being a witch, came to the house, and, during the course of conversation, asked which of the two cows gave the greater quantity of milk. The one which was indicated was then with calf. Upon the following day the two cows were driven, as usual, into the fields to pasture, but on attempting to drive them home, later in the day, the milch cow was found lying helpless upon the ground. The farmer, upon hearing of this, went into the field with his sons to endeavor to get the animal upon her feet. The sons took hold of the horns, while the father grasped the tail, but all attempts to move the cow were ineffectual. The father then directed the boys to gather some wood to make a fire, which was to be placed near the cow. During all this time the witch was standing on the portico of the farmer's house, watching the proceedings; but the instant she saw that fire was to be kindled, she came forward, and inquired after the purpose of the proceedings. The farmer accused her of bewitching the cow, but this she denied most vigorously. The witch then bade the farmer call his wife, who, upon her arrival, was told to take hold of the cow's tail while the witch went to the head. After a few caresses and the utterance of some words of endearment and encouragement, the cow rose from the ground, and walked away as if nothing had occurred.

Notes

1. [Hoffman is referring to the standard reference written by Robert Proud (1728–1813), *The History of Pennsylvania* (Philadelphia: Zachariah Poulson, 1797–98). —*Ed.*]

2. That a similar belief obtained in Great Britain is observed from the following passage in Tusser's *Poems* (printed 1744), quoted by Mr. Folkard in his *Plant Lore, Legends, and Lyrics* (London, 1884), p. 168, viz.: "It must be granted the moon is an excellent clock, and, if not the cause of many surprising accidents, gives a just indication of them, whereof this Pease and Beans may be one instance; for Pease and Beans sown during the increase do run more to hawm and straw, and during the declension more to cod, according to the comon consent of countrymen."

3. A similar belief obtains in Devonshire, England. Parsley was regarded by the Greeks as a funeral herb, and they frequently strewed the tombs of their dead with it.

4. "Do not kill your pig until full moon, or the pork will be ruined," is a West Sussex superstition. *Folk-Lore Record,* [London], 1878, vol. 1, p. 11. [This belief reported by Hoffman was collected by Charlotte Latham in 1868. —*Ed.*]

5. This information, not published in the Reports *in extenso,* was given to the writer by a gentleman present at the trial and practising before the court.

6. Hollis *v.* Wells, opinion by Judge Banks, Common Pleas of Lehigh County, August Term, 1845.

7. A New England saying, noted in the *London Folk-Lore Journal* (1884, vol. 2, p. 24), is, "He who proposes moving into a new house must send in beforehand bread and a new broom."

8. In one part of Germany it is customary "for the bride to place flax in her shoes, that she may never come to want" (*Flowers and Flower-Lore,* by Hilderic Friend, vol. 1, p. 134). Another custom, from the same authority, is to the effect that a bride will "tie a string of flax around her left leg, in the belief that she will thereby enjoy the full blessing of the married state." "Flax is the symbol of free and abundant vegetable life" (*Mythologie des Plantes,* by Count A. de Gubernatis, vol. 2, p. 199).

4

Folk Custom and Medicine of Chinese Americans

Stewart Culin

Stewart Culin (1858–1929) was "the friend of all the persecuted Chinamen," the *Philadelphia Inquirer* declared in 1887. The paper continued:

> Mr. Culin is one of the few Americans who have mastered the jaw-breaking elements of the celestial language, and being able to converse with the Chinamen in their native tongue, is appealed to whenever the colonists get into trouble. Mr. Culin's researches in this line have been presented during his business hours, more from a love of the subject than from any desire for notoriety or gain. He is still a young man of studious habits with prospect of a brilliant future before him.

And brilliant it was, filled with gold medals for outstanding exhibits and kudos for his many publications. He became, with Otis Mason, the leading exponent for studies of, as he put it, the "material culture of mankind."

Culin would also become known for his studies of American Indians and European peasants, but his first notoriety began with his studies with the Chinese. The Chinese were an unusual sight for Americans; besides their distinctive racial features, their customs, dress, and societies appeared clannish and exotic. They exuded the "mystery of the Orient" to many Americans; to others they threatened the fabric of American society. Chinese immigration flowed into America in the second half of the nineteenth century, forming virtual ethnic "colonies," as Culin called them. Their numbers nearly doubled to 105,000 from 1870 to 1880. They worked cheaply and their presence increasingly caused labor as well as racial strife. In 1882, the Congress restricted Chinese immigration for ten years, but the question of the role of the Chinese in American civilization became a fiercely debated issue through the end of the century.

To this debate, Culin, seen as a white man able to crack traditional Chinese secretiveness, contributed with exposés of Chinese religion, literature, customs, crafts, secret societies, rituals, drugs, and games. In 1887, he published two pamphlets, *China in America: A Study in the Social Life of the Chinese in the Eastern United*

States and *The Religious Ceremonies of the Chinese in the Eastern Cities of the United States.* He followed with many essays in both popular periodicals and scientific journals, for example, "Chinese Secret Societies in the United States," *Journal of American Folklore* 3 (1890): pp. 39–43, and "The Gambling Games of the Chinese in America," *Series in Philology and Archaeology* 1, no. 4 (Philadelphia: Publications of the University of Pennsylvania, 1891). This chapter combines three related essays by Culin: "Customs of the Chinese in America," *Journal of American Folklore* 3 (1890): pp. 191–200; "Chinese Drug Stores in America," *American Journal of Pharmacy* 59 (1887): pp. 593–98; "The Practice of Medicine by the Chinese in America," *Medical and Surgical Reporter* 56 (1887): pp. 355–57.

For background on Culin, see my "Stewart Culin, Museum Magician," *Pennsylvania Heritage* 11 (Summer 1985): pp. 4–11, and for later-day studies that follow Culin's trail into Chinese customs, see Jon Lee, "Some Chinese Customs and Beliefs in California," *California Folklore Quarterly* 2 (1943): pp. 191–204; Janet Langlois, "Moon Cake in Chinatown, New York City: Continuity and Change," *New York Folklore Quarterly* 28 (1972): pp. 83–117.

*   *   *

The subject of this paper is the life of the people of the little Chinese colonies that have recently been established in our cities, with especial reference to the modifications in language, dress, diet, religion, and traditions that have arisen among the Chinese in this country. But first I would like to say a few words as to the meagreness of our printed data concerning the social life of the Chinese. The opinions of their philosophers have been translated and discussed by the scholars of every European clime. Their country has been explored and the main features of its natural conformation have been recorded. The ethnological characteristics of the people themselves have been carefully noted, while those externals of their civilization, such as laws and system of government and the forms of ceremonial and religious usages, have been earnestly and successfully studied. But concerning the life of the people, of the millions who till the soil and ply the loom, of those humble craftsmen whose peaceful invasion has alarmed the dwellers upon our coasts, and furnished new problems to our politicians and law-makers, we find much less available information.[1] Most observers have been content to record only those features which appeared to them strange and unusual, and where they have not been influenced by prejudices of race and religion and thereby led to dwell upon and exaggerate all that is bad and disagreeable, and pass lightly over all that is good and admirable in Chinese life and character, their results are usually too general to be accurate, and too superficial to convey a correct impression of the genius of the people.

It is the especial province of the student of folk-lore to collect and bring together these neglected elements in the history of nations, and a fitting illustration of the value and importance of his work is found in its application to the problems arising in the question of restricting Chinese immigration. What an interesting field is here presented, especially as I feel assured there is more folk-lore to be gleaned from any one of the sallow-faced Chinamen we see shambling about our streets than could be collected among our entire native population.

The popular notions about the Chinese, which may be considered as part of our own folk-lore, would form an entertaining subject for discussion. The Chinaman has become a well established character in our popular literature; the professional humorist has paid his regards to him, and the playwright has made him figure as an amusing personage in the drama, from the halls of vaudeville in the Bowery to the theatre in Madison Square. In most cases the popular conception, with all its errors, has been perpetuated. Thus the well-known minstrel songs make the Americanized Chinaman talk, or rather sing, in *Pigeon-English,* when, in point of fact, he is usually altogether unfamiliar with that jargon, as most of the immigrants come from districts remote from the cities where it serves as the trade language in communications with foreigners.

A desire to learn the language of his adopted country seems to be one of the highest ambitions of the Chinese immigrant, and his English speech is often strongly marked with the local peculiarities of the place where it was acquired. He realizes the intrinsic value of such knowledge, for it may enable him to obtain a well-paid position as interpreter in some shop in Hong Kong or Canton, upon his return to China, and so he studies his native text-books,[2] attends Sunday-schools, and tries to glean a word or two from every foreigner with whom he comes in contact.

There are several local patois spoken by the immigrants. These vary from the dialect of Canton city, sometimes in the sound of a few words, and sometimes, in those from remote districts, in the sound of almost every word in the language.[3]

The people from each district have their peculiar local customs and traditions. Men from the same village usually associate together, and certain shops thus become the headquarters for people from the same neighborhood. The little territory from which they all come is in greater part known as the Sám Yup, or "Three Towns," and the Sz' Yup, or "Four Towns." The Sz' Yup people, who are in the majority, are not so well educated as those from the Sám Yup, and seem much more susceptible to foreign influences. The professed converts to Christianity are chiefly from among them, and they comprise almost the entire membership of the secret society that has for its object the overthrow of the present Chinese dynasty.

The influence of the clan is strongly felt among the Chinese in this country. Those of the same family name are often able to trace their relationship, although it may be many times removed, and in disputes they usually side together.

The differences in speech and traditions, and the influence of the tribal sentiment, serve as elements of discord in the Chinese communities. They divide them into little cliques, that are constantly quarrelling, as the disputes of each individual are apt to be taken up by his relatives and compatriots. These quarrels give rise to endless talk, and often so engage the communities that for the time everything else is forgotten. They are usually only a war of words. In fact, I know of an instance where a man was brought here from a distant city, and all his expenses paid, simply to say bad things at the other party in a trifling dispute. The Chinese here seldom, if ever, come to blows. They are not given to crimes of violence, and such assaults by Chinese as are reported in the daily press are usually committed by professional criminals, who are held in detestation by all the better class of the immigrants.

Home customs and traditions govern the life and regulate the conduct of most of these people. They show a marked indifference to our laws, much greater in fact than for their own code, which rests for its enforcement upon the public sentiment of their little communities. No organized form of self-government exists in any of the Chinese colonies in our cities. In Philadelphia the merchants occasionally meet to discuss some question affecting the welfare of the colony, and a bundle of slips of bamboo is kept for the purpose of calling such meetings together. The object for which the meeting is called, with the time and place, is written upon the smooth side of the tablets, one of which is sent to each shop, and serves as the credential of its representative. These tablets are said to be used in voting. In New York city the merchants support a guild hall, entitled the *Chung Wá Kung Sho,* or "Chinese Public Hall," which is in charge of a person of approved character, who is elected to the office annually. This custodian has been described in our newspapers as the "Mayor of Chinatown."[4] He really has no executive powers, but quarrels are laid before him for settlement, and he acts as peacemaker in the Chinese community. He receives a salary of $30 per month and the profits on the incense and candles sold to worshippers in the guild hall. The election for this office is held just before the Chinese New Year, when the new manager is driven in a carriage to each of the Chinese shops. His deputy precedes him on foot, with a bundle of red paper visiting cards about a foot in length. Two of these, one bearing the name and the other the official title of the new manager, are handed to each storekeeper.

Complete autonomy exists in all the Chinese communities in the

East. The Six Companies exercise no authority whatever, and there is little intercourse or sympathy with the consular and diplomatic representatives of the Chinese government. No people of greatly superior position or education, other than might be found in any village, exist in these colonies. They are practical democracies, that make their own laws, regulate their own affairs, and resent the interference of any outside power. They have no priests of any religion. Many laundries and shops contain small shrines, often with the picture of the God of War, before which incense and candles are burned, and large and expensive shrines to the same deity, with implements for divination, are found in all their guild halls and lodge rooms. No great importance is attached to the worship of this god among the Chinese here. It is looked upon as a mere matter of custom. Gamblers make offerings before him to secure good luck, and he is appealed to by many at the season of the New Year, in order that the will of Heaven may be learned when they throw the divining blocks; while the presence of the shrine in the halls of lodges and public guilds is regarded as giving dignity and solemnity to their proceedings. Stories of the miraculous appearance and intervention of Kwan Ti, the God of War, and Kwan Yin, the Goddess of Mercy, are told as having occurred among the Chinese in Havana, but nothing of the kind is reported here.[5]

Much more serious consideration is paid to the spirits of the dead. No tablets are erected here to ancestors, but in almost every shop a small tablet of orange-colored paper is placed on the wall just above the floor, inscribed, as is the custom in Hong Kong, to the "Chinese and Foreign Lord of the Place." He is regarded as the ruler of the ghosts, himself the ghost of the first person who died in the house, and for his benefit a small pent-house is erected over the tablet, and tea and rice often placed daily before it, that his good favor may be secured and the other household ghosts kept in subjection. There are few among the immigrants so brave or philosophical as to be fearless of ghosts, and many stories are told among them of midnight visitations, which they usually attribute to the unlaid spirits of foreigners, the objects of their greatest dread and detestation.

The popular feeling about the dead is shown by the custom of putting dying people without the house in order that the place may not be contaminated. Sick people are frequently removed to remote places, where they cannot receive proper food and attention; but this is done through ignorance and fear rather than from lack of human feeling.

Foreign undertakers are always called upon to care for the dead. Little if any attention is paid to the character of the site selected for the grave or to the direction in which the body shall rest. At the funerals brown Chinese sugar and a small coin, a cent or five-cent piece, is handed to each person present immediately after the body is interred.

In one instance incense was burned in the doorway of the house to which the mourners returned, and all were requested to pass through the smoke, it was explained, for the purpose of purifying themselves. The graves are usually visited in the spring-time, during the third Chinese month, when dishes of roast pork and cooked fowls are placed upon them, and incense and candles burned as an offering to the spirits of the dead. About the middle of the seventh Chinese month, which falls during our autumn, paper clothes, *i chi,* are burned by many in their laundries and shops, a rite said to be performed for the spirit world at large, both Chinese and foreign ghosts being propitiated or honored.[6]

Many of the most curious and interesting of folk-customs are those connected with infancy and childhood, but the small number of women and children and the seclusion in which the former are kept serve to prevent extended observations being made among the Chinese here. None of the usual rites are observed when Chinese intermarry with foreigners, as such men usually live apart from their countrymen, and adopt foreign customs. The children of native mothers are the objects of the greatest attention, not only on the part of their parents, but among the entire community. On the thirtieth day after their birth, or usually, rather, upon the next nearest Sunday, the father gives a dinner to which he invites all his acquaintances and friends. At such a dinner, which I attended, at the conclusion of the feast the father brought the child into the room in his arms. It was dressed in a red robe and wore a red skull-cap, with a gold ornament, in the shape of the "Genius of Longevity," on the front. Every one immediately placed a red paper package, containing several dollars in silver money, upon it, so that its dress was quite covered, after which the father carried the infant back to its mother, and the guests dispersed. It is not easy to obtain much information from the Chinese men concerning the games and sports of their childhood. They regard the subject as too trivial for discussion, and always burst into loud laughter when one, more good-natured than the rest, attempts to explain them. The subject is a most interesting one, and the patient inquirer apt to be well rewarded. The games of tossing "cash," of which there are several, appear to be the exact counterparts of the games that East Indian children play with cowries. A game of "shinny" is known, much resembling the one played in our own streets. "Hide and seek" appears to be as generally known as it is popular, and here it must be remarked that the immigrants constantly refer, when questioned, to the differences that they say exist in the customs of different villages. The children of each village, they inform me, have their own ways for playing certain games, as well as their own verses and counting-out rhymes. As an illustration of this I give three versions of a counting-out rhyme that appears, in one form or another, to be generally known. The first was related to me by Lí Ch'un Shán, of Hohshan.

> 'Tím tsz', nit nit
> Ch'a fan lok típ
> Yat yan, yat un
> Ho hü nit.

The second was related to me by a physician from Sin'hwui, named Wan Yuk.

> Tím tsz' nit nit
> Múi fá lok tip
> Kam chí fú yung
> Kam chí pái típ.

The third version was related by a man named Le Yam, from another village in the same district.

> Tím tsz' nit nit
> Mui fá lok típ
> Kam chán ngan p'ún
> Ngan shau sé tsz'
> Kam shing hau shau ní.

These rhymes appear to me to consist of words and phrases strung together without connected meaning, and such, also, is the opinion of Lí Ch'un Shán, who has carefully compared them.

The games played on lines with counters, pawns, or chessmen, which are known under the generic name of *k'í,* are very numerous, and vary from the simple *pong t'au k'í,* or the "mattock" game, to the classical *wai k'í* and the Chinese form of the Persian game of chess, called *tséung k'í,* which is played with thirty-two men. The last two are about the only games that are looked upon as dignified and respectable. *Tséung k'í* is sometimes played by clerks and elderly people in the shops, but gambling with dominoes, *fán t'án,* and a lottery, called *pák hòp piú,* are the common diversions of most of the immigrants. Gambling is carried on by well organized companies, and constitutes the principal occupation of the people who compose the Chinese quarter of our Eastern cities. Exceptions, of course, are found among the merchants and their employees, but many of them take shares in the gambling companies as the most convenient and profitable investment. No foreign games are played except cards, poker being a favorite amusement. I have never seen Chinese cards played except at the season of the New Year.

The New Year and the Mid-Autumn Moon Festival are the only native holidays generally celebrated by the Chinese in this country; but other days, such as the birthdays of the gods and the days set apart to the founders of their order, are observed by the organization called the *í hing,* the secret society to which I have already referred. At the last Chinese New Year they displayed a large triangular banner over their headquarters on Race Street in Philadelphia. This flag was red, with a jagged white border. In the centre was a large symbol composed of the character *fú,* "tiger," and *shau,* "longevity," which Gustav Schlegel, an authority on the subject, describes as the secret character for "age."[7] Above this was inscribed on the margin, *chün tái ting shau,* which Schlegel states to be a mutilation of the characters *shun t'ín hang tŏ,* "Obey Heaven and act righteously." On either side of the centre character, *kam láu kít í,* "In the Golden Orchard we have pledged fraternity." The banner agrees very closely with the one described by Schlegel as "the great flag of the city of Willows."[8]

The dinner is the principal feature of all holiday observances, and at such dinners every one eats to repletion. Two meals a day are usually eaten, one in the morning and one at about four in the afternoon. The food itself, the table service, and methods of cooking, are always exclusively Chinese. Beef is avoided and bread is not eaten, rice taking its place as in China.[9] Salt is now served on the tables in some restaurants, but formerly the salt *shí yau,* or *soy,* was expected to supply its place. Round cakes, containing a number of kinds of fruit and nuts, are made and sold in the restaurants and shops at the time of the Mid-Autumn Moon Festival.

On the 5th of the fifth Chinese month, dumplings called *tsung tsz',* are always served in the restaurants in commemoration of the death of K'ü Yüan. Oranges are usually handed to guests at a ceremonial dinner before beginning the feast. This is always done at the supper on the night before the New Year. It is customary to have a jar of sweetmeats, made of betel leaves and nuts preserved in syrup, to offer New Year's callers. Recently I have noticed the fresh leaves of the betel pepper, said to have been brought from the Hawaiian Islands, offered with lime and the dried nut on these occasions. Betel (*pan long*) is given to enemies as a token of reconciliation.

The Chinese in this country retain their native habits in the use of alcoholic drinks. They are only taken at meals, and drunkenness is very uncommon. At dinners the wine, or spirits, rather, is served in large bowls, into which all dip their cups. In drinking, the cup is raised to the person on the left, and then with a circular sweep of the hand to the others around the table. The usual salutation is *yam tsau! yam tsau!* "drink!

drink!'' to which the others make the same reply. Libations are sometimes poured, the wine being thrown backward toward the right.

Foreign whiskey and gin are occasionally used, on account of their cheapness, but native rice spirits are much preferred. Of these there are many kinds, differing in potency and flavor. Some that are served on dinner tables are regarded as medicines, and taken at such times as aids to digestion. The habit of taking medicine seems to be as strong and deeply rooted as that of smoking tobacco or eating rice. The Chinese here are constantly taking medicine, but the aromatics and demulcents that compose the greater part of their pharmacopoeia at the worst do them little harm. The folk-lorist finds an interesting field in their practice, and especially in the drugs they employ. Magical properties are attributed to some of them. The bezoar stone and many other reminders of the mediaeval pharmacist find place with tigers' bones and fossil crab shells in a collection than which none more appropriate could be taken as a beginning for a folk-lore museum. Every object would have its story. The Chinese are unwilling to take our medicines, which they pronounce too strong and powerful. They only call on foreign physicians as a last resort. They will not go to hospitals if they can help it, as there is a general belief among them that when a man goes to the hospital he always dies. They say there is a devil there that catches and kills people.

The uniformity that is characteristic of their native dress is preserved in those articles of foreign attire which as a matter of convenience they adopt here. Nearly all wear the broad brimmed black felt hat which we have come to look upon as their especial property, yet it is borrowed, as is shown by its having no special name, being simply known as a *fán mo,* or "foreign hat." It is also customary to make the foreign trousers, for which they abandon their own loose lower garments, of blue or black broadcloth. It may be that they thus perpetuate customs already fixed in the English settlement of Hong Kong. Those that adopt foreign dress often abandon it during the very hot weather of summer, and the extreme cold of our winter.

It is not customary to wear amulets or charms, except the jade wristlet, which is regarded by some as giving strength to the arm. One that has been recovered from a grave is most highly valued, and thought to furnish protection to the wearer against evil spirits. Light blue is regarded as the color of mourning, and the death of a relative is marked by wearing blue stockings, or braiding a blue string in the cue. The custom of shaving the head is continued, and at the New Year almost every one appears clean shaven. The Chinese barbers, who are always resorted to, shave the entire face, including the inside of the ears. They use foreign razors. The barber is an indispensable personage in every community, and often a most interesting one. He usually visits his customers in their laundries, but one in Philadelphia has a shop. He is reputed to be the most skilful calligrapher in the colony. Almost every one preserves his cue, although a few have recently taken to wearing wigs in order to hide it. The notion current among us that a Chinaman who has lost his cue would be put to death should he return to China is probably due to the fact that the cutting of the cue forms part of the ritual of the rebel secret society in which membership is punished with death by the government.

The Chinese here use their own calendar, and record all events as occurring in the year of such an emperor, in such a month, such a day, just as is the custom in China. They reckon time by the clock in the foreign manner, as in China, where clocks are now generally used.

They perform all arithmetical calculations by means of the abacus, which they are so accustomed to depend upon that they are often unable to make the simplest calculation without it. A person going to market, it is said, will either count upon his fingers or arrange coppers in the form of the counting instrument.

The migratory instinct, which seems to be found almost exclusively among the southern Chinese, and which in part has led them to seek their fortune in so many distant lands, does not desert them here. They never seem to hesitate to abandon any place and go where they can better themselves, no matter what the distance may be. They are constantly travelling from city to city, making long journeys to visit relatives and friends. They are probably by far the most generous patrons of railways, in proportion to their number, of any of our foreign population.

They make great use of both the post-office and the telegraph, going with reluctance out of the lines of communication with their kindred, and thus maintaining solidarity and concert of action.

Foreign inventions, and in fact our entire civilization, they look upon as a matter of course, seldom expressing comment or surprise to foreigners, and seldom rising, I fear, to a just appreciation of the many benefits we imagine we would confer upon them. They appear willing to borrow from us whatever they think will aid them in securing material advancement, just as they have borrowed in the past from all the nations of the East. From them they have accepted traditions and religions as well as useful arts, but with all their accretions they have remained an almost primitive people. How long will they so continue in this restless Western world, where change crowds change, and we, more conservative it may be than the rest, must join in united effort to preserve the customs of our very fathers from oblivion?

Not the least interesting feature of the Chinese quarter in our American cities are the drug shops which these conservative people have established for the sale of their native drugs in connection with their general stores.

These shops reduplicate the herbalists' shops of Hong Kong, and their native villages. They are usually conducted by a separate company from that of the store with which they are associated, and their supply of drugs arranged on one side of the shop, apart from the other wares. The sign of the company, a green or black tablet with the felicitous name invariably selected for such enterprises, inscribed in gilded letters, is suspended within the shop.

The drugs, such as are frequently called for, are contained in boxes or drawers ranged in tiers behind the counter. These boxes are usually divided into four compartments, and their contents indicated by neatly written labels of red paper, or sometimes, in lieu of labels, a tablet is suspended in front of the shelves, upon which appears a plan of their multitudinous contents. Powders are kept in tin or brass boxes in a drawer beneath the counter; a series of bottles contain nuts and mineral substances; while poisons, and some of the more rare and valuable drugs, are dispensed from a locked case with glass doors. Piled high above the cases are innumerable packages, each with the name of its contents written on the projecting end, which constitute the reserve supply of drugs, or contain barks and herbs seldom called for by the practitioners here. . . .

The medicines are all imported from China, either from Hong Kong or Canton, and reach here in their crude state, the herbs and barks in large pieces, and the tubers and roots usually entire. It is customary to cut the former in small pieces, and slice the latter in delicate segments, before placing them in the drawers and boxes for sale. A large cleaver, *yeúk ts'oi k'ap,* mounted with a hinge upon a slightly inclined table, is employed to chop the grasses and herbs in convenient lengths, while the tubers are sliced upon a instrument resembling a carpenter's plane, *yeúk p'ò,* inserted in a long bench upon which the operator sits, the pieces falling through upon a tray placed beneath. A canoe-shaped mortar of cast-iron, *yeúk shün,* is employed to reduce some of the more refractory nuts and minerals to powder. It stands upon four legs, and a heavy disk of iron is rolled backwards and forwards within it by means of a wooden axle to which the operator applies his feet, while his hands are free to perform other work.

The clerks who dispense the medicines have usually had some experience at home. They are paid from twenty-five to thirty dollars per month, with their board and lodging, the current wages among the Chinese here for unskilled labor; but their work is light, and they sometimes assist with the lottery drawings for which they receive additional compensation. They frequently act as bookkeepers, and, in common with the shop-keeping class, are brighter and better educated than the mass of the immigrants. Their knowledge of medicine is derived almost entirely from experience, no books on the subject being used or studied by them and the *Pún tso,* or Herbal, is not to be found in any of their shops.

The prescriptions furnished by the native doctors, which are usually written upon Chinese letter-paper and a foot in length, contain only a list of the names and quantities of the medicines required, with concise directions for their preparation, no date or signature being appended. Upon being presented to the clerk over the counter, he weighs out the ingredients, and places them separately upon a large sheet of paper, going over them carefully afterwards to prevent any possible mistake. A hand balance, *lí tang,* is used, consisting of a decimally graduated, ivory rod, from one end of which a brass scale pan is suspended by silk threads. The smaller kind weigh from one *lí* to five and one-half *léung,* or Chinese ounces,[10] and are remarkably accurate.

Various simple expedients are resorted to by the clerk in the preparation of the medicines. Some are powdered in the upright iron mortar, *chung hòm,* and others in the porcelain mortar, *lúi ún;* certain roots and seeds are roasted in a pan, while others are steeped for a few moments in Chinese rice spirits. The package of medicine is carried home to be boiled, and the infusion taken at one dose by the patient. Some *hak tsò,* Chinese prunes, are usually furnished to be eaten at the same time. The prescription, of which no record is kept, is returned with the medicine.

The practice of medicine by the Chinese doctors here is confined almost entirely to what is called by the Chinese *noi fo,* or internal medicine. *Ngoi fo,* "external practice" or surgery, which constitutes a distinct branch of their healing art, is little understood by them, and their patients seldom make greater demands upon them than for a cure for a cold, indigestion or headache. But slight as may be their ailments, the Chinese of our cities are constantly taking medicines. Well, they resort to prophylactics, or try to improve their digestion; ill, they take one prescription after another, and drink quantities of unpalatable tea every night, usually, upon their own testimony, to little advantage.

No less than four shops supply medicines to the little colony in Philadelphia, and day and night their clerks are busy, weighing and pounding and tying up packages for the relief of their suffering countrymen. Nor are the drugs regularly prescribed by their physicians the only medicine used by them; almost every shop furnishes an assortment of pills and teas compounded by Canton pharmacists.

First among these are the *Wai Shang Ün,* or "Life Preserving Pills," which are taken by both the sick and well on account of their supposed vitalizing properties. In common with many other Chinese pills they are enclosed in a shell of vegetable wax, upon which is stamped the name, with that of the makers, in vermilion and gold. One of these boluses— they are nearly an inch in diameter—is taken at a dose. The usual price for the best kind is one dollar apiece. They are said to be composed of *yan sham* (Manchurian ginseng), *luk yung* (deer's horns),[11] and other expensive drugs. A cheaper kind is entitled upon a printed advertisement, *Yan sham luk yung ning shan po shan ün*—(ginseng and deer's-horn pills for tranquilizing the spirits and strengthening the kidneys). These also purport to contain *yuk kwai,* a precious cinnamon, the bark of the *Cinnamomum Cassia*(?), one of their most highly valued drugs. That used by the Chinese pharmacists here is imported in boxes covered with raw silk, each containing one piece, about fourteen inches in length. The price varies with the quality, from two dollars and a half to five dollars for one *léung.*

Sú hòp ün (rose mallows pills), are taken to relieve flatulency; *king fung ün* are intended for children; *ying im ugán ün* (the well approved eye pills), are dissolved in water and used as an eye lotion; *Shan hau pak chuk ün* purport to be a remedy for a certain disease, and *Shan hau hung ün* (Divinely efficacious red pills), are taken as a prophylactic against the same complaint. Occult and magical properties are claimed for nearly all of these compounds, and they are not regarded with much favor by the regular physicians.

Several varieties of ginseng are sold in the shops. The American root, sold under the name of *yéung sham* (foreign ginseng), is the cheapest, the current price being 40 cents per *léung.* Next in value is *kat lam sham,* said to be obtained from Korea, costing 50 cents per *léung. Kò lai sham* (Korean ginseng), is the kind most used here, and costs from $2.50 to $3.50 per *léung. Yan sham,* Chinese or Manchurian ginseng, the most precious and famous drug of the Chinese pharmacopoeia, is seldom, if ever, to be found in the stores. Occasionally one sees small roots purporting to be *yan sham* kept wrapped in raw cotton in tin boxes; but the enormous price asked for them, often from sixty to one hundred dollars for one *léung,* prevents their use except in extreme cases, or as a matter of luxurious extravagance.

With a desire to learn something of the method of treatment and obtain some practical knowledge of the Chinese *materia medica,* I recently called upon a doctor connected with one of the principal Chinese stores in Philadelphia, and requested him to prescribe for a cold on the chest from which I was suffering.

The doctor was pleasant-mannered man of about forty years of age. Resting my hand upon a book, he carefully felt my pulse, first on the left wrist and then on the right, delicately compressing the artery and gradually relaxing the pressure. Then, without inquiring about the symptoms of my complaint, he wrote the prescription, a facsimile of which is herewith reproduced. The fifteen medicines called for are all of vegetable origin. The following is a transcription of their names, with some notes on their properties, and the quantities indicated in the prescription.[12]

Shau wu (a root highly valued as an aphrodisiac, said to have received its name from Ho Shau Wu, a resident of Szechuan, who lived unmarried until the age of 54 years, when he discovered the peculiar qualities of this root. He then married and had several children, and his life was prolonged by its use to the ripe age of 110 years). 4 *ts'in* (15.08 grams).

Un chi (a root from Szechuan, a tonic), 2 *ts'in* (7.54 grams).

Kau chaok (a plant of hair at crown of root from Fukien province) 4 *ts'in* (15.08 grams).

Kat kang (belwort, root of the *Platycodon grandiflorum,* a tonic and stomachic), 3 *ts'in* (11.31 grams).

Pak cheuk (root of *Poenia albiflora,* a tonic, sedative, and alterative), 2 *ts'in* (7.54 grams).

Pak shut (a sweetish sort of root; a tonic much valued as an aid to digestion; from Chekiang province), 2 *ts'in* (7.54 grams).

Ts'z'shat (the seeds of the *Euryale ferox;* a tonic; from Kiangsu province), 4 *ts'in* (15.08 grams).

Ch'ün pui (a demulcent; from Szechuan province), 3 *ts'in* (11.31 grams).

Ün ts'am (a root used to check internal hemorrhage and for coughs and colds; from Chekiang province), 3 *ts'in* (11.31 grams).

Chák sé (a root taken for diseases of the kidneys, as its name implies, a diuretic), 3 *ts'in* (11.31 grams).

Ts'un k'au (dried roots of the *Gendarussa,* given in cases of rheumatism and fever), 3 *ts'in* (11.31 grams).

Tsò yan (seeds of a species of *Rhamnus,* probably the *Rhamnus soporiferus,* a soporific), 2 *ts'in* (7.54 grams).

Tung fa, "Winter flower" (flowers of a plant resembling the chrysanthemum) 4 *ts'in* (15.08 grams).

Song pak (the white skin from the roots of the mulberry tree), 4 *ts'in* (15.08 grams).

Hau p'ok, "thick bark" (the bark of a tree from Szechuan), 3 *ts'in* (11.31 grams).

A clerk in the store weighed out the different articles with a small Chinese balance, and deposited them together on a piece of paper, first powdering the *ch'ün pui* in an iron mortar, and roasting the *tsò yan* in a pan; the *pak cheuk* was moistened with whisky before being placed with the mass. All was then put in a pot with four large cups full of cold water, and boiled for half an hour. The decoction I was enjoined to drink warm before going to bed.

Should this medicine have failed to relieve me, the doctor, upon my next visit, would have varied his prescription. The charge for the medicine was fifty cents, the price of each ingredient being computed separately. The doctor's fee was one dollar, this being the usual charge for each consultation. . . .

A slight knowledge of medicine is general among the people. They have been accustomed to take medicines from their childhood, when their mothers, by a kind of sortilege, selected some simple prescription to relieve their infantile complaints. . . .

While the Chinese in our eastern cities are superstitious, and cherish many of their native beliefs, they do not worship any particular god of medicine, and the practice of medicine among them is comparatively free from superstitious observances. Sick people sometimes burn copies of the charms found in the popular works on divination and magic, and drink tea made from the ashes, but this is done with very little serious belief in the efficacy of such treatment.

In cases of prolonged illness, a friend of the sick person is sometimes sent to the local shrine of Kwan tai, the divinity generally worshipped, to burn incense and ask the will of heaven as to his recovery by throwing the divining sticks.

Diseases which do not succumb to the treatment after being correctly diagnosed and the right medicine administered, are looked upon as due to the influence of a spirit or devil. Hysteria is generally regarded as an evidence of demoniac possession.

The people as a class are very healthy; venereal diseases and the complaints resulting from an excessive use of opium are the most common. They call upon their own doctors when ill, but are much averse to taking foreign medicines or submitting to the treatment prescribed by American physicians. They regard opium as a specific for colds and many complaints, and in slight disorders resort to their pipe before consulting a doctor. Chinese ginseng is highly valued for its supposed strengthening and life prolonging qualities (it is not looked upon as an aphrodisiac), and is taken in the form of pills or made into a tea by many of the older men in the spring of the year. American ginseng is seldom if ever used here.

Calomel is prescribed in syphilitic diseases. Quinine is known as *kam kai náp,* doubtless a Chinese transcription of *cinchona* and that sold in their stores is imported from China. It is prescribed for violent chills, and is looked upon as a very strong and dangerous medicine. With a few exceptions, mineral remedies are seldom employed, and roots, barks, and herbs, administered in the form of teas, constitute the principal drugs used. Many of these are not regarded as possessing any particular virtues, and some are retained solely through a tradition of cures once effected by them. Custom has ordained that a prescription shall contain a number of ingredients, of which, may be, two or three only are considered to have any direct effect.

The doctors show much solicitude about administering any medicine that may cause a fatal result, owing, no doubt, to the penalties inflicted in China upon such misadventures, so that their treatment in general, if not beneficial, does no particular harm to their patients.

Notes

1. The *Social Life of the Chinese,* by Rev. Justus Doolittle, New York, 1867, is a most valuable source of information, but it is based upon observations made at Fuhchau, where the customs vary from those of Kwantung, whence all of our immigrants come.

2. These consist of Chinese and English vocabularies and phrase books. Those in common use are printed from blocks with the English text cut in script, with its sound represented by Chinese characters beneath. The valuable dictionary of Kwong Ki Chiu, which is most highly esteemed, has not come into general use here on account of its high price.

3. These dialects are being made the subject of a series of studies by J. Dyer Vall, Esq., of H. M. Civil Service, Hong Kong, who has just published an admirable monograph on the San Wúi dialect in the *China Review.*

4. *The Evening Telegraph,* Philadelphia, January 16, 1890.

5. *The Religious Ceremonies of the Chinese in the Eastern Cities of the United States.* By Stewart Culin. Philadelphia, 1887. p. 5.

6. Ibid., p. 20.

7. *Thian Ti Hwui. The Hung League.* Batavia, 1866, p. 36.

8. Ibid., p. 40.

9. Neither milk nor butter have come into use among the Chinese here.

10. 1 *lí* = .57984 grains, Troy
    10 *lí* = 1 *fan* = 5.7984 grains
    10 *fan* = 1 *ts'in* = 57.984 grains
    10 *ts'in* = 1 *lèung* = 579.84 grains

11. Two deer's horns exposed in the window of a Chinese shop in Philadelphia are said by the proprietor to have cost ninety-five dollars for the pair.

12. The writer is indebted to the Catalogue of the Chinese Imperial Maritime Customs Collection at the United States International Exhibition, 1876, *Shanghai* (1876), for much of the information used in preparing these notes.

5

"A Retarded Frontier":
Appalachian Material Culture and Folklife

George E. Vincent

George Edgar Vincent (1864–1941) taught in the sociology department at the University of Chicago, which was especially renowned around the turn of the century for its bold statements on social life and reform. At the school, Vincent applied ethnological ideas of "survivals" to the understanding of societal development. In this essay, he points out the remarkable persistence of old British traditions in the mountain settlements of eastern Kentucky by giving special attention to the region's folk foods, furnishings, crafts, and houses. The survival of old English customs in the United States was one of the "fields" declared by the American Folklore Society at its founding, but Vincent adds an important concept, one that is at the heart of later folklife approaches, to the understanding of these survivals. In Vincent's words, this concept meant "a method of observation, which seeks to gain a conspectus of all social activities in their interrelations, not to scrutinize separately one department of life." In addition, Vincent wanted "to exhibit qualitatively, not quantitatively, the various factors of social life as they appear at different stages of social organization." Appalachia, he noticed, retained an early stage of social organization, and he saw in the folk material culture and customs of the region expressions of how this social organization is lived out.

Appalachia has held a special romantic lure for Americans especially since the late nineteenth century, when the region's preserved environment and old folk ways suggested the nation's primitive past, back, in fact, to the innocence of original settlement. Almost a decade after Vincent's pathbreaking study, Emma Bell Miles published her romantic account of Appalachian life, *The Spirit of the Mountains* (1905), and in the following decade Englishman Cecil Sharp left his mark by publishing survivals of "archaic" English folk songs from Appalachia in *English Folk Songs from the Southern Appalachians* (1917).

In this description of Appalachian life, Vincent closes with an appeal for students to "drop their books" and receive a social education by experiencing different kinds of societies and their customs first hand. This call expresses Vincent's life-long efforts to spread cultural education. During the late nineteenth century, he was vice-chancellor of the Chautauqua system; he went on to become the president of the University of Minnesota in 1911, and in 1917, president of the Rockefeller Foundation, where for a dozen years, among other initiatives, he oversaw educational programs in Appalachia and an expansion of ethnological studies.

This essay is reprinted from "A Retarded Frontier," *American Journal of Sociology* 4 (1898): pp. 1–20. For Vincent's ideas on social development, see George E. Vincent and Albion W. Small, *An Introduction to the Study of Society* (New York: American Book Company, 1894); it is the source for the quotes I used here. For the romantic lure of Appalachia, see Henry D. Shapiro, *Appalachia on Our Mind: The Southern Mountains and Mountaineers in the American Consciousness, 1870–1920,* and for the historical role of folklife in social studies and programs in the region, see David E. Whisnant, *All That Is Native & Fine: The Politics of Culture in an American Region* (Chapel Hill: University of North Carolina Press, 1983).

*   *   *

American history has been described as very largely a record of the westward movement of a frontier; not a geographical boundary, but a type of social life which has reacted upon and modified the ideals and political insitiutions of the nation. Beginning in earnest after the Revolution, and getting a further impetus with the close of the war of 1812, this frontier swept on like a wave seeking channels of least resistance. It followed water courses—the Hudson, the Mohawk, and the Ohio; it penetrated mountain passes, pouring through Cumberland and Big Stone gaps into Tennessee and Kentucky, and sweeping around the foothills of the Blue Ridge into Alabama. Having passed the Appalachian barrier, it spread over the prairies of the Mississippi basin until it broke against the Rockies. But this on-rushing tide left quiet pools in the mountains of Virginia, North Carolina, Kentucky, and Tennessee. There the frontier has survived in practical isolation until this very day. Only recently have we fully realized this fact, made vivid by the stories of Miss Murfree, Mr. John Fox, Jr., and other writers.

It was from a desire to see something of this old frontier life that I recently undertook a very short journey in the mountains of eastern Kentucky. In this descriptive article I shall simply jot down certain impressions and indicate a few lines of investigation which this interesting social survival suggests. It is hardly necessary to say that I have attempted no sweeping generalizations on the basis of a four-days' ride through parts of three counties.

Kentucky is divided into "Pennyroyal," "Bluegrass," and "Mountain." The boundaries of these popular provinces are somewhat vague; but in general it is a division into western, central, and eastern sections. The mountain region is bounded on the east by the Big Sandy river and the Cumberland mountains, from which the hills, gradually descending, die away westward into the rolling Bluegrass country. This district of eastern Kentucky is drained by the Kentucky and Licking rivers and by tributary streams of the Big Sandy. The structure of the country is such as to form many narrow, isolated valleys, communicating with each other only by means of wide detours along the water courses, or by sharp and difficult ascents of the steep divides. The drainage system, therefore, as in most hilly country sides, creates social groupings, determines lines of travel, fixes the location of little settlements and county seats, and furnishes a means of local designation. There is an odd analogy between the address of the Londoner and that of the Kentucky mountaineer. Instead of the main thoroughfare, side street, and lane of the complex English description, we have the "fork," "creek," and "branch" of the Kentucky direction.

The region, originally well wooded, has in many places lost the most valuable of its trees, among which are poplar, oak, elm, ash, hickory, and walnut. Lumber companies and individuals are cutting timber rapidly and floating the logs down to the mills along the rivers. In many valleys whole mountain sides have been desolated by "girdling" the trees and leaving them to die and fall. Such areas are appropriately called "deadening." But in spite of all this, there are large districts of beautiful forest land, made more delightful still by a dense undergrowth of laurel and rhododendron. Throughout the western counties of the region there is abundance of bituminous coal and considerable deposits of excellent cannel. On many of the farms in Breathitt, Perry, and Knott counties it is not an unusual thing to find family coal pits from which fuel is dug as it is needed.

There are three general types of farms in this region: the valley farm, with its fields spread out along the bottom lands; the cove farm in the cove or hollow at the mouth of a "branch"; and the hill farm, pushing its corn fields up the steep slopes, sometimes to the very top. It was a hill farmer who, according to mountain tradition, fell out of his corn field and broke his neck. These three types are by no means clearly defined. Oftentimes the valley farm creeps up the mountain side, for the valleys at best are very narrow, and only where the stream has swept round the long curves and deposited a generous "bottom" is there chance for level tillage on a considerable scale.

The highways oftentimes set out pretentiously from the county seats, but when they leave the main streams and turn up the creeks there is rapid degeneration. The bed of the stream becomes the roadway for much of the distance, and in many valleys the fording is so frequent as to seem well-nigh continuous. Riding is almost the only means of travel. Saddle-bags are as commonly used as they were by circuit riders and other travelers in Indiana and Illinois fifty years ago. Wagons are relied upon only for transporting farm products and store goods. Oxen are generally the chief draught animals in the more remote regions. In the springtime a heavy rain of a few hours will cause "a tide" which for a day or more effectually puts a stop to travel. In the summer the creeks are very low, and offer no obstacles save the loose stones which cover their beds.

The population of this region is singularly free from what we are wont to call "foreign" elements. The mountaineers are predominantly, if not exclusively, of English, Irish, and Scotch origin. They came in the westward movement from Virginia and North Carolina. Such names as Noble, Allen, South, Strong, Combs, Sewell, Hargis, Stacy, and Mullins tell of British stock.[1]

By intermarriage for three or more generations the ties of kinship have been extended along the forks and creeks, until one is struck by the frequent recurrence of the same name. The family ties seem very strong and arouse, perhaps, the keenest sense of social solidarity to which the mountaineer responds. This tribal spirit has been a powerful factor in the feuds and "wars" that have played so striking a part in mountain life during the last thirty years.

The typical mountain family very considerably must exceed the numerical average for the country as a whole. It is by no means an unusual thing to find a family in which ten children have been born, while the number rarely falls below five or six. The general health, so far as one gets impressions from casual inquiry, seems to be exceptionally good. One mother asserted with pride that she had raised twelve children without losing one, and without so much as having a doctor in the house. She spoke learnedly of certain potent herbs, but she summed up her medical theory and practice by saying that when the children were sick she kept them in bed until they got well.

The houses of the mountains, outside of the county towns, are almost without exception built of hewn oak logs, dovetailed securely at the corners. The crevices are filled with mud, and generally a split oak strip is spiked between the logs. The pitched roofs are covered with long, hand-made shingles, irregular and curled. The chimney, except in the case of the poorer cabins, is made of stone, frequently carefully cut and fitted. The crudest form of chimney is built cob-house wise of small sticks, smeared inside and out with clay. Along the front of many cabins there is a covered "gallery" or porch. In the older houses there are no windows, all light and air being admitted through the door, or through the chinks between the logs. A "double" cabin is really a combination of two cabins under the same roof. Sometimes there is an open space or hall between them. Again they are simply built end to end, the doors of both opening on the same gallery. In the latter case, although there seems no real separation, each room, from the standpoint of the other, is spoken of as "t'other house." Families of social pretension have, in addition to the two rooms of the main cabin, a cook-house at the rear, and in one establishment we found a dining-room beside. In a vague way, so far as there is any social stratification, it is reflected in the number of rooms of the family domicile. The one-room cabin represents the lowest stage, while the possession of four or five rooms confers real distinction.

The furniture of the cabins is primitive and simple. A sufficient number of bedsteads, sometimes of the old-fashioned four-poster type, often rough home-made products; a few hickory splint-bottom chairs, a table or two, and shelves for blankets or "kivers," complete the average equipment. In many houses there are old Connecticut clocks. In one cabin we saw two clocks side by side, keeping time exactly together. The old man pointed with pride to them and to the shadow of the sun upon the floor as it approached the noon mark.

Agricultural and industrial processes are relatively crude. The chief crops are corn, a little oats, potatoes, tobacco, and sugar cane. These supply all the staple products necessary to the family life. The list of domestic animals includes horses, cows, mules, sheep, pigs, geese, and chickens. The sheep and geese are kept for their wool and feathers, and are rarely killed for food.

The mill is the only mountain industry which has been specialized in any marked way. At intervals of a few miles along the streams there are log dams and small grist-mills, which look more like rustic summer houses than places of manufacture. Although the family ordinarily depends upon the water-mill, now and then there is a hand-mill near the cabin door, as a last resort in case the domestic economy, never very carefully organized, has failed to maintain its supply of corn meal. Iron working is largely given over to log blacksmith shops in the small settlements and at the crossroads. But on many of the isolated farms there are forges for domestic use. Tanning seems to be a rare industry among the mountaineers, who have come to depend for saddle and harness upon the storekeepers. Portable steam saw-mills have almost wholly superseded the old-time saw pit, with its "top-sawyer."

By far the most interesting industry is the making of textile fabrics. The men are now more rarely clad in home-made jeans, which they have exchanged for "store clothes." But the women still wear very generally, and always for common use, "linsey" gowns of their own weaving and making. Almost every cabin among the older mountaineers has its spinning-wheel and hand-loom. Many of the younger generation show a disposition either to buy store goods or to depend upon older and more skillful neighbors for the weaving of their cloth, if not for the carding and spinning of their wool.

The linsey is not, as we had fancied, a plain dull brown or gray. The yarns are dyed brilliant red, green, yellow, and blue, and are oftentimes woven in really complex patterns of checks and stripes. The rather brilliant, crude colors of the new material yield gradually to water and sun, softening frequently into pleasant and subdued tones. The mountaineers also raise small quantities of cotton and flax for muslin and linen. The coarse muslins of the stores, however, are too cheap to permit this industry greatly to enlarge. The mountain product of woolen dress goods, on the other hand, is held in high esteem and nothing could be more contemptuous than the references of the Kentucky housewives to the machine made cloth of the storekeepers.

But linsey forms only a part of the mountain weaving. Blankets and coverlets, known as "kivers," come in considerable numbers from the household looms. The wealth of the housewife is reckoned in "kivers." The mountain bride brings as her dowry a collection of these treasures, to which she adds as many as she can to pass on to her own daughters. In several families we were shown thick, well-woven quilts which had come down from a great-grandmother, and were cherished with something like Roman awe for household gods. We heard much complaint of the modern dyes sold in the stores. They were compared disparagingly with the more permanent colors given by the bark and berry dyes of the earlier days. Yet, so far as we could discover, the analine products are very generally used.

The art impulse of the women seems to find its chief expression in these textile fabrics. The patterns are spread by imitation up and down the valleys, the old traditions being constantly modified by suggestions from the mill goods of the towns. There are, besides, inventors and authorities who make innovations and set fashions going. In one cabin, among a dozen brilliant linsey "kivers," we found one with yellow, white, and red stripes—a veritable Roman blanket. It was quite unlike anything we had seen on our journey. The only suggestion as to the origin of the idea was the simple statement of the maker that she thought the colors "would look pretty." In another case a woman spread out for our admiration a quilted coverlet of store cotton. On a ground of blue she had sewed large conventional red figures. It was so utterly different from the other things we had been shown that we expressed surprise and curiosity. With a smile of triumph she let us into the secret. She had copied the jig-saw scroll work on one of the more pretentious houses in the nearest county seat.

The whole subject of domestic industry, especially the textile side of it, can just now be studied to great advantage in eastern Kentucky, and it seems unfortunate that someone is not taking advantage of this opportunity. Every year, with the modernizing of the region, the conditions become less primitive and simple.

The food of eastern Kentucky ought not to be confused with that of the Bluegrass and Pennyroyal regions. Corn pone, bacon, and fried chicken are appetizing enough in print, but they vary in attractiveness with different parts of the South. The mountaineers have preserved all the primitive processes of the real frontier. Their cooking is correlated with all the other elements of their life, and they seem to thrive upon a diet which to the stranger from without makes the call to meals the gloomiest of summons. We were too early for chickens, which were served only two or three times during the trip. But, as far as we could learn, the rest of the *menu* was thoroughly typical. The staple article is corn bread. It is made by mixing coarse corn meal and a dash of salt with cold water, until the whole is a pasty mass. This is pressed into a frying pan, or skillet, three or four inches deep. The pan is then covered with an iron lid and thrust into the open fire, where glowing embers are piled upon it. It is left only long enough to form a crust or skin upon the surface of the bread. The center of the loaf is never cooked. After the allotted time the bread is turned out upon the table, sometimes broken into pieces on a plate, sometimes left whole to be plucked away as needed by the hungry family. Biscuits of wheat flour and soda or baking powder are sometimes served. They are usually heavy and yellow, and exhale an unpleasant odor. Potatoes are usually boiled or baked. Sometimes they are mashed and given a brown color by the liberal use of ham fat. "Ham meat" is for the most part fried in irregular pieces, which float about in a flood tide of grease. Occasionally the meat diet is varied by roast spare ribs, and, in the season, it is, of course, relieved by "chicken fixings." The butter is a white cottage cheese, very much like the butter made by the Bedouin goatskin churns in Palestine. The coffee is ordinarily a black, uninviting liquor, boiled for a long time in a large pot. This pot is a type of perpetuity. It seems never to be cleaned. Before each meal a little more ground coffee is added and the same amount is drained away into the cups. Thus there is a constant, slowly changing sum of coffee grounds which lives on year after year. Milk is rarely used by mountaineers for their coffee. In the remote districts only "long sweetenin' " is to be had, *i.e.,* molasses made from sugar cane raised on the farm. "Short sweetenin'," a cheap grade of brown sugar, is found on the tables of the well-to-do who live nearer to the county seats. Eggs, usually fried in the ham fat, are looked upon as something of a luxury. Sweets and preserves have a place upon most of the tables. Apple-butter and various preparations of dried fruits are common; and sometimes a pudding of dumplings and fruit is attempted. It would be hard to imagine anything more unattractive than either the food itself or the way of serving it. The table is sometimes covered with brown oil-cloth, and frequently with a piece of cotton spotted with coffee and grease stains. Two-tined steel forks, steel knives, and pewter spoons are, of course, the rule. One of the most pressing needs of this region seems to be education in the simplest domestic economy—and yet the people are healthy in spite of "hog and hominy."

The hospitality of the mountains is proverbial, and what is more to the purpose, seems still to be offered with genuine good will. To be sure, in the county towns and along the more frequented highways there are signs of commercialism and traces of cautious suspicion. But in the more remote valleys the traveler is received with a welcome in which the "quarter" he pays for his meal and his horse's corn seems to be a small factor. Yet we heard from one or two cynical old people that the times have changed, and that it is no longer an unusual thing to be refused a night's lodging, or even a meal. One of these praisers of the past told of a whole afternoon spent in one valley in a vain attempt to find a place of shelter for the night. Finally, he said, he just stopped asking and got down and went in and stayed. He knew they wouldn't put him out if he once got in.

But we met with almost no rebuffs. Our own sense of delicacy prevented our spending one night in a single-roomed cabin where three persons were down with the fever. On another occasion we were refused a meal for what seemed a very urban reason. The cook had gone away. With these exceptions we were welcomed quietly, not effusively, at every house where we dismounted. We would ride up to the fence of the yard about the cabin, tether our horses, climb over the rails—there was rarely a gate—make our way to the "gallery," and ask for a meal. The request was readily granted, with conventionally diffident remarks about the larder. Boys unsaddled our horses and took them to the rambling log barn for their meal of corn. After dipping into the wash-basin, we sat talking with out host, while the women of the household prepared the meal which we needed and at the same time dreaded.

The decorations of the cabin were confined ordinarily to cut-paper fringes on the shelf above the fireplace, or on corner brackets nailed to the logs. In several cases the inner walls were covered with pages from illustrated magazines and papers, and with advertising posters in brilliant colors. It was a rare thing to find pictures of any other kind, and photographs and tintypes seemed almost unknown. In many of the cabins there was a small shelf of books, chiefly school texts, owned by the younger people, and it was not uncommon for the host or hostess to point with half-apologetic pride to the decorations of the room as the work of the "gals." The interiors of the cabins, especially the sleeping rooms, were given an odd look by the lines of garments hung along the rafters above the beds. There were no chests of drawers, or boxes for clothes, but simply ropes stretched from one side of the cabin to the other, and nails driven into the beams above. From these hung linsey dresses and store clothes, and now and then a bright "kiver," a pair of winter boots, strings of dried apples, bunches of yellowish green tobacco, and other odd-looking articles. The general effect of the room was a little that of a pawnshop in Petticoat Lane.

The conversation turned, for the most part, upon personal topics, and we felt it necessary to give a fairly detailed account of ourselves. No one ever seemed surprised at our desire to see the mountains, and we tried not to betray any consciousness of the unusual conditions in which we were placed. Whenever the talk turned from personal matters, it easily worked around to theological discussions, in which most of our entertainers seemed to take keen pleasure. One man said that he was regarded as a dangerous character in his valley, a sort of freethinker, a mountain Ingersoll perhaps, because he had avowed his doubts about predestination. Another was an orthodox member of the Baptist church, and took strong ground against "fiddling" and "frolics."

We had heard so many stories of the ignorance of the mountaineers that we were somewhat disappointed by their familiarity with a good many things we had expected them not to know. We did not, for example, find a person who had not heard of the explosion of the "Maine." There was a good deal of desultory interest in the possibilities of a war with Spain. But the whole question seemed remote, and was so thought of by the people themselves. As one old man said: "I reckon we mountaineers wouldn't know much about a war if there was one."

The chief contact with the outside world is through the lumbermen who go down the river on their rafts as far as Frankfort, or even to the Ohio, or through the merchants who make periodical trips to the "settlements," as the towns and cities of the Bluegrass region are called. In one or two places we heard of sons who were in the army or navy, and of their letters which were handed around from house to house, or reported by friendly gossip. A few papers, chiefly agricultural journals and religious weeklies, are to be found in the more accessible cabins. But we spent the night with one family that had not seen a paper for months. They were ten miles from the nearest post-office.

The mountaineers in the county towns are fond of telling anecdotes to illustrate the ignorance of the backwoods-men. Many of these have been embodied in the stories of mountain life. The jests are passed about with great glee by the storekeepers and petty lawyers of the little towns. The tale that had greatest vogue at the time of our visit was of the mountaineer who complained that he could not sleep because of the electric light in his hotel room at Lexington. When he was asked why he didn't blow it out, he replied that he couldn't, "because they had the blamed thing in a bottle." Most of the stories have about them a suggestion of newspaper origin.

It is perfectly obvious that these mountain folk must have only the most shadowy ideas about the world outside. We found middle-aged and old women who had never been outside the valley in which they lived, and had not so much as visited the little town at the lower end of it. One boy knew of Chicago only as the source of an arnica tooth soap which he highly prized and imported into his valley. A woman whom we met on the outskirts of Jackson replied, to our eager inquiry for war news, that her old man had heard somebody say, who had read it in a paper, "that England and France were goin' to begin a war tomorrow morning." And she added, with apprehensive uncertainty: "There be a France, ain't there?"

The young people, however, are clearly gaining in general information from attending the district schools established throughout the region, and the public schools and academies in the county seats. The district school is "kept" in the typical log-cabin schoolhouse, with rough benches, an open fireplace or a huge iron stove, and oftentimes with plain planks for a blackboard. The efficiency of the teachers has steadily improved, and although the schools are in session for only a short period, the character of the work has advanced in a marked way. It is through the school system and the young that connections between the national life and this partially isolated region are being more intimately established. The most influential single agency which is attempting this task is the college at Berea, Ky. Here is the point of contact between the great social tradition of the wider world and the narrow life of the Kentucky uplands. The young mountaineers resort in increasing numbers to this college, where manual dexterity, intellectual training, aesthetic standards, ethical and religious ideals are communicated by earnest and devoted teachers. The plans of Berea, so far as one may judge from its publications, are based upon a careful study of the peculiar conditions and needs of the region, and have already resulted in setting at work refining and elevating influences in many a mountain cabin.

The aesthetic impulses of the mountaineers have already been hinted at. The dress of the men has almost no suggestion of tidiness, to say nothing of taste. It was not unusual to find relatively well-to-do citizens going about in worn or tattered garments. The storekeepers, lawyers, and doctors were the only exception, and many of them had a shabby look.

The women, on the other hand, especially the younger of them, show an art feeling in their linsey dresses of bright patterns, their ruffled white and pink sun bonnets, and bits of bright ribbon at their throats. Their shoes, however, are in many cases very large and coarse, and obtruded themselves painfully from beneath the linsey gowns. The older women seem to care much less for appearances. They have a worn and faded look, the inevitable result of years of child-bearing and unremitting work over the blazing fire, at the loom, and, it may be, in the field.

The interest of these people in theology and church organization is keen. The "meeting" offers an opportunity for sociability hardly second to the singing school and the frolic. One Sunday evening, in the court-house of a small town, we heard a traveling evangelist, at the close of an earnest sermon, beg the people to go quietly to their homes and not to stop and "visit" as they usually did. We could infer from this how important a function of sociability the church renders among these folk.

Theological discussion satisfies the appetite for metaphysics, and offers opportunity for intellectual exercise and discipline. Along with this fondness for theological dogma, we found traces of a tradition of folklore and superstition which seemed to offer an inviting field of study to the student of folk-psychology.

The moral standards of the mountaineers have been modified in a marked way of late. Probably in popular thought the chief associations with the mountains are "moonshine" and feuds. It was something of a surprise to us to learn that all three of the counties through which we rode had adopted a no-license policy, and that for a considerable period a regular feud or "war" had not been known. Nor was this change chiefly the result of outside pressure. It grew out of a popular reaction against the uncertain, lawless, terrifying régime of whisky and bloodshed. The conviction gradually gained ground that liquor was the source of the evil. In creating this feeling missionaries and temperance workers took an important part. So far as we could learn from conversations with all kinds of people, the prohibition sentiment is wide-spread and vigorous. Several old men discoursed very rationally about the dangers to life and property, and the disgrace to the mountains, which the old system involved. The sending of state troops a few years ago seems to have made a perceptible impression upon the people. They realized then as never before the existence of an external authority which cannot be ignored.

To be sure, whisky is still made in violation of the revenue laws, but the traffic is now doubly under ban. In our four-days' ride we saw "moonshine" only once, and then in such circumstances as testified to the reality of the sentiment against its use.

The "feud," which Mr. Fox has described so vividly in his story, *A*

Cumberland Vendetta, seems to be typical of mountain "wars." In the little county town of Hazard we heard details of the famous Franche-Eversole feud, which was suppressed only a few years ago, after sixty or more lives had been sacrificed. The account was full of ambuscades, of firing from the cover of cabins, of besieging the courthouse and stores, of pitched battles in the streets. One story was of a woman who, learning that her husband had been surprised by his foes, filled her apron with cartridges, seized a Winchester, and rushed through the fight to her "old man." Once armed he fought his way out in safety.

Although these tales are related with great gusto, there is no expression of regret that the times have changed. We were impressed everywhere with the popular dislike of the old order of things and a sense of relief from the dread and uncertainty of other years.

Public opinion in the mountains often finds expression in a rude fashion. Night riders or Kuklux constitute themselves arbiters of conduct and visit the cabins of real or supposed offenders. We heard frequently of these parties, several of which seemed very active at about the time of our visit. Whatever of good the system may involve theoretically seems more than counterbalanced by the opportunity which it affords for irresponsible persecution and private revenge. We heard murmurings against the practice, and the hope was more than once expressed that the law would be invoked to stop it.

Somewhat akin to "Kukluxing" is the plan of leaving letters of warning at the doors of idle or vicious persons. The community tries to protect itself in this way against imposition or moral contagion. So long as a family is in real need, neighborly aid is never withheld; but once let the suspicion get abroad that a lazy husband is trying to shirk his share of work and depend upon his neighbors, and he will find a letter some morning under his door giving him a week in which to show signs of industry. Failing in this, he will have his choice of a flogging or of being driven out of the valley. There are no poorhouses in the mountains. The worthy poor are cheerfully aided; the idle are compelled to work or to go away.

I hope I have succeeded in giving at least a general idea of the interesting field for social study which this retarded frontier affords. Here the economist, the anthropologist, the linguist, the historian, and the sociologist may find materials for special studies which would be of great value. A series of monographs on the chief aspects of this curious social survival ought to be written before the life, now being modified so rapidly, has lost its comparatively primitive character. Let students of sociology leave their books and at first hand in the Cumberlands deal with the phenomena of a social order arrested at a relatively early stage of evolution.

Note

1. Professor William I. Thomas, who spent several summers in the Cumberlands, gathered from the daily speech of the mountaineers a list of three hundred words obsolete since about the sixteenth century or surviving only in the dialects of England.

[William Isaac Thomas (1863–1947), Vincent's colleague in the University of Chicago's sociology department, spent more than a few summers in the Cumberlands. He studied and taught there through the 1880s, and his interest in folk vocabulary probably stemmed from his teaching of English at the University of Tennessee in Knoxville. Thomas's list of words from the Cumberlands does not appear in his bibliography, although later, many investigators reported the "archaic" nature of Appalachian folk speech. See James Watt Raine, *The Land of Saddle-bags: A Study of the Mountain People of Appalachia* (New York: Council of Women for Home Missions and Missionary Education Movement, 1924), pp. 95–124, and Gordon Wilson, "Regional Words," *Kentucky Folklore Record* 17 (1971): pp. 10–18, 31–39; a challenge to this approach to eastern Kentucky speech is offered in Raven McDavid, Jr., "The Folk Vocabulary of Eastern Kentucky," in his *Varieties of American English* (Stanford, California: Stanford University Press, 1980), pp. 92–113. Although William Thomas did not write specifically on the folklife of Appalachia, he was influential in promoting among sociologists ethnological methods and attention to "folkways." See his "The Scope and Method of Folk-Psychology," *American Journal of Sociology* 1 (1896): pp. 434–45, and his bibliography of folklore in his *Source Book for Social Origins* (Chicago: University of Chicago Press, 1909), pp. 736–50. A list of Thomas's works, many of which cover folkways of eastern European immigrant groups, is found in Edmund H. Volkart, ed., *Social Behavior and Personality: Contributions of W. I. Thomas to Theory and Social Research* (New York: Social Science Research Council, 1951), pp. 319–22. —*Ed.*]

6

Folklife of American Children

Fanny D. Bergen

Fanny Dickerson Bergen (1846–1924) loved nature. As Americans during the Gilded Age realized that factories were crowding out plants and animals, Bergen offered them accounts of a romantic folk still close to nature, and closer to them than their Indian "ancestors" they were hearing so much about. That romantic folk was their children. Museums of natural history had taught Americans that Indians and other "savages" lived a life in commune with the environment, but Bergen connected the customs of children with primitive life. Children were uninhibited, clannish, instinctive, and wild. Oral tradition was at the heart of their lives; they were conservative about retaining tradition, and yet at the same time they seemed unabashedly creative.

In Bergen's studies children and nature meshed. Following the natural history model of evolution, the primitive youth of the entire "race" could be seen in traditional childhood practices. But even more significant to her age, and to her studies, was the feeling that in childhood was where one's true nature lay hidden. In childhood, people were free to express themselves and feel their humanity. It was not all a pretty picture, however, because Bergen's studies also conveyed a certain ambivalence. Childhood, she recognized, was superstitiously irrational, hardly the model for an advanced civilization marked by scientific rationality. Yet amidst the rapid social change and strict conventions of Victorian society, the traditions of childhood—so persistent, so regenerative—offered some sensual, indeed natural, vitality to Victorians. Indeed, with the close of the nineteenth century, reformers called for more nurturing of children. They insisted that this time of primitive innocence needed to be enjoyed as a foundation for the development of rational, "civilized" behavior.

In this essay, Bergen explores the traditional ways that children have toyed with, and eaten from, nature. In her study of this neglected material culture was a valuable addition to the more common collections of children's songs and games. This essay is reprinted from "Pandean Pastimes," *Atlantic Monthly* 77 (1896): pp. 526–30, and "Nibblings and Browsings," *Atlantic Monthly* 72 (1893): pp. 373–78. To her credit, Bergen also published a related book-length collection of folklore for the American Folklore Society, *Animal and Plant Lore: Collected from the Oral Tradition of English Speaking Folk* (Boston: Houghton Mifflin, 1899). Bergen's contributions to folklore scholarship are discussed in W. K. McNeil, "A History of American Folklore Scholarship before 1908" (Ph.D. Dissertation, Indiana University, 1980), pp. 802–5. For studies of children's folklore during Bergen's time, see William Wells Newell, *Games and Songs of American Children* (1883; reprint, New York: Dover, 1963), and Alexander F. Chamberlain, *The Child and Childhood in Folk-Thought* (New York: Macmillan, 1896). And for changing attitudes toward children's culture and nurture, see Bernard Wishy, *The Child and the Republic: The Dawn of American Child Nurture* (Philadelphia: University of Pennsylvania Press, 1968).

*   *   *

Pandean Pastimes

The old god of nature is not dead, as we have been told. Pan yet lives in the hearts of some children. They still do him reverence; make shrines unto him, and place thereon their little offerings. They seek the willows by the river and the hickories on the upland, to make pipes with which they salute the early spring. Spring is youth's own time; summer and autumn belong quite as much to grown people, but the child has an especial hold on the awakening year.

Ah, the blessed lawlessness of the strolling country boy! He seeks not always, but he is sure to find, in his intuitive wanderings. Brook or creek, running full after the going of the ice, may call him thither, bearing rod and line, both perhaps of some improvised fashion, a bent pin answering as hook. But the angling is of small moment. Besides the few small fishes the boy brings home with him unknown treasures. The real delights of the day, to be remembered in far-away years, are the rambling stroll to and from the stream, and the long reveries, as, lulled by the babble of the water and the low undertone of awakening life, he lies, face down, silently watching the sunlit ripples and little swarms of minnows at play above the yellow and brown sands. Such a young dreamer seems unconscious of his surroundings, yet in some way he must be sensible of every detail of the scene; else how, a score of years after, can he recall the flutter of white when a yellow-hammer flew from the dead limb of an old apple-tree in a neighboring orchard, or still see the meadow lark perched on a tall fence-stake in prolonged fakir-like meditation, while the child lay on the upspringing meadow grass? How else remember the very insects hovering above the brook, whose shadows startled the minnows and "silver-sides"? And the whole sweet picture may be brought back by a bluebird's note, by crows cawing in the distance, or by the odor of a freshly broken willow twig.

What a delightsome succession of out-of-door plays and labors make busy, for the country child, the months, from the first hint of the wondrous glowing haze of the maples' bloom until the nuts are garnered! Numberless traditional diversions, bits of childish artisanship, including the fabrication of playthings, weapons, even musical instruments, fill up the too swiftly passing days.

Children are as fond as savages of beads, and of playing with them. How fascinating little girls find the tedious employment of stringing glass beads for their own adorning or that of their dolls! How much of the pleasure depends upon the love of color, or how much upon being provided with something to do, it is impossible to say, but the taste is very general. They are quick to utilize as beads any berries, fruits, blossoms, or stems which they find in their path. Will reflection from plate-glass mirror of a white throat set off with necklace of Etruscan gold, or perchance of sparkling jewels, ever give the enjoyable vanity of looking well that irradiated the face of the little girl who, after throwing over her shoulders her necklace of scarlet rose-hips, Eve-like sought the margin of some quiet water, to gaze long at the sun-kissed face and neck decked with the splendid rosary? Visions of dryads and fairies, of noble ladies risen from low degree, flit through the child's mind, the mingled impressions that are left from fairy-tales, and she half fancies that somehow, some day, these dreams may come true in her own real life. Ah, that limpid brown water, overshadowed, with bending boughs must have been a magic looking-glass, the face it reflected was so satisfied, so glad, so full of hope!

More graceful and more classic than the adornments of bright berries are the wreaths woven from forest leaves, usually those of the oak or maple. How easily secured are the light crowns of interlaced stalks of bedstraw (*Galium*), which, childish tradition says, have a magical power of curing headache! Many little shoulders have gracefully borne the gentle freight of a necklace made by stringing the small flowers that compose the great plumes of the homely old purple lilacs. Another favorite ornament is the slender chain with such patience fashioned from pine needles. I know a little city-reared maid who is fond of stringing bracelets for her lady friends from the cheerful red-and-white four-o'clocks. Her doll's spring bonnet is a violet leaf with a blossom fastened in the crown. A grass-plat in the back yard, where chickweed, clover, and dandelions generously bloom, is her "little wild garden."

Children on the eastern shore of Maryland have a saying that in the meat of every persimmon seed there is a little tree, and they amuse themselves by cracking open the brown seeds to find the miniature image of a tree which they fancy the plumule to resemble. This is no recent notion, for Cotton Mather says, in a pseudo-scientific treatise: "[Leeuwenhoek] will give us to see, a small particle no bigger than a sand, contain the plant, and all belonging to it, all actually in that little seed; yea in the nux vomica it appears even to the naked eye in an astonishing elegance.'' The seeds of the wild balsam are not always allowed to bide their time, and to be scattered, when ripe, by their own ingenious device for that purpose; for what child can pass a clump of these jeweled plants and resist nipping the translucent green seed-pods, to see them pop out their freightage? The velvety capsules of the garden balsam afford the same amusement. In some places little girls use the lune-shaped parts of the latter as earrings, for their own elasticity will fasten them for a time to the ear, after they are once put in position.

Some of us, thank God, will never become old enough to outgrow the pleasure of popping rose petals on the forehead. Petals of the peony, and perhaps those of other flowers, are sometimes used in this way; but nothing equals the soft, fragrant petals of roses for puckering up between the thumb and finger into the tiny bag that bursts with a whiff of perfume when violently struck against one's brow. Were it in a palace garden, could one ever pass morning-glory vines without wishing, for the sake of old times, to gather and burst, one after another, the withering blossoms, whose trumpet mouths the sun has so quickly closed? A pink or purple morning-glory never fails to bring to me remembrances of farmhouse windows curtained with Aurora's chosen flowers, which made graceful tracery on whitewashed walls within; and at the thought of the vine-draped windows there comes back a medley of beloved sights and sounds and odors beyond them,—dewy fields, umbrageous orchards, the breath of cinnamon roses, sweet strains from some sparrow's matins, and robins caroling as if their hearts would burst just because it was day. In those days we too adored the dawn.

I have heard of a play among the children in a village in central Illinois that I never chanced to meet with elsewhere. On a veritable hand-loom, in which the fingers act as warping-bars, long grasses are woven into loose baskets, which the children call rabbits' nests, and which they put in secluded places to receive the eggs of the wild rabbits (hares).

Children find many nature-made playthings ready to hand. There are various sorts of rattle-boxes, notably small ripened gourds, whose light seeds are easily shaken against the shell. Where the splendor of the American lotus lights up Western rivers and ponds, its great flattened receptacle, when ripe, is also gathered for a rattle-box. And I have often seen the cows driven home for milking to the patter of the dry seeds in their rounded pods, scattered along the wandlike racemes of what we called rattlesnake weed (*Cimicifuga*).

Many kinds of seeds are used as toys. The lavender-tinted Job's-tears, the castor-oil bean with its wondrous resemblance to a shining beetle, the polished gray lens-shaped seeds of the Kentucky coffee-tree, of alluvial river valleys, and others of peculiar coloring or markings attract the attention of observant children. The ripened seeds of the garden lupine bear a strangely close likeness to the head and face of a small wizened monkey; hence, in our part of the country the plant was somewhat generally known by the name of "monkey-faces." Japanese boys and girls have a game something like our jackstones, which they play with the seeds of the camellia and the lotus. The "twin turtle-doves" in the columbine, beloved by little folks in England, are less familiar to our children, though Miss Ingelow's reference to the pretty fancy has led many schoolgirls to seek and find the cooing pair both in our graceful scarlet-and-yellow wild species and in the cultivated garden varieties. A quaint little Hindu man in full trousers may be fashioned out of a flower of the pink-and-white garden dicentra.

A favorite toy in many parts of the country is made by running a common pin through a green currant or gooseberry. Equal lengths of the pin are left projecting from the berry; the point of the pin is then placed in one end of a clay pipestem held in a vertical position. By blowing through the other end of the pipestem the tiny figure will be made to dance in the air, just above the end of the stem. In Boston the schoolchildren have used the fruits of the linden to fashion the manikin, which, while dancing, may easily be imagined to resemble a monkey. It has recently been suggested to me that this child's play may have given rise to the Boston name of "monkey-nut" for the linden fruit.

What delightful memories are awakened by the word "playhouse"! It was a dear imaginative little world by itself, whither one could swiftly flee from the trying practicalities of every-day life, such as drying dishes, gathering chips for the kitchen fire, or watching a slow kettle boil. It was all one's own, and within it as nowhere else was free play for individual taste and fancy. There one could be busy, or dream, or even indulge in breaking and destroying, if seized by an iconoclastic mood. At will our tiny world was desolate or peopled. Besides real dolls there were within the playhouse various kinds of little folks, such as the fine ladies fashioned from gay poppies or from the tawny flowers of the old-fashioned day-lilies. Poor marionettes, some of such ephemeral lives! What busy lives they led us! What opportunities for invention were afforded by the furnishing of their rooms and the storing of their larders! In addition to the ordinary house duties there was the preparation of manifold confections: some genuine delicacies, others as purely for show as were the gayly painted plaster-of-Paris fruit baskets that often used to form the central ornament on the parlor tables of country homes. Then the joyous trips to the woods to gather velvety moss for carpets and bright berries for decorations; for children, like the bower-birds, enjoy a bit of color in their surroundings. But it would make too long a story here to recall the hundred-and-one glad happenings connected with this interesting part of the make-believe side of child-life.

The playhouse was not by any means monopolized by girls, and many a bearded man is now glad to remember his own part in playhouse life. The playhouse was, I think, less of a fairyland, may I say less of a temple, to boys than to girls, but they enjoyed all the practical part of it,—the seizure of a suitable spot, the carpentry, and especially the primitive masonry involved in the making of a fireplace. The real feasting, too, they were ready to enter into; leaving, for the most part, to the girls and dolls the Barmecide feasts of mud pies, cakes, and like dainties, announced by the soundless ringing of the rose-of-Sharon dinner-bell. But there is, beyond the playhouse, much sylvan handicraft that keeps boys happily exploring wood and pasture. Now it is to select a good piece of ash, hickory, or hemlock for a bow; again, hornbeam or hickory for hockeys, otherwise known as shinny sticks. The city boy, who goes with his half-dollar to buy a machine-made polo stick, or with several times the sum to get a varnished lancewood bow, wots not how he is cheated of his own. He has not simply lost the choosing from numberless growing saplings or shoots one shapely enough for a bow, or grubbing about their roots to find one suitably curved for a shinny, meantime marking others for future working. There is the going through bramble-lined lanes to the woods, tasting and chewing at this and that, as the country boy saunters along, darting off to quench his thirst at a brook or spring, where he draws up the water through a tall stem of meadow rue or flower-stalk of dandelion; or, if spring and lily-pond chance to neighbor, he must needs seek the latter to get the painted stem of a lily-pad for a drinking tube. He may be turned aside from the nominal quest of the day by any one of a score of casual allurements, varying according to the time of year. It may be to chase a chipmunk; to follow the martial call of a bluejay; to club a chestnut-tree, whose frost-opened burrs display tantalizing peeps at browning fruits within. Long vines of the wild grape must be selected for skipping-ropes, and the same may serve as rope for harness. Western lads have found that good string can be made from the tough-barked slender twigs of the pawpaw.

To the boy's mind it is even worth while to take pains in selecting the sticks which they sharpen at one end, and from which, either simply as an amusement or in petty warfare, they delight to hurl crab-apples or potato-balls. I have heard described a real Homeric play of boys living on the bluffs overlooking an Illinois creek-valley. Each chose with care a good supply of spears from the thickets of giant ragweed (*Ambrosia*), then armed himself with a buckler made from a flour-barrel head, to which were tacked stout leather straps through which the arm could be thrust. Thus equipped, the young heroes rushed to the fray.

Various innocent divinations are handed down from generation to generation of children.

It is an interesting bit of psychology that it is chiefly the girls, great or small, who practice charms or ceremonies intended to reveal one's fate, notably as regards marriage. It is they, mostly, who will patiently hunt for a four-leaved clover to tuck inside shoe or gown as a love-charm or as a luck-bringer. Yet boys do not wholly despise talismans or distrust their virtues, for in eastern New England they are much given to carrying in their pockets a lucky stone, as they call the little white serrated bone found in the codfish's head, and I am pretty sure that somewhat of talismanic power is attributed to the horse-chestnut, or double or peculiarly shaped nut, or grotesque root that frequently forms a part of the furnishings of a boy's pocket. I have heard one say, caressingly touching such a pocket piece, "I have carried that two years," or so many months or years. An amusing custom is found among the peasant children in the neighborhood of Skibbereen, Ireland. If, on their way to school, they linger along the ditches and roadsides gathering their "fairy thimbles" (the flowers of the foxglove), or peering among the grass to catch sight of a skylark's nest, or engaging in some other happy idling, as they approach the schoolhouse they seek for a plant which they call "In-ge-na-blame," to secure a bit to secrete in their pockets, to act as a charm against punishment for tardiness. I fancy their colloquial name for the plant is a corruption for "I'll get no blame," from their faith in its potency to save them from merited reproof.

Don't you remember hurrying out before breakfast to where the sunflowers grew, at the back of the garden or in some waste bit of land behind the house, to see if each great yellow-rayed disk had turned during the night so that it might face the east? Our half-reverential watching throughout the day to see the gradual following of the sun's course was akin to the spirit of the sun-worship. We had been told that sunflowers slowly turned as the sun moved, and we believed it, and were interested to behold the miraculous behavior of the stately plants. We liked to tell younger children of the wonder, and to point out the changed position of the blossoms; and our faith never wavered, however many times some perverse flower failed to follow the ritual. And again, in the late autumn, as we separated the ripened, metallic-looking seeds from the chaff, to put them away as food for the fowls, we recalled the mysterious power of orientation possessed by our sunflowers. For by this time the happy credulity of childhood had quite wiped from our memories the exceptions, so many times exceeding the cases in which our supposed law had been obeyed. The imagination of a child is a rather conscienceless faculty, I suppose, but were it otherwise, of what would not only childhood, but the world be robbed, that we would not have eliminated!

The lilliputian baskets which schoolboys carve out of peach, plum, and even cherry stones are sometimes really works of art, and when such a little ornament, given as keepsake a generation ago by some deft-fingered schoolfellow, turns up, in clearing out a bureau drawer or an old box, there are brought to mind a host of associations of the old-fashioned district school, where one learned much of greater value than book-lore. There come back the morning walks to school along dewy roadsides; the noon-times in the adjacent woods; the swings made by interweaving low-hanging beech boughs; the going, at the call of school, with one's particular comrade to some well or spring to bring a pail of fresh water. What teacher with a heart might not be placated by a nosegay of wild flowers, if the water-carriers did take their own time! From the opening of the first bloodroot, how sweet we made the bare schoolroom with flowers from garden, roadside, and woods! The teacher's desk overflowed with them, and empty ink-bottles served the girls as vases for their desks. When the petals fell from poppy or peony or fragrant rose, it was a rest from partial payments or the meaningless chant of "I write, thou writest, he writes," and so, to put them to press inside a book. The dried leaves, petals, wreaths, or what-not, of no herbarium worth, had a value of their own to us young things; they were the symbols of what youth sought, ever will seek, and ever should find,—the bloom, the color, the perfume of life. To-day, when on opening a long-disused book one chances upon them, grown brown with the lapse of years, one feels like kissing them and the discolored pages. Dear ashes of roses!

One of the last of the long pageant of out-of-door amusements was the making of pumpkin lanterns, in early autumn. We counted it a great frolic to carve out the grotesque faces, without the knowledge of the elders of the family; then, after nightfall, to steal out, light the candle within each head, and suddenly hold the grinning hobgoblin, with its fiery eyes and mouth, in front of the window of a room where sat some of those who were not in our secret. Oftentimes we decorated the top of each post of the front gate with one of the flame-eyed monsters. After the home fun was over, perhaps we might dance off, carrying our illuminations to some of the neighbors. Then home at last, with pulses all a-tingle, to go to bed in an unconscious rapture over the soft darkness, full of nameless autumnal scents, that we had just left, to lie building air-castles, while through the now half-sere morning-glory vines crept in the entrancing pathos of the music of myriads of crickets; starting now and then, as slumber stole on, when an apple fell to earth with a dull thud.

Thus waned the sylvan year. The long evenings came, when we sat about the home fireside, playing morris or fox-and-geese, with red and white grains of corn for men; cracking nuts; eating apples and counting their seeds, while we repeated the old divination rhymes; telling oft-told riddles; between whiles recalling the good times of the past season, planning new ones for next year, and reckoning the months until the opening spring should begin another round of rural pastimes.

Nibblings and Browsings

In a neighboring botanic garden, the other day, I saw a spicebush, with its early gold buds, opening into tiny blossoms, clustered in bunches along the fragrant brown twigs. The mere sight of the bush left a pleasant taste in my mouth. Its smell and flavor both suggest the Orient. Then, too, the appearance of the entire shrub or of a single flowery branch is like a Japanese flower picture. I remember that my grandfather, himself an old pioneer, told me, at the time when he first made me acquainted with the shrub, that in his childhood the pioneers in West Virginia and eastern Ohio said that when the spicewood began to put forth leaves a sharp lookout must be kept for the Indians, or, as he called, "the redskins," whose approach could from that time on be partly hidden by the increasing foliage, and therefore made more sudden and more dangerous to the white settlers. To my childish mind there seemed something conscious in the silent signal of the woodland sentinels, and the impression then received always revives when I meet this old favorite. I longed to break off a twig from the bush in the well-kept garden, and to nibble at its spice-flavored bark, both for its own sake and for old times' sake; but I doubt if, after all, the delicious flavor which memory recalls would have come back.

Every one whose early life was spent in the country can remember many flavors and tangs with which, in childhood, he became familiar by nibbling at scores of edibles of the woods and pastures that never found their way to any table. We can hardly call them edibles, either, for we did not seek them for real food, but rather as something to be tried, to be tested, and to be enjoyed. Children do not philosophize much, I suppose, but they are quick to see, and, with a sort of savage practicality, like to invent some uses for their finds. For children, as for other animals, one of the most obvious uses to make of growing things is to eat them. If, however, one could revisit the very spot where this or that wild tidbit grew, and could find the very same clusters, branches, roots, or what not, I fear the old relish would not be found; for one could not bring back youth with its divine glamour, and the external environment is not all. Nevertheless, one still likes these piquant, wilding flavors because one used to like them.

   The sassafras, a tree so beautiful at every season, whether with the greenish-yellow little blossoms that in April put forth on the leafless branches, or when clad with the wonderful scarlet and yellow leaves and brilliant fruits of autumn, that I wonder it is not planted more in parks and cultivated grounds, offers twigs clothed in tender bark with a very aromatic flavor. Not only is this delicious green bark chewed both by children and adults, but the young leaves are eaten by children, and the white pith is often removed from the stems, now to bite, sometimes again to play with. Above all, there is the pleasure of getting out unbroken, clean, pliable little pith cylinders of as many inches in length as possible. The use of the bark of sassafras roots for making tea, which farm and village housewives in various parts of the country advise as a healthful drink in early spring, is well known. This ruddy bark of the roots is also a valued ingredient of homemade "bitters," the villainous concoctions still widely used as spring tonics. A good old man, half self-made doctor, half lay preacher, whom I met in western Massachusetts some years ago, and who had doubtless wrought a deal of harm by his well-intentioned dabbling in herb-doctoring, told me that half a lifetime of observation and practice had made him certain that in the spring of the year the human system required "the bitter principle." It apparently mattered little what root, twig, leaf, or fruit supplied it, so long as this quality of bitterness was obtained. The sassafras root is probably added to the proverbial "bitters" for its aromatic quality, and it may be for the pungent astringency that gives an ameliorating tang to these remedial mixtures.

   In regions where the black birch grows, its young branchlets and their bark are chewed just as is the sassafras. Then, again, children obtain a more delicate morsel by scraping off the sweet, moist cambium layer found between the inner bark and the wood. By what subtle alchemy of nature have both this species of birch and the bright little checkerberry, plants in no way related, managed to produce from earth, air, and water the essential oil that gives to them a flavor and scent so like each other as to be almost indistinguishable? We find, too, a trace of the same flavor in the dainty white fruit of the exquisitely beautiful creeping snowberry (*Chiogenes hispidula*), a plant of less geographical range than its scarlet-fruited relative, the checkerberry. We have few indigenous plants with more popular names than this last-mentioned member of the heath family, whose shining green leaves and red berries gleam out in early spring, in woods and pastures, from underneath late-melting snows, and are gathered and eaten in various places all the way from Canada to Kentucky. Familiar as the checkerberry or wintergreen of New England, farther north, in New Brunswick and even in parts of Maine, it is popularly known as ivory, and it is the mountain tea of the beautiful hills of southeastern Ohio. The young plants, whose brown-green leaves are especially liked by children, are called in different parts of New England by the various names of youngsters, jinks, pippins, and drunkards.

Alongside of the familiar small fruits, berries for the most part, that are regularly gathered to be served, either raw or cooked, at table, there is a whole world of fruits known to country children, for which they forage and in which they revel. They have, happily, not yet become either too civilized or too busy to have outgrown simple tastes and instincts which take them close to nature, and would seem a universal heritage of mankind, but which, alas, both races and individuals too often barter for a mess of the huskiest pottage; though, sad enough to tell, even our children in the older settled parts of the country are losing much of the primitive knowledge of woodcraft, and of the natural child's delighted love of gathering and garnering the hundred nameless delicacies of every pasture, woodland, or fence-row. Teaching natural science in our schools can never restore this priceless gift, if once lost, any more than a scientific study of the poetry, the mythology, and the every-day arts of the ancient Greeks, or of the legends of our American Indians, can give the student their intimacy with nature, or change him into a genuine worshiper at the shrine of Pan. The teaching of science can do much, for it can help to open the eyes and hearts of the children whom an unhappy artificial civilization has robbed and blinded; but such teaching, though of the best, can never quite make up for the loss of the traditionary lore that is part of the inheritance of the country-bred child, though he cannot tell you how and when he obtained his initiation into sweet secrets concerning all manner of growing things.

Often neighboring with the checkerberry is the partridge berry, with equal grace creeping about the aromatic pine pastures of New England, or spreading a bit of green carpet in chosen spots in Western woods. Insipid and flavorless as are its pretty scarlet berries, the children seek them, and pronounce them "good to eat." Far less flavor than is demanded by the adult palate satisfies the unexacting requirements of children; at least so it would seem from the comparative tastelessness of various fruits that they universally appear to enjoy. The ground cherries (*Physalis*), queer little globes showing myriads of seeds through their translucent amber coats, are plucked and devoured by the boy, as he straggles through the orchard to fill his basket with apples, or darts here and there as he cuts through some cornfield on his way to the cow pasture. Then the great May apples, which follow the waxen blossoms on the stems of the "parasols" that little girls carry over their dolls, are eagerly watched in their growth, and, despite their sickish odor and taste, gathered with great care at the right time, and hidden in the haymow to ripen. "Eaten by pigs and boys," says Dr. Gray, with quaint cynicism, in the older editions of the Manual of Botany, in his description of the May apple. The hard, acid, wild crab apples, too, are often hidden in the hay to mellow, though it must be that their exquisite fragrance has something to do with their favor among children. This fragrance of the fruit suggests that of the lovely pink blossoms, and he who has never, in a gentle, warm May shower, crouched beneath the low-growing branches of the scraggy wild crab apple trees when they are abloom, and been deluged with the ineffable perfume, has not yet been all the way through Arcady.

Children perhaps, as a rule, take little cognizance of odors, but must unconsciously be more or less influenced by them; for in later years a whiff of some wild perfume recalls more vividly than can aught else happy scenes and experiences of one's early years. As you walk or drive to-day between the tangled thickets that line some picturesque by-road which dreamily winds in and out, up and down, and pause to breathe the subtlest, most evanescent of all sweet odors, that of the wild-grape bloom, are you not at once back on the outskirts of your own old woods, clambering after tendrils and crisp young shoots from the wild vine that draped the fence or made a natural arbor over some little oak, before you entered the mysterious shadows of the great trees to call together the straying cows and drive them home for milking? The dewy fragrance, the soft afterglow in the west, the gathering twilight, the sweet sounds from all the unheeded busy little people of grass and trees,—what fullness of life did they not all promise to youth and health!

Such hips and haws as deck every English hedgerow, if less abundant in our own country, still are scattered here and there. The wild-rose hips in Nebraska are chewed by the children under the name of rose-balls. Wherever in this incredulous land the fairy's own tree, the whitethorn, dares to grow, it calls the children round about to come and nibble at the high-flavored yellow meat of its scarlet fruit. Nor do they scorn the puckery choke-cherry, or the almost flavorless drupes of the prim little dwarf cornel, known in some of its habitats as bunch-plums, elsewhere as bunch-berries or cracker-berries.

Then there is the multitude of nuts and seeds, and of fruits commonly known as seeds, from the insignificant little morsel attached to its gauzy encircling wing, thousands of which are shaken to earth every spring from the swaying elm branches, to the great kernel within the beautiful brown sculptured peach-stone, which children watch for and gather, each in its own season.

Children have a happy facility in naming their flowers and fruits,— sometimes with visible reason, often without. In eastern Massachusetts they call the spikes of fruit of the sweet flag (*Acorus calamus*) critch-crotches, probably from the zigzag lines which mark the division between each member of the spike and its neighbors. But why Boston school children should call the round fruits of the linden monkey-nuts I cannot guess.

With us, the bitter meat of the pignut, the insipid achenia of the sunflower, the mildly sickening pumpkin and squash seeds, retain their hold only on the untamed appetite of the child; but in less civilized regions, as among the Cossacks of the Don, the grown-up young people while away the solitude of their long evenings by eating sunflower and melon seeds, as they sit around or on their great oven-like stoves.

But daintiest of all the multitudes of dainties of pasture, woods, or meadow is the nectar of flowers. The curved spur of the columbine, the delicate trumpet of the honeysuckle, and the slender tubular flowers of the red clover and thistle all yield their treasured drops to young red lips that part for the lilliputian draught. The oppressively sweet locust flowers and the smaller blossoms of the redbud also tempt children as well as the winged creatures to seek their nectar; but the shape of these blossoms makes them less popular than tubular flowers. I remember how, when a child, if I wished an Olympian feast, I sought the purplish flowers of the queer, ungraceful old "matrimony vine," which for some unknown reason obtained so much favor with housewives, who carefully trained it over porch or trellis, or against the side of the house, and yet were always complaining at the litter of the leaves so constantly shed, which they diligently swept away. By squeezing the short tube of a freshly opened flower—the faded buff ones were passed by   a generous sweet drop was secured.

Numberless are the relishes offered by vine and shrub, plant and tree, to the boy or girl foraging afield. Among them are the tender stems of the much-loved sweet-brier, stripped of their bark, or similar shoots of the wild blackberry or raspberry; the refreshing acid leaves of the oxalis and of the little rumex, both generally known to children as sorrel,— though in Pennsylvania I hear they call the oxalis sour grass; beechbuds and young sprouting beech-trees; while they still consist mostly of the thick seed-leaves, the buds both of spruce and of linden trees.

On Cape Ann and in other parts of eastern New England, children eat both the leaves and the young shoots of *Smilax rotundifolia,* which they call biscuit leaf or biscuit plant. Men reared in quiet old Concord tell me how, in boyhood, they regaled themselves, in early springtime, with the immature fronds of the great cinnamon fern, which they now remember as delicious. The cambium layer of the white pine affords a delectable mouthful to the children of evergreen woodlands. Where the spice-odored pink azalea, or rhododendron, as the botanists would now have us call it, sweetens pasture or swamp, children eagerly gather and eat the fungoid growths abundant on its foliage. Sometimes these pseudofruits are called swamp apples, again sweet-galls.

The dainty pouches or chalices, poised upon their beautifully colored hairlike stalks, which hold the spores of certain mosses, such as the bryums and polytrichums, are harvested under a dozen pretty names by browsing children here and there. No brookside bed of mint, no wayfaring plant of ragged hedge mustard, no glossy-leaved pipsissewa growing in however deep woodland shadows, will be passed unnoticed; and even the keenly biting smartweed is often nipped, half in daring, half to tickle the palate. With the cooling draught of slippery-elm water a fevered patient often quaffs refreshment which the physicians wots not of, for every sip recalls glimpses of glad noontimes when, with lithe-limbed school-fellows, he rambled off to the woods to collect strips of the clean, pliant bark with its indescribable fresh odor, which, readily yielding to the jack-knife, could be cut into bits and stored away in pockets for sly chewing in school hours. The "cheeses" of various mallows and the creamy column of united pistil and stamens of the dooryard hollyhocks are other mucilaginous delicacies.

Children show their remote kinship with the ruminants by their fondness for chewing all manner of things, apparently often for the mere sake of chewing, for one cud is dropped when a new one presents itself. Simple-mannered or old-fashioned ladies sometimes keep up a trace of this earlier taste for chewing. In some little white country church one may still catch a breath from the spray of coriander seed or sprig of southernwood or sweet fennel or bergamot in the hand of a pew neighbor. Besides the familiar resins of the spruce and larch, the beautiful translucent gum that frequently exudes from an injury on the trunk of cherry and plum trees is gathered by farmers' children. Country children in the Western States greatly enjoy chewing into a pulp the purple bloom of the thistle. They also chew wheat kernels until a sticky dough is formed. The wheat is generally winnowed out in the palm of the hand, from heads plucked directly from the unreaped grain field; and this without doubt has a sweet flavor not possessed by the riper grain on the barn floor which a boy may grab in threshing-time from the great heap that he is helping to measure and store away.

As numerous as the hidden hoards of the old fairy tales, buried at the foot of some forest tree by beast or elf or troll, and kept for the enchanted prince, are the underground treasures known to the real country boy or girl. From the first turning of the sod by the ploughshare in early spring till the ground is frozen in late autumn, young foragers are stirring the mould with fingers, knife, or improvised wooden trowel, to unearth some treasure trove. There are the sweet cicely roots in the garden, the tiny bulbs of the timothy in the surrounding fields, the wild potatoes,—as children, in some places, call the deeply buried tubers of the spring beauty,—the hot pepper root, *Dentaria,* the little tubers of the nutgrass, *Cyperus,* and even the ill smelling and worse tasting little wild onions, and, in coast regions, the roots of the beloved marsh rosemary. Will any East India preserve ever make your mouth water in older years as did the wild-ginger rootstocks that you dug with your own hands from the black woods loam in early days? Expeditions are planned to go for ginseng, sweet flag, goldthread, or Indian turnip. To be sure, all these, and more beside, are somewhat valued as medicines by mother or grandmother, and, when washed and dried, are often added to the store of roots and herbs kept in the attic; but I suspect the real reasons for the enthusiastic searching for them and their like are the love of strolling and the natural passion for digging. Thoreau remarks that agriculture, in its most primitive state, belongs alongside of the venerable arts of hunting and fishing, which, he says, "are as ancient and honorable trades as the sun and moon and winds pursue, coeval with the faculties of man, and invented when these were invented." The very smell of newly upturned soil arouses instincts and impulses that doubtless are heritages from our most primitive ancestors. Is it not the unconscious delight of sniffing in the nameless, revivifying odor of the fresh brown earth that leads children to the fields, to follow the furrows as happily as their companions, the cheerfully talking blackbirds, which come to seize the food providentially thrown up for them by the gliding plough?

Children fortunately often keep enough sweet savagery, so that if turned out of doors they go straight to their own. With little knowledge of names save those of their own coining or the popular ones of their neighborhood, many a time they could lead the scientist to the chosen retreats of rare local plants, and point out nest or lair of shy wild creatures. If anything could justify the common assumption that in childhood we relive the golden age of the race, it is the possibility of this unconscious but profound childish sympathy with Nature's heart.

7

"Manual Concepts":
Observations among the Zuñi Indians

Frank Hamilton Cushing

Frank Hamilton Cushing (1857–1900) was among the most colorful of the nineteenth-century ethnologists. A famous portrait of Cushing painted by Thomas Eakins shows the frail Pennsylvania native in Indian regalia, a large hoop earring conspicuous alongside hair that reached down to his chest. Below a dark headband, his craggy face sports glazed eyes looking over a long nose which overshadows a bushy mustache. His fist firmly holds a war club while in the background hangs an ominous-looking ceremonial shield. Apparently he was living up to his notoriety as the "Man who became an Indian." He set out in 1879 at the tender age of twenty-two to study the Zuñi Indians in northwest New Mexico for the Bureau of American Ethnology. By the time he left four-and-one-half years later, he had become a participant in, as well as observer of, their culture and even signed his letters "1st War Chief of Zuñi, U.S. Asst. Ethnologist." He took to attending functions in Indian attire, and at one lecture in Maine "gave forth with an extremely loud Zuñi war whoop that nearly frightened the audience out of their seats."

Once past this reputation as an eccentric, however, Cushing's contemporaries respected him for his comprehensiveness and his insight. In a popular series of articles for *Century Illustrated Monthly Magazine* published between 1882 and 1883, he covered modes of farming, food, dance, craft, courtship, and ritual. Cushing helped to make the Zuñis one of the most familiar Indian groups during the Gilded Age; indeed, many of the generalizations about Indian culture were made from observations of the Zuñi. Cushing paid special attention to matters of material culture; at the Smithsonian Institution and the University of Pennsylvania Museum, he especially was favored for mastering Indian crafts techniques, and reproducing genuine-looking artifacts. Related to this interest in traditional technique and design was Cushing's collection of folk tales, because he pointed out similar patterns of design. The patterns of culture could be discerned in its various forms, he offered, and the design and symbolism of these forms held clues to the connecting threads of worldview and belief.

This search for connection characterizes much of Cushing's work. In this essay, Cushing ponders the role of the hand in shaping various parts of Indian culture. The hand is more than the instrument for gathering and crafting, he argues; it provides the basis of numerical systems, ritual observances, architectural layouts, and artistic traditions. Bound to evolutionary thinking, Cushing surmised that the "course of man's development changed by use of the hands"; studying "primitive manual processes," he argued, offered answers to all-important questions of "man's mental development." Cushing's view reflects a common belief among the Victorian ethnologists in "empiricism"; that is, they thought that the character of culture evolved from man's first experiences. What he saw is what he got; sexual differentiation, for example, occurred because men originally paid more attention to tigers and falcons (thus becoming militant) while women originally followed the wasps and spiders (thus becoming domestic). The model of the hand, Cushing thought, provided a unifying concept underlying the culture he observed, and by extension, all of culture.

This essay comes from "Manual Concepts: A Study of the Influence of Hand-Usage on Culture Growth," *American Anthropologist* (old series) 5 (1892): pp. 289–317. My quotes from Cushing here come from a privately printed syllabus of lectures, "Primitive Handicraft and Arts of America," which he gave in 1895 at the Drexel Institute, Philadelphia. For background on Cushing and a selection of his other writings, see Jesse Green, ed., *Zuñi: Selected Writings of Frank Hamilton Cushing* (Lincoln: University of Nebraska Press, 1979); Frank Hamilton Cushing, *Zuñi Folk Tales* (1901; reprint, Tucson: University of Arizona Press, 1986).

*   *   *

Steps toward Man's Intellectual Development.

If we assume that there have been three great steps in the intellectual development of man, the biotic, the manual, and the mental—

(a) The Biotic

Then, during his biotic development, man, as a genus of animal species merely, had progressed so far as to have free hands. Though these may have been developed in climbing, yet had not now either to creep or to climb, but could walk erect; could fend and defend freely with these hands.

(b) The Manual

It was then that man began to develop extranaturally; no longer like the mere animal, by coercion of the direct forces of natural environment, but rather by making an environment of his own, and this, first, by means of his hands—that is to say, this experience in warding off the blows of nature with his hands gave rise to devising, in which is to be sought the beginning of formal mentation—that is, of conscious ratiocination, as compared to instinctive consciousness and volition. Therefore I have named this period of man's development from his ancestral animal species, both physically and mentally, the manual.

(c) The Mental

No one has better defined the next period of man's development than our true-seeing teacher, Major Powell, when he states that the mental step or stage depends on the ascertainment of *truth*.[1] The degree to which man, practically, intellectually, or spiritually, ascertains truth determines the degree of his security and conditions his fitness for survival and prevalence; but man attained to both the perception and formal ascertainment of truth first through the *use* of and then through the *using* of his hands. The survivals of this are as striking as they are abundant. Let us examine only a few of them—this more in the way of suggestion for, rather than as the results of, adequate study.

I think that man is what he is, even racially to a certain extent, through this same use and using of his hands, he having been domesticated thereby, or by himself unconsciously, so far as to have changed himself and the degrees and modus operandi of the causes in outside nature which affected his development as an animal. If this be true of man in a general racio-physical sense it is certainly and much more obviously true of him in more special ways; as, for instance, in so far as he has modified himself by persistent custom or usage—usage rendered persistently specific through the limitations of his organism—his members acting upon and acted upon by environment, according to his condition.

For example, learned treatises have been written from all sorts of standpoints to account for the universal right-handedness of our race. It has appeared to me that the essential usages of primitive life have made man universally right-handed, or at least emphasized and confirmed in him any organic tendency that way; so that no students can ever have found a tribe or nation of wholly left-handed or even ambidextrous people, nor trace of them in art remains, although in the latter we may look among the earlier for more frequent signs of such than among the later.

Man the savage fends for life principally with weapons for war and the chase, of offense and defense. His heart, the most vulnerable part, is in his left side, which he would therefore even emotionally turn away from danger and encounter; but, more than this, his condition of life implies always the shield and the club. He has naturally always carried the shield over the heart with the left arm and hand; the club, lance, or sword in the right hand. He has thus *acted* constantly with the right hand; *carried* as constantly with the left. It is only natural, then, that in ritualistic talk the Zuñi should have called the personified right hand the "Taker," the left hand the "Holder," going so far as to deify the left and right members of the Sun Father as the Elder and Younger God-Twins of War and Chance—A'-hai-yu'-ta and Ma'-tsai-le'-ma—one the deliberate, the counsellor, and maintainer; the other the impetuous, the proposer, and doer.

In this we already have an example of the agency of hand-usage in framing mind or forming both mythic concepts and religious beliefs, along the line of which one might follow far the upward growth of culture in a special people; but the example serves also to introduce to us a clearer, more distinctly graded line, each advance of which may be obviously traced and which is, in much greater measure, of universal applicability to studies of culture-growth in the entire human race.

The question has been asked, Why have we a cumbersome decimal system of enumeration when it is well known that a duodecimal system would be better? The question has been answered by Dr. Tylor and by many others, as by myself—we have the decimal system because we have pentadactylic hands.[2] Whether we would or no, despite our mind, these hands have imposed upon us both the names and the figures for our numbers and numberings. The need for knowing in number arising in primitive time, *they* first responded; the will to know, *they* formed the way of knowing—the knowledge itself, for that matter. However well understood this may be as a general statement, I do not think the process of it has ever been quite fully or far enough traced out. . . .

Influence of Hand Usage in Left and Right Finger-Counting on Ceremonial Successions, etc.

It is now possible to demonstrate the controlling influence of finger-counting on the successional arrangement of the cardinal points or world divisions, and therefore on the lines of succession and directions of turning in ceremonial circuits and serial-marshallings, and of organizations of these and other kinds, as well as of the structural arrangements appertaining thereto.

It is the same to-day as it was in times ancient with the Zuñi when he uses his fingers as indicators. When calling attention to a single object only, he points as we do, with the index finger of his right hand; but if indicating a series of objects, then he points out the first one with the *little finger* of his *left* hand, palm upward, and the second with both it (involuntarily) and the finger next to it, whilst the third object will be pointed at with the middle finger, the fourth with the index finger, and the fifth still with the index finger, but with the thumb extended and the palm turned upward. If, say, the third object be pointed at a second, third, or fourth time, invariably the middle or third finger will again be used as at first, and it is likewise with whatever finger agrees with the serial number pointed out or meant a second time or repeatedly. This forcibly shows the power of apparently trivial action-habits to survive throughout indefinite numbers of generations; for this peculiar usage in indicating can only be conceived to have arisen before the origin of adequate speech in the effort to indicate connection, succession, and rank or precedence by means of gestures; that it was thenceforward kept up in the relating of successive events, even after names for numbers had been developed, but while yet no words for first, second, third, and fourth had been evolved from them, is equally conceivable, and that the inception of all this was involved in the origin of finger-counting itself, is at once apparent; that it would also influence (through gesture indication and naming) the placement in succession of the cardinal points, etc., may be made evident if we consider some of the aspects of primitive man toward extraneous nature. To him, the all-important factor in the universe was the Sun. It was the Maker of day and Renewer of life each morning. As such its chief place was the point on the horizon whence at dawn it came forth. Therefore all other points of the horizon would at first be located or arranged with reference to this one; but with all ancient peoples who, like the Zuñis, normally developed their numerical system previously to or alongside of their ceremonial placing and naming of the cardinal points (or sources of the wind-phenomena and gods), these points were but naturally arranged serially and *leftwardly from* the east, or the region of the rising sun. With this in view—and itself already indicated by the mere gesture for the rising sun—the next point, or the north, was, of course, the first thereafter. Therefore it was necessarily indicated or counted (according to the usage I have described) with the little finger of the left hand, and consequently came to be referred as "the first finger [cardinal] point," and hence conceived of as the *first* cardinal point, a conception which, through mythical fitness, would surely prevail. In the same way the next cardinal point, or the west, being symbolized by the second or next leftward finger, became the second cardinal point, the south the third, and the east the *fourth*[3] instead of the first. Finally, with a people far enough advanced, the next point to this, because in the direction of the sun rising from it, was the zenith, and the next to this in turn (because following the setting sun to the world of night) was the nadir, whilst the first and seventh as well was this world itself, or the center of them all.

Each cardinal point was characterized by many things differentiating it from all the others: in the Northern Hemisphere the winds of the North were cold, bringing winter; those of the South warm, bringing summer. So the East was the land of day, of awakening and "life-completing;" the West the land of night, of sleeping and dreams, death and souls or "life-finishing," whilst the Above was the world of clouds, and the path of day the source of seed; the Below, that of darkness and its terrors, yet the place of fertility and growth and of all becoming.

Nevertheless, though one journeyed afar, this world remained measurably the same; for the north, the west, the south, and the east remained ever the same in relation to it. Their phenomena were ever present, yet *they* were ever beyond. They must, then, be Worlds or Regions by themselves, and must be peopled by great gods, the causers or commanders of their severally characteristic phenomena, whose representatives in this, our own world, or the Place of the Middle, must be the animals, mortal or phenomenal, specially resident in the northern, western, southern, or eastern parts of this world.

The Masters of all these Gods of the Spaces and God animals of the related regions were those of the North, because resident in the First region and because, therefore, the Elders, as among men the first are the Elders and Masters. For that reason, no doubt (thought the primitive Zuñi), they were the most powerful, hence the fiercest; the most implacable, hence the first (yet most difficult) to be propitiated.

Thus, too, the gods of the other regions assumed their ranks and supposed relationships, those in each of the series becoming the younger brothers of those in the last before it, and their relative powers and mutual dependencies were explained with unfailing and equal readiness. Thus, until the Gods of the North withheld their icy breath, how could those of the West or the souls there breathe moisture over the land? And until the moisture from the West came, how could things grow in the warm breath of Summer sent by the Gods of the South? How mature and ripen without the age-drying drouth and tempering breath of the Gods in Dawnland?

Now, in order that these Gods of the several regions might be properly approached and entreated, wise men (the Elders of clans related to or most nearly connected with the chief animals of these same several regions, hence named after them) must become their Protopriests, and since thus constituted the Protopriests, of, say, the North, they were in special favor with the Gods of the North. Being of the North, they must be the First, the Elders of the other Protopriests, as their Gods are the Elders of all the other Gods. They also must have a place named of the North, their next younger brothers a place named of the West, and so on. So also they must have followers of whom they are both Fathers or Protopriests and Chieftains, and these are the children of their own clans named after the animals of the North, and finally these children or followers must in turn have an abiding place, which shall be called the "Place of the North," in which shall be the precinct of these Protopriests of the Northern Gods, wherein they shall worship and keep their sacred "Powers and Medicines," their symbols and fetishes of Winter and the North, wherein to hold their secret assemblies. Thus, too, it must be with each other region—it must have its Protopriests and they their followings, all properly assigned in places cardinally named or "word-placed."

The number of regulations which such arrangements have given rise to with a people like the Zuñis is legion, dramaturgically affecting, as it has, absolutely all their ceremonial life and well nigh all their institutions and organizations, whether religious and sociologic or regulative and merely governmental; whether of the tribe, the clan, or the family, or whether in the arrangements of the town, the kiva, or the dwelling. As an instance, the order of all dances during the year must accord with this, for the clans take precedence in the times or seasons of the celebration of these, mainly with regard to the relation of their totems to the North, the West, the South, the East, the Upper or the Lower regions, and the relations of these in turn to the elements of wind, water, fire, and earth, and to winter, spring, summer, and autumn. Yet in each dance or celebration each region must be represented by appropriate leaders of sections, whose precedence is arranged with like due and scrupulous regard to the sequence of the several regions and seasons they also represent.

Formerly the greater divisions were far more pronounced than now, as may be inferred from the fact that the Zuñis are the descendants of dwellers in the celebrated "Seven Cities of Cibola;" for in these the totems of the North dwelt in a village by themselves, those of the West in another, of the South in another, and so of the Eastern, Upper, and Lower, whilst those of the Middle dwelt in another town, apart from all the rest, itself subdivided into wards or septs (as in modern Zuñi), itself also the tribal head—ceremonially ruling all the rest, yet ruling through resident protopriestly representatives of and from all the rest, in due order of precedence; only, here in the Midmost place, these were under the Sun or Father-Protopriest, and the Seed or Mother-Protopriestess, in at least all religious and ceremonial concerns. A curious prototype or parallel this, it would seem, of Cuzco with its upper and lower divisions, and therein paired wards of representatives and rulers from all the "Suyus," and over all its Inca Father of the sun, its Inti Mother of the earth.

Again, in at least the central town of Zuñi were (and are) six kivas; but in any one of them any ceremonials relating specifically to all the regions will be performed by the leading Protopriests of the North, West, South, East, Upper, Lower, and Middle regions, each duly placed within a division of a diagram on the floor made with prayer-meal (fig. 7-1) of all the kivas arranged around a central space so that all may be entered from the right ("east") leftwardly in a four-fold circuit or "procession of seating," first, of "The Four," then (second) of the Uppermost, then (third) of the Nethermost, and, finally and singly, of the Midmost "Father" or "Seater of All."[4]

In each of the great cities or aggregations of pueblos which we excavated in the Salado and Gila valleys, I found that these six kivas were there also aggregated, like the many pueblitos, into a temple kiva as it were, the home or storehouse and stronghold and the place of sacred assembly of the Protopriest rulers over the wards or pueblo divisions of those cities. Each of these structures, which I have heretofore perhaps injudiciously called temples, contained from one to six or seven superimposed *sets* of either five (as in the celebrated Casa Grande, fig. 7-2) or seven chambers or halls of ceremony (as in the great kiva mound of Los Muertos). If five, then the Northern and Southern were nearly twice as large as the others, to represent not only the Northern and Southern but also the Upper and Lower regional divisions. It is significant, too, that the circuit of these chambers was made from the east, and thence leftwardly to the north, west, south, and east, and finally from the east to the center, whence no connection by doorways was provided with any of the other rooms than the eastern (compare [plans below]). The temple of Vira Ccocha of Peru was built on a grander scale, but on this same plan, and it is safe to say that both kinds owed their origin and probably placement, as heretofore suggested, mainly to such placing and sequence of the cardinal points as I have referred to. It is not too much to assume that this placement was founded upon unavoidable prehistoric usages of the hand, whether or not it denotes identity of culture origin.

It has been my object rather to suggest that the hand of man has been so intimately associated with the mind of man that it has moulded intangible thoughts no less than the tangible products of his brain. So intimate, indeed, was this association during the very early manual period of man's mental growth that it may be affirmed to be, like so many other hereditary traits, still dormantly existent in the hands of all of us to a greater or lesser degree.

For the hands have alike engendered and attended at the birth of not only all primitive arts, but also many primitive institutions, and it is not too much to say that the arts and institutions of all early ages are therefore memorized by them. In other words, their acts and methods in the production and working out of all these arts and institutions survive as

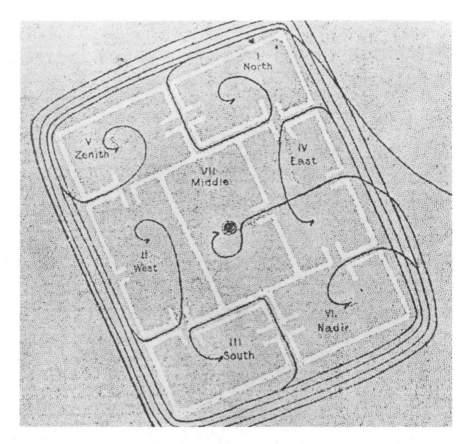

Figure 7-1. Ceremonial Diagram in Prayer-Meal of the Seven Ancient Spaces,
Showing Fourfold Circuit of Entrance

impulses within them, as do obsolete organs in changed animal species;
yet more, they survive according to well nigh the same laws of persistent organic inheritance.

It is chiefly through these survivals within the hands that the em-
bryology of the arts themselves may be traced and studied, a knowledge
of which subject is as essential to the proper understanding and classification of man's technical activities, at least, as was that of organic em-
bryology to the comprehensive view and modern classification of biotic
species.

The method of retracing these lost steps in the growth of the arts
surviving in the hands of man is comprised in simply turning these back
to their former activities, by reexperiencing through them, in experiment

Figure 7-2. Ground Plan of Casa Grande, Showing Orientation
(From survey made by Cosmos Mindeleff of the Bureau of
American Ethnology)

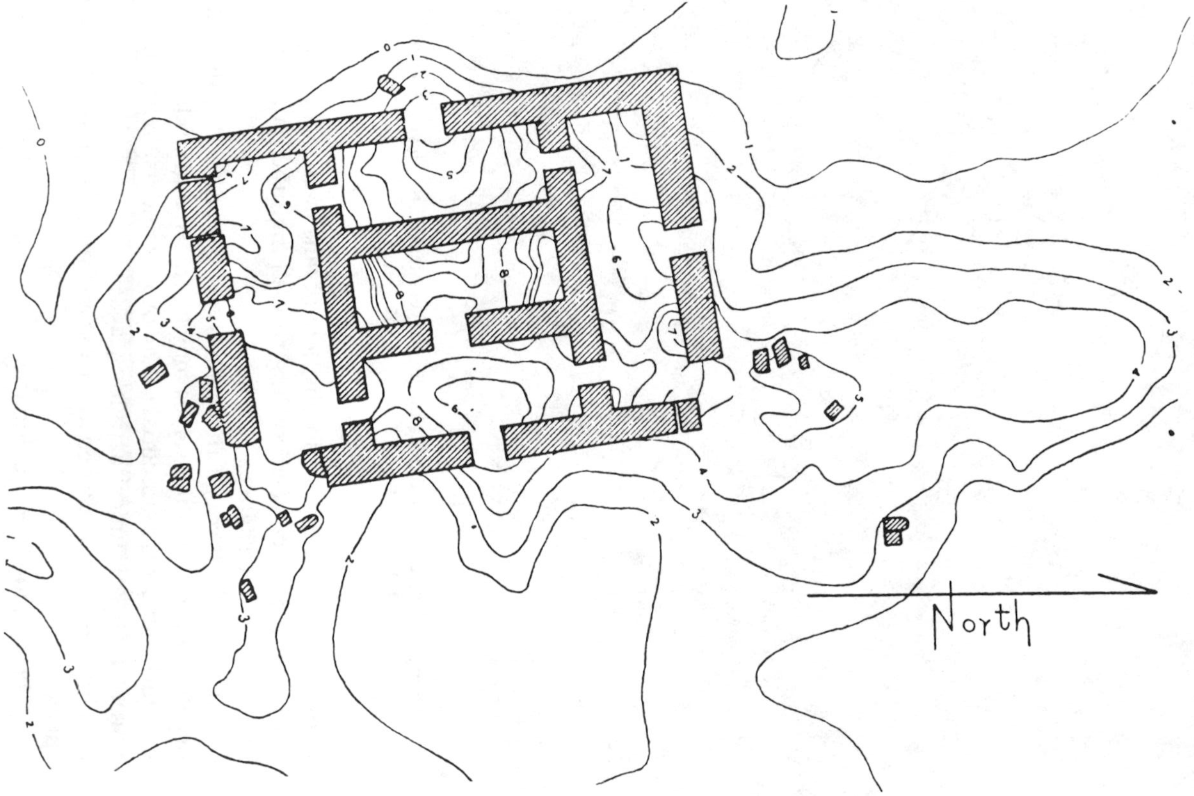

with the materials and conditions they dealt with in prehistoric times; times when they were so united with intellect as to have been fairly a part of it.

Notes

1. [Cushing is here referring to John Wesley Powell (1834–1902), founder and first director of the Bureau of American Ethnology, for which Cushing worked. Powell's ideas on mental development and the "ascertainment of truth" culminated in the publication of *Truth and Error* (Chicago: Open Court, 1898), but Cushing was probably thinking of Powell's many essays on evolution, including "From Savagery to Barbarism," *Transactions of the Anthropological Society of Washington* 3 (1885): pp. 173–96; "From Barbarism to Civilization," *American Anthropologist* (old series) 1 (1888): pp. 97–124; "The Three Methods of Evolution," *Philosophical Society of Washington Bulletin* 6 (1884): pp. 27–51. Powell's ideas on folklore are expressed in "The Interpretation of Folklore," *Journal of American Folklore* 8 (1895): pp. 97–105, and "The Lessons of Folklore," *American Anthropologist* (new series) 2 (1900): pp. 1–36. —*Ed.*]

2. [Cushing is here referring to Edward Burnett Tylor (1832–1917), the influential British anthropologist who broke new scholarly ground with the publication of *Primitive Culture* (1871). His discussion of the decimal system is found in *The Origins of Culture* (reprint of *Primitive Culture*). (Gloucester, Mass: Peter Smith, 1970), pp. 240–72. —*Ed.*]

3. As I have said, this seems the normal line of development, ceremonially, since it has characterized the greater number of ancient tribes and peoples, especially those inhabiting single regions for long periods. But there are exceptions. The nearest northern neighbors of the Zuñis, the Navajos, neither recognize the same number of regions the Zuñis do, nor do they name or range them ceremonially from the right leftwardly, but from the left rightwardly. This arose probably, as I have suggested, from the fact that their relative progress in ceremonially naming the world quarters and in naming their numbers was not the same. This would likely be the case with a wandering or unfixed people, with whom also in rare instances some factor, such as the direction whence they migrated, the source of something important to them, or a variety of other influences, would operate to render some one of the cardinal points more important mythically than another—that is, if the rising of the sun and its course rightwardly to the south and west had not already done so. Furthermore, the lack of the relative number-names up to four, either in gesture or speech, would leave the sequence also more likely to take a dextral turn, of course, than a sinistral tendency. This might and probably would be transformed to a sinistral succession after the development, in the ways I have described, of a more perfect number-phraseology, or the adoption of a more sedentary habit of life within a circumscribed area. The wandering or drifting peoples, at any rate, more often range the cardinal points dextrally than sinistrally, and their point of departure is usually also from the east or the rising of the sun, whilst the opposite is, in a like general sense, true of more settled peoples.

   In view of these facts, great importance attaches to a study of the particular conception and arrangement of the world quarters, characterizing any given tribe or people, or shown in monuments of such; for their former condition of life and often even their earlier habitat, or again, in case of vanished peoples, their grade of culture can be correctly approximated therefrom. Many lines indicative of this might be followed up, but I will here essay limitedly only one, because it seems to illustrate quite importantly yet another consequence of the sinistral arrangement as above accounted for. Naturally the wanderer locates the cardinal points by the sun, usually, therefore, making the east his first point, the south his next, and so on. No matter how far he may fare, his cardinal points, so far as he takes account of them, will be true to the sunrise at the time of year when he locates them. Not so, however, with a people long settled in one region, then migrating to and settling in another. Their chief cardinal point having previously become the north in ways already shown, they are far more apt to misplace it, either accidentally or intentionally, and accordingly all the other quarters, than are wandering people who locate theirs by the sun only: (1st) because, having a full sense of the cardinal points of their olden home, they will endeavor to adjust these old points to the new locality, and in doing this will almost unavoidably vary toward the left or west from the true north in this new country to the extent of at least the solstitial variation at the time, if not to a greater degree. In the latter case, they will claim and locate (2d) because of reasons which will presently be made evident, only *one* set of *quarters,* but *two* sets of *directions,* one—the sacred and "true," world-directions, the other those of the "new country" or of the people they find there.

Illustrations of this are not rare even in America. The Tusayan Indians of Arizona exemplify it in uniformly placing their sacred or world divisional north to between forty-five and fifty degrees west of north, and in constructing some of their kivas accordingly. For a kindred reason the great sacred citadel kivas or fanes in the ancient cities of pueblos in the Salado valley, discovered by me and excavated by the Hemenway Expedition, were found to have been placed with reference to a preconceived or else conventional set of directions. But this arbitrary placing of the world quarters was carried further, perhaps, by the ancient Incas (as shown not only by history, but also by the orientation of Cuzco itself and of the many sacred sextenary or septenary structures throughout Peru) than by any other people, except we turn to the old world. There the Chinese, whose sacred nomenclature shows either that they at one time almost completely reversed the points of the compass in their slow shifting from the west in Asia to the land they now live in as the midmost of the world, or else that they never varied an earlier conventional setting of these points according to or at least like the Babylonic system. This latter led to the well-known placement of the Babylonian and Assyrian temples obliquely to the cardinal points—that is, with the angles toward instead of the sides facing north, west, south, and east; and I think it originated—so far as exemplified in these temples—in the effort to arrange within them quarters to correspond serially and leftwardly to the six cardinal points or world regions outside of them. The reasons I assign for this may as well be briefly and simply explained here.

When a Zuñi Protopriest consecrates, or begins the planting of the father and mother seeds in the center of a corn-field, he makes a hole in the soil, usually in the middle of a circle of prayer-meal (fig. 7-1). Over this he marks a cross, also in prayer-meal, the four arms of which reach out toward the four cardinal points. At the extremity of each arm of this cross, beginning with the northern (i, fig. 7-1), he digs a planting hole. Then, moving his planting stick around and toward the left, outside of these, he digs a hole to the left of and slightly *below* (or south of) the northern hole and again moving his stick around the entire circuit, digs another hole to the right of and slightly *above* (or north of) the southern hole. Finally, moving his stick once more entirely around the circuit, he places it in the central hole.

Now, if an effort were made to construct a parallelogramic temple with quarters in it to represent, as do these seven holes, the seven regions, in which quarters ceremonial progressions or processions were to be performed (as they are dramaturgically performed by the Zuñi with his digging stick and afterwards with his corn grains) from the right (or east) side leftwardly, then the result would be the placing of the parallelogram obliquely and leftwardly to a line running north and south, in order that, as I have tried to indicate by the dotted lines in the accompanying diagram, the northern quarter (*i*) might be above or truly north of the upper quarter; that the southern quarter (*iii*) might be below or actually south of the lower quarter (see and compare . . . [the] plan of the "ancient spaces," figure 7-1, and of Casa Grande, figure 7-2).

4. In this may be seen either the origin or a development of the invariable four-fold circuit or procession four times leftwardly around the altar, shrine, or other receptacle of offerings—as a dramatic coming from or going to the six regions in succession—the four first regions being comprehended in a single circuit—as pertaining to the single plane of this world alone, whilst the visit to the *Middle* must have a circuit by itself as comprehending or representing all the rest in this world.

Types of Objects and Rites

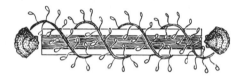

Primitive American Art and Ornament

Stewart Culin

Stewart Culin (1858–1929) stood at the dawn of a new century and addressed audiences on the evolution of art. Victorians patted themselves on the back for the glory of their artistic achievement, but the strength of design in the art of American Indians and other "savage" groups intrigued them. They asked ethnologists to tell them whether the restrained attitude toward art in Victorian society had a connection to the apparently ritual, grotesque uses of primitive art, and whether the excesses of decoration in Victorian society had links to the apparent simplicity of primitive ornament. Culin agreed with Britisher Alfred C. Haddon, who in 1895 suggested in *Evolution in Art* that "to understand civilised art we must study barbaric art, and to elucidate this savage art must be investigated." Haddon had mined the British colony of New Guinea for his examples, but Culin claimed for distinction the special investigation of American Indians. From his look at this material, and his previous studies of Oriental artifacts, Culin offered that culture is basically a unified whole. Similarities could be found around the globe, he found, and he suggested a natural evolution from lower forms to higher forms.

Although commenting on primitive art as a lower form, Culin recognized its "very essence" of humankind's "life and power." For Culin, his role as ethnologist, as an expert in material culture in a materialistic age, was to act as interpreter of "things made by man," "to make them speak and tell their story." For Culin, the so-called primitive objects possessed the "quality of life to quicken our minds and excite the creative impulse which we designate as art." He thought that as this quality passes with modern society's utilitarian advancement, the museum, and the ethnologist interpreter, had the opportunity to benefit society by providing the best examples of traditional art along with their interpretations to artists, designers, and manufacturers, who would use the primitive designs, or their "quality of life" in their work.

This essay is drawn from two addresses that Culin gave in 1900. The first is "Primitive American Art," which he delivered to the Biological Club on January 8, and which appeared in *University Bulletin* 4 (1900): pp. 191–96; the second is "The Origin of Ornament," which he delivered at the Free Museum of Science and Art (now the University of Pennsylvania Museum) on April 11, and which appeared in the *Bulletin of the Free Museum of Science and Art* 2 (1900): pp. 235–43. He developed his ideas on art at the University of Pennsylvania Museum, but his major exhibits on primitive art, including exhibits of Indian, African, and European peasant art were executed at the Brooklyn Museum, where Culin served as head of the ethnology section from 1903 until his death; see *The Brooklyn Museum Handbook* (Brooklyn: Brooklyn Museum, 1967), pp. 195–280; Craig D. Bates and Brian Bibby, "Collecting among the Chico Maidu: The Stewart Culin Collection at the Brooklyn Museum," *American Indian Art Magazine* 8 (Autumn 1983): pp. 46–53. In addition to Alfred Haddon, Frank Hamilton Cushing, by Culin's own acknowledgment, greatly informed Culin's thinking; see Cushing's essay in the previous chapter. Haddon's *Evolution in Art* has been reprinted (New York: AMS Press, 1979), and provides a sharp contrast to the relativistic argument of Franz Boas in *Primitive Art* (1927; reprint, New York: Dover, 1955); this is brought into perspective by Michael Owen Jones in "The Study of Folk Art Study: Reflections on Images," in *Folklore Today: A Festschrift for Richard M. Dorson,* ed. Linda Dégh, Henry Glassie, Felix J. Oinas (Bloomington: Research Center for Language and Semiotic Studies, Indiana University, 1976), pp. 291–303. For the influence of primitivism on American art and literature, see Robert Goldwater, *Primitivism in Modern Art* (revised edition, New York: Vintage Books/Random House, 1967); Michael Bell, *Primitivism* (London: Methuen, 1972).

*   *   *

In discussing primitive art from the conventional and customary standpoint, it is usual to refer to an early savage stage, in which the artistic instincts were entirely undeveloped; to illustrate by means of rudely chipped stones a period when man was just emerging from fellowship with the higher apes; and then to trace the gradual evolution of the aesthetic sense, as greater technical skill and increasing appreciation of form and color led him at last to the perfection of Greece or the sublimity of Egypt. The assumption is one that invariably passes unchallenged, but in point of fact we have little or no *objective* evidence of such an orderly progress among the American tribes. I am entirely unable (with all the resources of our great museums at my command) to discover satisfactory proofs of any considerable change in the character of the culture or the capacity of the race. Nothing that would justify a classification of paleolithic and neolithic man in America, or enable us to arrange in chronological sequence the remains that lie scattered over every hillside in our land.

Deprived, then, of the philosophic pleasure of assigning dates or reconstructing dynasties, the sane and conscientious student of American antiquities finds recompense in the light afforded by the antiquities themselves; in the new methods of study; and in the new theories of origins that are forced upon him as he traces, step by step, the logical development of our native institutions.

In any general survey of the American race, considering both its prehistoric remains as well as its surviving tribes, one is impressed with the fundamental truth laid down by my late master, the lamented Brinton, that it is practically homogeneous; and that, despite their many divergent languages, the aboriginal inhabitants of this country, past and present, have similar traditions, common modes of thought, and a symbolism practically identical in its expression.[1] We are therefore enabled to understand the people of a remote stone age, more remote than the Pyramids or that mound of Nippur, through the oral explanations of its surviving members.

These facts, the lack of any chronology, and the homogeneous character of the culture, premised, I proceed directly to my theme of primitive art.

Should one characterize the art of the Amerind in a word, it would be as *grotesque*. Man, beast and bird are represented, not always unskillfully, but ever with such a curious disregard of actual form and expression that it would seem some perversity of temper or intellect dominated the race; that the sense of beauty was absent; and that we saw here reflected a character either debased by superstition or unenlightened by any of the nobler sentiments of humanity. An explanation of this fundamental difference between aboriginal art, and art as we cultivate and understand it, involves not only the definition of art itself, but further, an explication of the mental processes of man in the stage which, as a matter of convenience, we call primitive. I shall not directly attempt this difficult task, but instead shall illustrate by actual examples the origin and development of certain typical forms, chiefly referring to the human figure. I must first state, however, that the basis of savage art is not aesthetic, but symbolic;—that the ornamental patterns, often repeated in pleasing designs, are always full of meaning; and even where this is forgotten, they are still employed because of traditional potency; that the color harmonies, subtle and elusive, are governed not by commingled taste and fancy, but by the requirements of an inflexible ritual; and that the sculptured form, though wrought in the semblance of a man, embodies the concept of an elemental power.

It is a common notion that our savage is near akin to a child. This true, his art might indeed have been the outgrowth of rude scribblings; but primitive man—savage man—master individually of all the tribal arts, the personal conservator of all the wisdom and experience of mankind, re-creating the world anew each year by his rites and thus saving it from darkness and oblivion—was childlike only in that egotism which centred the world in himself, and fancied his dwelling the navel of the universe. All nature to him was animated by a life akin to his own. The beasts of the forest were his blood relations; the trees, and even the rocks and stones, were endowed with a personality; nay—even the products of his handicraft became alive and invested with a potentiality of good and ill. The control of these omnipresent forces was supposedly secured by processes of sympathetic magic. Evil influences were averted and protection and fertility insured by dramatic dances, in which the auspicious influences were aided and encouraged, and the bad repelled. A jagged mark on the arrow, simulating the lightning, gave it the force and directness of the celestial bolt. This tooth—the tooth of a mountain lion—bound to the stick with which the arrow was thrown, imparted the tiger's energy to the lethal dart. The form and decoration of the food-bowl contributed to insure its constant replenishment. The art which arose out of such magical practices was naturally symbolic. Thus, for a bear, we have the print of his extended paw. For man himself, not the figure of a man directly, but usually one of two or three highly significant objects, which, first employed in their actual practical forms, were in time more and more conventionalized; and, slowly simulating the figure of the being they stood for, at last assumed the attributes of humanity.

The American Indian generally, at the time of discovery, was a migratory hunter. While, in Mexico and Peru he had built towns and cities, and, here and there, had become a settled agriculturist, planting corn and pumpkins, and even, as in Peru, domesticating the llama; yet, in general, he lived by the chase. He was a warrior, too: his tribal organization a federation of warriors. Both as hunter and warrior his chief offensive weapon was the arrow. This implement we find almost invariably marked to distinguish its ownership. The marked arrow designated the quarry, whether of war or the chase. His arrow, stuck in the prairie, identified the resting place of a fallen chief. In the estufa of the cult society, the arrow of an absent member stood in his place before the altar in the tribal ceremonies. The principal marks of identification were placed upon the shaftment (the part bearing the feather, next the bow); and we discover not only actual arrows, but this marked part alone, used as the symbol of a man. A bundle of these shaftments, each with its peculiar mark, thus came to represent the men of a particular war society, or all the warriors of a tribe or clan. In the tribal games, the contests were not only between the warriors themselves, but were waged with the warriors' weapons. These sticks which I exhibit, conventionalized shaftments of arrows, are the playing cards of one of the tribes of our Northwest coast. Again, among the representations of the gods upon the altars of the cult societies of our Pueblo Indians, are carved slats and wooden billets—both descendants of arrows which they have replaced. It may be interesting to learn the process by which I arrived at this conclusion.

A common—indeed, almost universal—American game is one in which a stick or stone is concealed under one of four differently marked arrow-derived tubes, the opposing side guessing under which it is hidden. In its elementary form the game is played with four marked canes or reeds. In the second form which I exhibit the cane is replaced by wooden tubes, distinguished, like the canes, by bands or ribbons. At the next step the bands disappear, and are succeeded by rude symbols of the gods of the four World Quarters. Finally, we have effigies of the gods themselves, corresponding both in name and form with those upon the tribal altars. These rudely carved billets are not to be considered as the direct attempts to represent the human figure, but rather as slow approximations from the practical arrow.

Everywhere essential to man's first steps along the path to civilization is that other all-important implement, used symbolically for a man, the stone axe. Like the arrow-head, the stone axe is found strewn over the length and breadth of the earth. It is to a peculiarly beautiful and luminous illustration of its use as the emblem of man's power I desire to direct your attention. There are two principal forms of the stone axe, one with a groove for hafting, practically confined to North America; the other, smooth and often highly polished, common to almost the entire world. These polished axes (or celts, as they are designated) are from a prehistoric cemetery at Nicoya, in Costa Rica. With them were found great treasures of jade and greenstone ornaments, gold images and other personal adornments. A majority of these carved stones are slices of pebbles, cut to simulate the practical axes, yet intended, as we know from analogy, as the ceremonial badge of the warrior. These imitation axes have, in some instances, carved upon them the marks of hafting cords, thus identifying them more closely with, and giving them substance and principle of, the real axe they stood for. Examining these simulated cord marks we perceive that, heightened and modified, they are used to convert the axe into the image of a man, with his hands folded across his chest. In some merely suggested, in others more pronounced, we trace this axe-figure until it reaches the stage of an image with head-dress, and legs cleft apart. Plated with gold, it yields this small image, which owes it peculiarities to its ancestor the axe; nor is this ancestry ever lost sight of. And thus to the end of the series we find a grotesque and unnatural element, which can only be explained by careful comparative analysis. Our axe-man (or axe-god) gives us a clue to the origin and meaning of some of the larger images. This figure (a large greenstone image from Mexico) is none other, and the great monolithic statues of Tiahuanaco, in Bolivia—remains that take their place with the walls of Balbeck and the Pyramids of Egypt—are doubtless also of similar derivation.

From man, the warrior, let us turn for a moment to woman, the mother and producer. This series of pottery vessels from the mounds of Missouri (modeled originally in imitation of the gourd) are seen to take on the face and figure of a pregnant woman, with whom the natural gourd is considered analogous.

Generally speaking, we find no attempt in America at anything like portraiture. From the identity of the exploits of the tribal heroes in the myths we conclude that these personages must be regarded, not as individuals, but rather as the personification of cosmical phenomena. In the same way the images and pictures should be considered, not as likenesses, but as embodying the attributes of these legendary heroes.

Very slight observation impresses one with the fact that the representations of animals in American art are more faithful and truer to nature than those of human beings. While man is depicted with animal head and limbs, or rather, while the lower creatures are frequently given human bodies and assimilated in forms to man, we also find the dominant beasts and birds copied directly from nature with amazing truth and fidelity. Their magical and vital power was something innate; an essence which man himself sought to borrow when he assumed their form in his masked dances, and thereby identified himself with the divine wisdom and strength supposed to reside in and emanate from these strange and mysterious creatures,—higher than man, midway between him and the gods, who were formed like them. But the animals are not always drawn from nature. We find them conventionalized past recognition save for beak or snout, teeth, claws, scales or tail; or again, so split and divided and wrought around and over some implement, utensil or weapon, to which it is desired to impart their personality, that only at the present moment, through the studies of Holmes, Cushing and Boas, have we come to recognize the meaning of what have hitherto been looked upon as the vagaries of an uninformed and unsystematized imagination.

And here I must leave the subject of form in American art. Color—equally strange in its application, following rules based upon the same system of reasoning, always significant and magical—I must also pass over, to say a few words in conclusion upon the value of our American studies in throwing light upon the problems of old world culture, as aids in the solution of the great riddle of humanity.

Man's beginnings were infinitely complex. His art is the product not only of the environment with which economists deal, but also of the interactions of that environment, and man's intellectual nature. The mental processes of man in America are precisely the same as those of man in Europe; and what we find existing to-day in America underlies all the higher civilization of the other continents.

When we examine the products of man's handicrafts, as represented both by his prehistoric remains, as well as by the rudest effort of the existing savage, we everywhere find evidences of an aesthetic sense, of an effort, not only at mere utility, but at decoration and ornament, analogous to that which is universal among cultivated people at the present day.

Considering our immediate surroundings, it is amazing how necessary and matter-of-course we have come to regard the use of ornament as applied to our houses, dress, implements and utensils. We flatter ourselves that it represents our keen appreciation of art, and look with undisguised superiority upon the people of ruder ages and less favored climes.

Enter one of our great department stores, and examine the fabrications of cotton and silk, of glass and metal, wood and lacquer; mere utility is quite insufficient to justify the profusion of form and color with which we are surrounded. Visit any of our art schools; the majority of the students are preparing themselves, not as disciples of Velasquez and Raphael, but to make designs for carpets or knife-handles. The mechanical processes of reproduction have of late enormously increased these tendencies. The general trend of our education is to encourage and foster what is regarded as the "art" instinct, and we have been led to view development of the so-called decorative arts as concomitant with the highest culture.

In studying the history of ornament, our task is simplified if we confine ourselves to the art of savage races. Our modern designs, while they chiefly repeat the past, are so mixed and conventionalized that it is often difficult to analyze them satisfactorily, or trace them to their ultimate origin. Students are ordinarily referred to Greece and Rome or the high cultures of Egypt, Persia and Assyria. While it is true that these countries stand as the ancestral sources of most of our arts, they are still far removed from the beginning. We must, indeed, leave the direct historic line and turn aside to the so-called sterile and unproductive cultures, if we are to correctly understand the beginnings of man, and unravel the tangled web of modern civilization.

In former lectures, here and elsewhere, I have pointed out that man's amusements were the outcome, not of some innate festal instinct or desire for play—but of religious and divinatory ceremonials. These ceremonies, repeated often at the same season of the year, after their meaning has been lost, or their necessity past, through man's better understanding of natural phenomena, have become the play of our children, the diversions of our youths and even, indeed, the fierce and irrepressible contests of the gaming table. It is my purpose, to-day, to prove an analogous derivation of art in general, and specifically of the decorative arts. To show that ornament and adornment arose, not from some deeply implanted love of beauty in the abstract, or were evolved from small beginnings, as for example, paint and feathers as means of sexual attraction; but instead, are the products of religious sentiment, of magic and superstition; of the reasoning, which led man to attempt through magic to control or influence the forces of nature.

It is safe to assume that the beginnings of ornament are to be found in personal decoration. We have been taught to take for granted that the main incentive here was the desire to please—the effort, both in man and woman, to find favor in each other's eyes; to apply the principles of selection, as illustrated in the plumage of birds, and regard the bright colors and grotesque patterns of aboriginal finery as removed only in point of taste and materials, from the choicest products of Paris and Vienna. It is true that the element of sexual attraction plays no small part in the origin of personal adornment, but the aesthetic was always secondary to the magical. Beauty or attractiveness was heightened not by the development of the natural graces, but by amulets and charms, to which indeed our very word "charm" refers.

A most interesting example of pregnant survival—connecting the old and traditional stage of personal ornament with that of the present day—is to be found in Egypt, in the jewelry worn by women. We are indebted to Lane, the learned author of "The Manners and Customs of the Modern Egyptians," for not only the names of the various jewels, but an explanation of their talismanic and magical significance. We learn, too, from the same source, of the survival of the custom of blackening the eyelids with antimony or kohl. The little jars for kohl, with other toilet appliances of an Egyptian belle of 4,000 years ago, are to be seen in the superb collection of Egyptian antiquities in this very museum. Beauty—aesthetic beauty was not the origin of this custom, for we know it sprang from an old religious rite—an opening of the eyes—that was practiced alike upon the mummies of Egypt, the carved and painted images of the Chinese pantheon and the grotesque idols of our Southwestern Indians. Face painting, and there is no form of personal decoration more widely distributed, was invariably ceremonial. In the effort man made to identify himself with his god, he endeavored to assume his visage; to mark himself as consecrated to the divinity, as set apart from other men, sealed with the emblem and signature of his protecting genius, or to cover his person with divinely revealed symbols that would render him safe against the attack both of mortal and spiritual foes. Tattooing follows painting, making the paint permanent, even after death and the accidents of time. Among the remains from that great sepulchre at Pachacamac, explored for us by Dr. Max Uhle, are the withered arms of old Peruvians, who died, ages it may be, before Columbus saw our shores, still bearing the indelible stains of their spiritual consecration to some divinity whose name is now entirely forgotten. A world of interest lies in the study both of the face and body painting and the tattoo designs. Often, as is the case with those collected by Mrs. Talcott Williams, in Morocco, and now exhibited in our collection, they have become so far conventionalized as to defy interpretation—retained merely as ornament, and yet perpetuated by an instinct that is at once the puzzle of scholars, and the prime factor in the continued existence of all our institutions. Other physical deformations belong to the same category. The Floridian Indians at the time of the discovery, in common with some of the existing tribes of Brazil, weighted their ears with pendants, so that they hung down over their shoulders. Dr. Furness found the same custom in Borneo, and again among the marks of sainthood in the images of Buddha are these pendulous ears enabling us to connect the custom with a religious and mythic ideal. The treatment of the hair, whether cut short, worn in a queue, or wrought—as do the maidens in Zuñi in symbolic designs, has depended upon the same underlying mythic notions, which, for more than mere material circumstances, have controlled man's actions and destiny.

Turning from the physical man to his costume,—apart from mere bodily protection, while the material depends upon his life,—of skins, if a hunter,—of wool, if a herdsman,—of cotton or silk, if an agriculturist, or of all combined, if a merchant and engaged in commerce,—all else seems determined by considerations which are neither practical nor aesthetic. An artist who visits this museum to study and admire the various products of aboriginal industry which are displayed here, frequently remarks to me that man pleases most when he is least conscious of his effort to please. He perceives that the charm and beauty of these fabrics and carvings, is not the result of any direct study or appeal to the senses on the part of their makers, and recognizes the presence of an instinct which is almost entirely lacking among professional designers at the present day. We have only to compare an Oriental carpet—no matter how cheap and relatively worthless—with the most ambitious product of our own looms. Let us turn to some of the pictures of our Indians, whose harmonious costumes and picturesque attitudes have been so successfully reproduced on canvas. Almost too late our artists have awakened to a knowledge of the wealth of material—soon to perish—ready to their hand,—on the narrowing reservations of the West. We find repeated the same marvelous color, the same bizarre combinations, the something we have long known and appreciated in the art of the East. But more, we find means to trace the secret of this art to its source, to learn its charm, to unravel its meaning from the very beginning—and not merely of the natural forms upon which it is based, but the reasons underlying their selection and employment. Contact with civilization has wrought many changes in this aboriginal art; the quill work has given place to beads, the gorgets of engraved shell to bosses of metal, and the rare plumage of semi-tropical birds to the dyed feathers of the hawk and chicken. But the spirit remains, nor will it be lost until the art itself unhappily becomes extinct. Let us consider one of the characteristic designs that we see repeated, with many agreeable permutations of color throughout the continent; the disks, white, yellow, blue, red, variegated, of which no more characteristic and pleasing example can be found than upon this beaded baldrick from the Sioux. These disks are, or were, protective amulets, analogous to the engraved shell gorgets now replaced by metal, and derived, I am well assured, from the ceremonial feather shields of Mexico and the south, shields of the all-protecting war gods of the four world-quarters, whose colors they retain through all their changes.

Apart from those inherent in the material, the colors of our aboriginal raiment are ordained by traditions amounting to laws, as permanent and inviolable as those which control the applied designs. The woven stuffs, wrought to the low singing of some magic song, are in themselves enchanted, and designed, not for mere pleasing show, but as spells against witchcraft and the powers of evil.

Turning our attention for a moment to some of the characteristic adjuncts of Indian costume, in the light of recent investigation we perceive that the plume of hawk or eagle feathers in the hair is intended, not as decoration, but to give the warrior the swiftness and lofty vision of the bird that originally bore them. So too, the necklace of bear claws or the mandibles of birds, the horns worn upon the head—all designed as charms of protection or offence. The weapons, too, are ornamented for other than aesthetic reasons. Man conquers, not by his own might, but with the aid of the divinity. This parang from Borneo is overladen with charms. Even the Japanese sword which we prize as a treasure of the highest art is in every part magical, from the Sanskrit inscription carved upon its blade, to the metal ornaments (fetishes) bound upon its haft. For what practical purpose did the smith bathe and fast, and protect his forge with sacred emblems? The sword so wrought was one that might not be sheathed until it had drawn blood.

One may see in the collection of pottery from the ancient cliff-dwellers of Mancos Cañon, in our American Hall, many illustrations of the use of symbolic design applied to even the common domestic pottery of an aboriginal people. As interpreted by Mr. Cushing, we perceive that the frets and spirals, so like the patterns on the Greek vases, refer to the clouds, the lightning and the rain, to the natural phenomena most vital and potential to the continuance of existence in an arid and desert land. Nor was architecture exempt from the influences which dominated personal and ceremonial adornment, nor even the plan of the camp, the citadel, nor as in Peru, the city itself.[2]

In a recent essay, Mr. W. J. Stillman has furnished us with a definition of the function of art, which covers and describes the unconscious art of the savage more completely, it may be, than the art of our own time.[3] "The primary function of art," he says, "is that of giving form to the ideals and emotions of mankind." He quotes, with approbation, Herbert Spencer's dictum, "ornament was before dress," and declares that the artistic impulse precedes all utilities. From another point of view, Mr. Stillman has reached the same conclusions as the eminent sociologist, conclusions which agree with those formed through comparative retrospective study. Let me quote a few lines from his charmingly written essay:

> It is a common illusion, that the first art-impulse derives, or ever did derive, from the desire to represent nature; and ingenious critics have professed to follow the evolution of art from crude representations of familiar objects. No doubt some of the first delineations we possess have been those of familiar objects with which the delineator had a certain sympathy, but the scientific tendency, as well as the artistic, precedes all our data regarding mental activity so long that we are unable to form sound conclusions as to their relative origins.

Yet it is apparent that the critic was unaided by the information comparative study affords, as to the fundamental instincts upon which art is based. For he continues, "We have sufficient evidence to show that art had its primitive *raison d'être* in the *love of decoration;* and its first work, in every case in which we are able to study it, is not a representation of natural objects, but in decorative arrangements of line and color, geometrical in the most naïve cases, and later with unsymmetrical but rhythmical arrangements.

Let us now consider the question of art and ornament from yet another side, and turning to a recent book by that industrious and intelligent English scholar, Professor A. C. Haddon,[4] review for a moment some of the results of applying the methods of the naturalist and biologist to the study of the arts of design. Mr. Haddon prefaces his classification of the incentives to artistic effort by the remark that the craving for decorative art having been common to mankind for many thousand years, it would be a very difficult task to determine its actual origin. The needs which have constrained man to art he groups under four heads: Art, Information, Wealth and Religion. Notwithstanding the fact that he places aesthetics, the study or practice of art for art's sake, for the sensuous pleasure of form, line and color, first on his list, he is constrained to admit that religion, the need of man to put himself into sympathetic relation with unseen powers has gathered unto it the foregoing secular triad. In his chapter on the application of biological deductions to the arts of design we find some interesting conclusions: that there is no spontaneous generation of design in savage art; that savages do not deliberately invent patterns, and that a design, no matter how simple, once started, is subject to vicissitudes analogous to those which beset the existence of any organism. One is impressed through Mr. Haddon's admirable work that mere objective comparison is in itself insufficient. The fundamental evolution we must consider is that of an underlying idea, which evolution, however, is intimately bound up with the symbol used for its expression. Referring to the variations of a design, he says: "While there is a certain amount of conscious selection, the variation as a whole of any design is an entirely unguided operation." This statement should be qualified with the information that variations are not necessarily accidental, and that the dominant idea, the underlying symbolism, often survives as a controlling and determining force long after it has ceased to be a conscious factor in mental processes. . . .

We have become so habituated to ornament, as to regard it as a matter of course in our existence. It is so old, so universal, that we speak of love of it, with dress and decoration as among the fundamental passions of humanity. A more correct appreciation of its origin and significance imparts a new interest to our immediate surroundings, and justifies the claims of our science, that, while it finds its material chiefly among savage tribes and in remote ages, the principles it formulates may be equally applied to the explanation of the phenomena of our everyday lives.

Notes

1. [Culin is here referring to Daniel Garrison Brinton (1837–99). Culin's reference to a "general survey of the American race" probably is Brinton's *The American Race: A Linguistic Classification and Ethnographic Description of the Native Tribes of North and South America* (New York: N. D. C. Hodges, 1891). Culin's argument is also informed by Brinton's "The Aims of Anthropology," *Proceedings of the American Association for the Advancement of Science* 44 (1895): pp. 1–17; *Religions of Primitive Peoples* (New York: G. P. Putnam's Sons, 1897). Culin honored his "late master" by organizing a memorial meeting for Brinton and publishing the proceedings and a bibliography of Brinton as *Brinton Memorial Meeting: Report of the Memorial Meeting Held January Sixteenth, Nineteen Hundred under the Auspices of the American Philosophical Society by Twenty-Six Learned Societies in Honor of the Late Daniel Garrison Brinton, M.D.* (Philadelphia: American Philosophical Society, 1900). —*Ed.*]

2. [Culin is referring to Frank Hamilton Cushing (1857–1900), who, Culin said, is credited with "the fundamental ideas" contained in his essay. Culin's reference to Cushing's work on pottery is probably "A Study of Pueblo Pottery as Illustrative of Zuñi Cultural Growth," *Fourth Annual Report of the Bureau of American Ethnology, 1882–1883* (Washington, D.C.: Government Printing Office, 1886). Culin's reference to Cushing's work on architecture is probably the "Manual Concepts" essay reprinted in this volume. —*Ed.*]

3. "Art as a Means of Expression," *International Monthly,* vol. 1, no. 2.

4. *Evolution in Art* (London, 1895), p. 4.

9

Folk Decoration of Southern Black Graves

H. Carrington Bolton
Ernest Ingersoll

For both H. Carrington Bolton (1843–1903) and Ernest Ingersoll (1852–1946), as for many Victorian writers, folklife study was a part-time pursuit. Both men were leading scientists, Bolton a chemist and Ingersoll a naturalist. Both men lived in New York City and were active in the New York branch of the American Folklore Society. Both viewed folk customs as interesting specimens shedding light on antiquity and both regarded the survival of these customs as strangely out of step with the advancement of a rational society. Traveling widely, both men took notes on folk customs across the country and contributed short descriptions to popular magazines and scientific journals.

Two such notes that attracted much attention related the decorations of black graves in the South. The notes aroused interest because during the nineteenth century, the culture of blacks was a subject open to much popular, and political, speculation. The incredibly well-received Uncle Remus books by Joel Chandler Harris, for example, offered a distinctive black brand of folktale that delighted American readers from 1880 to the beginning of the twentieth century, and they also stirred questions about the sources—and under the surface, the independence—of black culture. How much, readers wanted to know, did the stories, indeed the culture, owe to the African experience? And what was the relation of the race to the American experience? While a writer in *Lippincott's* declared in 1877 that "the folk-lore of Africo-Americans, as appearing in our Southern States, is a medley of fables, songs, sayings, incantations, charms and superstitious traditions brought from various tribes along the West African coast . . . ," another in *Atlantic Monthly* reported in 1891 that "the negroes on our Southern plantations have apparently adopted with marvelous rapidity the customs, language, and religion of the race that brought them into slavery a mere century ago." It is still a debated question.

The notes by Bolton and Ingersoll contribute to the dialogue of their day by offering observations on the practice of decorating graves with seashells and broken crockery—a practice, by the way, that continues to the present. In their notes can be read different concerns: Bolton marvels at the consistency between African and

American styles of decoration while Ingersoll uses the custom as an example of the "savage" and "childlike" state of black culture. Together, they also comment on the considerable amount of philosophizing on the ritual nature of death during the nineteenth century. Emerging from Puritan attitudes in the eighteenth century, Americans, as historian Karen Halttunen has pointed out, gradually shifted their focus from the "objective, physical fact of death toward the subjective response to death by those who mourned. . . . Mourning, the natural human response to the greatest human affliction, was held sacred by sentimentalists as the purest, the most transparent, and thus the most genteel of all sentiments." Victorians had devised elaborate mourning rituals, including the use of mourning stationery, pins, and pictures. Worrying about enhancing the deepness, the sentimentality, of feelings in their mourning rituals, Victorians read with great interest the emotional elements of "primitive" funerary rites. Indeed, Bolton's wife Henrietta contributed such a note in 1894 on "Curious Relics of English Funerals" to the *Journal of American Folklore*. Lillian Eichler, an etiquette manual writer in the early twentieth century, explained the appropriateness of modern-day funerary rituals by pointing to "primitive customs." Devoting, as many of the earlier guides did, an entire chapter to "funeral customs," Eichler commented that

> it was found necessary in tracing back to their source the manners and customs of man, to study the folklore and mythology of all countries, of all peoples. And you shall see in the pages that follow how both these factors—folklore and mythology—influence in a thousand little ways the things we do and say to-day. They are like mighty links, forged in the furnace of time, binding even us of the twentieth century to a chain of tradition that reaches far back into antiquity.

"Our fancy lingers for a moment with these people," she opined, and then underscored the tradition of decorating graves with flowers and wreaths, because it is "an old custom, handed down to us through many generations."

Because folklorists continue to encounter this practice, the notes by Bolton and Ingersoll still resurface. For an exhibit in 1978 of Afro-American decorative art at the Cleveland Museum of Art, John Michael Vlach reconsidered the black graveyard practice they found, and hypothesized that the decoration, working on an African cultural aesthetic, symbolically marked a transition to a different state of being. As he explained,

> Afro-American graves may thus be read as a kind of cosmogram: the world of the living above; the dividing line of shells; the realm of the spirits, which is not only under ground but also under water. The tradition for shell ornamentation is so strong that even in areas far from the ocean, like Kentucky, shells are sought for decorative purposes. Sometimes shells and water containers are combined into one symbol of transition. In Conway, South Carolina, I encountered a grave with a glass pitcher on it. The bottom of the pitcher had been knocked out, and the vessel had been set down over a conch shell. The layering of emblems is but another instance of an African sculptural aesthetic.

Of the persistence of the practice, Vlach points to areas where blacks have retained a certain amount of isolation, but he adds that "values and behaviors associated with death are so strongly felt that they manage to survive the pressures of social crises and perhaps serve as a source of ethnic identity and strength. The realm of the dead does truly have an impact on the living."

Bolton's note appears first; it is reprinted from "Decoration of Graves of Negroes in South Carolina," *Journal of American Folklore* 4 (1891): p. 214. Ingersoll's note comes from "Decoration of Negro Graves," *Journal of American Folklore* 5 (1892): pp. 68–69. They are typical of notes and queries on folklore that filled periodical reading during the Gilded Age. Bolton, for instance, also contributed notes on "Peculiar Methods of Counting in the Crockery Trade," "All-Fool's Day in Italy," and "Hop-Scotch Diagrams." His major folklore work was *The Counting-Out Rhymes of Children: Their Antiquity, Origin, and Wide Distribution* (1888; reprint, Detroit: Singing Tree Press, 1969); for biographical background on Bolton, see Danielle M. Roemer, "Henry Carrington Bolton: American Chemist and Folklorist," *Kentucky Folklore Record* 28 (1982): pp. 61–70. For readings of nineteenth-century essays on black folklore, see Bruce Jackson, *The Negro and His Folklore in Nineteenth-Century Periodicals* (Austin: University of Texas Press, 1967), which provided the quotes I used here ("Folklore of the Southern Negroes," by William Owens, *Lippincott's,* p. 145, and "Certain Beliefs and Superstitions of the Negro," *Atlantic Monthly,* p. 257); Victorian racial attitudes are covered in Christine Bolt, *Victorian Attitudes to Race* (London: Routledge & Kegan Paul, 1971). For an example of the debate on African sources for black folklore, see Daniel Crowley, ed., *African Folklore in the New World* (Austin: University of Texas Press, 1977), and for a discussion of African antecedents and meanings of southern black graveyard decorations (from which my quotes are taken), see John Michael Vlach, *The Afro-American Tradition in Decorative Arts* (Cleveland: Cleveland Museum of Art, 1978), pp. 139–47. For works on Victorian attitudes toward death and ritual (which provided the quotes I used), see Karen Halttunen, *Confidence Men and Painted Women: A Study of Middle-Class Culture in America, 1830–1870* (New Haven: Yale University Press, 1982), pp. 124–52; Lillian Eichler, *The Customs of Mankind: With Notes on Modern Etiquette and the Newest Trend in Entertainment* (Garden City, New York: Nelson Doubleday, 1924), pp. 559–97.

*   *   *

During a recent sojourn in Columbia, S.C., my attention was directed to the cemetery for the poorer negroes. It is situated on the edge of town, overlooking the Congaree; the numerous graves are decorated with a variety of objects, sometimes arranged with careful symmetry, but more often placed around the margins without regard to order. These objects include oyster-shells, white pebbles, fragments of crockery of every description, glass bottles, and nondescript bric-a-brac of a cheap sort,— all more or less broken and useless. The large number of medicine bottles on some graves has suggested that the bottles once held the medicines that killed the patients.

Inquiry of residents as to the origin and significance of this custom elicited no satisfactory explanation, and I was in doubt until the April number of the "Century" reached me. In Mr. E. J. Glave's article, "Fetishism in Congo Land," there is an engraving of the grave of a Congo chieftain that would do very well for the picture of one in the Potters' Field, Columbia, S.C. [fig. 9-1]. The author writes of this grave: "The natives mark the final resting-places of their friends by ornamenting their graves with crockery, empty bottles, old cooking-pots, etc., all of which articles are rendered useless by being cracked, or perforated with holes. Were this precaution not taken, the grotesque decorations would be stolen."[1]

The negroes of South Carolina are simply following the customs of their savage ancestors, and are unwittingly perpetuating the fetishism so deeply impressed. Some of the negroes on the coast islands still preserve an imperfect knowledge of the native dialects of their forefathers, and in decorating the graves of the departed they afford an illustration of the long survival of customs the meaning of which has been quite forgotten by those practising them.

The note by Dr. H. Carrington Bolton recalls to my mind with interest my own observation ten years ago in the Negro cemetery at Columbia, S.C., to which he refers. I made the matter then the subject of remark in a letter to the New York "Evening Post" (February 24, 1881). The paragraphs which apply are those following, and they give more in detail what Dr. Bolton has made note of, showing that the custom is not yet obsolete:—

I saw at Columbia, S.C., a practice in vogue among the blacks which exists nowhere else so far as I can learn, and is savage or childlike in its simplicity of idea. When a negro dies, some article or utensil, or more than one, is thrown upon his grave; moreover it is broken. If you go through a dilapidated weed-grown graveyard which straggles in and out of the hollows on a side hill covering the high bluffs along the river, you will see some very strange examples of this mortuary custom. Nearly every grave has bordering or thrown upon it a few bleached sea-shells of a dozen different kinds, such as are found along the south Atlantic coast. Mingled with these is a most curious collection of broken crockery and glassware. On the large graves are laid broken pitchers, soap-dishes, lamp chimneys, tureens, coffee-cups, sirup jugs, all sorts of ornamental vases, cigar boxes, gun-locks, tomato cans, teapots, flower-pots, bits of stucco, plaster images, pieces of carved stone-work from one of the public buildings destroyed during the war, glass lamps and tumblers in great number, and forty other kitchen articles. Chief of all these, however, are large water pitchers; very few graves lack them. The children's graves were really

Figure 9-1. Congo Chieftain's Grave
(From E. J. Glave, "Fetishism in Congo Land," Century [1891])

pathetic. There you could see doll's heads, little china wash-bowls and pitchers, toy images of animals, china vases, and pewter dishes, indeed everything of that sort that would interest a child.

The negroes themselves hardly know how to account for this custom. They say it is an "old fashion." In the case of the children, and partly in respect to adults, the articles thrown upon the grave are those of which the deceased person was especially fond—the baby's playthings for example. As for the shells, stone-work, stucco and that sort of thing, they are purely ornamental, as perhaps is all the rest. What the significance of so many cracked pitchers and jugs may be I do not know. They are found upon graves of all ages. Surely the negro of Columbia does not regard this particular form of earthenware with special admiration or affection. Can it have any allusion to the proverb that the pitcher that goes often to the well shall at last be broken? or better, be in memory of the prophet's line, "and the golden bowl shall be broken"?

Note

1. [Bolton is referring to E. J. Glave, "Fetishism in Congo Land," *Century* 41 (1891): pp. 825–36. —*Ed.*]

10

Primitive Inventions

George Wharton James

George Wharton James (1858–1923), an English immigrant who came to the United States in 1881, was a renowned missionary, author, and editor. For most of his life, he traveled across the Southwest taking notes on the natural wonders and the Indians who lived among them. He believed, as he wrote in *What the White Race May Learn from the Indian* (1908), that the traditional life of the Indians provided therapeutic lessons for pressured Victorians caught in the vise of modern industrial civilization. Many of his books invited Victorians to come to the Southwest for leisure travel. There, amidst primitive conditions, he insisted, they would get invigorated.

Before James's career was over, he had published forty-two books and edited four magazines. He was especially drawn to writing about Indian crafts, such as the making of baskets and blankets. In preparing these works, he was heavily influenced by Otis Mason (see chapters 1 and 12), who argued that Indian crafts could be placed on the bottom rungs of an evolutionary ladder leading up to modern invention. The social uses of crafts among the Indians, Mason informed James, were clues to cultural patterns that later emerged, such as differing work-related roles of men and women.

James admired the artistry, the sincerity, of the Indians, and he thought that their use of handwork could provide inspiration for manufacturers. With this attitude, he found himself aligned with elements of the American Arts and Crafts movement during the late nineteenth century. One of its leaders, Gustav Stickley, founded a magazine called *The Craftsman* (lasting from 1901 to 1916), in which he declared that "the introduction of machinery with its train of attendant evils has so complicated and befuddled our standards of living that we have less and less time for enjoyment and for growth, and nervous prostration is the disease of the age." Although Stickley admitted that "the age of handicraft is gone beyond recall, . . . the value of handicrafts for the numberless thousands of men and women who are leading ill-balanced, abnormal lives" was immeasurable. So, Stickley sought out information on peoples and places where the age of handicraft still persisted. James's accounts of Indian crafts and Southwest folklife were often featured in the magazine, and in 1904 James became associate editor.

Between Mason and Stickley, James in this essay from the *Craftsman* walks a fine line, and can't help but express ambivalence. It is an ambivalence between the moral force of primitive handicraft and the commercial efficiency of industry that both Mason and Stickley eventually had to admit to as well. Thus James would state that an Indian woman "made better, sweeter and more agreeable soap than comes from the French or English perfumer of reputation," yet "as we use the delicately scented Lubin's or Pears's soap, we are not liable to be grateful to the greasy little primitive woman of long centuries ago."

This essay is reprinted from "Primitive Inventions," *The Craftsman* 5 (1903): pp. 125–37. One can also look at his book-length studies of crafts: *Indian Basketry* (1909; reprint, New York: Dover, 1972) and *Indian Blankets and Their Makers* (1914; reprint, New York: Dover, 1974). An example of his travel-oriented literature is *Arizona: The Wonderland* (Boston: Page, 1917) and *New Mexico: The Land of the Delight Makers* (Boston: Page, 1920). For a discussion of the ambivalence inherent in the Arts and Crafts movement, see T. J. Jackson Lears, *No Place of Grace: Antimodernism and the Transformation of American Culture, 1880–1920* (New York: Pantheon, 1981), pp. 59–96; Edward Lucie-Smith, *The Story of Craft: The Craftsman's Role in Society* (Ithaca, New York: Cornell University Press, 1981), pp. 221–32. The quote from Stickley comes from an interesting essay, "The Use and Abuse of Machinery, and Its Relation to the Arts and Crafts," *Craftsman* 11 (1906): p. 205. See also Gustav Stickley, "The Craftsman Movement: Its Origin and Growth," *Craftsman* 21 (1913): pp. 17–26; Mary Ann Smith, *Gustav Stickley, The Craftsman* (Syracuse: Syracuse University Press, 1983).

*   *   *

When does the age of invention begin? Could we but look back into the far away dim ages of the past and watch the ascent of man from barbarism to civilization, how fascinating the occupation would be! Especially would our keenest interest be aroused at those epoch-making periods in which some small but important discovery was on the verge of being made; when humanity was stumbling toward some great fact that, once seized, was to revolutionize future methods. Who would not delight in such occupation, were he able to take with him into those dark days the light of present day knowledge?

How did men invent fire? When, where and how did they first make any kind of clothing or house? Under what circumstances did they fashion the first weapon? When consciously grind corn? Weave baskets? Make pottery? And the thousand and one other things that the little bronze women and men have handed down to us?

I can conceive of few things as interesting as these in all human progress. How one's heart would beat in high expectation, knowing what was to come, when the naked aborigine first began to shape a bow and arrow, a throwing stick, a war club, a battle-axe! How many attempts there were before success crowned the first efforts; or, alas! how often the thing had to be given up until some future time, perhaps centuries later! How the primitive inventor, prompted by some feeling, he knew not what, working solely for his own interest and profit, without thought of financial reward, or the higher incitement of doing good to his fellows, blindly groped along, confident that he could succeed where success had never yet beckoned; assured that he could accomplish, where none as yet had accomplished!

In the arts of hunting and war man has always been the inventor—those were his prerogatives. In the arts of peace, the domestic arts, woman was the pioneer; she was in her peculiar province. It is a tendency of our latter-day civilization that man claims chieftainship in the arts of peace; but in reality he is there an intruder, an usurper. Woman was the originator, the pioneer, the inventor. Man is the reaper, the enjoyer, and, sad to say, often the claimant and the boaster, forgetful that he inherited what he has and knows from his quieter and less arrogant female ancestor.

During the last few years a great wave of righteous sentiment has been aroused in favor of the North American Indian. As never before in our history, we are seeking to do justice to the peoples we have dispossessed. And not merely in the lower forms of justice—an honesty in treating with them about their lands—but in the higher forms, such as the recognition of what portion of our advancement we owe to their hitherto almost unrecognized struggle and labors.

We pride ourselves upon our advanced civilization, and in some things truthfully, if not wisely. But how many of us have ever considered the questions: To what do we owe our high position among the civilizations of the world? Where did our civilization come from? Who first groped the way out of primitive ignorance, and made our present methods possible? Someone had to begin. The trackless country is not built over with cities all at once. First, the explorer must go over it; then follow the pioneer and colonizer; finally, when everything is known to be reasonably safe, the multitudes pour in. So it is in the march of the world's civilization. There have been explorers to blaze the trails, and pioneers to suggest possibilities, and, in our race struggles, the little brown man and woman whom we know as North American Indians have played a noteworthy part. It is high time, therefore, that we recognize this and express our gratitude for what they have done.

We too often think of our primitive tribes as dull, stolid, unthinking, unimaginative. Nothing can be farther from the facts. They are quick-witted, observant, thinking, imaginative, poetic. They set the ball of progress rolling; indeed, they first made the ball, then started it and indicated its general direction.

Given a Franklin, a Joseph Henry, and a Morse, the work of Edison,

Gray, Bell, Marconi and Pupin is possible. But where would the second group have begun if the first had never been? One mind may influence millions. Stephenson and Fulton changed the history of the world; yet they were only men, not gods: men whose brains weighed but an infinitesimal fraction more than those of other men.

It is to the Indian that we owe the beginnings of the things we have carried to a greater or less degree of perfection. They were the original inventors, the suggestors, the "imaginators" (if I may coin an expression). We, the highly cultured and civilized, are the followers; they the leaders. We reap the rewards in the fields they grubbed, plowed, harrowed and sowed. A second crop is easy when the first hard work of clearing is done. So, while we complacently boast of the crops we now reap, let us not forget the day when our fields were wild swamps, rugged mountain slopes, or densely covered forest-growths. And in remembering, let us give due thanks to the long-ago aboriginal toiler, who, unconsciously working to improve his own condition, unconsciously worked to improve ours also.

This upward impulse is one of the most remarkable facts of all life. "Onward, ever onward! Upward, ever upward!" the hidden impulse urges, and the races have been compelled to obey. Necessity may have been the spur. That matters not. Something kept urging, and we are what we are to-day because of it, and because the little bronze man and woman obeyed imperative commands from some high and unknown power.

It must have been in the early days of the race that a vehicle for carrying was first discovered. The bird's nest, the tangled vines, the spider's web,—who knows?—may have suggested to the undeveloped mind of the early woman of the race the first net or basket, and aroused in her the desire to construct something that should enable her to carry many small things together. The desire awakened, she was forced to carry it out. How? What material could she use? What shape follow? At the very outset she was, by necessity, an adapter, an inventor. So she set to work, trying a variety of materials, experimenting again and again, until she found what she judged to be the best. And now we have learned that those native materials which she judged "best" for constructive purposes, modern science has accepted as having no superiors. Rapidly looking over the field of the Indian basket-maker of to-day, we find that she has tested every available material. She has covered the ground most thoroughly. The splint of willow, cedarbark, spruce-root, yucca-fiber, ash, hickory, slough-root, tule-root, cornhusk, squaw-grass, maiden-hair fern stem, redbud, and a thousand and one other vegetable growths cause the student to wonder at the wide reach of the Amerind's knowledge of materials. There is nothing that she has left untested. Every possible article has been tried and proven.

Having obtained the best possible material, the primitive woman proceeded to the invention of forms. Here Nature was her teacher. The primitive art-instinct is to imitate. The eyes fall upon some object that is pleasing. The object arouses a desire to copy it. True art inspiration can be best obtained in Nature. All the great masters of our later times have returned to the great source of life. Cloister-fed fancies may have pleased cloister-trained minds, but the great world has never been moved by anything but that which has been inspired by Nature. It is "one touch of Nature that makes the whole world kin." Our harmful divergencies lie in being artificial. The Amerind, fortunately, had no art schools; no teachers, with theories and systems deflecting the mind from undefiled sources of inspiration; no books confusing by their attempted explanations. No! she had nothing but pure, sweet, rugged, tempest-tossed, sun-kissed Nature. Nature in all her moods. Mother Nature; Father Nature; sunshine and storm; everlasting hills and earthquakes; waving grass-fields and tornadoes; flowing streams and tidal waves; towering trees and modest flowers. Here was her school of art and design; here were her models. She saw the spider's web, and she constructed the "reda" or net. She saw a gourd, and proceeded to make a water bottle shaped like it, and thus invented a shape structural and therefore permanent: at once useful and graceful. For, should this vessel fall from the saddle, such is its shape that it would immediately right itself, so that but little of its precious contents would be wasted: a desideratum in the desert, where water is most valuable.

Thus, one by one, nature-shapes were adopted, until now the number and variety of them are almost beyond enumeration. The shapes alone of a good basketry collection would number many hundreds. And, remarkable to say,—or, rather, it would be remarkable, were it not that Nature never errs, and that in copying Nature the Amerind has avoided our errors—there is not a single shape that is ugly or inappropriate to the work for which it is needed. Water-bottle, treasure-basket, cooking-basket, mush-bowl, carrying-basket, meal-tray, hat, roasting-bowl, gambling-plaque, fish-basket: all are perfect in shape, and in adaptation to use.

The Indian woman, having chosen her material and invented her shapes, next considered the kind of stitches to be put into her work. Nature did not give her models from which closely to copy here, so she experimented and invented. The spider web was to her a mere suggestion, but that is all. So also the bird's nest. Therefore, our patient inventor sat down, undiscouraged by her task, and, year after year, faithful and patient, she tried, again and again, every weave and stitch that occurred to her. Who can imagine what this meant? Which of us, to-day, would like to be required to invent a new stitch or weave? At first, one naturally thinks that there can be few varieties of stitches; yet the North American Indian invented the simple mat weave, and then played variations upon it by changing the order of intersection of the splints; she passed to the net weave, with its infinitude of changes; the plait or braid with its great diversity; the coil with its score or more of varieties; the web with its endless series of modifications. Indeed, it may confidently be said that there is not a single stitch or weave known to modern art, made with loom however complicated, that the Indian woman did not invent, and has not had in actual use for centuries. Is she not, then, entitled to our esteem and gratitude for her accomplishments in this direction, for what would the man of to-day be without his textiles varied? He is indebted to the Indian woman, as to other inventors of primitive times, for that which gives him his clothing, napery, bedding, and upholstery.

Basketry and fabric weaving are closely related. It is probable that basketry was invented first, and that weaving came much later. Undoubtedly, the first garments, after fig leaves, were skins of animals. Men killed the animals, and they, together with the women, dressed the skins; though, as belonging to the province of the hunter, it was purely optional with the woman whether or not she touched the skin. This division is clearly marked even to this day among the Havasupais: every man dressing the skins which are the result of his own hunting, and the women having no part in their preparation. The process is simple, yet perfect. No machinery or modern process can produce better, if as good, buckskin, as that which is made by these primitive people. Its quality is known and coveted by tribes a thousand miles away. The green skin is soaked in water until the hair is loose. Then, with a pair of *ji-vi-so-o* (bone knives made from the ribs of a horse), the skin is scraped until perfectly clean. Another brief soaking and the skin is ready to be dressed. This is done by pulling, stretching and working the skin between the fingers, hour after hour, until it is as soft and pliable as desired. Many a time at a pow-wow or council, I have seen the men occupied in quietly rubbing and stretching the buckskin which they had in preparation.

Among the Havasupais also, one may see the means still in use by which pottery probably came into existence. The term, "Basketry the Mother of Pottery," is more real than imaginative. The basket was the matrix of the pot. Not long ago I saw a Havasupais woman parching corn in a basket. This she lined with a mixture of sand and clay, in order to prevent it from cracking, and then threw into it a handful of corn and a scattering of live coals. Blowing into the basket, she kept the contents whirling by a circular motion of the hands, until the corn was properly parched. Finally, with a dexterous swing, the corn and coals were separated; the latter was thrown out, and the parched corn remained.

In due process of time the clay lining, under such treatment, hardens, bakes, and separates itself from the basket. What must have been the thought of the first Indian corn parcher when she found a new and convenient vessel, made without the labor of weaving, shaped and perfect at her hands, ready for carrying water or anything else that she chose to place therein? That was a triumph of accidental invention. But scientific research has shown that, voluntarily, for centuries, aboriginal pottery was made in basket or net moulds, and I have myself seen the Zuñi, Laguna, Hopi, Navaho, Acoma and other Indian potters, coiling the clay in ropes in exact imitation of their method of making basketry.

But now let us briefly return to textiles. Before skins were dressed, they were used for clothing: first, undoubtedly, in their rude entirety, afterward subjected to some process of cutting, and shaping to the body of the wearer. But this assumes the skins to be of a size large enough to be so used. What of the skins of smaller animals, such as the gopher, beaver, rabbit, raccoon, etc.? These are too small for garments. Something was necessary to make them broadly useful. So the wits of the primitive inventors were set to work, and how slowly or how rapidly the idea came we do not know, but, eventually, we find the aborigine taking the small skins, and sewing or tying them together until he had a long rope; then, on a crude frame, actually weaving them into a blanket.

Later came the spinning and weaving of vegetable fibre, and what a memorial we owe to the long forgotten, if ever known, discoverers of these processes! My heart has often thrilled at the sight of the great monuments of the world erected in honor of the slayers of mankind, our warriors; and I have silently shed tears as I have watched loving hands strew the graves of unknown soldiers with flowers. But now when I see the mausoleums, triumphal arches, columns, statues, memorial bronzes, I say to myself: "How unjust, how foolish is mankind! Scores of monuments to the slayers of men, and nothing but curses and anathemas for the busy-minded inventors of the arts of peace. If we must honor the slayers, by no means let us forget the conservers of life."

How did the primitive spinner work? Watch him to-day. He is a Navaho,—he or his wife, sometimes one, sometimes the other. The process followed is the primitive one invented in the dawn of history. The Navaho and his neighbor, the Hopi, grew and spun cotton long before a white man's dreams saw a passage to India by way of the North West. When Spanish colonization began, and sheep were brought into this Western world, three hundred or more years ago, Hopi and Navaho were quick to see the advantage the long, fine wool staple had over the fibre of the cotton. But originally it was yucca-fibre and cotton. And the spinning wheel? It is a smooth stick on which a circular disc of wood is fastened. It is held in the left hand and rapidly twirled on the knee, with the cotton or wool in the right hand; so that the yarn can be stretched to the required thickness.

Everything is now ready for the weaving. The loom on which the skin blanket, already described was made, was, perhaps, the most primitive of all. It is still in use by several tribes of Indians of the Southwest. It consists of four pegs driven into the ground to hold the four corners of the article to be woven, and completely around these one strand of the skin rope is tightly stretched. This forms the edge for sides, top and bottom, and the top and bottom strands also act as bases for the stretching of the warp strands. As soon as these are in place, the weft strands are woven over and under the warp, until the whole square is filled. Little by little, improvements on this primitive loom were made. The heddle was invented, and an article of many pages, with many illustrations, could be written upon this subject alone. The primitive loom as it is used by the Navaho and Hopis of to-day is a crude and simple, yet most effective contrivance. On it the most marvellous blankets are woven. I have carried water seven miles in a blanket of Indian construction. Yet the whole affair is made by the Indian woman weaver with a few poles cut from the nearest grove, and a couple of raw hide ropes. Using two of the heaviest poles as uprights, she fastens the third across the top, and a fourth across the bottom. Below the upper crossbeam, another beam is suspended by lashings of rawhides, and to this the yarn beam is fastened. On this yarn beam the vertical threads of the warp are tied to a corresponding beam answering the same purpose at the bottom. The rawhide above serves to draw the threads tight, and when thus fixed, the loom is ready for the weaver.

With her different "shuttles" of yarn she sits on the ground, tailor fashion, and, thrusting a stick through the warp, divides the cords, so that she can run through them without delay the different threads of the wool. The "shuttle" is a simple piece of stick, on the end of which the yarn has been wound. As soon as the thread is placed in position, a "batten stick" (which, like the woof stick, is always kept in the warp) is brought down with such great force as to wedge the thread into a firm and close position. And thus every thread is "battened down" with such energy that one does not wonder to find the blanket, when finished, impervious to the heaviest rains. . . .

The popular conception of the Indian is that the man, the buck, is a monarch, rude and savage, and the woman, the squaw, is a slave, abject and servile. Like so many other "popular" conceptions based upon ignorance or superficial observation, this is an error. Almost without exception, the higher class of explorers, Livingstone, Speke, Burton, and others, tell of the freedom and equality of the primitive woman. The general error seems to have had its birth and growth from the failure of early writers to recognize the fact that among the Indians a distinct division of labor was invariably observed, and that neither sex ever intruded upon the work of the other.

Even to-day misunderstandings of this character are constantly liable to arise. Suppose a person unacquainted with the customs of the Hopi [witnesses the following scene]: a score of women are seen engaged in building a house. They mix their own mortar, gather or quarry their own stones, are their own hod carriers, and neither seek nor expect the slightest help from the men,—who sit calmly smoking near them. With such a scene before him, the unacquainted observer would grow angry at the indolence of the men, and their brutality in compelling their women to do such hard work while they sit idly by.

But this would be a waste of sympathy, and a clear evidence of the observer's ignorance. Hopi women, in building their houses, do not desire aid from the men. The women are the owners of the domiciles; therefore, what more natural than that they shall build them?

This very act of house-building is a proof of the Hopi woman's equality with her husband, and, possibly, her superiority over him. For within the walls of the house she is supreme. Except the personal, ceremonial, hunting and war belongings of her husband, everything brought within belongs to her, or is under her control. Even the corn of the field, planted and gathered by her husband, once put into the corn-storage room, is no longer at his disposal.

With the neighboring nomad Navaho the same equality of the sexes obtains, and I can imagine the laugh of scorn that a person would meet, who would question the Hopi or Navaho woman as to her degraded and subordinate position.

Among the aborigines, the sex division of labor was instituted according to the law of natural selection of work; woman, the home-maker, the child-bearer, remaining behind, while the men went abroad to hunt or to make war.

As the food provider, the Indian woman has always been the beast of burden. She has not only been compelled to find the food, but also to transport it to her home (to this the results of the chase are the main exception, woman never having been a hunter). For methods of transportation alone we owe many valuable inventions to primitive women, and bearing upon this subject, Professor Mason of the Smithsonian Institution has written a lengthy illustrated article of great interest and value.[1]

The food having been carried home, it was necessary for it to be prepared; and here was large scope for the exercise of the primitive inventor's faculties. How was corn to be ground? How cooked? How preserved? Aboriginal woman was the first miller. She took a flat slab of rock, sloped it to a convenient angle, took a smaller slab to act as a grinding stone, and, placing the corn between the two, rubbed the one rock over the other, until the grain became meal. Every Indian of the Southwest to-day uses these primitive mills.

Some grains were found unfitted for grinding. They were better crushed by pounding, and the Indian women invented the mortar and pestle. Many of the mortars still in use are made from tree trunks cut off near the root and hollowed out, so that the gnarled twistings at the bottom form a solid pounding base.

Later, mortars were cut out of solid rock. The process was slow and laborious, and a well prepared mortar meant the hard work of many months. On Santa Catalina Island, just off the coast of Southern California, a primitive quarry of these mortars was recently discovered. The material is a kind of soap-stone, and bears the marks of the excavation of many mortars. Others were in the process of removal at the time of the abandonment of the quarry. If one could draw back the veil of the past, what interesting disclosures might this abandoned quarry reveal! Was it war or pestilence that moved the quarriers and left their work uncompleted? Did they start to cross to the main land in their frail boats, and meet death in some sudden storm? Alas, we can only conjecture, for there is no record to tell us how this change came about.

The food ground, how must it be cooked? Here primitive woman had to use her faculties, and she became an adept at broiling, boiling, steaming and baking. Although still without pottery or metal utensils, the Indian woman of to-day boils water in a basket, heating it far more quickly than can be done by the means of gas stove or electrical apparatus. At her camp fire she always keeps a number of fair sized stones, and close by is her basket full of water. As soon as the stones are heated thoroughly, she takes a stick with a loop at one end, and, with a dextrous twist, picks up one of the stones upon the loop and throws it into the basket. As long as it "sizzles," she stirs it to keep it from burning the bottom of the basket. When it is cooled, it is rapidly jerked out and another hot stone takes its place. In this way the water is made to boil quickly. Many times I have seen acorn and other mush cooked in this way; the hot stones being stirred into the food until it was thoroughly cooked.

Even in the invention of necessary toilet articles, the primitive woman has had her share. As we use the delicately scented Lubin's or Pears's soap, we are not liable to be grateful to the greasy little primitive woman of long centuries ago.

But we are so indebted. It was she, and our refined ancestors, who invented soap. They have invented new methods of preparing it, but the finest and best soap made even to-day, is the same as that which was prepared by the bronze woman of the wilds. She took the root of the amole (a species of yucca), bruised and macerated it, and then beat it up and down in her bowl of water. She thus made better, sweeter and more agreeable soap than comes from the French or English perfumer of reputation.

I have thus rapidly outlined a few of the things which we owe to primitive woman. The list might be lengthened ten times. I have said nothing of the instruments for making fire, the hand drill, the making of skin and birch bark canoes and other vessels, the work in metals, the taming of wild animals, the cultivation of plants, the discovery of medicines and of their methods of application.

But even with these things the list would be inadequate. The inventiveness of the primitive woman was never more wonderfully shown than in religion and philosophy. She devised a system of religion to account for all the fearful phenomena that she observed. She was the inventor of the story-telling art, and, indeed, the first teacher of language. She excelled in the art of representing human thought by picture-writing, out of which the alphabet was slowly developed. Therefore, it is not too much to say that we owe a vast amount of gratitude to the ignored women of the dawn of history. If, in future, we find ourselves unable to speak a good word for the Indian, our American representative of a primitive race, we shall no longer be able to plead ignorance. We shall at least "have awakened our senses, that we may better judge."

Note

1. [James is referring to Otis Mason's *Primitive Travel and Transportation,* Report of the United States National Museum for 1894 (Washington, D.C.: Government Printing Office, 1896). It is also obvious that James was influenced by Mason's *The Origins of Invention* (1895; Freeport, New York: Books for Libraries Press, 1972). —*Ed.*]

11

Folk Foods of the Rio Grande Valley and of Northern Mexico

John G. Bourke

John Gregory Bourke (1846–1896) received a taste for folklife study while serving in the United States Army. For a dozen years he was aide-de-camp to General George Crook in the Southwest, where he took extensive notes on the Indian tribes there. He caused a sensation by publishing books, usually with long, inviting titles, about exotic rites experienced first hand. In 1884, under the impressive imprimatur of Charles Scribner's Sons, he published *The Snake Dance of the Moquis of Arizona: Being a Narrative of a Journey from Santa Fe, New Mexico, to the Villages of the Moqui Indians of Arizona, with a Description of the Manners and Customs of This Peculiar People, and Especially of the Revolting Religious Rite, the Snake-Dance; To Which Is Added a Brief Dissertation upon Serpent Worship in General.* He followed with his best-known work, *Scatologic Rites of All Nations: A Dissertation upon the Employment of Excrementitious Remedial Agents in Religion, Therapeutics, etc., in All Parts of the Globe. Based on Original Notes and Personal Observation* (1891).

It is worth speculating that Bourke's interest in food habits is related to his work on the ritual uses of excrement. But his survey of Mexican-American foods downplays the rites involved and he treats the foods more as objects whose form and use are to be described. In this essay, food emerges as a distinctive genre of folklife, and indeed, he states that he planned a lengthy "dissertation" on the topic. The material for the essay probably stems from his posts in Texas from 1891 to 1895. In between he served in the Latin-American department of the Chicago World's Fair. By 1896, he had become president of the American Folklore Society, and had to his credit a series of articles in the *Journal of American Folklore* on the folklife of the Rio Grande Valley; it included accounts of folk medicine, folk drama, folk speech, and folk belief. He never brought them together for a book because he fell ill and died in that year.

Bourke's collection of Mexican-American culture had the purpose of preparing his army soldiers for their hostile surroundings. His post suffered occasional attacks, and Bourke reflected that "it might perhaps happen that an officer would find himself beleaguered, and supply trains cut off, in which case there would be no alternative of surrender or retreat, unless he could provide food for his troops from the resources of the country." At the same time, knowing the existing customs could help Americans "elevate" Mexican culture, Bourke condescendingly assumed, to "aid her struggle upward and onward in the path of civilization." In keeping with evolutionary doctrine, his approach is to seek survivals of "savage" foods, and Bourke is not shy about offering his critical opinions on these survivals. He cites, for example, the "depravity of taste due to long usage," the "appalling liberality" of garlic, and the "recklessness" of chile usage.

This essay is reprinted from "Folk-Foods of the Rio Grande Valley and of Northern Mexico," *Journal of American Folklore* 8 (1895): pp. 41–71. For background on Bourke, see W. K. McNeil, "A History of American Folklore Scholarship before 1908" (Ph.D. Dissertation, Indiana University, 1980), pp. 332–42. And for background on the region that Bourke describes, see William Madsen, *The Mexican-Americans of South Texas* (New York: Holt, Rinehart and Winston, 1964); Richard Bauman and Roger D. Abrahams, eds., *"And Other Neighborly Names": Social Process and Cultural Image in Texas Folklore* (Austin: University of Texas Press, 1981). For an update on official attitudes toward Mexican-American folk foodways, see Judy Perkin and Stephanie F. McCann, "Food for Ethnic Americans: Is the Government Trying to Turn the Melting Pot into a One-Dish Dinner?" in *Ethnic and Regional Foodways in the United States: The Performance of Group Identity,* ed. Linda Keller Brown and Kay Mussell (Knoxville: University of Tennessee Press, 1984), pp. 243–47.

*   *   *

It was with no intention of invading the literary province which Brillat-Savarin has made so eminently his own that I began the compilation of this series of notes upon the habits of life of the race which almost exclusively populates our southern boundary; my purposes were more strictly military than those which animated the brilliant author of "La Phisiologie du Gout." I figured to myself that should history repeat itself, and an army from Europe attempt to overthrow the government of Mexico, it should be again the policy and duty of the Americans of the north to push to the rescue of the sister to the south, and aid her in her struggle upward and onward in the path of civilization. It might perhaps happen that an officer would find himself beleaguered, and supply trains cut off, in which case there would be no alternative of surrender or retreat, unless he could provide food for his troops from the resources of the country.

Could all this thorny jungle and chaparral have been created in vain? No, I answered to myself, the more we examine into the great scheme of nature, the more do we see that nothing has been made without some purpose. What all these woods can supply I will try to discover. And thus I began, and continued in a more or less desultory way, to learn little by little, and not always with intelligent certainty, what that vast country was good for, and then the thought came to me that after all man's noblest pastime is not in constant and irritating preparation for war, but in adding all in his power to knowledge which might, to some extent, make men wiser and happier.

It is only necessary here to say that most of the cultivated fruits of Mexico were introduced principally by the Franciscan monks, who established missions everywhere in the days immediately succeeding the conquest. They brought over peaches, apples, pears, plums, cherries, quinces, figs, dates, pomegranates, walnuts, olives, nectarines, apricots, paper-shelled walnuts, almonds, sugar-cane, coffee, Spanish grapes, oranges, and perhaps lemons and bananas, as well as horses, donkeys, cows, sheep, chickens, and goats, together with wheat, oats, and barley, and many vegetables. About 1581 the Jesuits entered upon missionary work in that country, and followed the rule established by the Franciscans. Both these bodies gave earnest attention to the study of native foods, and improved upon the cooking of the natives. Chocolate, which plays so important a part in our domestic economy to-day, was obtained from the Aztecs, and so were the tomato and the pineapple. The potato grows wild in the higher altitudes of Mexico, but has never attained, in the dietary of the people, the importance it merits. There is in existence a quaint volume entitled, "A New Survey of the West Indies," by Thomas Gage, an English Dominican monk, who spent some fourteen years of his life in Guatemala and Mexico. He upbraids his brother monks for being addicted to the inordinate use of candied pineapple. The Carmelite nuns, who had convent schools for girls in nearly all towns of any size, seem to have been great cake and candy makers, and vestiges of their skill remain to our own day in the name of a Mexican candy much in favor, known as "Carmencillo de leche." Perhaps our own toothsome caramels may perpetuate the experiments with chocolate of some gentle, discalced Caramel-ite, who now occupies a long-forgotten grave.

In the equable climate of Mexico, where irrigation is applicable, all forms of vegetable life yield abundant returns.

With the rapid extension of her great railroad systems, and especially with the completion of the Trans-Continental line across the Isthmus of Tehuantepec, Mexico must soon become the polar star for thousands of immigrants from the congested agricultural regions of Europe.

The great depreciation of silver may act as a temporary drawback to the prosperity of Mexico, but in no country are the rights of invested capital more jealously guarded, while the fullest protection is guaranteed the laboring classes. General Porfirio Diaz, the present President, is a man of extended experience, fertility of resources, broad-minded sagacity, and uncompromising firmness of character. Under his administration Mexico has made wonderful advances, and the limit of her prosperity no man can predict.

In arranging a list of the aboriginal fruits and vegetables of Mexico and the Mexican portion of the United States, it seems to me to be proper to begin with those which have become cultivated, at least since the advent of the Castilian. Each of these will be described in its turn; and then the fruits which are still gathered in the wild state, and receive no attention from the hand of man, will be set down in as careful and complete a manner as I was able to obtain them.

The Piñon and Pecan, although indigenous to Mexico, may now be fairly classed among its cultivated foods. The pecan, which is said to be found in places from Wisconsin and Northern Virginia clear down to the Isthmus of Tehuantepec, is the best of all nuts, the almond not excepted. The Mexicans are very fond of a candy made from it with sugar caramel; this candy in appearance closely resembles our own ground-nut candy, which is also known to the Mexicans under the name of "Dulce de cacahuate." The Pecan-tree is one of the most beautiful of all that grow; it is tall, graceful and umbrageous; some of the most graceful are to be seen in that part of San Antonio, Texas, called Maverick Park or Grove, in the lawns surrounding the residences of Hon. B. G. Duval and other prominent citizens. One of the most interesting, historically considered, is still in full vigor in the old city of Monclova, in the Mexican State of Coahuila; the people there call it "El arbol del Padre" (the Priest's or the Father's tree); because when the Spaniards had taken the patriot priest, Hidalgo, prisoner, and were carrying him off to Chihuahua to be executed, they passed through this old city with their prisoner, and remained here one day. Father Hidalgo wrapped himself in his cloak and went to sleep under the branches of the pecan which records this incident in its name.

Then come the Sapotes, Chirimoyas, Chilcoyotes, Guayavas, Tunas, or Cardones, the fruit of the Nopal, or Indian Fig Cactus, Bananas, Mangoes, Jicamas de agua, Chié, Chile, Chilchipin, Alicóchis, improperly called pitahaya, Coyotillo, Granjeno, Sunflowers, Squash, with its seeds, Watermelon, Chapote, Mamé, Spanish Bayonet, Mango, Aguacates, Black Ebony beans, Acorns, Anacahuita nuts, Frijoles, another plant also called Frijol, Guadalupan, Mescal, Sotol, Tomato, Biznaga, Chicharrones, Mezquite, Guayacan, Lechuguilla, Amole, Onions, Sauco, Tejocote, Grapes, Socoyonostre, Pitahaya, Maguey, Corn, Strawberries, Mangostins, Ciruela, and also the true Plum (in certain districts), Cocoanuts (seen in Morelia only; all others were brought up from Tampico or Vera Cruz by rail, and need not be discussed).

There are several kinds of *Sapotes,* but they bear no resemblance to any northern fruits with which I am acquainted.

The *Chirimoya* is a large, dark green fruit, about as big as one of our Duchesse pears, and somewhat of the same shape, full of black seeds, with a pith the consistency of custard, which tastes like a mixture of pineapples, strawberries, and raspberries.

Chilcoyote looks much like the Chirimoya; if eaten by a person who is heated, will bring on chills and fever.

The *Guayava* or *Guava* is sufficiently well known to American readers through the palatable jelly made from it in Havana and imported into our country.

The *Tuna* or *Nopal* grows wild and is also cultivated; in the wild state it can be found, in an attenuated and shrivelled form, as far north almost as vegetation exists south of the Arctic Circle; in Mexico it seems to claim possession of the whole country, and is properly accepted as the principal figure of the present national coat-of-arms, as it was, we might say, in that of the Aztecs. It figures in the myths, traditions, and life of the country. The wild varieties bear fruit of different colors, generally red and purple and yellow. The cultivated variety bears a yellow fruit, very much larger and very much sweeter than the wild; it is piled up in the market-places and sold in quantities at all hours of the day and night. The Apaches say that the use of this fruit must be attended with some precautions, as it predisposes to fevers; their women collect it in great baskets carried on their backs, suspended from bands which pass around the forehead, and spread the split fruit out on rocks in the sun to dry. The outer skin being liberally supplied with acutely pointed thorns, the squaws have devised a brush of stiff hay, with which they knock off these spines before taking the fruit in the hand. Both wild and cultivated kinds are eaten raw, dried, baked, or boiled down into a stiff marmalade, which is sold in all the plazas under the name of "Queso de Tuna,"—Tuna Cheese. This is most agreeable to the taste, and might be mistaken by one ignorant of its true nature for a piece of preserved quince.

Not only is the fruit eaten; the large plate-shaped leaf is brought into use for both man and beast. Grated down into a coarse powder, after having been skinned, the meat of this leaf is added to soups to give a mucilaginous thickening. Travellers through the southern portions of Texas, and almost all parts of Mexico, can see in the earliest hours of the morning, fantastic figures dancing about in the smoke and flames of fires kindled for the sole purpose of burning off the spines of the nopal and letting draught oxen feed upon the leaves. Cattle, pigs, sheep, goats, and horses, running at large in the chaparral, do not wait for any such preparatory process, but take the plant as they find it. It is one of the sights of the Rio Grande to come suddenly upon a large, patriarchal, white goat with beard and breast dyed a blood red, from the juice of the tuna, and nostrils filled with the thorns of the fruit and leaf. Indeed, so well known is this peculiarity of all domestic animals in that region, especially during seasons of great drouth, that butchers will not accept orders to supply beef tongues, saying frankly that the meat is so full of ligneous fibre that it would be impossible to carve it upon the table.

Anti-scorbutic properties have been attributed to the nopal, and I have eaten the leaves fried, but am not able to express myself very warmly upon its merits, either as a medicine or an addition to the bill of fare.

Cut into strips, and thrown into a bucketful of turbid water, the nopal will cause the sedimentary matter in suspension to be precipitated to the bottom. This expedient was resorted to with success during our expedition to explore the Black Hills of Dakota in 1875. The juice of the nopal mixed with a small quantity of lime and a sufficiency of bullock's blood and river sand will form a cement finely adapted for flooring, as I have seen tried a number of times in Arizona and Texas.

Finally, the leaf, after being peeled of its thorny coat, is considered a valuable remedy as an embrocation in rheumatism, or as a plaster.

Whether or not bananas are indigenous to Mexico, I am unable to say, but I incline to the opinion that they were introduced by the Europeans; be that as it may, they grow wild in many parts, especially on the Rio Panuco, and do excellently in every place with a very slight amount of attention.

The same remarks apply to the sugar-cane; it becomes a reed, and one need not pay any attention to it; replanting is necessary only once in nine or ten years.

Mangoes might be mistaken for a small canteloupe; the fruit is rather insipid to my taste.

Chié is a peculiar seed, not unlike our linseed, but possessing properties worthy of commemoration. Several years since, I was paying a visit to the ruins of the grand old monastery of Atotonilco, and was received most cordially by the priest in charge, Padre Silva, who, seeing my heated and exhausted condition,—I had made a long ride over from San Miguel de Allende,—declined, to my great surprise, to let me have a drink of cool water from the "aljibe" (cistern).

That is always the way with you Americanos," he said gently; "you come down here and rush all over the country in the hot sun and dust, and when you reach a house the first thing you do is to call for cold water, and drink a quantity of it; the stomach cannot stand such treatment and rebels against it, and the sick man blames our climate. Now let me show you how we Mexicans do; take it easy; take off your coat and collar and cool off, while I send Pépé here after some chi-é."

Pépé soon performed his errand, and brought back from one of the old Indian women a small package of the seeds, which the padre immersed in a cup filled with water; the seeds swelled up and the water became slightly mucilaginous.

"Now," said the padre, "you must not gulp down this mixture all at once; it would give you a chill if you did; take one third at this moment; another third in ten minutes, and the remainder in ten minutes more."

The results surprised me very much; not only were my feverish symptoms alleviated, but my voice became very clear and strong. What this chi-é was I never could ascertain. The Padre told me that the plant grew all over northern Mexico and, he thought, in southern Texas also, but I never had another opportunity to learn anything about it.[1]

The Chiricahua Apaches, who have lived nearly always in Mexico, and pretty far down in the Sierra Madre, have a gens named the "Chi-é," a word which I never could get interpreted to my satisfaction; it has probably some connection with the plant which I am here attempting to describe.

Atotonilco is one of the out-of-the-way spots in America well worthy of a visit from the scholarly or the curious; it would be well to remember that one must go provided with food and blankets, as the padre may have other guests, and in that case a dependence upon the kind-hearted Indians of the adjacent village would be attended with most unsatisfactory consequences.

Chile, called "Aji" and "Quauhchilli" by the Aztecs, was the condiment used in all the feasts of the aborigines at the time of the landing of Cortez; there are several varieties,—the red, white, green, sweet, and bitter. No Mexican dish of meat or vegetables is deemed complete without it, and its supremacy as a table adjunct is conceded by both garlic and tomato, which also bob up serenely in nearly every effort of the culinary art.

The *Chilchipin* is the fiery berry forming the basis of Tabasco sauce; it can be found in a wild state just after you cross the Nueces, going south, and from that on no jungle is without it; the bush is of the same general size and shape as one of our rosebushes, with foliage light green in color. It is used both in the green and ripe, or red, state.

The *Alicóchis,* to which many people persist in giving the name of Pitahaya, is a cactus, resembling the Biznaga, or Turk's Head, but much smaller, and growing close to the ground; it yields, in the early days of summer, a fruit the size of a small plum, green in color, filled with fine black seeds; the skin is quite thin. This is generally regarded as the most delicious of all the wild fruits. It rivals the strawberry or the raspberry in delicacy of flavor and in the graciousness with which it submits to every mode of treatment. It seems to be equally good whether served raw, stewed, in pies and puddings, or in ice-cream; it makes an acceptable addition to juleps and lemonades.

The *Coyotillo* is a small bush, the sweet black berry of which is an agreeable food, but if the little seeds be swallowed, paralysis of the lower limbs results.

It is well known that the kernels of the delicious peach, plum, almond, and nectarine contain the deadly poison hydrocyanic acid, and something of the same nature may be the explanation of this peculiarity of the coyotillo. Mr. MacAllan, who was educated at Columbia College, New York, and at the University of Virginia, stated to me that he had made experiments at his father's ranch (Hidalgo County, on the Rio Grande, Texas), which proves the popular belief in regard to the Coyotillo, to be true; it paralyzed the hind extremities of goats, sheep, and pigs, upon which he experimented.

The *Coma* is a small, black, or deep blue berry, much like our own whortleberry, but dead sweet in taste; it grows on a stunted bush, and is ready for use from June to August.

The *Granjeno* is a parasitic bush, which entwines itself about a tree or larger bush, and grows, whenever possible, in the shape of a corkscrew; from the odd shapes often assumed under these conditions, it is a favorite wood for canes; the small, pinkish-red berries are not unpalatable, but the most that I feel at liberty to say in their favor is that they are not poisonous.

Sunflowers are not, to my knowledge, used as a food by any part of the Mexican population claiming an infiltration of Caucasian blood, but they are a favorite article of diet with many, if not all of the Indian tribes, in both Mexico and the United States. So much was this the case, that a quarter of a century ago, or less, the Moquis, Apaches, Navajoes, and Pueblos used to plant them; under cultivation, the seed-disk attained enormous dimensions; I have seen them in the fields of the Moquis and Ava-Supais at least a foot in diameter; the seeds, when mixed with corn and ground into a meal, make a cake which is believed to be highly nutritious.[2]

Not only are squashes and watermelons eaten by the Mexicans, but the seeds also are utilized as a food in many districts, especially by the Indian element.

The *Chapote* is the Mexican persimmon; the tree is small, with a smooth, white bark; the fruit, dead sweet to the taste, the size of a cherry, black and pulpy.

Mamé looks like a Nellis pear; has a smooth, russet skin, and an insipid pulp of firm, creamy, red matter, tasting much like a boiled sweet potato, and has a large black kernel.

The *Spanish Bayonet,* called *Datil,* or sometimes *Sotol.* The fruit, shaped like a banana, has a sweet, rather thick skin, and is filled with a mushy pulp, in which are imbedded a great number of black seeds, arranged symmetrically about the vertical axis. In Arizona, where it fills wide areas, it is much used by the Apaches, and the squaws dry it in the sun to keep for winter's use. It has a decidedly pleasant taste. The Rio Grande Mexicans do not make much use of the fruit, but take the young central shoot and bake it in live coals; it is not unlike a watery half-boiled sweet potato in flavor. From this same baked shoot they distil a variety of mescal, said by experts to be even more soul-destroying than the genuine.

Mango resembles a yellowish large cucumber.

Aguacate, or Alligator Pear. So much has been written about this that only a word seems to be a necessary here. When the custard-like pulp is beaten up with egg, oil, vinegar, and spices, it makes a most delicious salad, and when sliced seems to be equally good. This fruit resembles a pear in shape; is purple in color; the pulp is sweetish and can be eaten raw.

The *Black Ebony* grows all over the country now under discussion; the beans, when in the milk, are highly considered as a vegetable when boiled with milk, pepper, and salt; after becoming hard and black a coffee is made of them, but I am in no humor to say much in its praise. It has a rather unpleasant, terebinthine taste.

Acorns, which enter so largely into the dietary of the native tribes of the Pacific coast and the interior basin from Utah down to Texas, are used, to a slight extent, by the Mexicans of Caucasian derivation, and can occasionally be seen in the markets, but hardly in quantity sufficient to attract attention; allusion to them seems to be proper in an article of this kind.

The *Anacahuita,* a variety of the dogwood, bears a nut highly relished by pigs and goats, and used, to some extent, by the Mexicans; it is light-greenish in color, and grows in clusters.

The *Frijole,* or Mexican Bean, of both red and black varieties, is a plant indigenous to this continent, but all American readers are now so well acquainted with it, that reference only seems to be necessary; it is by far the most toothsome of all the pulse, and is cooked by the Mexicans in a half dozen different ways; stewed or boiled to a pulpy paste, it appears at almost every meal, and well deserves its title of "El plato nacional," the national dish.

There is another plant called "Frijol," which attains the dimensions of a tall bush; the long, thick pods are stewed in milk or water and eaten like the true bean. Some specimens which I sent to Professor Otis T. Mason, of the United States National Museum, Washington, D.C., were identified by Mr. George Vasey as the *Canivalia obtusifolia.*

Guadalupan is a plant which I have never personally tried; I relate only what others have told me. In appearance, as I saw it first, growing at the Rancho "La Grulla," Starr County, Texas, in 1891, it is of the size of a rosebush, with a bright red, pulpy fruit.

Of the *Mescal,* I have written so much, at so many different times, that I may well be excused from adding another line upon the subject. As a food, it has for centuries been in high repute among the nomadic tribes depredating along the northern border of Mexico. Dr. Gustav Bruhl has identified the word "chichimec" as a compound of two words, meaning "mescal eaters," which would do something in the way of demonstrating that the wild tribes included under that designation, from whom the Aztecs, and after them the Spaniards, suffered so much, were of the same general type as our Apaches, Navajoes, and Comanches.

The Apaches used to make regular pits or ovens of heated stones, covered with earth, in which the stalk and leaves of the mescal were buried for three days, and when then taken out yielded a sweet, palatable, and nourishing but slightly laxative food. The laxative quality is accounted for readily, the Mescal, like its big brother, the Maguey, being a member of the Aloe family.

When these cooked leaves are bruised and allowed to ferment, a fiery liquor can be distilled from the mass, although the same result is obtained in another way by collecting the juice from the pit left after extracting the central shoot, allowing that "miel" or juice to ferment, and then distilling.

The whole process, as described by me among the Tarascoes of southwestern Mexico, was so crude that it opened my mind to the suggestion that distillation was a primitive art, and must have been known to the aborigines of Mexico prior to the coming of the Europeans. The grated root of this plant is also used as food.

A North American who has never traversed the vast areas covered by the Mescal and the Maguey in the wild state, cannot comprehend how valuable they were, and are, to the people as a source of food supply. Besides this, the central shoot was utilized as a lance-shaft, or was used to form the side walls of huts, while the leaves made a fair to middling good thatch, and the strong thorn at the end of a leaf, with the attached filament, served the Apache squaw, or warrior on the trail, with a substitute for needle and thread. Of the central shoot of the Mescal the Apaches made their fiddles.

The *Tomato,* in the wild state, is not very much bigger than a cherry, but in both green and red state is made to enter into salads and sauces of all kinds. It is also dried in the sun.

The *Biznaga,* of Turk's Head Cactus, cut in small, slender strips, and boiled for several hours in syrup, makes a candy of which the people are very fond and which is on sale at every street corner, in almost every town.

Chicharrones are a variety of peas, and need no description.

The *Mezquite* has been recognized as a food of the American aborigines ever since the Spaniard Alarcon ascended the Rio Colorado, in 1541; the form of the loaf of bread made from its meal remains the same among the Apaches to-day as it was when he wrote his notes. Some of the tribes, the Pimas, Opatas, Papagoes, and others, used to make a kind of effervescent beer from the beans, but this does not seem to be much in demand of late years.

There are two varieties of the Mezquite; that with the screw pod, which grows only in the valley of the Colorado, and that with the flat pod, of more extended distribution. Both are palatable, and are very fattening to horses and other live stock.

These are the American representatives of the Acacia family, and the gum exuded from the trunk equals the best gum arabic.

Guayacan (lignum vitae), lechuguilla, and amole are spoken of here, not as foods, but as important aids in the Mexican household economy; their powdered roots are detersive, and supply the place of soap, and possess the valuable peculiarity of not shrinking flannel; they make a good dentifrice and a fine hair wash. The use of the Guayacan root is avoided, when possible, because it burns the hands.

Onions grow wild in parts of Mexico, as they do everywhere in the great West of our country; they are, however, so far as my experience goes, much more plentiful in the extended plains near the Yellowstone than they are in the regions farther to the south. In size they are very diminutive, not much bigger than a cherry, and very pungent. When General George Crook made his celebrated "Starvation March" down from the Yellowstone to the Niobrara, in 1876, his officers and men were glad to discover patches of these onions, which furnished a most agreeable addition to the stews made of the horse meat captured from the hostile savages.

Of the *Sauco,* or elderberry, I have not much to say beyond the fact that it is edible.

The *Tejocote,* or bud of the wild rose, is eaten by Indians and Mexicans, and is on sale in the markets.

The *Grape* may be regarded either as a wild fruit or as one of the cultivated sort; when Spanish missionaries and explorers first penetrated into Northern Coahuila and Chihuahua, they were surprised by the luxuriant growth and fine flavor of the wild grape, and one locality, Parras, in Coahuila, derives its name from this fact. Here for more than two hundred years has been made a wine which is highly considered by the

Mexicans, and has a taste intermediate between that of port and sherry, with a decided body.

This district, as well as its close neighbor, El Paso, or, as it is now styled, Ciudad Juarez, in Chihuahua, is noted for its crop of fruits of all kinds; the El Paso grapes and onions have no superior anywhere in the world, but of course I do not wish to be understood as saying that these are the wild varieties. In all likelihood, after it was learned that these two localities, Parras and El Paso, were naturally well adapted for viticulture, the Spaniards brought over cuttings from Xeres and the Madeira and Canary Islands.

The *Socoyonostre* is a variety of cactus much appreciated for its juice, which makes an especially good candy; the Mexicans, particularly those living well towards the centre of the republic, say that this is the best kind of cactus candy, but, so far as I could determine from the taste, it is no better than the biznaga, perhaps not quite so good.

In the beginning of this article, it was shown that the Mexicans of the Rio Grande Valley improperly applied the name Pitahaya to the cactus, which should be known as the Alicóchis, and which yields a fruit of surpassing sweetness and delicacy. The true Pitahaya is the Candelabrum, the Organ, the Giant, or the Saguara cactus of various writers; it has sometimes been called the umbrella cactus. There are two varieties: that growing in Arizona attains a height of from twenty-five to thirty-five feet, although, in extreme cases, the height has been put at as much as fifty-five feet, as determined by myself and other officers who measured one by its shadow near old Camp McDowell, Arizona, in 1870.

The difference between the two varieties is very slight; each shows in cross-section a number of ribs arranged at equal distances around the vertical axis of the stems or arms, the intermediate spaces being filled with a watery, stringy pith, the whole encased in a thick green skin, bristling with curvated spines.

From rib to rib, in the Arizona variety, the skin bulges outward, or assumes a convex surface, but in the variety found more to the south, in the Mexican States of Michoacan and Guadalajara, this same surface is concave.

The fruit, which grows at the very top of the high branches, is a big pear-shaped greenish pod, which, opening at the time of ripeness, discloses an interior filled with a ruby red pulp, in which are many tiny black seeds. The ripening of the pitahaya in Arizona used to be the signal for the arrival of great flocks of chattering birds, which fought for the rich spoil of the fruit, and of the downcoming from the mountains of bands of Apache Indians, who gathered the dainty feast and at the same time made war upon their hereditary enemies, the Pimas and Papagoes.

My first trip with Apache Indians was to assist them in a hunt for several jars of the preserve which their squaws knew how to make by boiling down this pulp of the pitahaya; in the present instance it had been necessary to hurry up matters and bury the jars containing the preserve, as a large war-party of Pimas had discovered the presence of the Apaches in the Pima country, and compelled them to take flight.

Maguey. All that has been said of mescal applies to its relative the maguey, excepting that when the central stock or shoot of the latter is cut out, the cavity made rapidly fills with a very sweet juice, which, under the name of "miel" (honey), is sold in all the market-places of Mexico.

Corn should be discussed under the title of cooked foods; the shucks carefully dried and rubbed smooth make the favorite wrapping for the Mexican cigarrittos. Corn-meal parched with a trifle of "pelonce," or coarse brown sugar, is one of the staple Mexican foods. Without the sugar, it was in use among the Aztecs. A similar preparation of parched wheat is called "atole." The nourishing properties of both these have been highly praised by writers who knew little about them. I had once to live on pinole for three days, and have never been able to arouse myself to enthusiasm over it.

Strawberries grow wild in the mountains, and are also carefully cultivated; in the neighborhood of Celaya and Queretaro they yield all the year round, or almost all the year, and a trade of some importance is springing up with the American cities to the north. The Mexican strawberry, as a rule, is of extremely delicious flavor, and growers have not fallen into our error of sacrificing taste and aroma to size and color.

Mangostins seem to be a variety of the mangoes.

Ciruela. Under the name of plum, one finds in the neighborhood of Toluca, Mexico, and in other places, a fruit which possesses very little merit, although not bad to the taste. It is yellow in color, of size of an egg, with a large stone inside.

Plums. The true plum, the same as that with which we are familiar in the United States, can be found in the vicinity of Linares and other small cities along "the Tampico Route," in Morelia and other places. The climate and soil of Mexico and Texas would seem to be very well adapted to the cultivation of the prune and the green gage, but no great amount of attention has thus far been paid to them.

Cocoanuts. Very few of these grow in the region which I am describing in this article; they do grow in Morelia, and in the country not far from Tampico, from which places they find their way on railroad trains and by wagon transportation to points farther inland and farther to the north, but without offering any peculiarities worth mentioning.

Sicamas. These are also called Xicamas de Agua; they look like a rutabaga; after being skinned they can be eaten raw, but should be followed by a drink of mescal to ward off chills and fever.

Having attempted to lay before my readers a list of the more prominent articles of food which attracted my attention while serving in this southern border country, it may not be amiss to venture upon a few references to the modes of preparing them which are peculiar to the people, beginning with those presented for sale at every street corner, and advancing from those to the supposedly more elaborate collations of the various "fondas," and the confessedly more cleanly and tempting refreshments offered in the hospitality of private houses.

The abominations of Mexican cookery have been for years a favorite theme with travelers rushing hastily through the republic, and pages have been filled with growls at the wretchedness and inadequacy of the accommodations offered in the hotels and restaurants.

I certainly have no desire to appear as the champion of the Mexican hotel, be its guise or its title what it may; not even when, as was the case with a small affair at which I was obliged to put up near Queretaro, it may be under the patronage of Our Lady of Guadaloupe, whose picture hung in the "zaguan" or main hall.

Neither shall I rush impetuously to the defence of Mexican cookery in the abstract, or in its entirety; as a general rule, there is an appalling liberality in the matter of garlic, a recklessness in the use of the chile colorado or chile verde, and an indifference to the existence of dirt and grease, which will find no apology in these pages.

These drawbacks are attributable directly to the illiteracy of the poorer classes, from which the cooks are drawn, and to some extent to depravity of taste due to long usage.

Once, when I had strongly urged upon a landlady in Camargo that the presence of garlic was inexpressibly repugnant to me at all times, she promised implicit obedience in the preparation of the dinner ordered for myself and friends, but when it appeared upon the table, "ajo" seemed to be the main feature of every dish.

Perhaps my temper got the better of my judgment, and led me to hasty expressions, which I would now gladly recall; but Señora Ornelas remained imperturbable. "Caramba!" she exclaimed, "one must have *some* garlic!"

But after all these disagreeable features have been conceded, there remain not a few excellences in Mexican cookery which occupy pleasant niches in the memory, and are deserving of preservation and imitation.

I will go farther than this, and say that the natural aptitude of the Mexicans in the culinary art is so pronounced, that I think it would be a wise policy for the general or state governments of that country to institute cooking-schools, and instruct classes in the chemistry and preservation of foods, with a view to aiding in the future establishment of factories for the canning of fruits, meats, and vegetables, or the making of the delicious "cajetes," "almibares," and "jaleatines," which will be referred to in other pages of this paper.

In justice to the cooks of Mexico, we should also remember that they are hampered by lack of proper utensils; as a general thing, food is prepared with a minimum of appliances, and the modest array of pots, pans, and kettles to be seen even in very well to do "fondas" and private houses throughout the republic would empty half the establishments of New York of their servants without a moment's warning.

A *cazuela* (stew-pan) or two, an *asador* (spit), a *cucharron,* or ladle, a *tenedor,* or big fork, a bundle of twigs for stirring atole, one or two bricks upon which to support a pan, and perhaps, but only in the case of families of some social pretensions, a *hornito* or Dutch oven, and you have the sum and substance of the paraphernalia of the Mexican kitchen.

Even in the most opulent houses in the City of Mexico itself, stoves and ranges are unheard of, their place being supplied by an architectural contrivance of brick, arranged for burning charcoal, the draught being regulated by an energetic use of a fan of feathers in the hands of a sweltering cook.

This was the cooking-stove of the Romans, although sheet iron boxes exhumed from Herculaneum and Pompeii are to be seen in the Museum of Naples.

The Mexican is tenacious of old usages; this because he is the descendant of five different races, each in its way conservative of all that had been handed down from its ancestors; these races, it needs no words to show, were the Roman, the Teuton, the Arab, the Celt, and the Aztec.

From no source did I receive greater help or encouragement in the preparation of this article than from the ladies of Mexico and southern Texas whom it was my great good fortune to meet; I found them eager to impart information, ready to concede deficiencies, anxious for the introduction of accessories of which they have heard more than most Americans would imagine, and possessed in an eminent degree of that true home spirit which impels every lady to the desire of becoming a "lafdig," lady, or loaf-divider.

He who has "nosed around" Mexican towns, as I have, without guide-book, and generally without a companion, is sure to yield to the temptation of indulging in historical restrospection and conjuring up in memory those centuries when the Spaniard was essentially the Roman, and the Roman had degenerated into a creature of "panem et circenses."

Bread and circuses are the mainstays of the Mexican population today, and no municipality is so poor that it does not attempt to provide open air concerts of some kind twice or thrice a week for all of its citizens.

The music is never really bad, and very frequently is as good as can be found anywhere, and no words of praise seem to me to be excessive for a policy which affords to the poor as well as the rich the most refining of all enjoyments, as well as an opportunity of coming in contact with one's neighbors. But to this policy we cannot give more than brief reference, and must pass on to describe the venders of street foods, who on such occasion throng the streets, and afford the traveler, the anthropologist, and the folk-lorist a never-ending source of interest and reflection in their wares, their usages, and their cries.

While there were many exceptions to the rule, yet the rule seemed to me to be that each street vender confined himself to some particular line of goods; there were those who dealt in candies only, while their neighbors hawked cakes of many kinds; some dispensed liquid hospitality, and others again had little portable ovens near their tables, and kept in readiness all sorts of savory compounds of meat, eggs, coffee, pastry, and vegetables.

It will be convenient for our purposes to consider this rule as absolute, and describe each in its turn.

Morelia may be selected as the typical Mexican town in this connection, but all such selections are matters of taste, and I should have no cause of complaint or dissent were some reader of these pages, experienced in Mexican matters, to take issue with me and defend the superior claims of Toluca, Patzcuaro, Chihuahua, Hermosillo, Queretaro, San Miguel de Allendo, Celaya, or San Luis Potosi.

In the streets of Morelia one finds no less than thirty kinds of candy carried about by the "dulceros"; this list includes all those to be seen in the cities farther to the north, such as San Antonio de Bexar in Texas, Laredo in the same state, Matamoros in Tamaulipas, Monterey, Monclova, and Chihuahua.

The number of cakes seems to go on *pari passu* with that of the candies. The reason for this preeminence in the matter of toothsome confections, as given to me by an intelligent Mexican gentleman whom I met, is that in Morelia and some other cities there were in olden days convents of Carmelite nuns, who devoted much attention to the making of cakes and candies, and instructed many of the young native women in the same art; the same rule would apply to the beautiful "drawn work," or "perfilada," for which many of these towns are famous; but in each case there is good reason for supposing that there was a substratum of native knowledge and aptitude upon which to build.

Included in the list of candies, we can fairly place candied fruits, and of these Morelia has to sell delicious candied bananas, apricots, figs, oranges, lemons, limes, pineapples, pears, apples, and almonds.

There are also candied slices of *Camotes* (sweet potatoes) and *Calabazas,* or pumpkins; and the favorite *biznaga* and *socoyonostre* candies are really nothing more or less than candied cactus.

Then come the candies of the pecan, *piñon,* and ground-nut, *cacahuate,* of which mention has already been made.

In the line of dried fruits sold by these peddlers of small wares, we find *tortas de higo,* a sort of fig paste, not at all bad, the *queso de tuna,* already fully described, *platanos pasados.* or dried bananas, but none of the dried Spanish bayonet fruit, so often seen among the Apaches, and none of the dried tuna itself; dried peaches, apples, and quinces are frequent, but rather among the street venders of groceries and the small *tendajones* than among the "dulceros" proper. The name *orejenes* (big ears) is commonly bestowed upon dried fruit of all kinds, from a supposed resemblance to the human ear.

Whether it be considered as a candied fruit or a cake by itself, I think I should here introduce the name of the *chaloupa* (sloop) or sweet potato hollowed out in shape of a small boat, fried in syrup and filled with a cargo of slices of the same material. It is very palatable and much relished by the Mexican *muchacho,* into whose good graces I have on several occasions forced my way by a diplomatic presentation of a mouthful.

With such an infinitude of material, I may be pardoned for selecting only those things which appear to me to be the most important. These are the *Carmancilla de leche,* a striated cream candy which will hold its own with any that can be found farther north. Next comes *Torreon de almendra,* a nougat of almond, and the *Charamusca,* a kind of sugar taffy, of all three of which, as of the pecan candy, my children sent me enthusiastic and appreciative praise from Omaha.

Charamusca is also applied to a cake much resembling our old-fashioned horse-cakes or gingerbread.

Marcasotas are a variety of tea buns, quite good in their way. The anise-seeded little cakes of our own tables are known to the Mexicans.

Puches are identical with our doughnuts, and *marramos* and *ojarrosca* in general resemble our cakes, but I cannot recall exactly which ones.

In the larger cities and towns there are pretentious *dulcerias* and *neverias* for the sale of sweetmeats of all kinds and of ice-creams. In these can be found about the same class of goods to be seen in New York,

Washington, Philadelphia, Chicago, or St. Louis. The prices are reasonable, and every attention is given to patrons; but for me these places possessed only slight attraction, as my desire was to watch the doings of the half-clad candy men of the street corners; so beyond acknowledging gratefully that the cream puffs which I found in Monterey, the City of Mexico, and other cities, were equal to the best anywhere, I will escort my reader back to the company of our friend, Don Procopio Ramirez, whom I should say we left dozing at the corner of the plaza soothed into a half slumber by the strains of the military band, which was rendering "En Sueño seductor" while the somnolent Procopio was trying to drive away the buzzing flies with a fly-flapper of paper.

Boys are boys the world over; those of Mexico are as mischievous as any, and a band of them, promenading restlessly around the plaza, listening to the music, soon espies the unfortunate Procopio, and is on him in a minute, flinging the greasy caps of unwary comrades in his face, and yelling in his ears the soul-disturbing epithet of "*Cucaruchero!*" or cockroach breeder, in allusion to the superstition prevalent among the boys of Mexico that all these street candies are made for the purpose of raising that domestic insect.

Don Procopio takes after them with an energy which does him great credit, but it is written in the annals of fate that rheumatic legs never shall catch the bad boy, and so poor old Procopio soon is back at his little table, under the flickering oil lamp, mechanically waving his "*flapper*" and droning out his monotonous song:

> Charamusca! Charamusca! Carmencillo de leche! de leche!
> Torreon de almendra! Almendra! Algo de Fruta! Algo de dulce!

When the sun is in the dog-star, when the days seem to be at their hottest, little tables are erected everywhere, and old men and women, and sometimes young ones too, engage in a lively trade in selling every conceivable kind of liquid refreshment. There is the inevitable *pulque,* smelling much like half-turned buttermilk, but cooling, palatable, refreshing, and nutritious. One penny will buy a big glassful. Alongside of it comes the pink *colonche* or cider of the tuna; this is an exceptionally good drink. Then you can buy lemonades, limeades, orangeades, pineappleades, and sometimes a pomegranateade, but all made with brown sugar or pelonce, white sugar not being any too plentiful in Mexico. The lemonade may be colored with rose, and is then called "limonada rosa," or it may, perchance, have a strawberry or two thrown in just for luck. More rarely, you may find fresh milk, of which I saw great quantities going by train from Lerma to the markets of the City of Mexico, or the acidulous *leche de mantequilla,* called *jocome* in the State of Michoacan, and known to us as buttermilk.

A fair to middling good ginger ale is made in Monterey, but it strikes upon the American palate with a peculiar taste, because it is nearly all flavored with rose or strawberry.

In the same city, and in Toluca and Patzcuaro, beer is made which as yet is only mediocre in quality; time will certainly improve it, and a great trade by developed, because the Mexicans are very fond of beer, and import quantities of it from Germany and Scandinavia; of late years, the American breweries of St. Louis and Milwaukee have had things all their own way, and send down train loads of their bottled product which commands a ready sale, despite the duty. Indeed, in the States of Sonora and Nuevo Leon I have seen Mexicans drinking beer for breakfast; but it is well to remember that the Mexican custom is much like that of the French in the matter of breakfast, and these people were travelling.

In the extravagant use of all these lemonade and other "ades," the Mexicans reveal the Moorish strain in their blood, and this is still further shown by the variety of *orchatas* (orgeats), which, of course, are not of American origin. Orchatas are made of the seeds of the melon, when those of the almond are not obtainable, and flavored with anything that suits the taste; they are pleasant and cooling and sold in great quantities, especially on such occasions as "La noche del Grito" (15th–16th of September), in the City of Mexico.

If one be not satisfied with these mild beverages, or with the honey water of the maguey (*agua de miel*), he can enter the nearest *pulqueria* or *cantina,* and drink to his heart's content of pulque itself, or the more alcoholic mescal, of the brands, "Legitimo Bacanora," "Legitimo San Carlos," "Legitimo Apam," all the while gazing upon the walls covered with highly colored representations of the Sacred Heart, the Good Shepherd, and other holy subjects, this being a perpetuation of the custom introduced by pious friars in the early days immediately succeeding the Conquest, the idea being that the sight of these sacred themes would distract the liquor-inflamed mind from thoughts of strife and blood.

Pulque and mescal are often "curado" or flavored with juice of the strawberry, pineapple, or orange, and with the peel of the last and of lemon; sometimes with the juice of pomegranate.

As I have shown in a paper on the Rio Grande, published in the "Anthropologist" of Washington, the mescal is adulterated with lime-water, a practice which was sternly prohibited by the Emperor Charles V as far back as 1528.

The mescal "curado" with the orange peel and lemon is very palatable, and loses much of its fiery taste, which is also diminished by the curious Mexican custom of placing a pinch of salt upon the tongue before swallowing the draught of liquor. In all the *cantinas* in Sonora, Guadalajara, and Michoacan the proprietor of the *cantina* offers to each patron a scoopful of salt to use with his drink.

On the streets in the towns one can see conveyances passing from point to point loaded with pigskins filled with pulque or mescal; at times, bladders are used for the same purpose. A good-sized pigskin will hold from twenty-five to thirty gallons.

Very little American whiskey is to be found, and that nearly always of the poorest quality and heavily adulterated; but there are the heavy native wine of Parras, already mentioned, the "aguardiente de caña," or sugar rum, and the "aguardiente de uva," or colorless grape brandy, also of Parras, and the fearful, fiery Catalan. The last had better be avoided.

French brandy, none too good, is on sale in many places, but it is not deserving of much attention, excepting in Matamoros, where it can always be found of excellent quality.

Mexicans of wealth are extremely fond of liqueurs, and many are in use among them which are unknown to Americans; among them may be mentioned "Crême de Rose," "Dessertine," "Crême de Menthe," "Crême de Nougat," and the Arabian liqueur prepared from wormwood, called "Byrrh."

In the centre of the plaza—that is to say of the principal plaza, if there be more than one, in a Mexican town—can always be seen rows of tables set out with some care, lighted with rather dingy oil lamps, and provided with hot coffee, hot chocolate, excellent bread, and many dishes, hot or cold, which are retailed in liberal portions at a moderate price; so moderate, indeed, that during the hotter months these tables serve all the purposes of the "trattoría" of Venice, and supply to families excellent food, already cooked, at prices which make it cheaper to patronize them than to depend upon servants.

Few tourists can have forgotten the "chile stands" of San Antonio, Texas, once a most interesting feature of the life of that charming city, but abolished within the past two or three years in deference to the "progressive" spirit of certain councilmen.

At these one was always tolerably sure of getting a cup of excellent hot coffee, or one of equally good chocolate, for the making of which the Mexicans are deservedly famous; tea, strange to relate, was never to be had, and milk only infrequently.

But, "chile con carne," "tamales," "tortillas," "chile rellenos," "huevos revultos," "lengua lampreada," many other kinds of "pucheros" and "ollas," with leathery cheese, burning peppers, stewed tomatoes, and many other items too numerous to mention at this time, were always on sale.

The farther to the south one went, the more elaborate was the spread to be noted on these street tables, until at or near San Luis Potosi it might be called a banquet for the poor.

I may save time and space by condensing my remarks and referring to what my note-books relate of the display upon the Grand Plaza of the City of Mexico, during the great national *fiesta* of September 15th and 16th, 1891.

It may be well to say that on this particular night of the year the fullest liberty is given to the boys and young men to make all the noise they wish, and a more conscientious discharge of a semi-constitutional privilege it has never been my fortune to witness. The walls of the public buildings seemed about to crack with the din of horns, the shrieks of *muchachos,* the howls of sandal-shod Indians saturated with pulque, and the cries of the men and women at the stands, imploring passers-by—I should not say passers-by, because no one could pass by, the jam being so fearful, but let us say standers-by—to walk right up and buy their wares.

"Do you not hear me? I am selling the best pulque in the republic of Mexico, and it is only a centavo a glass; come right up and taste it."
"This mescal comes from Apam; you'll never drink any other if you once try this."
"Arroz con leche! Arroz con leche!"
"Nieve! Nieve! para regalarse!"
"Algo de Dulce! Aglo de Frutal"
"Charamusca! Charamusca! Carmencillo de leche! Torreon de almendra!"
"Agua fresca!"
"Limonada rosa!"

And a thousand other yells, cat-calls, shrieks, whistles, snorts, blowing on horns, ringing of bells, and other diabolical noises which the small boy the world over can be relied upon to furnish if he be given half a chance.

To come to the tables or stands: they were loaded with chocolate, coffee, agua de miel, pulque, mescal orchatas of several kinds, all the lemon and other "ades" already described, as well as all the cakes and candies, chile con carne, tamales, tortillas, fresh bread, rolls, cheese, fruits, sandwiches of all kinds, spare-ribs, stewed kidneys, stewed heart, fried liver, pork chops, hogs' head cheese, salad of the aguacate, and another salad made of boiled potatoes, sliced, with shredded ham, lettuce, beets, and sardines. There were enchiladas, chaloupas, fried chicken, cold turkey, and I dare not say what else; there were so many things on exhibition, the sight became bewildered.

There was *arroz con leche,* or rice stewed to a pulp in rich milk, of which the Mexicans never seem to become tired; it is sold in little cups as custard, made into pies and cakes, and also without any addition at all; I found it very agreeable in all its forms, and I believe it to be a most nourishing food.

Sausages are very much in favor in Mexico; they are possibly the only "survival" now discernible of the Teutonic part of the lineage of the Mexican people. They bear names differing according to some peculiarity of shape or composition; the "longaniza" is the long thin variety most resembling our own "link" sausage; the "chorrizo" sells in largest quantity; it is made by boiling pork in strong vinegar, and then chopping it up with chile colorado and onions.

Chile con carne is meat prepared in a savory stew with chile colorado, tomato, grease, and generally, although not always, with garlic. Chile sauce is a sauce made of chile colorado, tomato, and lard. Chilchipin sauce is made on the same general principle.

Enchiladas are practically corn fritters allowed to simmer for a moment in chile sauce, and then served hot with a sprinkling of grated cheese and onion.

Tamales, a dish derived from the Aztecs, are croquettes of beef or chicken boiled in corn-husks.

Tortillas, as is well known, are corn cakes prepared by soaking maize in lime-water until the outer skin comes off, and then rubbing the softened kernels to a paste on a "metate" or stone mill.[3]

Puchero is a stew of any kind; it resembles an "olla;" when made of tripe, it is called by the name "menudo."

Boiled squash is sold and eaten seeds and all, just as is the case among the Yumas and Cocopahs of Lower California.

Huevos revueltos are eggs fried on both sides, and served with chile sauce.

Cabra lampreada and "lengua lampreada" are goat meat or tongue fried in egg.

Frijoles, it goes without saying, appear on every one of these tables.

The Mexicans have very excellent taste in the matter of preserves; several cities, notably Celaya and Morelia, make great quantities of the "cajetes," or wooden boxes of conserves of guavas, quinces, "leche quemado," and others which, in my opinion, will command a good market among the Americans as soon as they become acquainted with them.

In Monterey there are made three or four kinds of preserves such as were in vogue in the United States in our grandmothers' days: peaches, quinces, and pears, in glass jars; they are exceedingly good. The bread of Mexico is equal to any in the world; the "panaderias," or bakeries, are well patronized, very few families in the towns baking their own supply.

Coffee, in many sections, is made in the original Moorish or Arabic manner, as an "extracto," and in Michoacan, in the coffee districts, the servants do not ask you to take coffee, but to take "extracto." This "extracto" is kept in glass bottles, and a teaspoonful is enough, when mixed with hot milk, to make a cup of palatable coffee. The coffee of Mexico possesses both strength and fine flavor.

Chocolate is usually served with an egg foam on the top of the vessel; this is produced by rapidly revolving between the hands an instrument of wood made for that special purpose, and kept on sale in the market-places.

At Celaya and Morelia can be found a peculiar dish called *jaleatin,* or jelly, made by stewing pigs' feet in red wine; it is like our calves'-foot jelly, and is both cooling and refreshing.

In the early hours of morning, and especially of Sunday morning, a run through the markets of a Mexican town will always be found replete with interest and information.

The more prosperous tradesmen occupy large stalls or booths, but the poorer brethren are content with a mat or two upon which to spread piles of grapes, oranges, "cardones," "aguacates," "queso de tuna," and other fruits, vegetables, and table necessaries.

Each tries to drown the voice of his neighbor; but the Mexican men and women coming out to make purchases pass through the din apparently unmindful of the bawling of the vociferous costermongers who surround them on every side, or line the streets along which they are to pass.

> "Will you look at me? Here I am throwing away the finest cardones in San Luis; six for five cents!"
> "Perrones! Perrones! [big pears] here, only a medio for six; come up and carry them away!"
> "Can't keep me here all day: I want to go home; I am throwing onions, fine, fine onions in the street; I am not selling them; I am giving them away!"

and much more of like import.

But suddenly all this tumult was hushed, not a voice was raised, and every shouting street vender was kneeling on the stones of the street, and most of them with bent heads, devoutly crossing themselves.

"What is the matter?" I asked of the man nearest me.

"Señor, do you not see that carriage coming down the street; it contains a padre, who is bearing the last sacrament to a dying man."

"Is he a friend of yours?"

"Ah, no, señor, I don't even know where he lives; but it is some pobrecito who is about to die."

I confess to having been deeply touched by this proof of the existence, in all this fierce struggle for bread, of a bond of common humanity, but I was not left much time for indulgence in such reflections; the carriage, with closed curtains, rolled slowly by, and the noise of traffic became worse than ever.

"Will you never listen to me? Sixteen great big pears for a shilling, and the finest cardones and tomatoes thrown in the street; I am not selling, I am giving things away," etc.

Before leaving these street venders, who always possessed a particular attraction for me, mention should be made of the "nevero," or ice-cream man, who passes along the streets at certain hours of the day selling a palatable ice-cream, in those towns large enough to possess ice machines, or in communication by rail with their more fortunate neighbors.

They carry their wares on top of their heads in buckets, which are frequently painted in the national colors, green, white, and red. This cream is as good as one could expect from frozen milk, which is all it usually is; sometimes the maker seeks to enrich it by the addition of butter and cinnamon; it is then called "Amantequillado," and is a trial to both palate and stomach.

Once, in Monterey, a great *funcion* was in progress, and elaborate preparations had been made by all these dealers in street cakes, candies, fruits, and other refreshments, but a cold north wind coming up unexpectedly, with a shower or two of rain, proved a great disappointment, however, I was one of those who determined to make the effort of getting down to the Plaza Cinco de Mayo, where the most of the entertainment was to be held. At the entrance stood a "nevero," who manifested great distress on account of the heat of the weather; he was vigorously mopping his forehead with a red bandana, which might have been cleaner without hurting anybody's feelings, and at the same time calling out in a loud tone of voice:—"Caliente! Caliente! Ah, que caliente hay! Per aqui 'sta nieve tan dulce para resfrescarse, para regalarse!" (Oh! how hot it is! Oh! how hot it is! But here you have sweet ice-cream with which to refresh yourself, with which to regale yourself!)

His language was so emphatic and vociferous, his acting so life-like, that like numbers of others I was deluded into believing that the weather was indeed hot, and forgetting the "Norte," I bought cinco centavos' worth of his compound, and had nearly finished it before I realized that I had been duped.

In my contact with the street peddlers, and the keepers of the small stores of *tendajones,* I became impressed with the wonderful fact that the smaller and more insignificant the latter appeared to be to my un-practiced eye, the more consequential was the name borne upon its sign, because I wish to inform such of my readers as may never have had the opportunity to travel among Mexicans, that every store and magazine bears a title; it used to amuse me to see that the Store of the Two Hemispheres was probably not over two yards square of our measure-ment, and that the Magazine of the Globe was carrying a stock worth not a cent more than twenty-five dollars at the outside; but one must ac-cept each country as he finds it, and I am compelled to say that in the larger cities of Mexico there are numbers of finely stocked emporia of different classes of goods.

The position of clerk in one of these great mercantile establishments is much in demand, for what reason it would be hard to say, excepting that the comparative seclusion of the young women makes it somewhat difficult to meet them often, unless one be a special attendant in a dry-goods store, in which case conversation is allowed to flow unreservedly.

If the clerk be young, handsome, well-mannered, bright, and of good family, it generally takes about four hours for a young lady to buy a paper of pins; an intelligent clerk may have a great amount of information to impart upon the subject of pins if the intending customer have dove-like eyes, a gentle voice, tiny, soft hands, and a rich old daddy. There are long pins, short pins, black pins, white pins, American pins, English pins, French pins, and many other varieties, all of which I have heard described at length, but I never found it in my heart to grumble at the delay, and always have murmured, "Bless you, my children, bless you," leaving the more earnest expressions of disapproval to the cross old "dueñas," for whom my antagonism dates back to the days when I was a lieutenant in Arizona, ever so many years ago.

Sometimes one will enter into a gorgeous establishment and feel a vague sensation of distrust at seeing some such firm name as that of "Patricio O'Dowd Hijos" (Patrick O'Dowd's Sons, Monterey).

The original Patrick has long since been gathered to his fathers, but his prosperous business is energetically carried on by descendants of decidedly Castilian appearance, whose only sign of a Celtic derivation lies in their name. And so with the banking firms of MacManus in Chihuahua, and Milmo in Monterey, or MacElroy in Tamaulipas, founded by enterprising, intelligent, quick-witted Irish and Scotch ancestors, who married among the natives and left influential families behind them.

In all these mercantile establishments there is the singular custom of *pelon,* which apparently counterbalances any attempt at overcharg-ing on the part of the proprietors. When you become a regular customer, a tiny tin cylinder is provided and hung up in the store in full view of everybody, marked with your name and number. Every time that you make a purchase, a bean is dropped down into the cylinder, and at stated times these are all counted, and for every sixteen or eighteen, depending upon the commercial generosity of the firm, you are allowed six cents in money or goods.

This custom must be one of great antiquity; the word "pelon" means a stone, or other crude weight, with which in Spain it was in ancient days customary to balance the scales used in the markets.

Under the name of "l'agniappe," the very same thing exists among the Creole French in Louisiana. Perhaps the Romans had in their "bonus" a custom of similar import.

Once a week the beggars, the lame, blind, deaf and dumb, take possession of Mexican stores; there being very little, if any, organized charity in the republic, such a system is undoubtedly as good as any that could be devised. The merchants good-naturedly submit to the tax, and an employee doles out to each mendicant the "limosnita" determined upon in his case.

But I was astonished and amused one day, after listening to a beggar's whine:—

"Limosnita, señores, limosnita, por el amor de Dios, y de Nuestra Santa Madre, Maria Santissima, siempre Virgen, concebida sin pecado, madre de Dios, y de los santos Apostolos Pedro y Paulo, y Santo Tomas, San Buenaventura, San Antonio de Padua y San Juan de Dios. Dios se lo pague, señores," etc., and so on to the end of the recitation, which is always carefully committed to memory by the suppliant.

("Alms, just a trifle of alms, gentlemen, for the love of God, and of Our Blessed Mother, Mary, Most Holy, every Virgin, conceived wihout sin, Mother of God, and of the Holy Apostles Peter and Paul, and Saint Thomas, Saint Buenaventura, Saint Anthony of Padua, and Saint John of God," etc.)

"Get out of here, you scoundrel," shouted the irate proprietor. "Get out of here, and go where you belong; you get your alms over at Samaniego's."

From the Mexican restaurant to the Mexican home is only a step, but a big step. There may not be such a great difference in the dishes served or in the manner of cooking, but a Mexican home presents a warm-hearted hospitality which he who has once been fortunate enough to encounter finds hard to forget. While much could be written upon this part of the subject, there are reasons why much must be left unsaid for fear of wounding the sensibilities of people whose homes have been visited. Then much that might properly be said here has been anticipated in the earlier paragraphs, such as those which treat of the stoves and kitchen furniture, as well as the character of the bread to be found on all Mexican tables.

The Mexican housewife does not copy the extravagant habits of her sister to the north of the Rio Grande; all nations belonging wholly or in part to the so-called Latin stock adhere to the one plan of food supply for domestic purposes. Only the amount needed for each day's use is purchased at one time, and very generally just the quantity required for the particular meal; in Teutonic or Northern nations, on the contrary, there is a more apparent tendency to purchase supplies in gross and lay them aside for a rainy day. But Italy, France, Spain, and Mexico never have a rainy day; theirs are the lands of perpetual sunshine; they have little, if any ice; and not being possessed of means of preserving food for more than a few hours, buy exactly what is needed for the occasion. With Northern nations, the reverse obtains: snow and ice and cold may be looked for at any time after winter has once begun. Food if bought can be preserved indefinitely, and unnecessary journeying to and fro avoided. So, our prudent little Mexican housewife sends her "Maria" or "Manuela" to buy in the plaza or from a passing vender a small bunch of fresh onions, tomatoes, and parsnips, with a diminutive slice of pumpkin and one of cabbage; all of which will cost her five centavos. This would be the duplicate of the package which I bought in Monterey, greatly to the surprise of the dealer, who could not altogether make out what a man wanted with such things. Or, she may do as I did in San Luis Potosi and buy for six cents a small-sized collection embracing juicy, sweet, scarlet tunas, with one or more each of chirimoyas, bananas, figs, apples, oranges, grapes, and mangoes, with a small slice of "queso de tuna." But when she sends out for meat, she will scarcely be so fortunate; it is true that she may be offered a choice of ham, goat, kid, sheep, beef, or hog meat, but it will be butchered in a way that will scarcely commend it even to an Apache Indian. The Mexican butcher is generally a fraud, a delusion, and a snare. He worries himself very little about questions of roasts, joints, and chops, but boldly cuts his meat in a manner to suit himself. "This piece you can have for a medio; that one will cost you a real, and that lomo will come to two reales." In the outlying districts beef is very frequently used as "carne seca," or jerked, a form which is far from agreeable to the American palate. Four and one half pounds of lean, fresh meat, free from bone, will make one pound of "carne seca," which has about as much taste as an equal bulk of shavings dipped in bullocks' blood.

Most of the dishes to be found on the tables of private families resemble our own sufficiently well to pass without special description; where there has been a difference, it has been indicated in the reference to foods on sale in the streets and plazas.

Some of the Mexicans have four meals daily, somewhat in the French style; there is a *desayuno* or early breakfast of strong coffee and rolls, or sweetened bread; the more elaborate *almuerzo,* which is a full meat breakfast at noon, after which follows the afternoon siesta; then *merienda* or *collacion* at about five in the evening, consisting of chocolate, sweet cakes, and milk, and the *cena* at 8.30 or 9 P.M., in which figure chile con carne, frijoles, tortillas, cabbage (soup made with onions and tomatoes), cheese, preserved peaches, guavas, quinces, or tunas, and black coffee.

At a fashionable wedding in Saltillo, Mexico, which I witnessed in company with my friend, Captain Francis Hardie, in 1891, there was a very unique procession of servants bearing to the house of the bride great platters upon which were chickens and ducks, roasted, but with the heads replaced and gilded, and decidedly barbaric and Oriental in their magnificence. At the wedding of the beautiful Miss Varrios and Mr. Yturri, in Laredo, the banquet, served in the open air, under canvas sheeting, was very much in the style of such things in the United States. There were cold dishes of turkey, chicken, ham, fried oysters and fish from the Gulf of Mexico, salads, fruits and vegetables of several kinds, cakes of a dozen kinds, rolls, bread, coffee, chocolate, sherry, claret, brandy, whiskey punch, champagne, and cigars. The bride very graciously sent for all the gentlemen who approached in single file and were made the recipients of rosebuds from the bridal bouquet. In the cathedral, the groom, at the words "With all my worldly goods I do thee endow," presented his bride with thirteen coins, in memory, so the local Solons assured us, of the twelve Apostles and their Master, but this is not so; the custom, called by a word of Arabic derivation the "jarras," came into Spain with the Moors, and is still known in Algeria and Morocco, as I find stated by an English writer in a late number of "All the Year Round."

The above will, no doubt, give a fairly clear idea of the foods and culinary methods of the Mexican people and the Americans living nearest to them; much more might be added, but it would be in the nature of surplusage. There remain to be described only two or three dishes which are peculiar to the country and somewhat different from those to be found in the United States. One is made of chicken, first parboiled and then roasted and stuffed with chopped onion, chile, tomatoes, and seeded raisins. Another is a salad of cucumbers sliced very thin and served with an Italian dressing to which are added hard boiled eggs, chile, a pinch of curry, and some chopped onion. This salad may have been introduced from the Creole portion of Louisiana. During the holy season of Christmas, the women on the Rio Grande make the "buñuelos," a fritter or fried pancake, moulded into form on the cook's knee; in "The Medicine-Men of the Apache," in volume IX, Annual Report of Bureau of Ethnology,

Smithsonian Institution, I made an attempt to demonstrate the identity of this cake with the "Crispillae" of the Normans and Romans, as described by Ducange in his "Glossarium." Something of the same sort is still prepared among the Algerians, but without regard to seasons.[4]

To make this article perfectly complete, there should be added some few paragraphs descriptive of the great love borne by the Mexicans for birds and flowers, but an elaborate extension of the subject would demand too much space.

There are very few houses in Mexico proper which cannot boast of half a dozen cages filled with mocking-birds or some others of the feathery tribe, and rarely can one pass through the "zaguan" or main entrance hall of a Mexican residence, and not see in the "patio" or inner court more than a dozen different varieties of flowers in successful cultivation and bloom.

The flower market of the City of Mexico will suffer but little, if any, in comparison with that of the Madeleine in Paris, or Covent Garden, London; there is always a fine display of Jacqueminots, Marshal Neils, tuberoses, mignonettes, pansies, "no me olvides" (forget-me-nots), orange blossoms, and other beautiful and fragrant flowers, to be had at your own prices. For example, an irreproachable bouquet of all the above flowers made up sells for two bits in Mexican money, equivalent to about sixteen cents American.

The same agreeable exuberance of floral vegetation is manifest in Morelia, Saltillo, San Luis Potosi, Hermosillo, and nearly every other town of any consequence in Mexico, although from the fact that Mexican houses are built to enclose the garden or "patio," the transient visitor to a town may not always promptly see what is to be seen of this kind.

But there are very few towns which do not maintain public flower gardens in the main plazas; some of these, notably that of Hermosillo, in Sonora, when I was last there; that of Chihuahua, and those of San Luis Potosi, Linares, and many other places, were well worthy of imitation; there were growing maguey, bananas, dates, oranges, and lemons, roses, oleanders, jasmins, lilies, and many others.[5]

This rule obtains not only in the southern and central parts of the republic, but in the extreme northern boundary as well; the Jagous, Mac-Manuses, Leals, Isaguirris, Young-MacAllans, and Biscayas, of the Rio Grande valley, make commendable efforts to raise everything in the floral line worth raising. In the Biscaya garden, Matamoros, I noted pinks, roses, bananas, geraniums, jasmins, oranges, lilies, mignonettes, lemons, peaches, grapes, forget-me-nots, tulipans, magnolias, heliotropes, carnations, and such exquisite flowers, all at their best.

In all that part of Texas where the Mexicans once had settlements the same rule holds good, although I am far from attributing it to former occupancy solely.

San Antonio, Houston, Victoria, San Diego, Laredo, Corpus Christi, each claims the banner. The "Battle of Flowers," in San Antonio, held on the first day of May or the last of April, is a sight well worth miles of travel to see. All equipages are decorated from pole to hind wheel with beautiful buds and foliage; the horses are equally favored, and the ladies and gentlemen driving wear boutonnières and bouquets, or wreaths or parasols of flowers. It is one of the great attractions of Texas.

Most interesting of all these gardens, to my mind, was the Cactus garden of Mrs. Miller, near the Havana ranch, on the Rio Grande, in Starr County, Texas. This indefatigable and intelligent lady keeps under cultivation no less than seventy-eight different varieties of this wonderful family. I was astonished at what she had to show, and would certainly enter into a longer relation of all that I there noted, did I not know that the more prominent cactologists of the United States and Canada are now in correspondence with her.

The great zone of territory of which I have been trying to make a description—from the river Nueces, in Texas, to and below San Luis Potosi, in Mexico, about a thousand miles in a direct line from north to south—has, until within the past few years, been a sealed book to the botanist, the folk-lorist, the anthropologist, and the explorer generally, and even with the construction of the International, the "Tampico Route," the Mexican National, and other lines, much remains to be desired in the way of easy communication, and great districts can as yet be traversed only by pack-mules, or slow-moving "carretas."

There is good reason for believing that within the next two or three years further extensions of existing lines, or the construction of new ones, will be made a matter of state expediency; and once begun, there is no telling where the work of progress will stop, since the more the country is known, the better will it be appreciated.

Colonization on a large scale is not to be recommended, except in the one case of sericulture, where the superior knowledge of the Japanese might be used to excellent advantage.

Colonies will always be looked upon, in any country, with a good deal of suspicion and mistrust. Where they do well, the natives feel that they are losing profits which belong to them by the right of prior occupation. Where they fail, they become a menace to existing institutions.

Small bands, or small colonies of skilled laborers, will be just what Mexico wants. If composed of such trades as that of the carpenter, the iron-worker, blacksmith or machinist, the painter, the stone-cutter and builder, the telegraph operator, the railroad and bridge engineers, they will enter at once into the nation's life, as they supply exactly what it needs, and if composed, to some extent, of young men who will seek wives among the respectable families of the neighborhood in which they settle, so much the better.

Notes

1. In her interesting and charming work, *Life in Mexico* (London, 1843), Madame Calderon de la Barco has much to say in regard to a drink called "chia," which possibly is the same with "chié." But unfortunately she leaves much to be inferred. She speaks of the crowds in the city of Mexico who "were quenching their thirst with orgeat, chia, lemonade, or pulque," and says that chia is "a drink made of the seed of the plant of that name" (page 110). See again on page 228. Again, on page 292, it is alluded to as one of the drinks used for cooling purposes in very warm weather: "Booths, with ices and chia, were erected all down the lane leading from the church."

2. Francis Parkman (*Pioneers of France in the New World*) says that the Indians of Canada made a hair-oil from the seeds of the sunflower.

3. Among the rustic Mexicans, especially those living in the remoter mountain regions, knives, forks, and spoons are dear and scarce; food is generally dipped out of the dish with a piece of folded tortilla. The above described custom of the rural Mexicans of dipping their tortillas into the dish is certainly Asiatic in origin; perhaps our Lord himself knew of it: "And he answered and said unto them: it is one of the twelve that dippeth with me in the dish." Mark xiv. 20.

4. Lack of space must be offered as an apology for failure to refer to various game birds which resort in great numbers to portions of Mexican territory: ducks, geese, turkeys, quails, doves and "Chachalacas," or to fishes which, of the finest flavor, throng the waters of the Gulf of Mexico. Where, in all the world, for example, can one pass in review such a list of delicate fish? All along that gulf coast from Tampico, in Mexico, clear to the Capes of Florida, the waters are the chosen home of the oyster (Ostion), the shrimp (Cameron), the red snapper (Corbina), the sheepshead (Sargo), the rock (Robalo), the croker (Gruñate), and many others, not omitting exceptionally large and fat green turtles (which are abundant in the estuaries), and frequent catches of the delicious "pompano," and the Jew fish. The last named is as tender as the most delicate spring chicken. In the City of Mexico itself, there is encountered a totally different kind of fish in the "Charrara," or tiny white fish, which I have seen caught by hundreds in the nets of the Tarasco Indians of Lake Patzcuaro, who immediately dry them on rocks in the sun, and ship them in crates of matting to the capital; the taste is much like that of a sardine. They were a favorite food of Montezuma.

    The banks of the Rio Grande are lined with the soft-shelled tortoise, and its waters yield liberally of the "Piltonte," or cat-fish, in great demand among pious and impious Mexicans of the border states during Lent, when (at least in Holy Week) squads of young men start for the river banks at night, marching to the music of guitars. Speaking of fishing, the Mexicans are also fishers of men, as I had occasion to learn several years since, when a little boy was drowned while bathing in the treacherous current of the swollen Bravo del Norte. No trace of his body could be found, as his young comrades were too frightened to give a very intelligible account of the sad accident. "But why can't these Gringo Americanos get the body of the defuncto?" queried the indignant old Mexican women; "doesn't everybody of any sense know that all you have to do is to get a blessed candle, light it, and put it on a shingle, and the shingle will surely float to the spot where the boy's body is, and there remain? Caramba! what stupidity!" Well, they did take the candle, light and place it upon a shingle, and the shingle did circle around over the concealed whirpool, which had sucked the little boy down into its death-dealing embrace, and his body was recovered and buried, to the lasting and triumphant gratification of the "viejas," who wanted to know what the "Americanos" had to say to that?

5. Madame Calderon de la Barca alludes to the tenacity with which the Mexicans adhere to the Aztec custom of using flowers on all occasions, and the decorating of the church altars with them. See her *Life in Mexico,* London, 1843, page 95.

Interpretations from
Museums and Collections

Traps of the "Amerinds":
Classification and Study of Folk
Technology from the Vantage of the Museum

Otis T. Mason

Imagine Otis Mason (1838–1908) contemplating his task as the newly appointed curator of ethnology at the Smithsonian Institution. Looking over the collections on a balmy summer day in 1884, he estimated that 500,000 cultural artifacts, mostly inadequately documented, lay chaotically before him, while new accessions steadily poured in. From these disorganized collections he was asked to prepare numerous exhibits for mass consumption at world's fairs while maintaining service to specialized scientists. And from his supposedly exalted position in the nation's capital, he was expected to set the standard for ethnological study, and to wield social influence and power. All this, of course, was to come about with staff, funding, and space in short supply.

Mason shut himself in the museum with his objects and set about to provide a classification and subsequent interpretation that would provide dignity and order to his division. Mason gave the job of fieldwork to others; upon himself, he took the responsibility to sort, organize, and interpret the collections. Working from the assumption of the unity of culture, Mason lumped objects collected from various cultures into neat categories of technology. During the next ten years, he published a series of museum reports on some of these categories, including "basketwork," "cradles," "bows, arrows, and quivers," and "throwing sticks." With each work, he underscored the similarities of designs and uses across the globe; once arranged and compared, Mason enthused, the objects taught "the progress of the race."

An exhibit of the division's Eskimo collections in 1886 showcased Mason's ideas to the public. Although attention to the cultural areas was evident, Mason cautioned the visitor that "it must be distinctly understood that these areas are wholly secondary to types and material." Walking along one axis of the exhibit, the visitor viewed the range of invention in an arbitrarily defined cultural region; moving on the other axis, the stronger route, allowed the visitor to follow a single invention. "With all the objects in the Eskimo collection being placed in their appropriate boxes," Mason thought, visitors could appreciate the rigor and clarity of natural science taxonomy applied to culture. The emphasis on object types suggested the goal of tracing backward—in time and in culture—through converging lines the origins of modern technology.

Mason's essay on traps reflects many of these concerns that were common to the museum evolutionists. It gives a succinct example of the importance of classification to the cultural interpretation given to the public. Even the essay's organization reflects Mason's museum orientation; it is divided into many sections, and each section labels an idea. The importance of the trap, according to Mason, is that it "teaches the whole lesson of invention." Following the idea of empiricism—that is, that technology arose from imitations of nature—"the trap," he argues, "is an invention in which are embodied most careful studies in animal mentation and habits." Yet there is a difference between this essay and his early reports on technological objects; in this later work, the mystery of cultural varieties and the influence of environment overshadows the unity of culture theme.

Mason closes with a relatively weak section on distribution, which was probably a token nod to some of Franz Boas's concerns. Boas did not believe in the unity of culture and rocked Mason with the argument that similarities resulted from migration of people or from the migration of inventions through passing contact. Unlike causes, Boas pointed out, can cause like effects. Boas wanted Mason to classify the artifacts by cultural groups to teach that "civilization is not something absolute, but that it is relative, and that our ideas and conceptions are true only so far as our civilization goes." Boas insisted, therefore, that Mason not study the unity of a capitalized Culture, but rather study the integrity of specific cultures, and the particular historical and social contexts that influence the diverse character of technology.

Mason took into account in this essay "culture areas" and "contacts," but Mason budged little from his natural science taxonomy. Boas eventually left museum work for the university, and, from his academic post, spread his relativistic thinking until it became dominant in anthropology. The senior Mason still saw system and unity, while the junior Boas saw uniqueness and individuality; Mason stressed the objects while Boas stressed their contexts; Mason served the mass public while Boas served the specialized student. In 1900 when this essay appeared, Mason was capping his career, speaking for a Victorian brand of folklife study, while Boas was looking ahead to the dawn of a new age in the twentieth century.

This essay comes from "Traps of the Amerinds—A Study in Psychology and Invention," *American Anthropologist,* new series, 2 (1900): pp. 657–75. It appeared at a pivotal time, because it marked one of Mason's last studies, while at the same time Boas began assuming control of, and spreading influence from, the American Folklore Society and the anthropology program at Columbia University. For background on Mason's ideas on invention, see his *The Origins of Invention: A Study of Industry among Primitive Peoples* (1895; reprint, Freeport, New York: Books for Libraries Press, 1972); J. W. Powell, "Technology, or the Science of Industries," *American Anthropologist,* new series, 1 (1899): pp. 319–49. For the Mason-Boas debate, see John Buettner-Janusch, "Boas and Mason: Particularism versus Generalization," *American Anthropologist,* new series, 59 (1957): pp. 318–24; Curtis M. Hinsley, Jr., *Savages and Scientists: The Smithsonian Institution and the*

Development of American Anthropology, 1846–1910 (Washington, D.C.: Smithsonian Institution Press, 1981), pp. 94–100; George W. Stocking, Jr., *A Franz Boas Reader: The Shaping of American Anthropology, 1883–1911* (Chicago: University of Chicago Press, 1974), pp. 1–20, 61–67.

*   *   *

> *That unicorns may be betrayed with trees,*
> *And bears with glasses, elephants with holes,*
> *Lions with toils and men with flatteries, . . .*
>   *Let me work;*
> *For I can give his humour the true bent,*
> *And I will bring him to the Capitol.*
>   *Julius Caesar,* II, 1

Meaning of the Term Amerind

America, in this connection, embraces all of the Western Hemisphere visited by the native tribes in their activities associated with the animal kingdom. It might be allowed to exclude a small number of frozen or elevated or desert regions untrodden by human feet, were it not for the fact that most of these were the favorite resorts of zoömorphic gods and all creatures of the aboriginal imagination. Most certainly the name America must in this study include those oceanic meadows or feeding grounds, stretching out from the continents often more than a hundred miles, whereon were born and nourished innumerable creatures, vertebrate and invertebrate, which dominated the activities of the littoral tribes, penetrating far inland, and carrying back in the shape of live animals, including fish, birds, and mammals, the by-products of terrestrial activities.

Amerind, or Amerindian, is merely an abbreviation of the phrase "American Indian," which has fastened itself on our literature despite the errors which it involves.

Definition of the Term Trap

A trap is an invention for the purpose of inducing animals to commit incarceration, self-arrest, or suicide. In the simplest traps the automatism is solely on the part of the animal, but in the highest forms automatic action of the most delicate sort is seen in the traps themselves, involving the harnessing of some natural force, current, weight, spring, and so on, to do man's work.

The climax of invention in any direction is automatic action. The human hand comes first as efficient in human work, and its own movements are supplemented and intensified by devices, but gradually it withdraws itself, its activities being at last performed by apparatus which function in its absence.

These assertions hold true in the devices for capturing animals, which in their simplest forms are merely taking them with the hand just as in gathering fruits. By a second step they are harvested with devices—scoop-nets, dippers, seines, hooks that are substitutes for the crooked finger, reatas, dulls, bolas, and many more. A third step leads to active slaughter with clubs for bruising, knives and axes for cutting and hacking, and with a thousand and one implements for piercing and retrieving. In these the hunters are present and active, making war on the animal.

In the matter of automatism there is no great gulf between the trapper and the hunter. At both ends and in the middle of the trap's activity the man may be present, but not to the victim. Not waiting for the victim to go to its doom of its own will, the hunter, having set his trap, proceeds to entice and compel the game; he has learned to imitate to perfection the noises of birds and beasts—it may be of those he is hunting, of others hunted by them or their enemies;—he knows the smells that are agreeable and the dainty foods most liked; on the contrary he also knows how to allay suspicions in one direction, to arouse them in another,—always with the trap in his mind.

The action of the trap itself is also frequently assisted by the hunter out of sight. He releases the pent-up force of gravity, of elasticity.

Finally, the result of the trap's action is to hand the victim over to the hunter to carry away or to kill. Often the trap does the killing outright, and the result is raw material for the elaborative industries; but in other cases the hunter must be near by to give the *coup de grâce:* the instances are many where the victim must be dispatched at once, or the trap will be destroyed and the result lost.

The Trap as an Invention

As intimated, the trap teaches the whole lesson of invention: At first it is something that the animal unwittingly treads on (Middle Low German, *treppen,* to tread; tramp is a kindred word) in its tramps and walks or falls into durance; at last it is a combination of movement and obstruction, of release and execution, which vies in delicacy with the most destructive weapons. Gravity and elasticity are harnessed by ingenious mechanical combinations. It is possible to trace the new and useful additions in each class, which in the Patent Office would be called inventions.

To follow these in savagery and barbarism, before there were monopolies and patents, is an interesting contribution to the history of empiricism.

The Term Psychology

In this paper the term psychology stands for all those mental processes that are caused and developed by trapping. There is the mental activity of the animal and that of the man; the trap itself is an invention in which are embodied most careful studies in animal mentation and habits—the hunter must know for each species its food, its likes and dislikes, its weaknesses and foibles. A trap in this connection is an ambuscade, a deceit, a temptation, an irresistible allurement; it is strategy. Inasmuch as each species has its own idiosyncrasies, and as the number of species was unlimited, the pedagogic influence of this class of inventions must have been exalting to a high degree for the primitive tribes.

The variety of execution to be done by the trap, irrespective of the species of animals, was very great. It had to inclose or impound or encage, or to seize by the head, horns, limbs, gills; to maim, wound, crush, slash, brain, impale, poison, and so on, as though it had reason—that is, the thought of the hunter had to be locked up in its parts ready to spring into efficiency at a touch. As population increased, wants became more varied and animals made themselves more scarce. They also became more intellectual and wary. If any reader of this may himself have been a trapper he will remember the scrupulous care with which he proceeded at every point—to make the parts stable or unstable, to choose out of innumerable places one that to a careful weighing of a thousand indications seemed best, to set the trap in the fittest manner, and at last to cover his tracks so that the most wary creature would not have the slightest suspicion.

The Amerind knew that the beaver makes for deep water when caught, so he fastened to the trap a heavy stone which held the creature under until it was drowned; he knew also that the beaver would amputate its own leg when it found itself seized, so he must provide for that. The beaver's objection to the smell of anything human is also strong, so the most aromatic substances have to be mixed with castor to sink the weaker into the stronger scent. The savages making a coöperative onslaught upon a village of beaver anticipated their plunging into the stream by rows of stakes driven close together, and killed the beaver while trying to make their escape. To catch a fox it was necessary to win its confidence, and this the savage knew; so he prepared a trap that was perfectly harmless, and let Reynard walk about over the ashes or fresh earth or chaff, picking up dainty bits, until all suspicion was removed. Then was the time to conceal the trap; but all vestiges of human hand or foot must be removed, and the apparatus must be cleaned and smoked most effectually.

Parts of Traps

The trap, like all other inventions, has classes of parts, namely, the working part, and the mechanical, manual, animal part. The victim finds itself in a pound, deadfall, cage, hole, box, toil, noose, or jaw, on a hook, gorge, pale, or knife, and so on. This dangerous element, to repeat, may not need any accessories. The fish swims into a fyke, the animal walks into a pit or pound, the bird or climbing animal finds itself in a cage with racketed entrance to prevent egress; that is all.

In a higher stage of invention, where the forces of gravity and elasticity are invoked to do the incarceration, arrest, or execution, there has to be found between the lure and the execution a host of devices, and these form an ascending series of complexities. The simplest of these intermediary inventions is an unstable prop or support of some kind; the slightest pull at a bait removes the ticklish thing, and weight or noose or other deadly part is set free. The trigger and the catch are more complicated and varied; the secret of them all, however, is that an unstable catch is released by the animal in passing, in prying curiosity, or in rubbing; this is connected by means of sticks and strings to the last release, since the operation of releasing is in connection with the device in which the force is confined and by which the work is to be done. In the highest forms of weight-traps and spring-traps there are veritable machines, since they change the direction and the effect of motion. It is on these that most ingenuity has been expended, and in them is exhibited that wonderful threefold play of working force, work to be done, and processes of reaching the end. Variations in the materials utilized will play no mean part also in a continent covering all zones save the antarctic, all elevations at which man can live, and all varieties of vegetal phenomena growing out of temperature and rainfall. To proceed with some order it will be necessary to divide the Western Hemisphere into convenient culture-areas; the following will serve for a provisional list:

Amerind Culture-areas

Areas	Peoples
1 Arctic	Eskimo
2 Canadian	Athapascan
3 Atlantic slope	Algonquian-Iroquois
4 Mississippi valley	Siouan
5 Louisiana or Gulf	Muskhogean

6	Southeastern Alaska	Haida-Koluschan
7	Columbian region	Salish-Chinookan
8	Interior basin	Shoshonean
9	California region	Very mixed stocks
10	Pueblo region	Tanoan-Tewan and Sonoran
11	Middle American	Nahua-Mayan
12	Cordilleran region	Chibcha-Kechuan
13	Antillean region	Arawak-Caribbean
14	Upper Amazonian region	Jivaro, Peba, Puno, etc.
15	Eastern Brazilian region	Tupi-Guarani, Tapuya
16	Mato Grosso and southward	Mixed people of Brazilian and Andean types
17	Argentina-Patagonian region	Chaco, Pampean, and Patagonian stocks
18	Fuegian region	Aliculuf, Ona, and Yahgan

The inquiry will not be raised here whether the traps not made of metal and found in the hands of the American savages are entirely aboriginal or whether there has been acculturation. A good knowledge of the traps as they exist or existed will go far toward settling the question of origin.

Classification of Traps

Traps are variously classified according to the concept in the student's mind. If it be the natural element in which they work, there will be—
Land traps for mammals, birds, reptiles, and invertebrates,
Water traps for mammals, birds, reptiles, fishes, and invertebrates,
Air traps for birds and insects.
With reference to their parts, either mechanical or efficient, there are a multitude of names which will appear in a separate vocabulary. In the setting they are man-set, self-set, ever-set, and victim-set.

For the purposes of this paper traps may be divided into three groups, namely, (a) inclosing, (b) arresting, (c) killing. In each of these we may begin with the simpler forms—those with the least mechanism—and end with those that are more intricate.

a. Inclosing Traps

(*a*) Pen—dam, pound, fyke.
(*b*) Cage—coop, pocket, cone, fish-trap.
(*c*) Pit—pitfalls.
(*d*) Door—with trigger, fall-cage or fall-door.

b. Arresting Traps

(*e*) Mesh—gill, toils, ratchet.
(*f*) Set-hook—set-line, gorge, trawl.

(*g*) Noose—snare, springe, fall-snare, trawl-snare.
(*h*) Clutch—bird-lime, mechanical jaws.

c. Killing Traps

(*i*) Weight—fall, deadfall.
(*k*) Point—impaling, stomach, missile.
(*l*) Edge—wolf-knife, braining-knife.

A. Inclosing Traps

Inclosing traps are those which imprison the victim, most of them without doing any further bodily harm, though there may be added to these some other devices which will injure or kill. There are four kinds of inclosing traps: (a) pen-traps, (b) cage-traps, (c) pit-traps, (d) door-traps.

(a) *Pen-traps.*—These include pounds or corrals on land, and dams, fish-pens, and fykes in the water, the idea being simply to inclose. Traps of this sort have no tops and therefore are not useful for birds. In connection with other forms, small inclosures of this kind are used to surround the bait and to guide the victim in a certain direction. The pen or pound is like a farmyard—it is an inclosure in which animals are shut. How the animal gets in, how it is kept in, and what is done to it afterward will decide whether the pound is a trap or a corral, or whether it is a reservoir, an abattoir, or a domesticating device. The simplest form of pound is of brush or reeds and confines whatever enters, large or small; but the perfected form, in whatever element it is erected, has interstices carefully adapted to retain certain species and to allow others to escape, or holds the adult individual in and lets the small and young out. The savage tribes understood this process well and, further, could make movable walls of reeds and long nets; indeed, the great impounding nets are the last word in the series. There is a vast deal of natural history and learning in them: they are on land or in the water; above water-level or submerged; in still water or in running water; facing the current or with the current; mouth upward or mouth downward; man-closed, self-closed, or victim-closed,—all the result of good intellectual exercise. Add to the pound an entrance, and there begins another set of inventions around the notion of shutting. A gateway or an entrance may be closed by nature or by device: the tide falls and leaves aquatic creatures imprisoned; animals get under some obstacle and cannot surmount it—they corral themselves. A gateway may be guarded by sentinels also; but gates may be intentionally shut, or a pound-shaped barrier be set up so that the return of those which pass in is impossible. Most pounds, whether in water or on land, have some natural or artificial lane for conducting the game to the gateway. On either side may be precipices, trees with ropes or wattles between wing-nets, or something of the kind along which animals pursue their natural course and are lured or driven to the pen.

(b) *Cage-traps*—In this class must be grouped all forms of coops and strong house-traps on land, and a great variety of cones, pockets, and fish-traps in the waters: all of these are designed for climbing, flying, or swimming creatures. The cage- or coop-trap, completely inclosed on every side, is a step in advance of an open pen, whether on land or in the water. The majority of cage-traps have funnel-shaped entrances, into which the animal passes easily and unrestrained, but exit is prevented by means of a pointed strip of wood or other substance acting as a rachet; or, in the case of nets, the small end of the funnel consists of a series of string gates, which the animal passes, and these close the mouth of the net so as to prevent escape.

Among the Eskimo a unique contrivance for catching foxes was a net which was made to be set around a burrow. Stakes were driven into the snow to support the net, which was about five feet high; in the corners were long pockets, opening wide into the net but gradually contracting until the fox could go no farther; endeavoring to turn back, it became hopelessly entangled and died of fright and cold.

(c) *Pits.*—The digging of pits was not common in America before the discovery, owing to the lack of metallic excavating tools. Pits partially dug out and partially built up were seen here and there as a blind for the hunter, who concealed himself therein. Boas, quoting Lyon, describes an Eskimo fox-trap in the snow into which the animal jumped and was unable to extricate itself; it was like a small lime-kiln in form, having a hole near the top in which the bait was placed; the foxes were obliged to advance over a piece of whalebone which bent beneath their weight and let them into the prison.

The central Eskimo, according to the same authority, dig a wolf-trap in the snow and cover it with a slab of snow on which the bait is laid; the wolf breaks through the roof, and as the bottom of the pit is too narrow to afford him jumping room, he is caught.

The Cree in the Saskatchewan country place at the end of their deer-drives a log of wood, and on the inner side make an excavation sufficiently deep to prevent the animal from leaping back.

Pitfalls are said to have been used by the Indians of Massachusetts. They are described as oval in shape, three rods long and fifteen feet deep.

The Concow Indians of California are said to catch grasshoppers for food by driving them into pits. The Achomawi, or Pit River Indians, dug deer pitfalls, ten or twelve feet deep, by means of sticks, and carried the earth away in baskets. In southern Brazil, also, wild beasts were caught in pits dug for that purpose and covered with leaves.

(d) *Door-traps*—The last form of inclosing trap to be mentioned here is also the most mechanical; it includes those in which a gate or door falls and incloses the whole of the animal, or in which a cage, one side of which is held up by an unstable prop, falls and incloses the victim.

Among inventions of capture in which the operator is present, the inclosing trap resembles the inclosing net or seine.

Parry describes a small house-trap, made of ice and used by the Eskimo for foxes, at one end of which was a door made of the same material to slide up and down in a groove. This door was sustained by a line which passed over the roof and was caught inside on a hook of ice by means of a loose grommet to which the bait was fastened. The fox, pulling at the bait, released the door of ice and found itself in prison.

Crantz describes a house-trap, used by the Greenlanders, in which a broad stone forms the movable door. I have seen a trap of similar mechanism, used by folk in eastern United States, in which a cage or basket is propped up with a loop of splint; this, pulled inside by the animal tugging at the bait, brings down the cage upon the victim. Doubtless this form of imprisoning animals designed to be taken alive was quite well spread over the continent.

B. Arresting Traps

The arresting traps are designed to seize the victim by the neck or gills or feet, resulting in death but not killing it outright.

(e) *Mesh nets.*—The mesh net is based on the fact that birds, beasts, and fishes, by the conformation of their bodies or by the set of the hair, feathers, or gills, may ratchet themselves; that is, they can move in one direction into the net, but cannot withdraw themselves. To this class belong "toils" for land animals, trammels and gill nets for aquatic animals.

Among the archeologic treasures of our National Museum are many net-sinkers, which would lead us to the conclusion that netting is an old art among the aborigines. The great majority of meshing devices are for aquatic animals, but tribes on the coast of British Columbia suspend long nets between long poles in order to capture migratory geese and ducks. The Eskimo make nets of sinew, of rawhide, and of baleen; these nets are set across the rivers in the open water, but more ingeniously under the ice by means of holes cut at such distances apart as to enable the fishermen to draw the net out and in by means of very primitive tackle. In order to set the net, the line is put over the end of the pole and thrust under the ice and in the direction of the other hole, from which another pole with a hook on the end is run. The upper edge of the net has floats and the lower end sinkers.

A device somewhat in the nature of this is doubtless used by the Eskimo of Point Barrow for catching seals: four holes are drilled through the ice about a breathing-hole; from these a net is set under the breathing-hole, the lines being worked through the four corners of the space; the net is hung under the ice, and the seal coming to breathe is entangled therein.

Gill nets are set for seal after the ice forms along the shore. Murdoch reports that smaller seals are captured also in meshing nets of rawhide set along the shore in shallow water; he refers to many authorities on the same subject, but thinks that the meshing nets in northern Alaska came from Siberia.

The use of gill nets is universal throughout Alaska, whether it was an aboriginal invention or not. Elliott illustrates Eskimo women catching salmon in a gill net consisting of a pole and a triangular net attached. The pole rests on a stone at the water-line, while the net sinks in the water; as soon as a fish strikes, the women lift the pole, extricate the fish, and reset the net.

Mesh-fishing is also quite common among the Athapascan tribes, both on the Yukon and on the Mackenzie. Charlevoix states that in St. Francis river, Canada, the Indians made holes in the ice through which they let nets five or six fathoms long; he also describes the taking of beaver by means of nets.

(f) *Set-hooks.*—These may be employed on land or in the water for taking mammals, birds, or fishes. A toggle or gorge may be so baited or placed that a duck or a goose, by diving and swallowing it, may be held under the water and drowned. A single hook may be set for vermin, or baited and left in the water, especially for large fish; for the smaller fish, the trawl or trot-line holding several hooks may be stretched across a body of water, and thus the game may be secured in the absence of the fisherman.

In one sense, most hooks used in taking birds and fishes are traps. They are baited and cast into the water or placed in such position on land that the hunter is out of sight. A line is attached to hooks of this kind, one end of which may be held in the hands of the hunter or tied to a buoy or other signal device.

Anything like a comprehensive treatment of this capture invention would far exceed the limits of this paper; but it is interesting to note that fish-hooks are not found in many American areas—large regions are entirely devoid of them, and even in ancient mounds and works all such relics are wanting. No picture of a fish-hook is seen in any Mexican or

Maya codex, and Von den Steinen notes the entire absence of fish-hooks from large places on the affluents of the Amazon. The simplest form of this class of devices was seen by Lumholtz among the Tarahumari in northern Mexico; they catch blackbirds by tying corn on a snare of pita fiber hidden under the ground; the bird swallows the kernel, which becomes toggled in its esophagus, and cannot eject it.

Another simple form of hook used in catching fishes, reptiles, and birds is a spindle-shaped toggle with a string attached to the middle; the animal swallows the gorge, as it is called, and is thus securely caught.

In the order of complexity—a removal from the mere action of hand-hooks for capture—hook-traps may be divided into the following classes:

The seed on a string.
The gorge.
Hook at the end of string; squid hook.
Baited hooks.
Compound hooks.
Barbed hooks.
Automatic hooks.

(g) *Noose.*—This is a most interesting class of traps. A string or thong or rope, or a bit of whalebone and sinew, may have one end looped around itself so as to slip with perfect ease; the other end will be fastened to some object. This noose may be so placed that the animal will run its head or its foot into it and be caught; or it may be attached to a bent sapling or some form of springe which is held down by a device, to be liberated by the animal coming to seize the bait or lure. In order to prevent the animal from gnawing the snare, perforated sticks may be suspended just over the knot, thus making a very complicated device. The noose may be used in the air for birds on the wing, on the land in many ways, and sparingly in the water.

Boas says that among the central Eskimo water-fowl of all descriptions are caught in abundance in whalebone nooses fastened to a long whalebone line or to a thong. The line is set along the edge of a lake, particularly near the nesting-places. At shallow points these lines are placed across the water to catch the diving and swimming birds. Hares, ermines, and lemmings are also taken in whalebone snares. E. W. Nelson describes a noose for catching Parry's marmot, which involves a form of release mentioned also as used among the Iroquois. The victim enters the leadway as usual, and instead of pulling at the bait to release the spring, it gnaws in two a string which holds the snare-down and which has something on it appetizing to the animal. In the Iroquois rabbit-trap the string is steeped in salt.

The simplest nooses at Point Barrow are made of baleen and set around where fine gravel has been placed to attract the birds. Accounts are also given of nooses of whalebone set in water along the shores where ducks dive for their favorite plants, and which catch the birds by the neck. This reminds one of the use of the mesh net for the same purpose in California. From Nelson and other observers among the Eskimo, and from the examination of collections in the museums, it is learned that the methods and places of setting a noose are limited only by the habits of the different animals.

In the Mackenzie river country, and wherever the Hudson Bay Company's people have prosecuted their work, the snare and the springe are very commonly employed. Even reindeer and moose are strangled by means of snares set in their way.

Father Morice figures a great variety of applications of the noose. In a form called the hedge-snare an open gateway in the hedge is flanked by two stout posts, each of which has a notch near the top; the noose is placed open so as to fill the space between the posts; above the noose is fastened a stick just fitting across the gateway, the ends resting in the notches of the posts. The animal runs its head into the noose, releases the toggle, and the spring flies up. The insertion of the long stick or pole into the lines above the noose is very common in the northern Athapascan area.

In Wood's *New England Canaan,* we have the quaintest description of a New England trap: "The Salvages take these in trappes made of their naturall Hempe which they place in the earthe where they fell a tree for browse and when hee roundes the tree for the browse if hee tread on the trap he is horsed up by the legg by means of a pole that starts up and catcheth him."[1]

The Gentleman of Elvas[2] gives the following description of the trap among the Autiamgue tribes: "With great springes which lifted up their feet from the ground; and the snare was made with a strong string, whereunto was fastened a knot of a cane, which ran close about the neck of the conie, because they should not gnaw the string."

Teit, in his account of the Thompson River tribes,[3] describes deer fences and springs used in catching large and small animals. Mrs. Allison describes snares for catching deer and birds in the same region. This custom prevailed also in California among many tribes described by Frost and Powers. Zuñi boys catch blackbirds with snares made of horsehair fastened to rope; these snares are laid on the ground and seeds placed between; when the birds alight they put their feet into the snare and are drawn up and captured. The older Zuñis drive sunflower stalks into the ground and fasten a noose on the top; when a hawk, watching for fieldmice, alights on the stalks, its feet are ensnared; being unable to rise, the hawk remains stupidly on its perch and allows itself to be captured.

The Tarahumari of Chihuahua are very ingenious in trapping rats, gophers, and deer. The ancient inhabitants of Copan caught quetzal birds in snares, and having plucked their beautiful feathers, set them at liberty again. In southern Brazil birds were snared by the feet, by the neck, and by the body. The Fuegians also use baleen nooses, which are set hidden in the grass for the purpose of catching partridges and other birds.

(h) *Clutching devices* are best exemplified by bird-lime, of which last there is not a specimen in the National Museum. The ordinary jaw trap of the hunters may be placed in this class; the common steel rat trap is a good example. It is possible that spring nets may have been used in certain parts of America before the discovery, but the principle involved in the metallic clutching traps was not known.

C. Killing Traps

The principles involved in killing traps are those mentioned under "hunting" as crushing, piercing, and cutting, giving a blow, a stab, or a slash.

(i) *Weight-trap.*—The simplest form of killing trap is the fall, or deadfall, in which a heavy weight drops suddenly upon the animal, destroying its life. The most interesting part of the deadfall, however, is not the crushing of the animal, which is a very gross and brutal operation, but the inventions for securing an unstable support of the weight and for releasing this support by means of the trigger or bait contrivance. There are few separate supplementary or accessory appliances to the deadfall, since the animal is slain outright.

The fall-trap was found in several of the areas mentioned. Essentially, in its least complex form, it consists of five parts: a heavy weight to crush the animal, a fixed support (perhaps a stake in the ground), an unstable support on which the weight rests, a catch which prevents the weight from falling until the bait is nibbled or the string pulled, and, lastly, the trigger itself. The whole weight then comes tumbling upon the animal. The central Eskimo form of deadfall has a slab of ice as a crushing weight, and the same sort of device is found among the western Eskimo. FitzWilliam[4] describes minutely a simple form of deadfall. The Hudson Bay Company's native trappers have a great variety of this particular type. Strachan Jones says the Kutchin caught foxes, wolves, and wolverines in the deadfall.

Maximilian figures a deadfall used for bears in Pennsylvania: the animal walks between two logs; above are two logs fastened firmly together; these are held up by a crossbar supported between two sticks;

a lever attached to the logs passes over the crossbar and is held down at either end in a ratchet, where there is a bait. The bear crouches between the logs, pulls the trigger, and releases the lever, which flies up and lets the ring that supports the fall slip off; then comes the tragedy.

Similar traps are noted in British Columbia and throughout the southwestern country, but I have no reference to a fall-trap in middle America or in South America. I am told by Dr. [Walter] Hough that the Hopi of Arizona have two very primitive forms of deadfall: one, for foxes, consists of a heavy stone slab worked between two upright slabs for wings; one end of the prop rests above against the stone, the other end rests on a cobblestone beneath; the least touch of the prop rocks the cobblestone and lets the weight down upon the fox. In this case the proverb of the rolling stone is reversed. In another form, used for taking birds, the box and the fall or stone slab are similar. The release consists of the following parts: first, the upright and the notched catch; to the bottom of the notched catch a short string is tied, having at the other end a small wooden toggle which is held by a little rod resting against it and caught at its other extremity in the grains of the sandstone slab. This is, indeed, a ticklish support, and the least touch overcomes the friction between the trigger and the slab; this sets free the toggle, which unwinds from the post, the hook-catch flies up, and the weight falls.

(k) *Point-traps* of the highest order were not common in America; that is, the use of arbalist or bow for the purpose of driving an arrow or bolt into the victim or for impaling, or the use of sharpened sticks in the pathway of land animals; but the throwing in the way of carnivorous animals of sharpened whalebone splinters wrapped in fat was practiced.

Bancroft mentions a bear trap, used by the Aleuts, consisting of a board two feet square and two inches thick, furnished with barbed spikes, which was placed in Bruin's path and covered with dust. The unsuspecting victim stepped upon the smooth surface, when his foot sank and was pierced by one of the barbed hooks. Maddened with pain, he put forth another foot to assist in pulling the first away, when that, too, was caught. When all four of the feet were spiked to the board, the beast fell over on its back and its career was soon ended by the hunter.

The wolf-bait, made of a piece of whalebone sharpened at both ends and doubled up, has been mentioned by Boas, and examples of the same device were brought to the National Museum by Nelson from St. Michael, Alaska.

Lumholtz says that the Tarahumari catch deer by putting sharpened sticks in the track and stampeding the animals with dogs.

(l) *Edge-traps.*—There were in America two forms of knife or cutting traps of the most ingenious character. One may be called the wolf-knife. A sharpened blade was inclosed in a frozen mass of fat, and stuck up in a block of ice; the wolf, licking the fat, cut its tongue; the taste of the blood infuriated the animal, so that by licking the knife more it caused a larger flow of blood. All the other members of the pack were attracted to the same spot, devouring one another for the sake of the blood, till all were destroyed.

Another form of edge-trap is found in Alaska, where the blades are attached to one end of a lever, the other end of which is inclosed in a torsion spring of rawhide. The animal stops to pick the bait, pulls the trigger, and releases the unstable hook-catch; the knives fly over and the victim is brained.

Distribution of Traps in America

To trace minutely each of the twelve types of traps throughout the eighteen culture areas of the Western Hemisphere would transcend the limits of this paper. Some of the types were confined to narrow limits, others were used quite universally.

The occurrence or non-occurrence was first of all owing to the presence or the absence of certain animal forms; again, it depended on material for making traps. Deadfalls, for example, could not be employed where there were no trees or stones, but pitfalls might replace them.

Much must be attributed to the ingenuity of one tribe or another, to their contacts and suggestions, and to the demands made on them. A rigorous climate was more stimulating than one that was enervating. The demands of trade, first native and then European, provoked the inventive faculty immensely in such areas, for instance, as the Hudson Bay territory.

So the study of the distribution of traps is also a study of Amerindian intellect and of the primitive mind in its earliest struggles with problems in mechanics and engineering.

Notes

1. *New England Prospect,* Prince Society; Boston, 1883, p. 202.

2. Hakluyt, *Voyages,* vol. 3, p. 114.

3. *Memoirs* of the American Museum of Natural History, Anthropology, vol. 2, pp. 247–49, figs. 228, 229.

4. *The Northwest Passage by Land.*

13

Sacred Objects of the Navajo Rites

Washington Matthews

Washington Matthews (1843–1905) was an army surgeon who used his post at Fort Wingate, New Mexico, to document Navajo folklife. Like Otis Mason, Matthews was concerned with the interpretation of specific objects. But unlike Mason, Matthews sought meaning for his objects primarily from field observation in the context of a single culture. His descriptions of apparently "simple trifles" showed that in use among the Navajos, the objects take on a great cultural significance. In his view, the objects were part of elaborate rites, whose spiritual and ceremonial meaning the natives understand, but would not be clear from the kind of evolutionary technological comparison across cultures that Mason employed. Interpreting the objects from the rites thus means, in museum terms, that "the label is more important than the specimen." The object, in other words, does not speak for itself; the culture speaks to it.

Matthew's thinking on the interpretation of these objects can be traced from his first studies of material culture to his last works on rituals. Matthews began by publishing detailed descriptions of Navajo silversmithing and weaving for the second and third reports of the Bureau of American Ethnology from 1880 to 1882. In each, he addressed matters of origin, and offered that in the case of his silversmithing study, "it may serve not only to illustrate some aspects of their mental condition, their inventive and imitative talents, but possibly to shed some light on the condition and diffusion of the art of the metalist in the prehistoric days of our continent." The descriptions focused on techniques of manufacture, the form of the designs, and the practical uses to which the objects were put. In *The Mountain Chant: A Navajo Ceremony* (1887), Matthews moved deeper into Navajo culture and sought out the symbolism within native rites that was not immediately apparent from evolutionary comparison. In 1897, writing in *Navajo Legends,* he eschewed "the seductive paths of comparative mythology" and instead related their significance in Navajo life. He capped his career with *The Night Chant: A Navajo Ceremony* (1902), in which he concentrated not just on the character of a single culture, but on the symbolism of a single ceremony. The basket-drum and yucca drumstick that he describes in this essay belong to this ceremony; the objects have persisted, he argues, to serve spiritual needs. Indeed, Matthews might have irked some members of his audience by suggesting that the symbolism of the Navajo was "logical and elaborate."

Still, Matthews aligned himself to the evolutionists by pointing out the "primitive" nature of "this crude people," the reflection of the "thoughts and sentiments" of "lower races." Shying away from theoretical pronouncements or generalizations, Matthews was anything but forceful in his interpretations. In *Navaho Legends,* he wrote: "Resemblances between the tales of the Navahoes and those of other peoples, civilized and savage, ancient and modern, are numerous and marked; but space devoted to them would be lost to more important subjects. Again, many of the readers of this book may be prepared, better than the author, to note these resemblances." His modesty is also evident in this essay, in which he quietly defends his right to talk about the objects by claiming twelve years of "hard and oft-baffled" investigation. Nonetheless, his colleagues must have thought highly enough of his studies to elect him president of the American Folklore Society and vice-president of the Chicago Folklore Society. Writing Matthews' obituary in 1905, ethnologist James Mooney wrote, "By a faculty of mingled sympathy and command he won the confidence of the Indian and the knowledge of his secrets, while by virtue of that spiritual vision which was his Keltic inheritance, he was able to look into the soul of primitive things and interpret their meaning as few others have done."

This essay comes from a lecture delivered to the Third International Folklore Congress at the Chicago World's Fair in 1893. It was originally printed as "Some Sacred Objects of the Navajo Rites," in *The International Folk-Lore Congress of the World's Columbian Exposition,* ed. Helen Wheeler Bassett and Frederick Starr (Chicago: Charles H. Sergel Company, 1898), pp. 227–47. For background on Matthews, see James Mooney, "In Memoriam: Washington Matthews," *American Anthropologist,* new series, 9 (1907): pp. 514–23: W. K. McNeil, "A History of American Folklore Scholarship before 1908" (Ph.D. Dissertation, Indiana University, 1980), pp. 325–32. For background on Navaho objects and rites, see Clyde Kluckhohn, W. W. Hill, and Lucy Wales Kluckhohn, *Navaho Material Culture* (Cambridge: Harvard University Press, 1971), and Clyde Kluckhohn and Dorothea Leighton, *The Navaho* (Revised edition, Garden City, New York: Doubleday, 1962).

*   *   *

Someone has said that a first-class museum would consist of a series of satisfactory labels with specimens attached.[1] This saying might be rendered: "The label is more important than the specimen." When I have finished reading this paper, you may admit that this is true in the case of the little museum which I have here to show: a basket, a fascicle of plant fibres, a few rudely painted sticks, some beads and feathers put together as if by children in their meaningless play, form the total of the collection. You would scarcely pick these trifles up if you saw them lying in the gutter, yet when I have told all I have to tell about them, I trust they may seem of greater importance, and that some among you would be as glad to possess them as I am. I might have added largely to this collection had I time to discourse about them, for I possess many more of their kind. It is not a question of things, but of time. I shall do scant justice to this little pile within an hour. An hour it will be to you, and a tiresome hour, no doubt; but you may pass it with greater patience when you learn that this hour's monologue represents to me twelve years of hard and oft-baffled investigation. Such dry facts as I have to relate are not to be obtained by rushing up to the first Indian you meet, notebook in hand. But I have no time for further preliminary remarks, and must proceed at once to my descriptions.

The Basket Drum

The first thing that I present to you is a basket. Wordsworth tells us of Peter Bell that:

> A primrose by a river's brim,
> A yellow primrose was to him,
> And it was nothing more.

To most observers this may seem a yellow basket, but it is much more to many an untutored savage. The art of basket-making is today little cultivated among the Navajos. In developing their blanket-making to the highest point of Indian art, the women of this tribe have neglected other labors. The much ruder, but cognate Apaches, who know how to weave woolen fabrics, make more baskets than the Navajos and make them in greater variety of form, color, and quality. The basket I show you is, however, of Navajo make, and it is skillfully fabricated; yet it is with one exception almost the only form and pattern of basket now made in the tribe. They buy most of their baskets from other tribes. But, having generally let the art of basketry fall into disuse, they still continue to make this form, for the reason that it is essential to their sacred rites, and must be supplied by women of the tribe who know what is required. It is made of twigs of aromatic sumac—a shrub which has many sacred uses—wound in the form of a helix. The fabricator must always put the butt-end of the twig toward the centre of the basket and the tip toward the periphery. A band of red and black, with zigzag edges, is the sole decoration. This band, it will be observed, is not continuous, but is intersected at one point by a narrow line of yellow, or, more properly speaking, of uncolored wood.

When I first observed this, years ago, I fancied that it had some relation to the ''line of life'' observed in the ancient and modern Peublo pottery, and that its existence might be explained by reasons as metaphysical as those which the Pueblos give for their "line of life." But the Navajo has at least one reason of a more practical character. The line is put there to assist in the orientation of the basket, at night, in the medicine-lodge when the fire has burned low and the light is dim. [As for] the law of butts and tips in Navajo ceremonies it must suffice to say that throughout their ceremonies careful discrimination is made between the butt and the tip, the central and the peripheral ends, and that the butt has precedence over the tip. This law applies to the basket before you as well as to other sacred things. The butt of the first twig, placed in the centre, and the tip of the last twig, in the edge, must lie in the same radial line, and this line is marked by the hiatus in the ornamental band. The rim of the basket is often so neatly finished that the medicine-man could not easily tell where the helix ended were not the pale line there to guide him. This line must lie east and west when the basket is employed in the ceremonies.

The most important use of the basket is as a drum. In none of the ancient Navajo rites is a regular drum or tom-tom employed. The inverted basket serves the purpose of one, and the way in which it is used for this simple object is rendered devious and difficult by ceremonious observances. To illustrate, let me describe a *few* of these observances belonging to the ceremony of the Night-Chant. This ceremony lasts nine nights and nine days. During the first four nights song is accompanied only by the rattle. During the last five nights, noises are elicited from the basket-drum by means of the yucca drumstick. The drum is beaten only in the western side of the lodge. For four of these five nights, the following methods are pursued: A small Navajo blanket is laid on the ground, its longer dimension extending east and west. An incomplete circle of meal, open in the west, of the diameter of the basket, is traced on the blanket near its eastern end. A cross in meal, its ends touching the circle near the cardinal points, is then described within the circle. In making this cross a line is first drawn from east to west, and then a line is drawn from south to north. Meal is then applied sunwise to the rim of the upturned basket so as to form an incomplete circle with its opening in the east. A cross, similar to that on the blanket, is drawn in meal on the concavity of the basket, the east and west line of which cross must pass directly through the hiatus in the ornamental band. The basket is then inverted on the blanket in such a manner that the figures in meal on the one shall correspond in position to those on the other. The western half of the blanket is then folded over the convexity of the basket and the musicians are ready to begin. But before they begin to beat time to a song, they tap the basket with the drumstick at the four cardinal points in the order of east, south, west and north. The Navajos say, "We turn down the basket," when they refer to the commencement of songs in which the basket-drum is used, and "We turn up the basket," when they refer to the ending of the songs for the night. On the last night the basket is turned down with much the same observances as on the previous nights; but the openings in the ornamental band and in the circles of meal are turned to the east instead of to the west, and the eastern half of the blanket is folded over the convexity of the basket. There are songs for turning up and for turning down the basket, and there are certain words in these songs at which the shaman prepares to turn up the basket by putting his hand under its eastern rim, and other words at which he does the turning. For four nights when the basket is turned down, the eastern part is laid on the outstretched blanket first, and it is inverted towards the west; on the fifth night, it is inverted in the opposite direction. When it is turned up, it is always lifted first at the eastern edge. As it is raised, an imaginary something is blown toward the east, in the direction of the smoke-hole of the lodge, and when it is completely turned up, hands are waved in the same direction, to drive out the evil influences which the sacred songs have collected and imprisoned under the basket.

The border of this, as of other Navajo baskets, is finished in a diagonally-woven or plaited pattern. These Indians say that the Apaches and other neighboring tribes finish the margins of their baskets with simple circular turns of the investing fibre, like that in the rest of the basket. The Navajo basket, they believe, may always be known by the peculiar finish described, and they say that if among other tribes a woman is found who makes Navajo finish she is of Navajo descent or has learned her art of a Navajo. They account for this by a legend which is perhaps not all mythical. In the ancient days a Navajo woman was seated under a juniper tree finishing a basket in the style of the other tribes as was then the Navajo custom, and while so engaged she was intently thinking if some stronger and more beautiful margin could not be devised. As she thus sat in thought, the good Qastceyelci tore from the overhanging juniper-tree a small spray and cast it into her basket. It immediately occurred to her to imitate in her work the peculiar folds of the juniper leaves and she soon devised a way of doing so. If this margin is worn through, or torn in any way the basket is unfit for sacred use. The basket is given to the shaman when the rites are done; he must not give it away, and he must be careful never to eat out of it, for, notwithstanding its sacred use, it is no desecration to serve food in it.

The Drum-Stick

The next thing to be examined is the drum-stick with which this drum is beaten. I show you now only the stick used in one rite—that of the night chant. The task of making this stick does not necessarily belong to the shaman, any assistant may make it; but so intricate are the rules pertaining to its construction, that one shaman has told me he never found any one who could form it merely from verbal instructions. Practical instructions are necessary. The drum-stick is made anew for each ceremony and destroyed in a manner to be described when the ceremony is over. It is formed from the stout leaves of *Yucca baccata,* a species of Spanish bayonet. But not every plant of this kind is worthy to furnish the material. I have seen an hour spent in search for the proper plant on a hillside bristling with *Yucca baccata.* Four leaves only can be used, and they must all come from the same plant—one from each of the cardinal points of the stem. All must be of the proper length and absolutely free from wound, stain, withered point, or blemish of any kind. These conditions are not fulfilled on every yucca. The leaves may not be cut off but must be torn off downwards, at their articulations. The collector first pulls the selected leaf from the east side of the plant, making a mark with the thumb nail on the east or dorsal side of the leaf near its root, in order that he may know this leaf thereafter. He walks sunwise around the plant to the west side, marks the selected leaf near the tip on its palmar surface and culls it. He then retreats to the south side of the plant and collects his leaf there but does not mark it. Lastly he proceeds sunwise to the north and culls his last leaf,—also without marking it. When the leaves are all obtained the sharp flinty points and the curling marginal cilia are torn off and struck, point upward, in among the remaining leaves of the plant from which they were culled. The four leaves are then taken to the medicine lodge to be made up. The leaves from the east and west are used for the centre or core of the stick and are left whole. The leaves from the north and south are torn into long shreds and used for the wrapper. But since the shaman cannot adequately explain in words, to the devotees who assist him, how the stick is made I shall not attempt the task for you tonight. I have learned how to make it; but I have, now, no fresh yucca leaves on hand to illustrate the process of making. So I shall say nothing more of the process. Any one who is not satisfied with this decision may come with me to the yucca-covered deserts of Arizona and there I may show him how to make a drum-stick. The core of the stick is divided, by a suture of yucca shred into five compartments, one for each night during which the stick is used. Into each of these sections are usually put one or more grains of corn, which, during the five nights that the implement is in use, are supposed to imbibe some sacred properties. When the ceremony is all over these grains are divided among the visiting medicine men, to be ground up and put in their medicine bags. On the last morning of the ceremony, at dawn, when the last song of sequence has been sung and the basket turned up, this drum-stick is pulled to pieces in an order the reverse of that in which it was put together. This work may only be done by the shaman who conducted the rites, and, as he proceeds with his work, he sings the song of the unravelling. As each piece is unwrapped it is straightened out and laid down with its point to the east. The debris which accumulated in the manufacture of the drum-stick and which has been carefully laid away for five days is now brought forth, and one fascicle is made of all. This is taken out of the lodge by an assistant, carried in an easterly direction and laid in the forks of a cedar tree (or in the branches of some other large plant, if a cedar tree is not at hand) where it will be safe from the trampling feet of cattle. There it is left until destroyed or scattered by the forces of nature. The man who sacrifices these fragments takes out with him in the hollow other fasces. As each willow is cut it is trimmed off to the proper length and the discarded top is placed, upright, among the growing willows, as close as possible to the stump from which it was cut. The stump is then rubbed with pollen and pollen is scattered in the air by the ascending hand, upwards from the stump in the place where the shrub grew, as if in sacrifice to the spirit of the shrub. The proper length for the wand is the natural cubit, measured from the inner con-dyle of the humerus to the tip of the middle finger and throughout this distance, the stick must be free from branch, knot, cicatrix or blemish. One stick measured on the arm is taken as a standard for the other sticks. The sticks are then denuded of their bark and each whittled to a point at the butt end, in order that it may be stuck in the ground. Each of the four sticks cut south of the river has then a facet cut at its tip end to repre-sent the square domino or mask worn by the female dancer in the rites. The sticks cut on the north side of the river have no such facet, their round ends sufficiently represent the round or cap-like masks worn by the male dancers. In numerous other articles made of sticks for the Navajo rites, this distinction is made between male and female. I have observed among the Moquis a similar feature in their sacrificial sticks or bahos; but I am not aware if a similar explanation is given by the latter people. The sticks are now painted—those of the south, blue, those of the north, black. Blue in all Navajo symbolism is the color of the south and of the female; black is the color of the north and of the male. The sticks that come from the south of the San Juan represent females; those from the north, males. I might read you a separate lecture on this particular symbolism; but I can now only take time to mention a few instructive points. From various analogies in Navajo myth and language, I am led to believe that the male is assigned to the north for the reason that the north is a land of rigor and fierceness to these people. Not only do inclement and violent winds, typical of the male character, proceed from the north; but the country north of the Navajo land is very rugged and mountainous—within it lie the great peaks of Colorado. And the female is assigned to the south because thence come gentle and warm breezes and the landscape of the south is tame compared with that of the north. However this may be, all through Navajo myth and ceremony the south and all its symbolism is associated with the female; the north and all its symbolism with the male. There is a special portion of the Creation and Migration Myth of the tribe which has relation to these sticks. It is told that when the Navajos lived in the nether world, a great river, the exact counterpart of the San Juan, flowed from east to west through their land. The two sexes of the tribe quarrelled and separated; the women took the south side of the river, the men the north. It is a long story, how they fared during their separation and how they were at last reconciled and came together again, and it need not now be told. But the shamans connect the custom of cutting these sticks on the San Juan—the female sticks on the south and the male sticks on the north bank with this ancient myth.

The black sticks are painted white at their upper extremities in accordance with a fixed law of Navajo hieratic art to which I shall again refer. The facet on each blue stick is daubed with small black spots to represent the eyes and mouth of the female mask, and at its bottom is the yellow horizontal streak seen on the female mask which symbolizes the Naqotsoi or land of yellow horizontal light, i.e. the last streak of departing daylight. The upper extremity of each blue stick is painted black to represent the hair of the female characters in the dance, which flows out freely, not being confined by the domino; while the hair of the male dancer is hidden by the cap-like mask. When the painting is done the sticks are decked with two whorls of turkey and eagle-feathers—each whorl secured by one continuous cotton string which terminates in a downy eagle-feather. The string must be twilled from raw cotton on an old fashioned spindle, the material manufactured by the whites would never do. It must remembered that this use of cotton shows no degeneracy of the rite, since cotton was grown and spun in New Mexico and Arizona from a remote prehistoric period and cotton fabrics are today found among the ruins of the cliff-houses. When the sticks are finished the debris of manufacture is carried to the north and thrown away among a cluster of willows on the north bank of a stream. As I have said, these sticks are, afterwards, stuck up around the sacred dry paintings and the sudatories, and when in this position the black are always erected in the north and the blue in the south. These sticks are permanent property of the shaman.

The feathers used in these plumed wands and in other more important implements of the rites must be taken from live birds. The smaller birds, whose feathers are used are captured on their nests at night. The eagles are caught in earth traps such as I have seen and described among tribes of the north a quarter of a century ago, and the Navajo eagle-hunt is accompanied by rites, prayers, and songs much like those of the same northern races. Each eagle plume must be provided with a well-developed hyporachis; otherwise, it must not be used.

Kethawns

But I must reserve a large share of my time for a description of the kethawns—the sacrifices and messages to the gods. These are perhaps the most interesting of all the sacred objects of the Navajo rites, for they are almost endless in variety and each one embodies concepts usually easy of explanation. Sacrifices of a character analogous to these are widely diffused. All the tribes of the southwest, to and beyond the Mexican line, use them or have used them, and I have found them employed by Indians residing within sixty miles of the British-American boundary. The inahos of the Ainos of Japan seem closely allied to the kethawns.

Navajo kethawns are of two principal kinds, viz.: Cigarettes made of hollow cane, and sticks made of various exogenous woods. Many of them are sacrificed with feathers, either attached or enclosed in the same bundle with them, and such are, no doubt, to be classed with the plume stick of the Zuñis. Much as these sacrifices differ from one another in size, material, painting, and modes of sacrifice, there are certain rules which apply to all, and these I shall describe at length when speaking of special kethawns. . . .

Sacrificial Cigarettes

I shall speak next of the sacrificial cigarettes. These are usually made of the common reed or *phragmites communis,* which grows all over the United States, by the shores of Lake Michigan as well as on the banks of the San Juan. The reed designed for sacrifices is first rubbed well with a piece of sandstone—this is done, no doubt, for the very practical purpose of removing the glossy silicious surface of the reed, in order to make the paint stick. It is next rubbed with a composite plant which grows abundantly in the Navajo country, *Gutierrezia euthamiae,* the tcililgizi or scare-weed of the Navajos—this is done chiefly for metaphysical reasons. The reed must be cut up with a stone knife or arrow-point, and it must be a perfect knife. If the point has been broken off, or if it has been otherwise mutilated, it is dead, "Just the same as a dead man," the shamans have told me—and must not be used in ceremonies which are intended to cure disease and prolong life. In cutting a reed to form a series of cigarettes the operator holds the butt-end toward his body, the tip-end toward the east, and cuts off first that section which comes next to the root; for the butt, as I have told you, has precedence over the tip. This section he marks near its base, and on what he calls its front, with a single transverse notch made also with the stone knife. The severed section he lays on a clean stone, buckskin or cloth (for it must never touch the earth, at least until it is sacrificed) and proceeds to cut off another section from the remaining part of the cane which is next the root. If it is the same length as the preceding piece he marks it with two horizontal notches, in the manner described. A third section he would mark with three, and a fourth with four notches. These notches are put on in order that, throughout all subsequent manipulations—particularly if they are sacrificed in the dark—the butt may be distinguished from the tip, the front from the back, and the order in which they were cut may not be disregarded. But in making the notches, the sacred number four must never be exceeded. If there are to be more than four cigarettes of the same size in one set, the fifth must form the beginning of a new series to be marked with one notch, and the operator must depend on his memory and his care in handling to keep the sets separate. The nodal part of the stem or culm must not be used; it is carefully excluded and split into fragments with the point of the stone knife before being thrown away, lest the gods, coming for their sacrifices, might mistake empty segments for cigarettes and, meeting with disappointment, leave in anger. The god, it is said, examines and smells the cigarette to see if it is made for him; if he is pleased with it he takes it away and rewards the giver.

The second section cut off is laid south of the first and parallel to it. The last section is placed furthest to the south; the order of precedence being from north to south when sacrifices are laid out in a straight line. If there is an order of precedence among the gods to whom they are given, the higher god owns the more northern sacrifice.

The cut ends of the section are next ground smooth on a stone and a splinter of yucca leaf is inserted into each, to serve as a handle while the cigarette is being painted. A thin slice of yucca leaf is also used as a brush, and curved sections of the leaf are used as saucers to hold the paints. The decorations in paint are in great variety, a very few only will be, at present, described and exhibited.

When the painting is completed, a small pledget of feathers is inserted into the hollow of each section at the tip end and shoved down toward the opposite extremity; this is to keep the tobacco from falling out. The feathers used here are commonly those of blue-bird and yellow bird, and an owl-quill is in most cases the implement with which the wad is shoved home. The sections are then filled with tobacco, not the tobacco of commerce, *Nicotiana tabacum;*—this does well enough for men, the gods despise it—but some of the species of native tobacco of the southwest. *Nicotiana attenuata,* the dsil-naco, or mountain tobacco of the Navajos, is the kind used in all the rites I have witnessed; but the Navajos tell me that *Nicotiana palmeri* is used in some ceremonies, and it is not improbable that other species are used. Pollen (usually of corn) is sprinkled on the open end of the cigarette, after the tobacco is inserted, the pollen is moistened with a drop of water and thus the cigarette is sealed. There are very particular rules as to how this water is to be collected, used and disposed of, to which I must now only allude. After the cigarette is sealed, it is symbolically lighted. To do this a piece of rock crystal is held up in the direction of the smoke-hole, or in the beams of the sun, should they enter the lodge; it is then swept down from on high and touched to the tip of the cigarette. On one occasion when I saw cigarettes prepared early in the morning, the sun rose just as they were to be lighted, and shot its ruddy beams in through the doorway of the lodge over the ragged blanket which hung there as a portière. The shaman caught these first beams on his crystal and then touched the crystal to the cigarette.

I have spoken of the front or face of the cigarette, this corresponds with the side of the internode on which the alternate leaf grows, and is marked at the base of the internode in winter by the axillary pit or scar which the Navajos call the eye, this is the side which is notched and which lies next to the ground when the cigarette is sacrificed or planted.

Throughout the work on the kethawns, songs appropriate to different occasions are sung. There are songs for the painting; songs for the filling, when the tobacco is put in; songs for the lighting; songs for the application of the sacrifices to the body of the patient; songs for the application of the pollen, and songs for the sacrifice when the kethawns are taken out to their hiding-places. Some of these I have secured on the cylinder of the Edison phonograph, and I hope, ere we part, to give you a sample.

I present you now a set of sacrifices which are all cigarettes. They belong to the morning of the third day of the ceremony of kledji-qaçal. This ceremony, or a portion of it at least, the myth tells us, originated in the Cañon de Chelly, in Arizona; hence, the reeds of which these cigarettes are made should be culled only in the Cañon de Chelly. The cigarettes may be either six, eight, ten or twelve in number. The shaman who is master of the ceremonies never prepares the same number at two successive ceremonies. He changes the number constantly, and so, too, he makes changes in the songs that accompany the manufacture.

In the Cañon de Chelly, Arizona, there still stands, in an excellent state of preservation, a remarkable ruined cliff-house, built of yellow sandstone. Its upper portion is painted white, horizontally. As it lies in a deep rock shelter, well overshadowed by the towering cliff above, the coating of white paint has been protected from rain and snow, and looks almost as fresh and white now as when first applied, many centuries ago. The Navajos call the edifice "Keninaekai," which signifies a stone house with a white horizontal streak. Freely translating this name the Americans call it the White House. Here, according to the myth, certain divine beings once dwelt, who practiced these rites and taught them to the Navajos. It is to this house, or more properly speaking, to the old divinities of this house, as the accompanying prayers indicate, that these sacrifices are offered:

> Kininaekaigi
> Qayolkal bilnàhacináhi.
> Qayolkal bilnaciçàha.
> Qastceyalçi.
> Nigel icla'.
> Naci hila'.

> In the House of Horizontal White,
> He who rises with the morning light,
> He who moves with the morning light.
> Oh Talking God!
> I have made your sacrifice,
> I have prepared a smoke for you.

Thus does the first part of the prayer begin and then the devotee following the dictation of the priest, mentions what blessings he expects to obtain in return for the present of a cigarette—restoration of all parts of his body, of his mind and voice, prosperity for all his people, increase of his flocks, long life and happiness. All these things and many more: but never one word of vengeance on his enemies or of evil to any one. Qastceyalçi, or the Talking God, is the chief in many groups of Navajo local divinities.

In the set here presented, there are two long and four short cigarettes. Like all other things made in the course of Navajo rites, they have a definite, if not a very accurate or scientific measure. The length of the small kethawns equals the width of three finger-tips: first, second, and third, pressed closely together. This measurement is much used and I shall call it three finger-widths; on my own right hand it measures about 1 ¾ inches. The longer kethawns, which are twice this length, are painted half yellow and half white, to symbolize this White House, as I have described it. The first kethawn is made white at its eastern extremity; the second is made white at its eastern extremity, for reasons that cannot be briefly explained. A cotton string is attached to each, at its centre, by means of a very peculiar knot in whose circles are included three feathers of the blue-bird (*sialia*), and three feathers of the Yellow Warbler, or of *Pipilo chlorurus*—caçoinogáli, "he who shakes the dew," the Navajos call it. One of each kind of feather is taken from a different wing of the bird and one from the tail. Five beads are strung along each string: one of white shell for the east, one of turquoise for the south, one of haliotis shell for the west, one of cannel coal for the north, and one more of white for the east. Beyond these a bunch of three feathers is secured, by means of the peculiar knot already referred to. One of these is a downy eagle feather, the second is the breast feather of a turkey, the third is a "hair" from the "beard" of a turkey-cock. The position of the five attachments on the string are determined by stretching out, on the latter, the digits of one hand—an attachment is made where the centre of each digit falls. The string is originally two spans long, but when it is tied to the kethawn and all objects are attached, the end is cut off, three finger-widths beyond the last attachment.

The four smaller kethawns are called Naakqaigi kethawn or cigarettes sacred to the original dancers of the last night of the ceremony. But as the original dancers all lived once in the Cañon de Chelly and danced at the White House, these cigarettes go with those just described. Two of the four are painted black to symbolize males, and each is marked, near its eastern extremity, or tip end, on the right side, with a design representing the two eagle-plumes and the bunch of owl-feathers worn to this day in the dance of Naakqai by the male dancers. I show this design; but when the kethawns are laid down on their faces to be sacrificed, the design comes only partly into view. The two other small kethawns are merely painted blue to symbolize the yebaad or female characters in the dance. The black and the blue kethawns alternate just as the male and female characters alternate in the dance.

When the kethawns are completed, each is put in a separate corn-husk with twelve different articles which I will not now name and the husks are folded around their contents in a particular manner. The kethawns are arranged in the order of their proper precedence from north to south (from above downwards). This is the order in which they are made, painted, placed in the husks, folded in the husks, lifted, sacrificed and otherwise manipulated.

It takes about an hour to prepare these sacrifices. When they are done the patient sits in the west of the lodge facing the east, with lower extremities extended and with hands open resting on the knees. The shaman first puts the bundles containing the two long cigarettes into the patient's hands and says a long prayer (part of which I have repeated) which the patient recites after him, sentence by sentence. The shaman takes then the bundles and applies them to different parts of the patient's body, proceeding upwards from sole to crown. Pollen is then applied to the patient and the bundles are given to an assistant who carries them out of the lodge. The shaman lastly collects the bundles containing the smaller kethawns and repeats with them all the observances mentioned as belonging to the greater cigarettes.

The long kethawns are thus finally disposed of. The bearer carries them, running in an easterly direction from the lodge to the foot of a perpendicular rock that fronts the west, and such rocks are not hard to find in the Navajo land. This rock, some say, typifies the high-walled White House itself; others say, the towering cliff on whose face the White House is built. He makes a faint mark on the ground with the outer edge of his foot from east to west, near the base of the rock. He lays down in this mark a bunch of composite plant, *Gutierrezia euthamiae,* usually collected *en route.* Taking the first kethawn from its husk, he places it on the *Gutierrezia,* at such a distance from the rock, that when the string is stretched eastward to its fullest extent its extremity will nearly touch the rock. He puts on the kethawn, in a certain established order, the twelve other articles contained in the husk and while crouching to do this he repeats in a low voice a short prayer. This finished he rises, measures off a foot's length to the southward of the first kethawn, makes at this distance, with his foot another mark, parallel with the first and places here the second kethawn with exactly the same forms which he observed in placing the first kethawn.

The smaller kethawns are also carried in an easterly direction from the lodge, until a piece of clean, level ground is found, representing the level surface on which is held the dance, wherein figure the characters symbolized by these kethawns. They are laid parallel, with their tips to the east a foot's length apart, in a row extending from north to south. In disposing of them, the observances connected with the longer kethawns are repeated. When the kethawns are all laid away the bearer returns to the lodge, observing the definite rules for return, and bearing back with him the empty corn-husks which are delivered up to the shaman to be later disposed of, according to established rules, the recital of which I shall now spare you.

I have referred to the outer or more obvious symbolism of these objects, but there is an inner and more recondite symbolism. The larger kethawns represent the White House where the devotee is supposed to stand in the centre of the world. The white cotton string is the *bike qajoni* or trail of happiness, mentioned so often in the prayers, which he hopes, with the help of the gods to travel. With all around me beautiful may I travel, says the prayer, and for this reason the string passes through beads which symbolize by their colors the four points of the compass. "With all above me beautiful may I travel. With all below me beautiful may I travel" are again the words of the prayer, so the string includes feathers of the turkey, the bird of the earth and lower world, and a feather of the eagle, the bird of the sky; "My voice restore thou for me," and "Make beautiful my voice" are expressions of the prayers, and to typify these sentiments the string includes feathers of warbling birds, whose voices "flow in gladness" as the Navajo songs say.

I shall next describe a set of sacrifices in which both cigarettes and hard-wood sticks are employed. The sacrifices are 52 in number; four are cigarettes cut from cane and 48 are pieces of exogenous wood. Of the 48 sticks, 12 belonging to the east, are of mountain mahogany (*Cercocarpus parvifolius*); 12 belonging to the south, are made of a small shrub not found much beyond the borders of New Mexico and Arizona, the *Forestiera Neo-mexicana,* the maiça or coyote—corn of the Navajos; 12 belonging to the west are made of juniper (*Juniperus occidentalis*); and 12, belonging to the north are made of cherry. Mountain mahogany is probably selected for the east because its plumose fruit is white—the color of the east. Forestiera may be chosen for the south because its small olive-shaped fruit (it belongs to the Oleaceae or olive family) is blue, the color of the south. Juniper is perhaps taken for the west because the leaves of its outer branches, have a tone of yellow, the color of the west. Cherry seems to be adopted for the north, because the fruit of *Prunus demissa,* the common wild cherry of New Mexico ripens black, and black is the color of the north.

The cigarettes are each three finger-widths, the sticks, four finger widths in length. All the pieces are not measured with the fingers; but one piece having been thus measured it is used as a gauge for others.

The four cigarettes are cut from a single cane and prepared with the usual observances. The first is painted white for the east; the second, blue for the south; the third, yellow for the west; and the fourth, black for the north; no devices are painted on them.

The wooden kethawns are painted on the bark, thus: those of mountain mahogany, white; those of Forestiera, blue; those of juniper, yellow; those of cherry, black. The outer or tip end of each male kethawn (every alternate one) is painted a contrasting color, i.e. the ends of the white sticks are painted black; the ends of the blue sticks, yellow; the ends of the yellow sticks, blue; and the ends of the black sticks, white. The tip ends of the female kethawns are painted black for reasons which I explained when speaking of the incia or plumed wands. The wooden kethawns as I have before intimated are made to represent, alternately, males and females, by means which I have described in speaking of the plumed wands, with this difference that the males are not painted black nor the females blue to symbolize sex. Only the facets, which symbolize the female masks worn in the dance, are painted blue. The bark is removed from each stick only at the butt end, where it is whittled to a point. This point should be one finger width in length, so should the facet which represents the mask.

The sacred basket, previously described[,] is used to contain these sacrifices. A little pile of corn meal is put in the centre of the basket and on this the four cigarettes are laid, one after another, in order of their precedence, from north to south. The painted sticks are laid in the same basket in four groups: the twelve white sticks are laid in the eastern quarter; the twelve blue sticks, in the southern quarter; the twelve yellow sticks, in the western quarter and the twelve black sticks, in the northern quarter of the basket. They are laid in one by one. The most northern white stick, representing a male divinity, is laid down first; the next white stick south of that, representing a female divinity, is laid down next. Thus male and female sacrifices are laid down alternately. When all the white sticks, sacred to the east, are put in place, the most easterly blue stick, sacred to the south, is placed in position and thus they proceed around the basket, in the direction of the course of the sun, until all the sticks are in the basket; the most easterly black kethawn, a female, being laid down last.

These sacrifices are made to propitiate certain local divinities called Qastcêayuhi. The four central cigarettes are for the chiefs, the sticks are for their humbler followers. They are prepared in the afternoon and laid away in a safe part of the lodge until night.

Soon after dark, four men begin to dress themselves as divinities. When their toilet is finished they leave the lodge. The kethawns are then brought forth and the shaman and his assistants begin to sing that set of sequential songs known in the rites as aga'hoàgisin or summit songs. These songs, some of which I have obtained on the phonograph, are sung unceasingly in their proper order until all the kethawns are taken out.[2]

The four divinities are Qastcèyalsi Qastcegogan, the Home or Farm God, and two Qastcebaad or goddesses. There seem to be no bachelor gods among the Navajos and, although they are a people who practise polygamy, their gods seem to be monogamists. Each has his one accompanying goddess and no more. Each god, too, has his own peculiar cry, meaningless and often inarticulate; but the females, contrary to the custom among mankind, are silent.

Soon after the first song begins, the Talking God enters, runs towards the patient and applies his quadrangular talisman (method of application exhibited). This done he runs out of the lodge and returns instantly without his talisman. Again he approaches the patient at a run, and, being handed one of the kethawns, he applies it to certain parts of the body (soles, knees, palms, chest, back, shoulders, head) giving his characteristic whoop with each application. This done he runs with the kethawn out of the lodge. The moment he disappears his goddess (a man dressed as a goddess) rushes in, takes another kethawn from the hand of the shaman and repeats with it all the acts of the Talking God with his kethawn, uttering, however, no sound. As the goddess rushes out, the Home God enters and repeats with a kethawn all the performances already described. He is followed in turn by his goddess, who does exactly as the first goddess did. In this order they follow one another and repeat over and over again these acts, until all the kethawns are taken out. Then the Talking God returns once more and applies his folding quadrangular talisman as he did in the beginning. As there are 52 kethawns to be disposed of, each one of the gods makes 13 entries and besides these there are two visits of the Talking God to apply his quadrangle.

The kethawns are taken out in the exact order in which they were placed in the basket, and the work is so arranged that the male divinities carry out male kethawns and the female divinities, female kethawns.

Each god, as he carries out his kethawn runs a short distance from the lodge (to the east when he bears a white kethawn, to the south when he bears a blue kethawn and so on)[,] holds the kethawn in a peculiar manner, but end foremost and face up, supported on the back of his index finger, and throws it away from him into the darkness.

This ends my descriptions. I am aware that I have made them minute to a tedious degree; but not otherwise could I have impressed on my auditors the character of these primitive observances, the thoughts and sentiments associated with these simple trifles which I have shown you. It may be some satisfaction for you, at the end of my discourse, to know that I have not told one half the particulars that I might appropriately have told you; but I trust I have said enough to show you how logical and elaborate is the symbolism of this crude people, and how, having once established for themselves a law of symbolism, they never lose sight of it, but follow it persistently and undeviatingly to the end.

Notes

1.   [This statement comes from George Brown Goode (1851–1896), head curator of the United States National Museum beginning in 1878. Goode stated: "An efficient educational museum may be described as a collection of instructive labels, each illustrated by a well-selected specimen." See "The Museums of the Future," *Annual Report of the United States National Museum* (Washington, D.C.: Government Printing Office, 1897), p. 249. A naturalist by training, Goode was the driving force to apply natural science methods to a museum on the history of civilization. Under his direction, ethnologists in the United States National Museum (such as Otis Mason) and at the Bureau of American Ethnology (where Matthews worked in 1885) prospered. See Edward

P. Alexander, *Museum Masters* (Nashville: American Association for State and Local History, 1983), pp. 277–310. —*Ed.*]

2. [Some of these phonograph recordings were transcribed in Washington Matthews's *Navaho Legends* (Boston: Houghton Mifflin, 1897). Matthews played these recordings at the international congress in a presentation, "Navajo Songs and Prayers, as recorded by the Edison Phonograph, with Sacred, Agricultural, Building, War, Gambling and Love Songs." —*Ed.*]

14

"Object Lessons":
A Folk Museum and Exhibit of Games
in the Columbian World's Exposition

Stewart Culin

In 1893, Stewart Culin's organization of a "folklore museum" drew the acclaim of the great chronicler of Victorian folklore studies, Lee J. Vance. Vance declared in *Popular Science Monthly* that Culin had created an "object lesson" in folklore. In the rhetoric of the day, this was a grand compliment, a sign of progressive education. It meant that Victorians were conveying ideas through the excitement of their material surroundings; they discovered in the things they saw a world of education that classical learning with its insistence on sitting and listening neglected. "In this busy, critical, and skeptical age," a leader of the Smithsonian Institution opined, "each man is seeking to know all things, and life is too short for many words. . . . In the schoolroom the diagram, the blackboard, and the object lesson, unknown thirty years ago, are universally employed." "Amid such tendencies," he concluded, "the museum, it would seem, should find congenial place, for it is the most powerful and useful auxiliary of all systems of teaching by means of object lessons."

Thus it was with great excitement that Vance described "The Folk-lore Museum established in connection with the Philadelphia chapter" of the American Folklore Society. "Many rare and valuable objects have been collected," Vance reported, and

these objects serve to illustrate myth, religion, custom, and superstition the world over. The collection includes idols and ceremonial objects from China, Japan, India, Thibet, Egypt, Polynesia, Africa, North and South America. Prominent in this exhibit are amulets and charms of paper and wood and metal. Very interesting are those implements used for divination and fortune-telling and those manipulated in games. Thus, the evolution of the playing card is shown; so too the games of chess and backgammon are displayed in their various forms or types. Nor have the games and toys and dolls been overlooked. They are all there—even Noah's ark, with its beasts and birds, two and two.

The museum was suggested by Culin to show the folk ideas conveyed by ceremonial objects. "As folklore deals with ideas," Culin argued, "so it would be the mission of the folklore museum to collect, arrange, and classify the objects associated with them." In his capacity as a curator at the University of Pennsylvania Museum and secretary of the Philadelphia branch of the American Folklore Society, Culin first publicly proposed the museum in 1890, and by 1893 he was able to tap the museum's collection to prepare an exhibit at the Chicago World's Fair. Soliciting objects from members of the American Folklore Society, Culin put together a collection that showed the global sweep of primitive belief, and the universal appeal of religious and gaming objects around the world. The objects suggested to Culin an evolutionary progression from religious uses to more playful activities, from superstition to science, from supernatural to secular control, and he arranged the many eye-catching objects into different cases to bring home the point.

Guides to the World's Fair invariably drew attention to Culin's gold-medal-winning exhibit which lined an entire wall of the anthropology building. "It is the greatest museum ever collected and is a spot of untiring interest. . . . Shrines, idols, amulets and ceremonial objects gathered from different parts of the world are the objects from which we must learn of the ancient religions," one guide declared. Another reported that "Prof. Culin has ransacked every country on the globe and every age of the world back to prehistoric times. . . . One of the neatest stories in his showcase is the evolution of playing-cards from dice, and of dice from the knuckle-bones of a sheep."

This scene was repeated in several other fairs, including Atlanta in 1895 and Buffalo in 1901. The world's fairs brought this new version of the usable past in the evolutionary lessons of folklore before millions of people. This interpretation of the past offered a comprehensible order to the social confusion caused by heightened immigration, industrialization, and transportation. And that order conveyed the expansiveness and superiority of Western Civilization over traditional peoples, and of industry and incorporation over handicraft and community.

Although the social message of the exhibits was mostly buried by the end of the Victorian age, the educational vision of the exhibits lasted much longer. Influenced by the exhibition techniques of Stewart Culin, Allen Eaton of the Russell Sage Foundation nonetheless had a different relativistic message to convey when he designed a blockbuster exhibit called the America's Making Exhibit during the 1920s to impress upon the nation the "immigrant gifts to American life." With his arrangement of objects divided into colorful displays of separate ethnic groups, Eaton suggested the rich diversity and worthiness of recently arrived immigrant cultures. Eaton's exhibit is but one example of the ways that objects, images, and arrangements increasingly became powerful forces to impress and educate through the twentieth century. And still debate rages on the proper messages that folk objects have to relate in a modernizing society.

This chapter presents the original proposal for a folklore museum and follows with the inventory of the famed exhibit at the Chicago World's Fair. The opening section comes form "Folk-Lore Museums," first appearing in the Philadelphia *Public Ledger* on September 3, 1890, and excerpted in the *Journal of American Folklore* 3 (1890): pp. 312–13. The inventory of the exhibit comes from Stewart Culin, "Exhibit of Games in the Columbian Exposition," *Journal of American Folklore* 6 (1893): pp. 205–27. The quotes on object lessons come from Lee J. Vance, "Folk-Lore Study in America," *Popular Science Monthly* 43 (1893): pp. 586–98; George Brown Goode, "The

Museums of the Future," *Annual Report of the United States National Museum* (Washington, D.C.: Government Printing Office, 1897), pp. 243–62. For the continuation of "object lessons" today, see John A. Kouwenhoven, "American Studies: Words or Things?" in *Material Culture Studies in America,* ed. Thomas Schlereth (Nashville: American Association for State and Local History, 1982), pp. 79–92. For Culin's studies of games, see *Games of the North American Indians* (1907; reprint, New York: Dover, 1975); *Games of the Orient* (1895; reprint, Rutland, Vermont: Charles Tuttle, 1958); Alyce Cheska, "Stewart Culin: An Early Ethnologist of Games," *Association for the Anthropological Study of Play Newsletter* 2 (1975): pp. 4–13. For background on folklife museums, see Howard Wight Marshall, "Folklife and the Rise of American Folk Museums," *Journal of American Folklore* 90 (1977): pp. 391–413; Ormond H. Loomis, "Organizing a Folklore Museum," in *Handbook of American Folklore,* ed. Richard M. Dorson (Bloomington: Indiana University Press, 1983), pp. 499–506. The social message of the fairs and their ethnological exhibits is discussed in Robert W. Rydell, *All the World's a Fair: Visions of Empire at American International Expositions, 1876–1916* (Chicago: University of Chicago Press, 1984); Alan Trachtenberg, *The Incorporation of America: Culture and Society in the Gilded Age* (New York: Hill and Wang, 1982). For the social message of Allen Eaton, and the present debate on the presentation of folk objects, see Eugene W. Metcalf, Jr., "The Politics of the Past in American Folk Art History"; Suzi Jones, "Art by Fiat, and Other Dilemmas of Cross-Cultural Collecting"; Henry Glassie, "The Idea of Folk Art," in *Folk Art and Art Worlds,* ed. John Michael Vlach and Simon J. Bronner (Ann Arbor, Michigan: UMI Research Press, 1986), pp. 27–50, 243–68, 269–74.

*   *   *

[A folk museum] would have an extended field, and might embrace a vast number of objects which do not ordinarily come within the domain of the collector, and yet are most valuable as illustrating customs, myths and superstitions.

Amulets, charms, implements for games, and objects used in divination and in religious and other ceremonies, especially among primitive peoples, would be included, as well as those natural objects with which man has associated some myth or legend, or has attributed with occult and supernatural properties.

Many illustrations of the latter class may be cited, such as the pierced pebble of natural formation, referred to by Jacob Abbott in one of those familiar children's classics, the Rollo Books, which children call a "wishing-stone," and cast with a wish into the nearest stream. The rabbit's foot to bring good luck, and the potato and the horse-chestnut carried to prevent rheumatism, belong to the same category, with many other articles, often quite uninteresting in themselves, and yet which, if properly arranged and labelled with their special story of signification, would form a vastly entertaining collection, and a valuable aid in the study to which the Folk-Lore Society is devoted.

Popular taste in collecting does not often receive the approval of scientific men, and the "curiosities" which many people treasure, valued often on account of their associations, and little prized by the critical student, who even condemns many of our public museums as mere depositories for bric-a-brac, useless in their present state for scientific or education purposes.

And yet these same curiosities would, if their true story was told, prove far more entertaining and possibly even as valuable and instructive as the series of flint knives and stone implements to which some enthusiastic scholars would devote all available shelf room.

No subject within the range of scientific investigation appeals more strongly to popular interest than that so well designated as "folk-lore," and the very instinct that underlies the custom of collecting strange and rare and curious objects is one through which much of this same lore may be accounted for. As folk-lore deals with ideas, so it would be the mission of the folk-lore museum to collect, arrange, and classify the objects associated with them. Such a museum would form an essential part of a museum of ethnology, and would serve an admirable part in supplementing the existing collections of art and archaeology.

It would include amulets and charms, not alone the admirable specimens of glyptic cut, such as are brought together by collectors of gems, but objects of paper and wood and metal, of which a great variety may be found among the people of the foreign colonies of our cities, as well as among the native Indians and our negro population. Many contributions relating to religious usages and ceremonies could be obtained among the same classes; while the subject of games, in itself practically inexhaustible, would furnish material for a museum of its own. . . .

Among the materials used in games, special attention might be paid to playing cards. No collection of playing cards exists in any of the public institutions of this country, and there are few, if any, private collectors, although in Europe they have been deservedly the object of serious study. The British Museum contains a superb collection, of which a special catalogue has been made, while other notable examples are found in the National Library at Paris. They have many points of interest, as, for example, their connection with the early history of printing; but they claim the particular regard of the folk-lorist, who may some day throw light upon the identity of the kings and queens around whom so many new traditions have grown since they commenced their long reign upon the pasteboards.

Toys would form another and most interesting department of the museum. How many of them must have lost their original significance, to be rediscovered, it is hoped, at the hands of the student of folk-lore!

The Noah's ark remains, with its birds and beasts two and two, and Shem and Ham and Japhet, with little round wooden hats, to illustrate and confirm the possibilities in store in the future investigation. Poor Noah's ark! The children of this generation have quite foregone such trifles, and it may well take its place, and that not too soon, in the folk-lore museum. The East is replete with toys that illustrate popular myths, like the Indian miracle toy of the rescue of Krishna, in which the water recedes when it touches the figure of the infant god; and the zoölogical mythology is also well displayed in the many creatures represented among children's playthings.

Coins, too, would have to have a place in the museum; not the treasures usually prized by numismatists, but the broken sixpences and love tokens, the "touch money," and the many pieces valued as charms to invite good luck or drive away bad fortune.

Primitive religions, and folk-lore, including games, are the subject of a special section in the Anthropological Building at the Columbian Exposition. This section, which is known as the "Section of Religions, Games, and Folk-lore," is located upon the main floor, where the exhibit occupies a series of cases on the south side and a line of flat cases which extend across the entire building.

Folk-lore is the name given to the material which has come down to us in the sayings and customs of mankind. Its study, for which no special name has been devised, is an important branch of the science of anthropology.

The chief object of the collection is to show things which illustrate folk traditions and customs. The field being a vast one, the collection has been practically restricted to the subject of games. The basis of the collection was formed in the Museum of Archaeology of the University of Pennsylvania during the past two years. The University's collection has been supplemented by exhibits from individuals and the leading manufacturers of games in this country.

The objects are classified and arranged for comparative study, games of the same general sort being placed together. They are contained in twelve table cases running from the southernmost entrance on the west side to the corresponding entrance on the east side. Puzzles and the simple games of children commence the series.

Case I. Puzzles, Children's Games, Mancala

The ingenious objects which we designate as "puzzles" are represented by about one hundred and twenty-five specimens exhibited by the

Museum of the University of Pennsylvania. They begin with a collection of East Indian puzzles "invented" by Aziz Hussan of Saharanpore, among which may be seen many types of puzzles that are common in Europe and America.The Chinese puzzles of wood, bone, and ivory follow them. Chinese puzzles, long a household word, are very limited in number. Those which are made for export are invariable in form, and consist of the familiar "Ring Puzzle," the "Geometrical Puzzle," and the "Dissected Cube." Their Chinese names are all descriptive, and the "Ring Puzzle," which they call "The Nine Interlinked Rings," was probably borrowed by Chinese from India. The number of types in the entire series of puzzles is surprisingly small. The one that was revived some years since under the name of the "Fifteen Puzzle," and which was described by an English writer some two hundred years ago, has suggested a large group. "Pigs in Clover," an American invention, is the most recent addition to the world's amusements of this character, and its wide diffusion and popularity is shown here in a great variety of specimens from different countries.

Some of the simpler amusements of children are suggested by the objects on the north side of this case. Here are to be seen Mr. William Wells Newell's "Games and Songs of American Children," and "The Counting-out Rhymes of Children," by Dr. H. Carrington Bolton, two books which may be regarded as classical in their particular field. Mr. Pak Yong Kiu, of the Korean Commission to the Columbian Exposition, has furnished the following interesting addition to the collection of children's counting-out rhymes:—

Hau al ta	Ku chi,
Tu al da	Pol ta,
Som a chun	Chong kun,
Na al da,	Ko tu ra,
Yuk nong,	Biong.

The wide diffusion of the custom of using counting-out rhymes among children, and the general resemblance they bear to each other, present problems of curious interest.

Among the imitative games of children, there are few more interesting than the Toros or mock bull-fight of Spanish boys. A wicker mask from Madrid, representing the bull's head, which is used in this sport, is suspended beside this case, within which may be seen the toy *espadas* or swords and the *banderillios*. Tops are shown to be of great antiquity and of very general use over the earth. Their age is illustrated by a wooden top from the Fayum, Egypt, discovered by Mr. Flinders Petrie at Kahûn, belonging to 2800 B.C. They were common among the American Indians, north and south. A number of balls of baked clay and stone, which were whipped in a game on the ice, represent the primitive tops of the Sioux, while a more recent Sioux top of wood with a peg of brass shows foreign influences. Among the Omahas tops were called *Moo de de ska,* a name which Mr. Francis La Flesche says is not descriptive. The explorations conducted for the Department by Mr. George A. Dorsey in Peru have contributed several interesting specimens to this collection. Two prehistoric tops from Ancon are identical in form with the ancient Egyptian top, while another from an ancient grave at Arica is distinguished by a spindle, not unlike the modern tops of Japan. The use of pop-guns among the ancient Peruvians is also shown by two beautifully carved specimens of wood contained in a llama skin pouch, from an ancient grave in Cañete valley. Pop-guns were used by many if not all of the American Indian tribes. Among the Omahas the children made them of willow branches, and then, by partly stopping one end, would convert them into squirt-guns. The toy squirt-gun sold in the Chicago shops is here shown beside the syringe from India used in the Hindu *Holi* Festival.

Jackstraws, which are known in England as "Spillikins" and in France as *Les Jonchets,* are next in order. The peculiar Chinese name appended to the Chinese specimens, "Eight Precious Things," suggests the probability that China was the country from which we derived them.

The remainder of this case is devoted to the implements for a game that holds an unique position among the world's games, and for which no place could be found in the series that follow. It is variously played with pebbles, shells, and seeds in holes dug in the ground, or upon a board with cup-like depressions. The game appears to be found wherever Arab influence has penetrated. It is very generally played in Africa, in Asia Minor, and in India. Two boards are exhibited, one brought from Jerusalem for the University Museum by Mrs. John Harrison of Philadelphia, and another from the Gaboon River in Africa. The Syrians in the Damascus house in the Turkish village in the Midway Plaisance know it under the name of *Mancala,* and it is a favorite game with the Chief of the Dahomey village, who frequently plays it with his son before his hut in the Plaisance. Among the so-called Dahomeyans this game is called *Madaji,* the board *adjito,* and the seeds which they use, *adji.* It is a game for two persons. As played in Syria, there are several forms of the game. One is called *lâ'b madjnuni,* or the "Crazy Game." Ninety-eight cowrie shells are used, which are distributed unequally in the fourteen holes in the board, which is placed transversely between the two players. The first player takes all the pieces from the hole at the right of his row and drops them, one at a time, in the first hole on the opposite side, and so on, continuing around the board until the last one is let fall. He thereupon takes all the pieces from that hole and distributes them one by one as before, until, arriving at the last piece, he takes all the pieces again in his hands. This is continued until the last piece dropped either falls into an empty hole or completes two or four in the hole in which it falls. In the latter case the player takes the two or four for his own as well as the contents of the hole opposite, and should there be two or four in the next hole or holes to the one at which he stopped, he also takes them with those opposite. The players continue in turn, and when the game is finished the one gaining the highest number of cowries wins. If a player's last piece falls in an empty hole, his turn is ended. Skill is of no avail in this form of the game, the result always being a mathematical certainty, accordingly as the cowries are distributed at the beginning.

Case II. Balls, Quoits, Marbles

The antiquity of the ball as an implement of sport is attested by the balls found associated with objects used in other games in old Egypt, where it was known at least 4,700 years ago. Games of ball are common among savage and barbarous people, and ball games of Burma, Siam, India, and Japan, as well as those of the North American Indians, are suggested in this case. With the ball games are the sticks used in a widely diffused game which we commonly know as "Tip-cat." Tip-cat is played with a block of wood, about six inches in length, which is struck with a small club or bat and knocked into the air. The rules for playing are somewhat complicated, and as far as they have been compared, appear to be much the same all over the earth. The oldest specimen is from Kahûn, Egypt, of 2800 B.C. Tip-cat is known by the Syrians in the Plaisance, who have contributed the sticks they use in the game they call *Hab*. In Persia it is called *Guk tchub*, "frog-wood," a name given to it, like our name "cat," from the way the small stick leaps into the air. In China the game is called *Ta-pang*, "to knock the stick," and the Chinese laborers in the United States call the "cat" *To tsz*, or "Little Peach." In Japan the game is called *In ten;* the small stick *ko*, "son," and the long one *oya*, "parent," In India the game is called *Gutti danda;* in Burma, *Kyitha*, and in Russian *Kosley*, " goat," a suggestive name like that of Persia and our own name, "cat."

The wicker baskets or *cestas* for the Spanish game of ball or *Pelota,* now so popular in Spain, are next shown, with the flat bat used by the Spaniards in ball games. A very ancient English bat for trap ball appears with them, and these are followed by the implements used in the current American and English ball games exhibited by Messrs. A. G. Spalding & Bros. of Chicago. Cricket, Baseball, Football, Golf, Polo, La Crosse and Lawn Tennis, Racket and Battledore and Shuttlecock, are displayed in order, and with the last are exhibited the Zuñi Indian and the Japanese form of this game and the Chinese shuttlecock, which is kicked with the toes. The tossing games comprise Jackstones, Cup and Ball, Grace Hoops, and Quoits, and ring games of various kinds, and include the iron quoits *Rayuelas,* used in Spain. The stone quoit games of the Zuñis, and of the Tarahumara Indians are also exhibited. The North American Indian forms of the Cup and Ball game comprise the *Ar-too-is,* or "match-making" game of the Penobscots, exhibited by Chief Joseph Nicolar of Oldtown Me., and the Sioux game played with the phalangal bones of the deer. The comparatively new game "Tiddledy winks" follows, leading up to a recent German game called the "Newest War Game," in which the men or "winks" are played upon a board upon which are represented two opposing fortresses. The games of tossing cowries and coins are next suggested, with the game played by Chinese children with olive seeds. Many natural objects are exhibited that are used by children in playing games resembling marbles, to which artificial objects they appear to lead. In Burma the seeds of a large creeper, the *Eutada pursoetha,* are employed in a game called *Gohunyin,* one of the commonest forms of gambling known in that country. In Asia Minor, knuckle-bones of sheep, which are often weighted with lead, are used in the same manner, and in Damascus and the cities in connection with marbles. Marbles themselves, in the varieties known to commerce, are next exhibited.

Case III. Bowling, Billiards, Curling, and Shuttle Board

The objects used to illustrate the games of Bowling, Billiards, and Shuffle Board were made for this exhibit by the Brunswick-Balke-Collender Company of Chicago, by whom they are displayed, and comprise miniature tables for these games of remarkable accuracy and beauty of finish. On the north side of the case may be seen the implements used in the game of Croquet as it is played at the present day. The first games of Croquet manufactured in the United States were made from an English sample in 1863. The Chicago Curling Club here displays a collection of representative objects, including three sets of Curling stones and the medals and trophies belonging to the club and its members.

Case IV. Merrells, Fox and Geese, Chess, and Draughts

An attempt has been made to bring together as large a number as possible of the simple board games like Merrells and Fox and Geese, with the hope that they would throw light upon that much discussed question, the origin of the game of Chess. The Chinese, Korean, Japanese, and Siamese, Malayan and Samoan forms of several such games are exhibited. it is curious to note that the peculiar board used in the Japanese Fox and Geese game, called *Furoku Musashi,* or "Sixteen Soldiers," is the same as one from Peru for a similar game. The inference is that they are both of Spanish introduction, which seems to be confirmed by the statement that the Japanese game was first known in that country in the sixteenth century. Merrells is displayed in a board made in the Damascus house in the Plaisance, where the Syrians call it *Edris,* and in a diagram obtained from Chinese laborers from Canton, who call it *Sám k'i,* or the "Three Game," as well as by European boards.

A Japanese board for that famous game which the Japanese call *Go* and the Chinese *Wei k'i,* or the "Game of Surrounding," follows. This is the game which is often erroneously referred to as chess, in China. The Japanese name of this board, *Go-ban,* has furnished the name which we have applied to the simple game of "Go Bang," which we also got from Japan.

A board and men for a highly developed game, somewhat like draughts, played by the Zuñi Indians of New Mexico, furnishes a striking object for speculation and research. The board is a square divided into 144 small equal squares, each of which is crossed by two intersecting diagonal lines. The moves are made one square at a time along those diagonal lines, the pieces being placed at the angles of the squares. Two or four persons play. They each start with six men, and their object is to get their men across to the other side and occupy their opponent's places, capturing as many of his pieces as possible by the way. A piece is taken by getting it between two others, as in the modern Egyptian game of *Seega,* and the first piece thus taken may be replaced by an extra piece belonging to the player who makes the capture, which may move on the straight as well as the diagonal lines and is called the "Priest of the Bow." This game, which was arranged and is exhibited by Mr. Frank Hamilton Cushing, is called *A-wi-thlák-na-kwe,* which he translates as "Stone warriors." Mr. Edward Falkener, in his work entitled "Games Ancient and Oriental," which he lent for exhibition here, has published a restoration of the ancient Egyptian game of Senat from fragments of Egyptian boards which have come down from 1600 B.C. The game as thus restored is in some respects similar to the Zuñi game, the men being taken as in *Seega* by getting them between two others. The Zuñi game, however, may be regarded as in advance of any other board game, even of our own civilization, until we come to the true game of Chess. Chess stands alone among games. We do not find the links that connect it with lower forms of board games, and the Indian game from which our own is derived almost without change is the source from which the many variants of the Chess game doubtless originated. Several of these offspring of the Indian Chess are shown in the north side of this case, including the chess games of Burma, Siam, the Malay Peninsula, China, and Japan. A Moorish board is exhibited with them, and European chessmen and boards follow. A finely carved ivory chess set represents the pieces that are made for export by the Chinese at Canton. Draughts, which in the opinion of Mr. Edward B. Tylor may be regarded as a modern and simplified form of Chess, now follow, and here are shown two sets of interesting German draughtsmen of the eighteenth century.

Case V. American Board Games, Games of Lots, Lotto, Chinese Lotteries

The games played on boards, like Merrells and Draughts, manufactured by Messrs. McLaughlin Brothers and E. J. Horsman of New York, and the Milton Bradley Company of Springfield, Mass., are found in this case. Many of them appear to have been suggested by the Oriental games such as are shown in the preceding collection.

These are followed by games of Lots, a class of games extremely common among the North American Indians. The Haida and other tribes of the northwest coast play with sticks which are painted and carved. According to Dr. Franz Boas the sticks are thrown down violently upon a hard piece of skin, and the object of the game is to pick out the unmarked sticks, which alone count. The designs on the sticks are of the greatest interest, and a set of plaster casts of a very finely carved set in the United States National Museum at Washington, which are displayed through the courtesy of Professor Otis T. Mason, exhibit these peculiarities. The wooden discs from Puget Sound are concealed beneath a mat, and the players endeavor to select a particular disc. Guessing games of various kinds were very general among our Indians. The two bones, one wrapped with thread, which were used by the Alaska Indians in such a game, are exhibited with similar bones from the Utes. They were held in the hands, the player guessing which contained the marked one. The balls of buffalo hair with which the Omahas play a similar game are also displayed, with the moccasins in which the object was sometimes concealed. These games were played with the accompaniment of songs. Miss Alice C. Fletcher exhibits the music of two of these gambling songs used by the Omahas, and in Dr. Washington Matthews' "Navajo Gambling Songs," a copy of which may be seen in this case, the songs sung in the game of *Kêsitce,* played with eight moccasins, in one of which a stone is concealed, are recorded. Among the Zuñis and Mokis, cups like dice cups were used to cover the ball. The Moki cups here exhibited have been used in a sacred game and then sacrificed with "plume sticks," as is shown by the small holes with which they are pierced.

Games can be made to throw much light upon the social and political institutions of many peoples. This fact is rendered conspicuous in the implements for the Chinese lotteries which are shown in this series. They comprise the paraphernalia of the *Pák-kòp-piu* or "Game of the White Pigeon Ticket," the *Tsz' fá,* or "Character Flowering," and the *Wei Sing* or "Game of Guessing Surnames." In the first, the tickets are imprinted with the first eighty characters of the *Tsin tsz' man,* or Thousand Character Classic, one of the elementary text-books of Chinese children. In the second, the writer of the lottery assists his patrons in their effort to guess the hidden character, by an original ode, in which it must be in some way referred to.

The third is the game of guessing the name of the successful candidate at the Governmental Literary Examinations. Upon them all the peculiar literary traditions of the Chinese people have left their imprint.

Case VI. Knuckle-bones and Dice, Dominoes, Evolution of Playing Cards, Chinese Playing Cards, Parchesi, Patoli, and Kab

No method of appealing to chance is more common than that of tossing some object in the air and deciding the result by its fall. A coin is often used at the present day, and many natural and artificial objects have found currency for this purpose. Nuts, cowrie shells, and the knuckle-bones of animals have been used from the earliest times, and the last, the knuckle-bones, have become the parent of many of our modern games. The American Indians across the entire continent played a game with marked plum-stones and other objects which had many points of resemblance with games played by other people with dotted cubical dice. The specimens of such games here exhibited comprise the game played with marked bone discs in a wooden bowl by the Penobscot Indians of Oldtown, Me., contributed by Chief Joseph Nicolar; a set of marked plum-stones and the basket and tallies used by the Sioux, and a similar set of marked bone and wooden pieces, with the basket, from the Arapahoes. Among the Pueblo Indians of the southwestern United States blocks of wood are used in the same manner as dice, and among the Arabs of northern Africa numerical values are attributed to the throws made with four and six similar pieces of reed. In India, cowries are used. Sortilege is also practised with the implements that are used in games. In China, the cleft root stock of the bamboo is commonly employed in fortune-telling, and the blocks, which form part of the accessories of nearly all Chinese temples, may be seen upon the altar of the Chinese God of War, commonly appealed to by Chinese gamblers, erected in this Section. Knuckle-bones or astragali present a most interesting subject for investigation. From a prehistoric knuckle-bone of terra-cotta from Cuzco, Peru in the collection of Señor Montes in this building it appears that they were used by the ancient Peruvians. The Peruvian Indians at the present day use four knuckle-bones as dice in a game. It is known in Kechua as *tava,* a word meaning four, which should not in the opinion of Señor Montes be confounded with the Spanish word for knuckle-bone, *taba,* from which he does not think it was derived.

Knuckle-bones were used in games in old Egypt, as was shown by the ivory specimens found with other gaming implements in the tomb of Queen Hatasu, B.C. 1600, and are constantly referred to by the Greek and Latin authors. Numerical values were attributed to each of the four throws, which among the Romans were designated as *Supinum, Pronum, Planum,* and *Tortuosum,* and estimated as three, five, one, and six. Among the Arabs, and at the present day throughout western Asia, the four sides receive the names of ranks of human society; thus among the Persians, according to Dr. Hyde, they are called *Duzd,* "thief," *Dibban,* "peasant," *Vezir,* and *Shah,* and so with the Turks, Syrians, Armenians, and other peoples. A pair of natural bones from the right and left leg of the sheep are commonly used, which among the Syrians of Damascus are designated respectively as *yisr* and *yemene,* "left and right." The transition from these *kabat,* as the Arabs call them, from *kab* meaning "ankle" or "ankle-bone," to the cubical dotted dice was an easy one. The same numerical values and social designations were attributed to four sides of the cubical dice, as are given to the knuckle-bones, and it is curious to note that the significant throws with cubical dice in China are those that bear the numbers assigned to the astragali throws. The modern East Indian dice which are exhibited will be seen from the arrangement of the "threes" to be made in pairs, like the natural astragali, and the pair receives in India the name of *kabatain,* the dual of *kab,* the name which is also applied to the pair of astragali. The Syrian dice used in *Towla,* or backgammon, are marked in the same way, as well as the Japanese dice used in the similar game of *Sugoroku* or "double sixes." A pair of ancient Roman dice which I purchased in Florence show that the Romans practised the same arrangement, and are especially significant. The invention of the cubical dotted die must have occurred at a comparatively early time. The oldest die of which I have any knowledge is displayed in this collection, a large pottery die from the Greek colony of Naucratis, Egypt, belonging, according to the discoverer, Mr. Flinders Petrie, to 600 B.C. The dice found in Babylonia and Egypt appear to have been associated with foreign influences.

Dice were carried over from India to China, where we find the next stage in their development. Here the twenty-one possible throws with two dice are each given a name, and in the case of the double sixes, double aces, double fours, and three and ace, these names are those of the triune powers of Heaven, Earth, and Man, and the Harmony that unites them. This change in nomenclature, in which the social terms of Shah, Vizier, etc., were replaced with cosmical ones, is characteristic of the way in which China adapts and absorbs foreign ideas. A game with two dice remains the principal dice game in China at the present day. In it the twenty-one possible throws are divided into two series, one consisting of the throws $\frac{6}{6}$, $\frac{1}{1}$, $\frac{4}{4}$, $\frac{3}{1}$, $\frac{5}{5}$, $\frac{3}{3}$, $\frac{2}{2}$, $\frac{5}{6}$, $\frac{4}{6}$, $\frac{1}{6}$, $\frac{1}{5}$, called *man*, "civil," and the other, $\frac{5}{4}$, $\frac{6}{3}$, $\frac{5}{3}$, $\frac{6}{2}$, $\frac{4}{3}$, $\frac{5}{2}$, $\frac{4}{2}$, $\frac{3}{2}$, $\frac{1}{4}$ and $\frac{1}{2}$, designated as *mò,* or "military." In the twelfth century, according to Chinese records, dotted tablets, i.e., dominoes, were invented. Chinese dominoes consist of 21 pieces representing the 21 throws with two dice of which the 11 pieces of the *man* series are usually duplicated to form a complete set, which numbers 32 dominoes. In southern China, long wooden dominoes are employed. when paper was used instead of wood we have the playing card.

The subject of Chinese playing cards has been illustrated in an admirable and exhaustive manner by W. H. Wilkinson, Esq., H. B. M. Consul at Swatow, who has lent for exhibition a series of Chinese cards, dice, and dominoes collected at no less than fourteen different cities in China, from Peking on the north, and Tai yuan, down along the coast at Nanking, Shanghai, Ningpo, Wenchow, Fuchow, Swatow, Canton, to Hongkong. Cards are also shown from various places along the Yellow River, from Chung King eastward to Nanking. The cards in this collection are arranged according to the symbols or marks distinguishing them, which Mr. Wilkinson divides into four classes, according as they are derived:

1. From the sapek or cash, and its multiples.
2. Through dominoes from dice.
3. From the Chinese Chess game.
4. From other sources.

A very complete account may be expected from Mr. Wilkinson, who has displayed here what is doubtless the most perfect collection of Chinese cards ever exhibited. The miscellaneous cards in this collection are drawn from western China and bear some resemblance, according to Mr. Wilkinson, to the "Proverbs" and "Happy Families" of Europe and America. They include the cards based on a writing lesson, cards based on numbers, and cards based on a lucky formula.

Returning to the subject of dice, the special implements used in dice divination in India are shown, as well as illustrations of the methods employed in telling fortunes with dominoes in China and Korea; these forming part of the material used in the investigation of the origin of dominoes. Japanese and Siamese dice are also exhibited with the East Indian and Chinese specimens, as well as dice made in various parts of Europe, comprising a pair of iron dice purchased at Perugia, which, although presumably modern, have the dots arranged with the 6-5, 4-2, and 3-1 opposite, like those of old Etruria, instead of the sums of the spots on the opposite sides being equal to seven, as is otherwise general. With the dice are the spinning dice of various countries, including the East India *Chukree,* the Chinese *Ch'e me,* and the corresponding dice of Japan and Siam. A variety of dominoes are also displayed, including those of Korea, which are identical with those of China, and the Siamese dominoes, which were also borrowed from the latter country.

The pair of knuckle-bones appear to be the parent of many of that large class of games which Mr. Tylor describes as the "backgammon group." With reference to dice-backgammon the evidence in this particular is very direct, but the similar games played with cowries and wooden blocks, for which even a greater antiquity may be claimed, there is a likelihood of independent origin. Several games of the latter class from India, North America, and Egypt, types of which have been referred to by Mr. Tylor, are exhibited in this collection. The first, *Pachisi,* is the most popular game in India. It is played around a board, usually made of cloth, in the form of a cross, according to the throws with cowries. Six or seven shells are ordinarily used, and count according as the apertures fall. When long dice of ivory are employed, the game is called *Chausar.* This game was introduced from India into the United States, where it was first published in 1860 under the name of Parchesi, and has become very popular. Mr. Cushing has set up beside the *Pachisi* a Zuñi game, which the Zuñis call *Ta sho lí wé,* or "wooden cane cards," and which has many points of resemblance to the East Indian game. The moves are made according to the throws with wooden blocks three inches in length, painted red and black upon their two faces, around a circle of forty stones which is broken at the top and bottom, and the right and left, by four openings called the "Doorways of the four directions." This game embodies many of the mythical conceptions of the Zuñis. It is played by two or four players, who use colored splints to mark their course around the circle. These splints, which are placed at starting in the doorway to which they correspond, have the following symbolism: At the top, Yellow, North, The Wind, Winter. At the left, Blue, West, Water, Spring. At the bottom, Red, South, Fire, Summer. At the right, White, East, Seed or Earth, Autumn. The colors of the two wooden blocks symbolize the two conditions of man: Red, Light or Wakefulness; Black, Darkness or Sleep. The throws with the blocks, which are tossed, ends down, upon a disc of sandstone placed in the middle of the circle, are as follows: 3 red count 10; 3 black count 5; 2 red and 1 black count 3; 1 red and 2 black count 1.

A count of three red gives another throw. when four play, the North and West move around from right to left, and the South and East from left to right. When a player's move ends at a division of the circle occupied by his adversaries' piece, he takes it up and sends it back to the beginning. It is customary to make the circuit of the stones either four or six times. beans or corn of the seven varieties being used as counters. This game forms one of the seven sacred games of the Zuñis, and its antetype, *Sho lí we,* or "Cane Cards," is one of the four games that are sacrifices to the God of War and Fate. The sacred form of the game is called *Tein thla nah na tá sho lí we,* or literally, "Of all the regions wood cane cards, and the blocks which are thrown in it bear complicated marks, consisting of bands of color on one side." In the sacred game, the players are chosen with great care with reference to their totem, and the region to which it belongs. A much more complete account of this game may be expected from Mr. Cushing himself, from the ample material which he has placed at my disposal. Side by side with *Ta sho lí we* is the corresponding game as played by the Apache and Navajos, which has been set up by Antonio Apache. It lacks the color symbolism, but the principle is identical. The Navajos call it *Set tilth,* which Captain John G. Bourke, U.S.A., tells me should be transliterated *Tze-chis,* or *Zse tilth,* and means literally, "stone-stick." The circle of stones, he says, is called *Tze nasti,* "Stone circle."

Lieut. H. L. Scott, U.S.A., has contributed the implements for a similar game of the Kiowas, which is known as the "Awl Game." It is called by the Kiowas *Zohn ahl,* that is, *Zohn,* "creek," and *ahl,* "wood." A detailed account of it will appear elsewhere, furnished to the writer by Lieutenant Scott, who states that the Comanches have a similar game which they play with eight *ahl* sticks, which are two feet or more long.

These games are all similar to the Mexican Patoli, as described by the early Spanish chroniclers. A picture of the latter game from an early Hispano-American manuscript, reproduced from the original in Florence by its discoverer, Mrs. Zelia Nuttall, is exhibited in this connection. The method of play among the Aztecs is here shown, and it is curious to note that they used a diagram or board in the form of a cross, like that of the East Indian Pachisi. In the Malayan archipelago, a stone is placed in the centre upon which dice are thrown in games, as among the North American Indians. Mr. Taylor has set forth the conclusions which may be drawn from these resemblances, but the matter is still open for discussion. Another game remains to be noticed, played with wooden blocks as dice: the Arab game of *Tab,* in which men are moved on a board according to the throws of four slips of palm. These slips, about eight inches in length, are left with one face of the natural color, and the other showing the whiter interior of the palm, these sides being called black and white respectively. The throws count as follows: 4 black, 6; 4 white, 4; 3 white, 3; 2 white, 2; 1 white, 1.

The implements displayed for this game were made in the Cairo street. No more curious ethnographical parallels are presented in the Exposition than that of the Arabs in the Plaisance, and the Navajos beside the South Lagoon, both playing these curiously similar games.

Case VII. Backgammon, Sugoroku, and the Game of Goose, East Indian, Japanese, and Siamese Cards

According to Mr. Tylor, dice-backgammon makes its appearance plainly in classic history. The game of twelve lines (*duodecim scripta*) was played throughout the Roman Empire and passed on, with little change, through mediaeval Europe, carrying its name of tabulae, tables; its modern representatives being French Tric trac, English Backgammon, etc. Among the ancient Greeks *Kubeia,* or "dice playing," is shown by various classical passages to be of the nature of backgammon. The pearl-inlaid backgammon board here shown is from Damascus, where the game is known as *Towla,* "tables." A Siamese board exhibited by the government of Siam, with other games, through its royal commissioner Phra Surya, has departed little from the ancient type. Backgammon is known in China as *Sheung Luk,* "double sixes," and in Japan by the corresponding name of *Sugoroku.* The popular games, both in China and Japan, however, are not played with men upon a set board, but resemble the games with many stations, which are common in Europe and America.

The most notable of the Chinese games of this class is the one which is called *Shing kun to,* or "The Tables of the Promotion of Officials," a game which has been known to scholars, through Dr. Hyde's account, as "The Game of the Promotion of Mandarins." It is played by two or more persons upon a large paper diagram, upon which are printed the titles of the different officials and dignitaries of the Chinese government. The moves are made according to the throws with four cubical dice, and the players, whose positions upon the diagram are indicated by notched or colored splints, are advanced or set back, according to their throws. The paper chart here exhibited was purchased in a Chinese shop in New York city. It was printed in Canton, and bears an impression about twenty-

three inches square. This is divided into sixty-three compartments, ex-
clusive of the central one and the place for entering at the lower right-
hand corner. The latter contains the names of thirteen different starting-
points, from *yan shang,* or "Honorary Licentiate," down to *t'ung shang,*
or "student," between which are included the positions of *t'in man
shang,* "astrologer," and *i shang,* "physician." These are entered at the
commencement of the game by the throws of "three, four, five, six,"
three "fours," three "sixes," three "fives," three "threes," three "twos,"
and three "ones;" and then in the same manner double "fours," and so
on down to double "ones."

The sixty-three compartments, representing as many classes of officials or degrees of rank, comprise three hundred and ninety-seven
separate titles, of which the highest, and the highest goal of the game,
is that of man *fá tín tái hok sz',* or "Grand Secretary." This, however,
under favorable conditions, can only be reached by a player who starts
from a favorable point, advancement in the game being regulated by rules
similar to those which actually regulate promotion under government.
Thus, a player whose fortune it is to enter as physican or astrologer can
only obtain promotion in the line of his service, and must be content
with a minor goal, as he is ineligible to the high civil office of "Grand
Secretary."

The dice are thrown into a bowl placed in the centre of the sheet,
the players throwing in turn, and each continuing to throw until he makes
a cast of doublets or higher. It is noticeable that "fours," as in Dr. Hyde's
account, constitute the highest throw. A pair of "fours," according to
the rules, is to be reckoned as *tak,* "virtue," and leads to a higher place
than those of the other numbers. Sixes are next highest and are to be
reckoned as *ts'oi,* "genius;" and in the same manner, in descending
degree, "fives" are to be reckoned as *kung,* "skill;" "threes" as *léung,*
"forethought;" "twos" as *yau,* "tractability;" and "ones," *chong,*
"stupidity." The game is much complicated by being played for money
or counters, which is necessary under the rules. By this means advancement may be purchased, degradation compounded for, and the winner
of a high position rewarded.

The main point of difference between the game as it exists to-day,
and as described by Dr. Hyde, is the number of dice employed, six being
the number mentioned by him. The enlarged form of the diagram is of
minor importance, as he himself says that the names of officials written
on the tablet are many or few, according to the pleasure of the players.
With the game of *Shing kún to* may be seen a copy of Dr. Hyde's treatise,
De Ludis Orientalibis, containing the reproduction of the chart of the
game which he made in London 200 years ago. The names of titles of
the Ming dynasty appear upon it, in curious contrast to those of the

present Tartar domination. The two-hundredth anniversary of the date of the imprimatur of this precious volume occurs on the 20th of September of this very year [1893].

There is a very great variety of games of this character in Japan, new ones being published annually at the season of the New Year. Illustrations of the more formal game played upon a board divided into twelve parts are figured in the Chinese-Japanese cyclopaedias. According to the *Kum mō dzu e tai sei,* the twelve compartments, called in Japanese *me,* or "eyes," symbolize the twelve months, and the black and white stones with which the game is played, day and night.

Italy contributes several forms of the dice game played upon a board having many stations. The oldest specimen in the collection, purchased in Parma, is a manuscript game bearing the title of *Oca Franchese.* Others printed in Florence bear the printed labels of *Giuoco dell' oca* and *Guioco del Barone,* while late examples more fanciful, both in name and design, appear as *Giuoco del Tramway* and *La Battaglia del 48.* A French game is shown under its proper title as *Jeu de l'oie,* beside which is placed a similar American game published as the "Game of Goose."

A number of packs of Oriental cards other than Chinese are contained in this case, among which are included several packs of East Indian Hindu cards which they call *Gungeefa.* They are all circular, varying in diameter in the different sets from 1⅝ to 3⅛ inches. One pack from Lucknow comprises eight suits, each composed of twelve cards, ten of which are "numerals," from one to ten. The two remaining cards are designated respectively as *Badsha* and *Sawar.* No satisfactory explanation has yet been afforded as to their origin.

The Japanese call the cards which are now current in Japan by the name of *Karuta,* a word evidently derived from the Portuguese *carta.* Those commonly used by gamblers, a pack of which is exhibited by Mrs. J. K. Van Rensellaer, are called *Hana Karuta,* or "Flower cards," and comprise forty-eight pieces, a number, it will be observed, identical with that of the present Spanish pack. They bear pictures, chiefly flowers, emblematic of the twelve months, four cards being placed under each. Their names are as follows: *Matsu,* "pine;" *Sakusa,* "cherries;" *Momidzi,* "maple;" *Butan,* "wild rose;" *Hagi,* Lespedeza; *Kiku,* "golden-colored daisy;" *Kiri,* Paulonia; *Fudzi,* Wisteria; *Soba,* "tiger lily;" *Ume,* "plum-tree;" *Yama,* "mountain;" and *Ame,* "rain."

The *Iroha,* or Proverb cards, also consist of ninety-six cards, half of which bear a picture and one of the forty-seven characters of the *Iroha,* or Japanese syllabary. Each of the other cards is inscribed with a proverb, the first word of which is written with one of the characters. There are several methods of play, the commonest being that of laying out all the picture cards face up. One of the older players reads the proverbs in turn, while the others endeavor to select the card from the table bearing the corresponding initial character. The *Uta Karuta,* or "Cards with songs," contain, according to Mr. Karl Himly, the well-known one hundred songs (*Hiyaku nin issiu,* 1235 A.D.), or the poems of the "Old and New Collection" (*Ho kin schiu,* 905 A.D.). The picture cards have the pictures of the poet or poetess, with the commencement of the poems. The rest is on the corresponding cards. The game is the same as that played with the *Iroha Karuta.*

Case VIII. American Board Games Played with Dice

The first of American board games played with dice is said to be the "Mansion of Happiness." This game is said to have been published in 1852, and copied from an English game. Thirty-three specimens of similar games published in this country are exhibited. They form a small part, however, of the entire number.

Case IX. Tarots, Tarocchino, and Minchiate. Types of Italian Cards. Manufacture of Playing Cards

The question of the origin of playing cards in Europe, whether they were introduced from the East, or an independent invention in France, Italy, or Germany, has been the object of much discussion. It may be regarded as conclusively settled that playing cards were invented in China in the twelfth century, and in view of the remarkable similarities between the card and card games of China and those of Europe which have been brought to light by Mr. Wilkinson, it may be profitable to suspend further consideration of the matter until the results of his studies are made public. Italy appears to be the oldest home of the playing card in Europe, and the earliest Italian packs are said to be those which the Italians call Tarocchi. Several types of these cards are found in Italy. According to Willshire these games are known as the *Tarots* of Venice or Lombardy, the *Tarocchino* of Bologna, and the *Minchiate* of Florence. The first of these, the old Venetian Tarot, he regards as the parent of all. The sequence consists of 78 cards, i.e., of 22 emblematic cards of Tarots proper, and 56 numeral cards made up of 16 figures or court cards, and 40 pip cards. The 22 Tarot cards bear emblematic designs which appear to be borrowed from a series of prints which are known to collectors as the *Tarocchi* of Mantegna or the *Carte di Baldini.* The emblematic cards in the Venetian series usually bear the following inscriptions: I. La Bagettel. 2. La Papessa. 3. L'Imperatrice. 4. L'Imperatore. 5. Il Papa. 6. Gli Amanti. 7. Il

Carro. 8. La Guistizia. 9. L'Eremita. 10. Ruot. della For. 11. La Forza.
12. L' Appeso. 13.   . 14. La Temperan. 15. Il Diavolo. 16. La Torre.
17. Le Stelle. 18. La Luna. 19. Il Sole. 20. Il Giudizio. 21. Il Mondo.
22. Il Matto.

No name is placed upon the 13th, which usually bears a skeleton with
a scythe, representing "death."

The second game, the *Tarocchino* of Bologna, though a direct
descendant of the ancient Venetian tarots, is not so old as the third game,
or *Minchiate* of Florence. The chief characteristic of the *Tarocchino,* its
name a diminutive of *tarocchi,* is the suppression in it of the 2, 3, 4, and
5 of each numeral suit, thus reducing the numeral cards from 56 to 40.
This modification of the tarot game was invented in Bologna, early in
the fifteenth century, by Francesco Fibbia, Prince of Pisa, an exile in that
city, dying there in 1419.

The third game is the *Minchiate* of Florence. It is more complicated
than the Venetian game, twenty additional cards being added to the
emblematic series. A pack of modern Venetian tarot made in Milan, which
are remarkable for their beautifully engraved and painted designs, a pack
of modern *Tarrocchino* from Bologna, and a pack of seventeenth century *Minchiate,* are displayed in the south side of this case. All of these
cards are in current use in different parts of Italy.

The suit marks of Italian cards consist of money, cups, swords, and
clubs, called *danari, coppe, spade,* and *bastoni.* The four court cards
of the numeral suits are known respectively as *Re,* King, *Regina* or *Reina,*
Queen, *Cavallo,* Knight, and *Fante,* Knave. The regular cards, as opposed
to those which include the emblematic series, are distinguished by certain peculiarities in the designs of the court cards in different parts of
Italy. The distinctive cards of Florence, Milan, and Naples are exhibited
in this case, together with several interesting packs upon which all the
designs, except an indication of the value at the top, have given place
to texts designed to afford instruction in history, geography, etc. A
remarkable pack of this character, exhibited by Dr. G. Brown Goode,
of Washington, is in manuscript and is intended to teach geography.

According to Chatto, on the earliest cards he had ever seen the figures
had been executed by means of stencils, this being the case both in the
cards of 1440 and those known as the Stukely cards. There are exhibited
in this case the stencils, brush, and unfinished card sheets from a card
maker in Florence, who still practises this ancient method of manufacture. The cards on the south side of this case, which in common with
all others not specially mentioned are exhibited by the University of Pennsylvania, represent the cards made at the present day in no less than
eighteen Italian cities by some twenty-nine makers. They were collected

for the University Museum by Mr. Francis C. Macauley of Florence. The cards of Florence, Bologna, Modena, Parma, Piacenza, Ferrera, Padua, Treviso, Udine, Novara, Turin, Sesia, Bergamo, Brescia, Genoa, Perugia, Naples, and Bari are included in the collection, in which an opportunity is afforded to observe the peculiarities of the cards of the different Italian cities. A distinctive character of the marks of the numeral suits of *spade* and *bastoni* is the mode in which they are interlaced or connected together in place of standing separately or apart. It is interesting to note that in the cards made in and for southern Italy this peculiarity does not exist, they being almost identical with the cards made in Spain.

The cards of Austria succeed those of Italy. The pack exhibited from Trent is like those of Italy, but the distinctively German cards predominate among those made in Vienna and the northern cities.

The suit marks of old German cards consist of hearts, bells, leaves, and acorns, which they call respectively *Herzen* (*roth*), *Schellen*, *Laub* (*grün*), and *Eichlen*. The court cards of the German pack are usually three in number, the peculiarity of the true German pack being that the queen is omitted and an upper valet or *Obermann* put in her place. They consist of the *König* or "King," the *Obermann*, and the *Untermann*.

Tarocchi cards are found in Germany under the name of *Taroks*, and a number of Tarok packs manufactured in Austria appear in this collection. Special names appear on their labels, as *Trieste Tarok*, *Kaffee Tarok*, etc., and the tarots proper bear a variety of emblems and designs different from those of Italy. They are usually numbered at top and bottom with Roman numerals from I to XXI.

Willshire has pointed out that the Italians early suppressed the emblematic cards in a game which was termed *Trappola*, in which the true tarots were abolished, as likewise the three, four, five, and six of each numeral suit. This game, he states, was still in vogue in Silesia when Breitkopf wrote (1784). An interesting Austrian pack of this character is shown under the name of *Trappolier Spiel*, in which the shape as well as the suit marks of the Italian tarots are displayed.

The German cards manufactured in Germany are prefaced by a series of reprints of German cards of the last century exhibited by Mr. Macauley. They were obtained by him through the courtesy of the Bavarian National Museum in Munich, for which they were made from the original blocks of the old Munich card makers that have been conserved in the Museum.

Case XI. German Cards (Continued), Swiss, Danish, Swedish, and Russian Cards. Spanish, Mexican, and Apache Cards

The collection of cards made in Germany comprises 53 packs, consisting chiefly of the current cards manufactured by card makers in Munich,

Altenburg, Frankfort a. M., Berlin, Leipzig, and Breslau. Among these is an extremely beautiful pack by B. Dondorf of Frankfort, with pictures suggesting the four quarters of the globe, after designs by Haussmann. Toy cards, patience cards, comic cards, trick cards, and cards which are labelled "Gaigel cards" appear, as well as cards made for special games, as the *Hexen* or "witch" packs. Many of the cards manufactured in Germany are seen to bear the French suit marks of *Coeurs, Carreaux, Piques,* and *Trèfles,* or "hearts," "diamonds," "spades," and "clubs," instead of the old German suit marks, and the court cards correspond at the same time with those of France and England. There are a number of packs with French suit marks, which bear pictures of Swiss scenery and costumes. The cards made in Switzerland are from Schaffhausen and Geneva, and comprise a variety of designs, including those which are especially designated as Swiss cards, German cards, and German Taroks. Belguim is represented by a German tarot pack, and imitations of English cards made for Oriental markets. Three packs of this character are shown, which were sent from Johore, in the Malay Peninsula, with another pack from Beirut, in Syria. The Russian cards in the collection, contributed by Madame Semetchkin, the representative on the Russian Commission of the "Institutions of the Empress Marie," are similar to modern French cards. The manufacture of playing cards in Russia is a monopoly of the state, and the revenues accruing are devoted to the support of the great charitable institution of which Madame Semetchkin is the distinguished representative.

Tarots or Tarocchi cards are not used in Spain, nor are they found among Spanish cards. The regulation Spanish pack now consists of 48 cards of four suits, called respectively *Dineros,* "money," *Copas,* "cups," *Bastos,* "clubs," and *Espadas,* "swords." The numerals run from one to nine, the ten being replaced with the *Caballo.* The court cards comprise the *Sota,* or "knave," the *Caballo,* or "knight," and the *Rey,* or "king." Cards manufactured at Vitoria, Burgos, Madrid, Barcelona, Valencia, Cadiz, and Palamos are displayed. Great antiquity has been claimed for cards in Spain, and it has been urged that this is the country through which Europe received cards from the East, but heretofore no Spanish cards of assured date earlier than 1600 have been known, and material evidence has been lacking. There was exhibited at the Columbian Historical Exposition in Madrid in 1892–93, a sheet of cards made in Mexico in 1583, which has been preserved in the Archives of the Indies at Seville, Spain, and which throw light upon the origin of Spanish cards. A copy made in water-colors by an artist in Madrid is shown in this collection. The original consists of an uncut sheet of about 11 by 17 inches, and bears on the back a pen and ink inscription with the date 1583. The face displays an impression from a wooden block of 24 cards each 2 by 3½ inches. They are colored in red, blue, and black, and represent the court cards and aces of the suits of money, cups, clubs, and swords, and ten numeral or pip cards of the suit of swords. There are but three court cards for each suit, instead of four as in the present Spanish pack. The marks of the numeral suit consist of crossed swords, instead of being arranged as on the Spanish cards now current, and strongly point to the Italian affinities of early Spanish cards.

Side by side with this early Mexican pack is a colored plate representing leather cards made by the Indians of South America, and an original pack of leather cards used by the Apaches. From the arrangement of the swords on both of these sets, which were copied from cards introduced by the Spaniards, it appears that they were initiated from the present type of Spanish cards. Such is not the case with the corresponding marks on a pack of native cards from the Celebes, which are also exhibited. Their Spanish origin is clearly indicated by their number, 48, and by the devices, which still bear a faint resemblance to those of Europe. The clubs and swords on both are represented by crossed lines which confirm the impression created by the Mexican pack. The Japanese "Hana Karuta," or "Flower Cards," are also shown here, as another pack of Oriental cards derived from those of Spain or Portugal. Their number, 48, and their name, *karuta,* from the Portuguese *carta,* clearly suggests their origin.

Case XII. French, English, and American Playing Cards. Fortune-Telling Cards, Dr. Buzby, Authors, and Miscellaneous Card Games

Tarocchi cards are called Tarots in France, and the French tarot pack is similar to the Venetian. The earliest specimens of French Tarots exhibited bear the name of Claude Burdel and the date 1751. There is direct historic proof that France possessed cards at a very early time in the accounts of the Treasurer of Charles VI, A.D. 1392. The earliest pack of French cards in this collection is one of which I have not been able to determine the date. It bears the name Pierre Montalan on the Knave of Spades and Claude Valentin on the Knave of Clubs. A variety of modern French packs are shown, including those made with Spanish suit marks and special cards for various games. The French suit marks reappear on English cards, and according to Willshire it is most probable that cards made their way into England through France. He states that the time is not known, but that we are safe in believing that cards were not in use in England until after the reign of Henry IV (1405), and that they were certainly employed before 1463. The English cards here displayed consist entirely of those of the present day, but this deficiency in historical packs is compensated for in part by Lady Charlotte Schreiber's folio volume on English and Scottish, Dutch and Flemish cards which she has loaned for this collection. The great work, of which this is but the first volume, contains fac-similes of the cards in Lady Charlotte Schreieber's private collection, and reveals the wealth of historical suggestions to be found upon playing cards, and their value, as thus collected, to the antiquary and historian.

America early received playing cards from Spain, and Spanish cards are still made and imported into Spanish American countries. In the United States English cards were naturally adopted. No very early packs are shown, but some interesting cards are found in the North American series, including a variety of cards with patriotic emblems of the time of the Rebellion, as well as caricature cards of the recent political campaigns. The collection closes with the souvenir packs of the Columbian Exposition at Chicago. Mrs. J. K. Van Rensellaer's work, entitled "The Devil's Picture Books," a copy of which is exhibited, contains many interesting particulars concerning cards and card playing in America. Several interesting card boxes are shown in this collection, with specimens of the old-fashioned "fish" or card counters of mother-of-pearl, among which are some that belonged to Robert Morris, the financier of the Revolution. Treatises on American card games, exhibited by Messrs. Dick & Fitzgerald, conclude the series of playing cards proper.

Among the notions concerning the origin of cards in Europe is one that they were first introduced by the gypsies, who used them in fortune-telling. It appears that they were early used for divinatory purposes in Europe, but according to Willshire their employment in fortune-telling gradually declined among the upper classes until the middle of the eighteenth century, "though it was prevalent, no doubt, among the lower grades of society frequenting fairs and the caravans of mountebanks. About 1750 divination through cards again became popular in Paris, at least, for in 1751, 1752, and 1753 three persons were publicly known as offering their services of this intention." According to certain writers, the emblematic figures of the tarot cards are of very remote origin, stretching back as far as the ancient Egyptians, from whom they have descended to us as a book or series of subjects of deep symbolic meaning. The discovery and explication of the meaning of the tarots employed in modern times was claimed by M. Count de Goebelin in 1781, who in his "Monde Primitif analysé et compare avec le Monde Moderne," gave a dissertation on the game of Tarots, in which he states that the tarot pack is evidently based on the sacred Egyptian number seven, and reviews the tarot emblems in detail.

The probable origin of the 21 tarot cards has already been suggested in connection with Chinese cards, and it is not surprising that the astrological notions associated with Tarots should find parallels in the speculations of the Kabbalists, who attached similar notions to the dice throws as are now found asociated with them in China, from whence the 21 Tarot cards doubtless came to Europe. An explanation is therefore found for some of the resemblances upon which M. de Goebelin lays such stress. His fancies, however, never subjected to very severe examination or criticism, were seized upon by a perruquier of Paris of the name of Alliette, who combined with his ordinary occupation the practice of cartomancy. He read the dissertation of Count de Goebelin, and, thereby enlightened, changed the letters of his name and prophesied under the name of Ettillia. His writings furnish the basis of most of the treatises now extant upon the subject of fortune-telling with cards, and his name is found associated with several of the modern French tarot packs published especially for fortune-telling, in the present collection. During the exciting periods of the first Consulship of Napoleon I, there lived, according to Mr. Willshire, a well-known diviner named Madame Lenormand, whose predictions gained great repute. Her name, with that of Ettillia, appears on the French cards here exhibited, as well as on those made in America. Several French and German fortune-telling packs of an amusing character are to be found in the present collection, as well as others published in the United States, which are designed solely for purposes of amusement.

The entire northern side of this case is devoted to the card games other than regular playing cards, which owe their existence to the prejudice against cards or to the demand for simple and instructive amusements for children and young people. Mr. Milton Bradley has contributed some interesting notes on the history of such games in this country. In 1843 Miss Annie W. Abbott, a clergyman's daughter of Beverly, Mass., offered to Mr. Ives, a publisher of Salem, Mass., a card game which she called "Dr. Buzby." This game, which was the first of its kind, was reluctantly published by Mr. Ives and met with an astonishing success, no less than 50,000 copies being sold in the following year. It will be remembered by many of the parents of the present day as among the earliest games ever learned and possibly played upon the sly through fear of reprimand. A pack of the original Dr. Buzby cards will be found at the beginning of this collection. The game of "Authors" was originated by a young man living in Salem, helped by some of his female acquaintances. The method of play was copied from "Dr. Buzby," but it contained an element of instruction and profit not found in the older game. He took it to a local publisher to see if he could have ten or a dozen packs printed, as it was too much work for him to print them. Mr. Smith, the publisher, saw the possibilities of the game and told him if he would let him make them, he would supply his needs gratis, to which he consented. This was in 1861, and the sale of this game has since been wonderful. Many modifications and improvements of the original game are shown in the collection.

Soon after the publication of "Dr. Buzby," a teacher in a young ladies' school in Salem devised a game of letters which has since become popular under the various names of "Spelling Puzzle," "Word Making and Word Taking," "War of Words," "Anagrams," "Logomachy," "Words and Sentences," etc. The publications of the Milton Bradley Company, McLaughlin Bros., and E. I. Horsman are here exhibited, and no less than 78 different card games are displayed. They are classified in groups according to the methods of play, which, in spite of the ingenuity displayed in the designs of the cards, are relatively very limited in number, the ideas in the main being derived from games already played with regular playing cards.

15

"Tools of the Nation Maker": Toward a Historical Interpretation of American Folklife

Henry C. Mercer

Henry C. Mercer (1865–1930) stood late in his life beside a museum bearing his name in his native Doylestown, Pennsylvania. Dedicating the structure, he called attention to "a new presentation of the history of our country from the point of view of the work of human hands." In it were tools and crafts, not from "savage" Indians or remote peoples, but from America's forebears. To Mercer, the rustic objects were evidence of a preindustrial folklife that revealed the soul of the American nation. With this museum, Mercer anticipated the spread of American folklife and living history museums across the country, as well as the interest in American antiques and folk art. The interpretation of his collections sprung far from the ethnological studies he had done in the late nineteenth century, and therein lies his importance as a transitional figure in folklife studies.

After graduating from Harvard, Mercer gave up a budding law career to join archaeological excavations around his home in Bucks County. Later he joined the staff of the University of Pennsylvania Museum where he came into company with Stewart Culin, Daniel Brinton, Frank Hamilton Cushing, and other well-known ethnologists. Fired with the enthusiasm of his colleagues for ethnological inquiry into humankind's distant past, in 1895 he explored the caves of the Yucatan peninsula to find "evidence of man's antiquity." Tired from the exhausting and only partially successful search, Mercer turned to his hometown roots. Speaking in 1896 to the Bucks County Historical Society, he offered a paper on "Folk Lore, Notes Taken at Random." He told his audience that "turning over the pages of note books which record the researches of several years past, I find stray allusions to that class of descriptive popular characteristics, which often escaping notice because everywhere in evidence, have found value in the eyes of science under the name Folk Lore." Mercer related a variety of German-American folklore, which probably came as no surprise to his Pennsylvania-German audience, but which lay the groundwork for his collection of folk material culture. Closing his address, Mercer contemplated the evolution of firemaking: "From the match to the flint and steel; from the flint and steel to the fire stick; from the fire stick to ignorance; a series of slow steps which we may best realize by turning to savage tribes in the stone age, still ignorant of the flint and steel, and therefore at the lowest stage of development of the most momentous and important of all human arts."

A chance encounter a few months later with a box of old Pennsylvania farm tools bought at a country sale made him rethink his archaeological work. In these tools he saw not a series of slow steps, but a large leap in living memory from the region's agricultural settlement to industrial town. Captured in these tools, he thought, was the historical experience of the United States. It was a saga, like the evolution of fire making, of man battling nature for supremacy, and coming away with a great cultural achievement. But he did not have to locate the savage tribes of the Stone Age to uncover this saga; he had his neighbors whose old tools represented to him centuries of consistent use until mechanization swept over the country. In their tools he also saw the rise of a distinctive American heritage, because while owing to European sources, he hypothesized, American folklife set against a unique set of conditions took on a character all its own.

Mercer's energies suddenly turned from the mysteries of antiquity around the globe to the neglected folk heritage of the nation. He avidly collected such things as powder horns, plows, and lard lamps; most of the things he found dealt with the implements of subsistence and arts of everyday life. The result was a ballyhooed 87-page catalogue entitled *Tools of the Nation Maker* (1897); it was designated as the first number of the Bucks County Historical Society's "Contributions to American History." Mercer immediately followed with published commentaries on American folk art in the form of Pennsylvania-German illuminated manuscripts (*fractur*) and decorated stove plates. Later he contributed a groundbreaking essay on the dating of log houses, and a large compendium on carpenter's tools. His museum was a series of texts to be read and experienced. Inside the strange-looking concrete structure were hung his preindustrial vehicles, tools, and crafts; outside could be found a setting preserving farm and village life. There on the grounds one could walk into an old log building or eat from a fireplace; this was "living history." "Feel what a moment it must have been," he offered, and realize the everyday experience that shaped the nation as much as its great events.

This chapter reprints his original introduction to the *Tools of the Nation Maker* catalogue (Doylestown, Pennsylvania: Bucks County Historical Society, 1897), and follows with his address ten years later on the collection. The address comes from *A Collection of Papers Read before the Bucks County Historical Society,* vol. 3 (Riegelsville, Pennsylvania: B. F. Fackenthal, Jr., 1909), pp. 470–81. For other prominent works by Mercer, see *The Bible in Iron: Pictured Stoves and Stoveplates of the Pennsylvania Germans,* ed. Joseph E. Sandford, 3d ed. (Doylestown, Pennsylvania: Bucks County Historical Society, 1961); *Ancient Carpenters' Tools,* 5th ed. (Doylestown, Pennsylvania: Bucks County Historical Society, 1975). For background on Mercer and his museum, see Donna Gail Rosenstein, "'Historic Human Tools': Henry Chapman Mercer and His Collection, 1897–1930" (M.A. Thesis, University of Delaware, 1977); Gary S. Dunbar, "Henry Chapman Mercer: Pennsylvania Folklife

Pioneer," *Pennsylvania Folklife* 12 (Summer 1961): pp. 48–52; Horace Mann, "The Museum of the Bucks County Historical Society," *Pennsylvania German Folklore Society,* Annual, 7 (1949): pp. 9–28; J. Alden Mason, "Henry Chapman Mercer, 1856–1930," *Pennsylvania Archaeologist Bulletin* 26 (1956): pp. 153–65. For background on living history and the uses of tools and folk artifacts in the museum, see Jay Anderson, *Time Machines: The World of Living History* (Nashville: American Association for State and Local History, 1984); J. Geraint Jenkins, "The Use of Artifacts and Folk Art in the Folk Museum," in *Folklore and Folklife: An Introduction,* ed. Richard M. Dorson (Chicago: University of Chicago Press, 1972), pp. 497–516. For a work that parallels Mercer's interest in domestic American objects, see Alice Morse Earle, *Home Life in Colonial Days* (1898; reprint, Stockbridge, Massachusetts: Berkshire Traveller Press, 1974). For the turn-of-the-century movement of tracing American heritage through everyday artifacts, see Elizabeth Stillinger, *The Antiquers* (New York: Alfred A. Knopf, 1980); Alan Axelrod, ed., *The Colonial Revival in America* (New York: W. W. Norton, 1985), pp. 184–240; Simon J. Bronner, *Grasping Things: Folk Material Culture and Mass Society in America* (Lexington: University Press of Kentucky, 1986), pp. 177–210.

*   *   *

Mechanical improvements in human handicraft at the beginning of the nineteenth century have suddenly transformed the American farmer from a pioneer relying for equipment upon his own skill and industry to a husbandman abundantly supplied with labor saving devices. To the latter the stern conflict with nature has become a rapidly fading memory. Already, though often less than half a century old, the disused home-made tools of wood or iron by which he felled the forest, expelled a weaker race, contended with the forces of nature, lived and enjoyed life, grow curious in his own eyes, while to the man of cities they are things unknown. Yet these castaways, gathered together, offer valuable suggestions on all sides. Manifold elucidations of nationality are in store for us as we study them. Leading us by way of an untrodden path, deeper into the lives of people, they give us a fresh grasp upon the vitality of the American beginning. At first, illustrating our humble story, they unfold by degrees a wider meaning, until at last the heart is touched.

From the sweet-scented herb store of the ancient garret to where the mill race washes the mossy machinery of the crumbling mill; from the dark recesses of a bake oven to where a north light wanes through dusty windows upon the granary or wagon house; from the smelter's iron heap to the wood pile, the search for these disused and neglected things has led us. The historian has overlooked them. The antiquary has forgotten them. But when we realize the value of the associations that perish, as they pass away in our midst, we commend them as heirlooms to be saved from destruction and set in a place of honor. . . .

What we see suggests often the interesting subject of the relation of Germany to the United States. This is because the collection has been made in an old settled region, half Germanized one hundred years ago, and including to the northward a district where fixed conditions, having escaped the encroachments of railways, die slowly. Here in Bucks county, rather than in Dutch New York, Puritan New England, or the more decidedly English or French regions of the South, we might expect to trace readily the leaven of various trans-Atlantic ingredients of nationality which by degrees should be detected amongst a group of objects fashioned by English, Irish, Welsh, Dutch or German hands.

But in the largest sense the store of Eastern Pennsylvania and of its Bucks county is that of the whole Nation. As often the founders of Indiana, Kansas, and Missouri have returned to the shores of Delaware to look with affectionate curiosity upon the birthplace of their ancestors; as the Kentuckian may trace the path of that chief of the American pioners, Daniel Boone, westward from the Schuylkill and Neshaminy, so the log houses of Bedminster and Plumstead, and the tools which made them, and came from them, differing unessentially in make and use from the contemporary tools of New England [and] the South, stand for the beginning of the Nation. They belong to a past claimed now by many millions of humanity, and are the inheritance of North, South, East, and West. . . .

The American pioneer, thrown for a time upon his own resources, turns back to conditions more primitive than those left behind in the Old World. Contenting himself with such makeshifts as the wooden plow, the hay drag formed of a branch, or the house of logs, which in his hands do not strictly represent stages in the general development of culture, his wits are quickened by necessity, until suddenly, towards the beginning of the present century, he casts aside the old tools and equips himself with machines. The latter are tributes to his energy and skill, but the simpler older implements, having long lain close to his life, reveal to us more of that humanity which outlives in interest all mechanism.

In the axe and the rifle, the hollow gum tree and the calabash, the flax break and the frow, the lard lamp and the bake oven, the dinner conch and the illuminated song book, we see the birthmarks of Adam, that must long stamp the citizen of the United States, whether he will or not, as a wayfarer upon the broad pathway common to many nations.[1] Immigrants from a variety of ancient communities, inheriting numerous advantages, the white Americans cross the Atlantic, and thrown together by stress of similar conditions, grow into a nation. . . .

Inasmuch as we may be asked some day to describe how, when, where and under what circumstances I made this collection, hanging above your heads, which has been called the "Tools of the Nation Maker" it would be well to begin with a date. . . . It was probably one day in February or March of the spring of 1897 that I went to the premises of one of our fellow-citizens, who had been in the habit of going to country sales and at the last moment buying what they called "penny lots," that is to say valueless masses of obsolete utensils or objects which were regarded as useless, or valuable only as old iron or kindling wood, things which fortunately have been preserved among us for two noteworthy reasons, first because of the existence in our country of several of these unthanked and non-mercenary hoarders, and second because of the abundance of wood and consequently of outbuildings such as are lacking in Europe adapted to the preservation of perishable heirlooms. The particular object of the visit above mentioned, was to buy a pair of tongs for an old fashioned fire place, but when I came to hunt out the tongs from the midst of a disordered pile of old wagons, gum-tree salt-boxes, flax-brakes, straw beehives, tin dinner-horns, rope-machines and spinning-wheels, things that I had heard of but never collectively saw before, the idea occurred to me that the history of Pennsylvania was here profusely illustrated and from a new point of view. I was seized with a new enthusiasm and hurried over the county, rummaging the bake-ovens, wagon-houses, cellars, hay-lofts, smoke-houses, garrets, and chimney-corners, on this side of the Delaware valley. When having gathered together a great mass of things, I first stored them in and upon our old room in the Bucks county court-house some of you very naturally rebelled and we had to go to Galloway's Ford and examine the objects again at the next meeting in the court-house at Doylestown in the autumn of 1897 and classify them and explain them before it was fair to expect you to keep them.

In a rough way as you now see them, I then classified them. Here is the cutting down of the forest and the building of the log cabin. There are utensils concerned with the preparation of food, that is to say cooking appliances together with apparatus for making and producing light. Next we have the production of clothing, illustrated by spinning and weaving and the adaptation of vegetable fibre for these purposes. Then comes the relation of man to animals, in the way of domesticating them or killing them and expelling them from the region. Agriculture is represented by a multitude of implements which stand at the very bottom of man's effort to keep himself alive, and we have next the great variety of utensils, home and hand made, produced by the man of the land on his own farm before the factory existed, before the country store came into being and before a wave of mechanical inventive genius took possession of the American people about the year 1820. By way of the fabrication of utensils of burnt clay we come finally to a lot of objects illustrating learning and amusement at a time when the pioneer had little time for aught save the removal of the forest and the general struggle for existence.

With much to say and but few moments to say it in, I would like to dwell strongly upon the significance of this collection for several reasons. Here we have history in the first place presented from a new point of view. Mr. [George] Bancroft wrote the history of the United States and dwelt with great vividness upon the Revolutionary War but no history can show as these things show, that during that war a hundred thousand hands armed with these sickles were reaping wheat and rye so as to make any kind of a war possible by the production of bread without which all the combatants on both sides would have been unable to fight. You may go down into Independence hall in Philadelphia, and stand in the room in which the Declaration of Independence was signed and there look up at the portraits of the signers. But do you think you are any nearer the essence of the matter there than you are here when you realize that ten hundred thousand arms, seizing upon axes of this type, with an immense amount of labor and effort made it worth while to have a Declaration of Independence by cutting down one of the greatest forests in the North Temperate Zone. You may go to hear a lecture on the subject of Naval Battles or the War of 1812 at the Pennsylvania Historical Society but do you think that you are more vividly confronted with the truth of the whole story than you are here when you realize, looking at those spinning-wheels, that once upon a time there was a vast noise of humming from the work of ten hundred thousand women at least, spinning upon these wheels that actually took place, and was needed to make it possible for men to be adequately protected from the cold so that they could go out and fight any battles at all by sea or by land.

[At this point the following objects displayed before the meeting were described and explained: A leaf fork used to collect masses of leaves from the woods for the bedding of cattle when straw was scarce. Disused in Nockamixon about 1860. A Bread tray adzed from a native log from Plumstead township antedating the country store and the year 1830. A pounding apparatus for mashing the outer husk of flax used before 1850 when linen was homemade. A flint lock gun; a shovel plow used for plowing newly cleared land, a sickle used for reaping wheat and rye, without important change between the years 1800 A.D. and 2000 B.C. The specimen typified those used in Bucks county until 1800. An axe of indigenous form evolved from the longer bitted English types of the first colonists—destroyer of the American forest and probably in general use by 1750. A spinning wheel as the successor of the still earlier distaff and spindle used by the wives of some of the first settlers.]

Perhaps these things can be included or adequately described by history but a sight of the actual object conveys an impression, otherwise indescribable. Moreover a multitude of words have passed out of the language and become obsolete since these objects ceased to be used and this too is history.

[At this point the following objects exhibited before the meeting were described, explained and compared: An ancient clay lamp of about 200 B.C. found in an Etruscan grave at Orvieto, and several bronze boat shaped lamps together with a standard reproduced from originals excavated at Pompeii and now in the museum at Naples, compared with a typical boat shaped lard lamp of iron found in an old farm-house in Plumstead township, Bucks county, and in use there until 1830. A typical sieve meshed with wooded splints from older Bucks county compared with an ancient type made of punctured rawhide from the Island of Inishnee, county Galway, Ireland. A potter's quern for grinding metallic colors by twisting one stone upon another used in New Britain township until 1880, compared with the painter's rubbing stone of old Bucks county and the pestle and mortar of the North American Indian, as a food grinding implement of immense antiquity and the origin of all modern flour mills. A dinner horn formed of a conch shell blown upon to illustrate the origin of forms of trumpet and horn of great antiquity where the sound is produced by vibration of the lips—as a musical instrument two or three thousand years old at least. Still in use to signal open lock on the Delaware canal. A light is struck on scorched linen with a tinder box after a method several thousand years old derived from the prehistoric striking of flint against native iron—in use in Bucks county until 1820.]

You may say that the history of man as exemplified and illustrated by his artefacts is after all archaeology and that we are already familiar with archaeology. So we are. But the archaeology of the museums of Europe and America begins at the past, presents us with the remains of man thousands of years old, and pretends to lead us to the present. Generally speaking you might say that they put the cart before the horse. But here on the other hand we look from the present backward to the past. Beginning at the doorstep of our grandfathers we go back to Roman and Egyptian times. This therefore is archaeology turned upside down, reversed, revolutionized. What seems obscure and dark in the museums which we have visited is here rendered plain. It is a very easy matter for friends of ours still living to explain the uses of these things to us. When they have done so we have learned more of archaeology, by means of the kindergarten method, as you might say in a few hours than we otherwise could have mastered by the study of books and museums, from the other point of view, in months.

Because a great number of these things before your eyes have been in use by man without any very important change since the time the pyramids of Egypt were built, because man reaped with sickles of this general pattern, made fire in this general way, wove thread, prepared the fiber of vegetables for spinning, dug in the ground, cooked food, practiced many of the common crafts of every day life after this manner for thousands of years, and because the child of nature, the primitive savage continues to utilize utensils of this sort at the present moment, for these reasons it may be said that having easily familiarized yourselves with the uses of these things, the whole range of your observation wherever in your travels you take a broad view of the panorama of human life will be much increased. Enlightened by this knowledge, whether in the cave of the troglidite or in the hut of the savage, whether upon the steppes of Tartary or upon the banks of the Congo, whether among the habitations of the Eskimo, or the forest dwellings of the Amazon, you are no longer a stranger. Everywhere you see familiar objects. The same story is repeated. You are at home again in Bucks county.

But if I fail in all else I hope I may succeed in impressing the thought that this collection is of significance because it is the child of a remarkable opportunity. I have tried several times to illustrate the fact that in so far as the equipment of man with tools and utensils is concerned a greater change has taken place in the last two or three generations than took place in any fifteen or twenty generations preceding. This sort of thing is very often said in connection with a great many events referred to in addresses of this sort. But in this instance no patriotism or desire to boast, or spirit of the Fourth of July oration, clouds the actual truth, namely that in this respect there is a greater difference between our lives and the life of George Washington than between his life and the life of William the Conqueror. Many of our lives reach back into this period which, though only removed from us by about a century, practically stands for an antiquity of a thousand years. Equipped as his ancestors had been for centuries in the old world with these very tools and utensils, the pioneer came to America. Armed with these things he cut down the forest, contended with the forces of nature, and worked out his life and destiny until about the year 1820, when a wave of inventive mechanical genius having seized him, he cast them all aside, and equipped himself with the products of a new machinery. If the followers of William Penn hunting about among the heir-looms of their time, three or four hundred years old, had tried to make a collection of this signficance, they could not have done so, inasmuch as the objects collected by them, no matter how old, would have more or less closely resembled the things in use at their own time, so that no vivid and startling lessons would have been taught. The conestoga wagon suspended above your heads presented to us by Mrs. Richard Hovenden used by her husband as a painter's model in the picture by him known as "Westward Ho!" in the capitol at Washington, stands for an immense change in the daily life of man, although it is not more than a hundred years old. Because a great many of us have outlived this change, because the transformation 'has taken place under our eyes as it were, it is none the less momentous and important, and the fact that we got to work to collect these perishable objects at this particular moment is what we should wish to set forth as a thing of great importance. This conestoga wagon standing for the whole westward march of the Anglo Saxon colonization, and the transportation of all merchandise over mountains and plains toward the setting sun, before the birth of railroads; these spinning wheels, these flax brakes, illustrating the whole equipment of mankind with clothing, these shovel plows, clover-strippers, rope-machines, leaf-forks, long bitted axes, flint-lock guns, cranes and bake-irons will never be made again. Because they come to an end so suddenly and so near our own lives, they are still within reach, but they are vanishing fast, and we must gather them together now or never. I have been told that if we tried to make this collection now after a lapse of ten years we could not do it, and the statement may be true, but whether absolutely true or not we know that the difficulty of gathering these things together has increased very greatly since they were first shown you at Galloway's Ford. For these reasons we say that this singular collection is the child of an opportunity which has not occurred until it did occur for the last thousand years, and which will certainly never occur again. And if we are convinced of this fact let us be inspired to cease destroying historical specimens, and further to realize that we now have only about ten more years, in which to note down first hand and save the unique and universal yet unrecorded information explanatory of these things still surviving in the memories of men now about eighty years old, but doomed to perish, if unnoted, as surely as perished the classical learning burned by Arabs in the Library of Alexandria.

Having said this much we may ask why has not someone else made a collection of this sort, and if we do we can not answer the question. We can only say that they have not done so. The series of volumes containing illustrations of similar objects, whether produced by the authoress to whom I have referred or the Pennsylvania German Society, do not stand for collections gathered together and classified.[2] The collections at Deerfield, Mass., and at Indian Hill near Newburyport are confined to objects of a more or less picturesque character relating to the household or cookery or to certain phases of village life and do not cover the broad ethnological field represented here. In Europe there is a gathering of peasant costumes in Sicily, of ancient lighting appliances in Vienna, and of certain peasant utensils and appliances in Munich, but neither in Italy nor Spain where a remarkable opportunity now exists for making a collection of this kind nor in England, nor Ireland, nor France, nor Holland has any such thing been done. One remarkable exception however must be cited. In the fact that somewhere about the time of the beginning of this collection, or earlier, although I never heard of the matter until last summer, Dr. [Hazelius], of Stockholm, conceived the idea of gathering together just such a showing as this.[3] The Swedish government came to his rescue, they granted him a large portion of one of the public parks and gave him money to lift up whole buildings of historic interest, place them within the inclosure and fill them with tools and implements of an earlier make and kind. Inasmuch as his fellow countrymen regarded it as a patriotic duty to help him, his collection increased rapidly and continued after his death until it has now become a source of pride and glory for his native city and country. If this collection at Stockholm were more important, or valued, or significant than ours, it would be no serious cause for lamentation, but when all is considered it may be fairly said without patriotism or boasting, that the collection before your eyes for the reason that it stands for a momentous and complete change in the destinies of a great number of European nations, brought together here in the United States and transmuted as it were in a great cauldron, conveys a broader object lesson than a similar collection would in Sweden where there has been no such influx of immigration or gathering together of other nations, and where Swedes have remained Swedes from time immemorial.

The last question of all in connection with the matter, namely, what are we going to do with the collection, ought to be answered practically. In the first place take up this wooden floor and replace it with a fire proof pavement, remove the useless, combustible ceiling and fire proof the roof itself, so that the collection can be augmented in this room by hanging more objects all over the beams of the ceiling, or supporting them above our heads upon columns. Safeguard the library from any possible chance from fire, get the wood out of the stair-case and bedrooms, and fire proof the whole building so that no one will ever be able to say to us that with the best intentions in the world he would be unwilling to deposit such and such a valuable collection in a building which was liable to burn down at any moment.

Over and above this we should have a keeper under a salary to preserve these objects, clean them, refresh their labels, care for and catalog new donations as they come in and protect what we have from danger and decay. We may make the mistake of turning our energies toward the collection of a library or joining forces with the town library, but there are a thousand and one other towns and other historical societies that have libraries and it will take us a long time to catch up to many of them. We may devote a great deal of time to genealogical research but the Pennsylvania Historical Society is far ahead of us there. We may work for the expensive publication of documents of historical records, etc, without realizing that in these matters we are in hopeless competition with a number of other organizations already far ahead of us, but the point I earnestly desire to make, even if I fail to convince you of anything else at all, is, that in this collection called "the Tools of the Nation Maker" we are ahead of everybody, we are original, alone and unique.[4] If any other historical society or individual shall undertake to compete with us we are so far ahead that with a reasonable amount of effort on our part it will be a hopeless task for them to catch up with us. If we were to say that this collection would be worth its weight in gold a hundred years hence, it would be no very great exaggeration, but we need not look so far ahead to imagine the time when if we do anything like our duty, the student of these things, whoever he may be, will not go to Washington, Boston, New York, Chicago or anywhere else in the country to study American history from this fresh point of view, but will be compelled to come to Doylestown.

Have you walked out upon the splendid enclosure which surrounds this building and now belongs to us? If so you have seen a beautiful natural amphitheatre where the Greeks would have built a theatre a thousand years ago. Fronting toward the south, looking over the roofs of modern American houses into the valley of the Neshaminy, the place would delight the heart of a botanist. Here is wet ground, dry ground, cold ground, warm ground, high ground, low ground, adapted for the planting of all sorts of trees, shrubs and flowers. We dreamed of this building a long time ago and the dream came true. Why not dream now of a wonderful garden, a botanical park devoted to the past, surrounded by a high wall behind which we can forget the railroad and the trolley, the modern newspaper and the telegraph, the automobile and the megaphone and look upon the trees and plants which were associated with the lives of the colonists and closely involved with his struggle for life, or upon the herbs which cured him of disease, or the flowers which he brought from the old world to embellish his new home in the wilderness until they themselves escaped from his dominion and ran wild in the woods. In the middle of this grove fit for the best meditations of a philosopher, upon an open sward the ethnobotanist might come to teach the uses of plants and their relation to humanity to his pupils. Is this dream a hopeless or impossible thing? We have the land and having fenced it in in a temporary manner for the present so that we are safe from pastured animals and the game of baseball, we are ready for the botanists, and the trees and the wall. What we want are friends. Let them lend a hand. Our small village in which many of us were born has a court-house with a handsome steeple, but so have a hundred other villages in this and other states. We have a certain number of banks, so have they. We are perched upon the top of a hill with a fine view and we may be more or less proud of some of these things, although we are not pre-eminent in any one of them, but here around and about us is something that is unique, an educational institution that no other town possesses, and if our citizens are not proud of it to-day their children and grand-children will be. Here is a rare and remarkable tree in good condition, just planted, watch over it, guard it, save it, prune and water it until it spreads its noble shade, not only over this little town and over this State of Pennsylvania, but over the whole nation.

Notes

1. [During the late nineteenth century it was a common literary convention to refer to the "American Adam." In this conception, Europeans who came to America's shores were innocents in a Garden of Eden. From their early struggles came a reborn civilization, an American one, fashioned from, but different from, European experience. See R. W. B. Lewis, *The American Adam: Innocence, Tragedy and Tradition in the Nineteenth Century* (Chicago: University of Chicago Press, 1955). —*Ed.*]

2. [The "authoress" referred to with some disdain is undoubtedly Alice Morse Earle, who published her groundbreaking book *Home Life in Colonial Days* in 1898. Earle had garnered a great deal of attention for her exploration of everyday life and folk objects in America, mostly drawn from New England sources. Mercer felt that his work in the field preceded Earle's and deserved more credit. During 1897, for example, Mercer published besides *Tools of the Nation Maker,* "The Survival of the Mediaeval Art of Illuminative Writing among Pennsylvania Germans," *Proceedings of the American Philosophical Society* 26 (1897): pp. 424–33, and "The Decorated Stove Plates of Durham," *Contributions to American History,* no. 3 (Doylestown, Pennsylvania: Bucks County Historical Society, 1897). The Pennsylvania-German Society to which Mercer refers was founded in 1891, and had among its interests everyday material culture and folklife. Mercer's vague reference to the work of the society in "his" field is probably F. J. F. Schantz's *The Domestic Life and Characteristics of the Pennsylvania-German Pioneer* (Lancaster, Pennsylvania: Pennsylvania German Society, 1900). This 97-page narrative described many folk crafts and utensils, and included photographs of objects, which Mercer claimed came from his collection. —*Ed.*]

3. [Mercer is referring to the work of Artur Hazelius (1833–1901), who developed the outdoor folk museum called *Skansen* during the 1890s. According to museum historian Edward Alexander, Hazelius was significant for instituting "field studies on the way the folk lived—their houses, gardens, and interior furnishings, household implements,

tools, and clothing as well as their beliefs, customs, and amusements. . . . His continuing aim was to use the past to inspire national consciousness in the Swedish people during a period of rapid industrial and social change." See Edward Alexander, *Museum Masters* (Nashville: American Association for State and Local History, 1983), pp. 241–75. Hazelius's ideas profoundly influenced the development of American folk museums. Hazelius, for example, used a national indoor museum, the *Nordiska Museet,* to erect interpretive exhibits devoted to the life of the nation's various regional groups. The emphasis was on the material culture, and especially the tools, evident in folklife. Mercer, in addition to conceiving of an outdoor site to relocate early folk buildings from his region, also designed and erected an indoor museum which opened in 1916, and which now goes by the title of the Mercer Museum. For further discussion of Hazelius's influence on American folk museums, see Howard Wight Marshall, "Folklife and the Rise of American Folk Museums," *Journal of American Folklore* 90 (1977): pp. 391–413. —*Ed.*]

4.   [Mercer's museum is no longer alone, although it certainly was ahead of its time. A sign of the growth of interest in the "tools of the nation-maker" was the founding of the Early American Industries Association in the 1930s. The association's magazine, *The Chronicle,* regularly carried reports on museums and societies dedicated to collecting early American tools and preserving folklife. See Horace M. Mann, "The Bucks County Historical Society" 3 (April 1945): pp. 23–25; "Henry Ford Museum and Greenfield Village" 11 (June 1958): pp. 13–17, 24; "Old Sturbridge Village" 8 (April 1955): pp. 13–16; H. K. Landis, "Landis Valley Museum" 3 (September 1945): pp. 43, 46, 49; Janet R. MacFarlane, "The Farmers' Museum in Cooperstown" 3 (December 1944): pp. 3–7. Of course there is a certain irony, or explanation, in the fact that many of these pioneering collections were formed by industrialists, most notably Henry Ford. Mercer was also an industrialist, engaged in the manufacturing of ceramic tiles. See Thomas J. Schlereth, "Material Culture Studies in America, 1876–1976," in *Material Culture Studies in America,* ed. Thomas J. Schlereth (Nashville: American Association for State and Local History, 1982), pp. 15–20; Warren Susman, *Culture as History: The Transformation of American Society in the Twentieth Century* (New York: Pantheon, 1985), pp. 122–49 (for Ford). Their interest in early American tools was closely aligned to the study of folklife; see H. K. Landis, "Local Folk Museums," *Chronicle of the Early American Industries Association* 2 (April 1939): p. 71. For further background, see Patricia Hall and Charlie Seemann, eds., *Folklife and Museums* (Nashville: American Association for State and Local History, 1987); Louis C. Jones, "Folk Culture and the Historical Society," *Minnesota History* 31 (1950): pp. 11–17; Warren Roberts, "Folk Architecture in Context: The Folk Museum," in his *Viewpoints on Folklife: Looking at the Overlooked* (Ann Arbor, Michigan: UMI Research Press, 1987). —*Ed.*]